Contents

LJUBLJANA P46

Welcome to Slovenia

A paradise of snowcapped peaks, turquoise rivers and Venetian-style coastline, Slovenia enriches its treasures with harmonious architecture, rustic culture and sophisticated cuisine.

A Matter of Taste

Slovenian cooking borrows a little something from each of its neighbours – Italy, Austria, Hungary and the Balkans – synthesising and reinventing dishes that emerge both familiar and unique. Slovenes have an obsession for using only fresh and locally sourced ingredients. The result is a terrific foodie destination, where you'll sample dishes in unusual combinations, featuring items like scrumptious pasta dumplings of potato, chives and bacon, salads drizzled with nutty pumpkinseed oil, and multi-layered *gibanica,* a wildly decadent dessert. Slovenian wine is an unheralded strength, and regional whites and reds pair well with local specialities.

Astounding Natural Beauty

From the soaring peaks of the Julian Alps and the subterranean magic of the Postojna and Škocjan caves to the sparkling emerald-green lakes and rivers and the short but sweet coastline along the Adriatic Sea, tiny Slovenia really does have it all. An incredible mixture of climates brings warm Mediterranean breezes up to the foothills of the Alps, where it can snow even in summer. And with more than half of its total surface still covered in forest, Slovenia does more than simply claim it's 'green'.

Architectural & Cultural Treasures

You might be forgiven for thinking that anything of beauty in this greenest of green lands is, well, all natural. But it isn't necessarily so. Where humakind intrudes is often to good effect, such as at Lake Bled, where a tiny baroque chapel on a picturesque island and a dramatic castle looming above complete a harmonious whole. The architecture is wonderfully varied: from the Venetian harbour towns of the coast and the rustic Hungarian-style farmhouses of Prekmurje to the Gothic churches of the Julian Alps and the art nouveau splendours of Ljubljana.

Outdoor Pursuits

Slovenia is first and foremost an outdoor destination. Local people favour active holidays, and you'll be invited – even expected – to join in. The list of activities on offer is endless, with the most popular pursuits being skiing, walking and hiking in the mountains, and increasingly, cycling. Fast rivers like the Soča cry out to be rafted and there are ample chances to try out more niche activities like horse riding, ballooning, caving and canyoning.

Why I Love Slovenia

By Mark Baker, Writer

Slovenia was the first guidebook I ever wrote more than a decade ago, and even back then I knew I was smitten. The location is hidden away just enough to be off the well-worn path yet still at the heart of Europe. Ljubljana strikes that ideal balance between urban energy and liveability, and who can forget the electric blue-green waters of the Soča River? Slovenes themselves seem to take all of the natural beauty, the unhurried pace, the food and the wine in stride. We visitors know how special and rare this unspoilt place really is.

For more about our writers, see p288

Above: Soča River (p116)

Slovenia

Soča River
Raft it from adventure capital, Bovec (p116)

Vršič Pass
Breathtaking, zigzagging Alpine pass (p115)

Mt Triglav
Slovenia's highest, most legendary mountain (p108)

Lake Bled
A lake, an island and a fairy-tale castle (p90)

Vipava Valley
Source of Slovenia's finest wines (p143)

Škocjan Caves
Gargantuan, dramatic underground canyons (p139)

Postojna Cave
A vast labyrinth of subterranean marvels (p131)

Piran
Slovenia's best-preserved medieval Venetian port (p153)

Predjama Castle
A fortress perched in a cavern's mouth (p134)

N 0 — 50 km
0 — 25 miles

Ptuj
Medieval town of red roofs
and narrow streets (p209)

Fürstenfeld

Feldbach

Heiligenkreuz

AUSTRIA

Leibnitz

Oriszentpeter

Goričko Hills

Šalovci

Mačkovci

HUNGARY

Arnfels

Selnica
ob Muri

Mura

Bad
Radkersburg

Moravske
Toplice

Dravograd Muta

Kobansko Hills

Radlje ob Dravi

Gornja
Radgona

Bogojina

Ravne
na Koroškem

Vuzenica

Vuhred

Drava

Selnica ob
Dravi

Slovenske Gorice

Murska
Sobota

Dobrovnik

Lovrenc na
Pohorju

Pohorje Massif

Ruše

Lenart

Banovci

Beltinci

Redics

Slovenj
Gradec

▲ **Velika Kopa
(1543m)**

Žigartov
▲ **(1347m)**

MARIBOR

Spodnje
Hoče

Bučkovci

Lendava

Mislinja

**Rogla
(1517m)**

Slovenska
Bistrica

Ljutomer

Mursko
Središče

Šoštanj

Zreče

Pragersko

Ptuj

Dornava

Velenje

Slovenske
Konjice

Poljčane

Kidričevo

✛ *Ptujska
Gora*

Ormož

Gioričak

Središče
ob Dravi

Šempeter

Žalec

Celje

Šentjur

Rogaška
Slatina

**Donačka Gora
(884m)**
▲

Cirkulane

Sotla

Haloze Hills

Rogatec

Maceljsko

Varaždin

Silavec ▲

Laško

Đurmanec

Podčetrtek

Krapina

Ljubljana
Vibrant capital with a
hilltop castle (p46)

Zidani
Most

Radeče

Sava

**Kozjansko
Regional
Park**

Bistrica
ob Sotli

Sevnica

Senovo

Kozjansko

🏰 *Podsreda Castle*

Boštanj

Orlica ▲

Brestanica

Posavje

Mokronog

Krško

Križevci

Šmarjeta

Brežice

CROATIA

Kostanjevica
na Krki

Terme
Catež

*Mokrice
Castle*

Dolenjske Toplice
Historical spa with modern
pampering (p169)

Krka

Šentjernej

✛ *Pleterje
Monastery*

🏰 Obrežje

Novo
Mesto

▲ **Trdinov Vrh
(1178m)**

Gorjanci Hills

⭐ **ZAGREB**

Dugo
Selo

Metlika

Božakovo

Podzemelj

Bela Krajina
Sleeping pods in
pristine nature (p176)

Črnomelj

Adlešiči

Kupa

Karlovac

Vinica

Zuniči

Črnomelj
Home to Slovenia's oldest international folklore festival (p179)

Petrinja

ELEVATION

2000m
1500m
1000m
750m
500m
300m
200m
100m
0

Slovenia's
Top 14

1

Climbing Mt Triglav

1 They say you're not really a Slovene until you climb Mt Triglav (pictured left; p108) and get 'spanked' at the summit. And it's all but stamped in locals' passports once they've made the trek up the country's tallest mountain. The good news for the rest of us is that Triglav is a challenging but accessible peak that just about anyone in decent shape can conquer with an experienced guide. There are several popular approaches, but whichever path you choose, the reward is the same: sheer exhilaration.

Ljubljana

2 Slovenia's capital city (pictured below; p46) effortlessly achieves that perfect pitch between size and quality of life. It's big enough to offer lively clubs, theatre, exciting exhibitions and great concerts, yet small enough to walk – or better yet, cycle – around at a leisurely pace. And no place in Slovenia waltzes through architecture so adroitly as does the capital, from its ancient hilltop castle and splendid art nouveau buildings to all of those wondrously decorative pillars, obelisks and orbs found everywhere designed by local boy Jože Plečnik.

ENRIQUE UGARTE/GETTY IMAGES ©

JUSTIN FOULKES/LONELY PLANET ©

JUSTIN FOULKES/LONELY PLANET ©

Piran

3 Venice in Slovenia? That busy merchant empire left its mark up and down the Adriatic coast, and Slovenia was lucky to end up with one of the best-preserved medieval Venetian ports anywhere. It's true that Piran (pictured above left; p153) attracts tourist numbers on a massive scale in season, but the beautiful setting means it's never less than a constant delight. Enjoy fresh fish on the harbour, then wander the narrow streets and end up for drinks and people-watching in a glorious central square.

River Adventures

4 Rarely does a river beckon to be rafted as convincingly as does Slovenia's Soča (pictured above centre; p116). Maybe it's that piercing sky-blue-bordering-on-green – or is it turquoise? – colour of the water, or the river's refreshing froth and foam as it tumbles down the mountains. Even if you're not the rafting type, you'll soon find yourself strapping on a wetsuit for that exhilarating ride of the summer. Outfitters in Bovec, Bled and Kobarid specialise in guided rafting trips. For gentler floats, try the Krka River.

Lake Bled

5 With its sky-blue lake, picture-postcard church on a tiny island, a medieval castle clinging to a rocky cliff and some of the country's highest peaks as backdrops, Bled (pictured above right; p90) seems to have been designed by the very god of tourism. But Slovenia's biggest draw is more than just a pretty face. There's a lively cultural calendar during the summer months and a raucous adventure scene too, with diving, cycling, rafting and canyoning, among other active pursuits. The town is blessed with excellent campgrounds, hostels and hotels.

Postojna Cave

6 The cave system at Postojna (pictured right; p131) is Slovenia's biggest subterranean attraction. The rather innocent-looking entrance might not look like much at first, but when you get whisked 4km underground on a train and only then begin exploring, you start to get a sense of the scale. The caverns are a seemingly endless parade of crystal fancies – from frilly chandeliers and dripping spaghetti-like stalactites to paper-thin sheets and stupendous stalagmites, all laid down over the centuries by the simple dripping of mineral-rich water.

ALEXANDER PINK/SHUTTERSTOCK ©

7

8

Ptuj

7 Its name might sound like a cartoon character spitting, but Ptuj (pictured top; p209) is no joke. Rather, it's one of Slovenia's richest historical towns. Everyone since the Romans over the centuries has left their mark here, and the centre is still a maze of red roofs and medieval streets, dotted with churches, towers and museums, as well as street cafes to enjoy the passing scenes. Ptuj has great hotels and restaurants and is within easy reach of some of the country's best wine-producing regions.

Crossing the Vršič Pass

8 Making your way – whether by car or (yikes!) on bike – across this breathtakingly scenic Alpine pass (pictured above; p115) that zigs and zags through peaks and promontories, it's hard not to think of the poor Russian WWI POWs who were forced in the dead of winter to build the road – now called the Ruska cesta (Russian road) in their honour. This summer-only roadway links Kranjska Gora with Bovec, 50km to the southwest, and includes a number of photo-op rest stops and several mountain huts along the way.

Predjama Castle

9 Slovenia is over-endowed in castles and caves, but one inside the other? Now that's something special. Few fortresses have a setting as grand as this, wedged halfway up a cliff face at the foot of the valley (pictured top; p134). The location has a story behind it that's equally dramatic: Slovenia's 'Robin Hood', Erazem Lueger, apparently taunted besieging troops here by hurling fresh cherries at them that he collected via a secret passage. He came to a swift and rather embarrassing end, however.

Škocjan Caves

10 Where Postojna Cave is entirely baroque, the caves at Škocjan (pictured above; p139) are positively Gothic. It's all about the melodrama here – think Jules Verne, Tolkien and Wagner rolled up in one. Forget crawling around in tiny underground spaces; the Murmuring Cave has walls reaching something like a hundred metres high, while the Cerkevnik Bridge crosses a gloomy chasm with a 45m plunge to where the Reka River carves its way through the rock. Visiting the caves is a truly awesome experience.

Folklore Festivals

11 Expect lots of booze, colourful costumes and accordion music as Slovenes let their hair down at centuries-old folklore festivals. The best known is Kurentovanje (pictured below left; p211), a rite-of-spring party celebrated at Ptuj in the days leading up to Shrove Tuesday and the start of Lent. Jurjevanje (p181) in Črnomelj in June celebrates an ancient Slavic deity called Green George and is Slovenia's oldest international folklore festival. The zany Cows' Ball in the towns around Lake Bohinj in September sees bovines trip the light fantastic.

Vipava Valley Wines

12 Slovenia is blessed with the means to produce some of the region's best wines and the Vipava Valley (p142) particularly stands out among the country's three wine-making regions. It enjoys a warm Mediterranean climate freshened by cold winter winds, making it the ideal destination for those wanting to treat their palates. Wineries with some of the best merlots in the world? Check. The best air-dried *pršut* ham? Yep. Pick up some local fruits and olives and you've got a Slovenian picnic to remember.

XSEON/SHUTTERSTOCK ©

Traditional Spas

13 A spa in Central Europe can often mean a fusty 19th-century royal relic with lots of great architecture but not much in the way of modern treatments. Slovenia's natural and thermal spas have the architecture, but more importantly they offer a wealth of high-quality wellness and beauty treatments, including massage, mud baths, saunas, warm sea-water baths and more. Most of the spas are situated in the eastern half of the country and usually offer in-house (or nearby) accommodation as well; Dolenjske Toplice (p169) is a fine spot to take the waters.

Rustic-Glam Accommodation

14 To enhance Slovenia's clean, green appeal to travellers, locals are embracing and redefining the art of 'glamping'. Unique sleeps are springing up in scenic locales; some are heavy on the clever camping element (sleeping in 'pods' in Bela Krajina) while others emphasise the glamour (safari tents with private hot tubs in Bled). Some are not-quite-camping but far from regulation hotel rooms: beds in wine barrels in Ptuj, haylofts in Logarska Dolina and even under the herb garden in the Vipava Valley. An inventive and fun way to escape the everyday.

Need to Know

For more information, see Survival Guide (p257)

Currency
Euro (€)

Language
Slovene (slovenščina)

Visas
Generally not required for tourist stays up to 90 days (or at all for EU nationals); some nationalities will need an entry visa.

Money
ATMs are widely available or exchange money at banks. Credit and debit cards accepted by most businesses throughout the country.

Mobile Phones
Local SIM cards can be used in European, Australian and some American phones. Other phones must be set to roaming to work, but be wary of roaming charges.

Time
Central European Time (GMT/UTC plus one hour)

When to Go

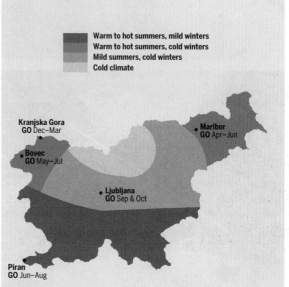

Warm to hot summers, mild winters
Warm to hot summers, cold winters
Mild summers, cold winters
Cold climate

Kranjska Gora
GO Dec–Mar

Maribor
GO Apr–Jun

Bovec
GO May–Jul

Ljubljana
GO Sep & Oct

Piran
GO Jun–Aug

High Season
(Jun–Aug)

➡ Mostly sunny skies with occasional rain.

➡ Crowds in Ljubljana and the coast; advance accommodation booking essential.

➡ Museums and other attractions open for business.

➡ Party atmosphere everywhere.

Shoulder
(Apr & May, Sep & Oct)

➡ Sunny, dry September is a great time for climbing Mt Triglav.

➡ Lower tariffs are in effect at many hotels.

➡ Rafting is great by late May; swimming is over by September.

➡ Best overall time for hiking.

Low Season
(Nov–Mar)

➡ Ski season runs from mid-December to March or even April.

➡ Christmas through New Year can be crowded.

➡ Attractions in smaller towns may close or have limited hours.

Useful Websites

Slovenian Tourist Board (www.slovenia.info) Info on every conceivable sight and activity.

Slovenia Times (www.sloveniatimes.com) Website of the independent quarterly magazine.

E-uprava (http://e-uprava.gov.si) Official info-packed government portal.

Lonely Planet (www.lonelyplanet.com/slovenia) Destination information, hotel bookings, traveller forum and more.

Important Numbers

Slovenia's Country Code	✆386
Domestic Directory Assistance	✆1188
Ambulance & Fire	✆112
Police	✆113 (emergencies)
Road Emergency or towing	✆1987

Exchange Rates

Australia	A$1	€0.65
Canada	C$1	€0.66
Japan	¥100	€0.78
New Zealand	NZ$1	€0.60
UK	UK£1	€1.14
US	US$1	€0.86

For current exchange rates, see www.xe.com.

Daily Costs

Budget: Less than €60

➡ Hostel dorm bed or low-cost guesthouse: €15–25

➡ Street food and self-catering: €10

➡ Train/bus tickets: €10

➡ Bicycle rental: €12

➡ Pint of beer: €3

Midrange: €80–120

➡ Room in a midrange hotel or pension: €40–60

➡ Dinner in a good restaurant: €30

➡ Train/bus tickets: €10

➡ Lipica Stud Farm entry: €16

Top End: More than €120

➡ Room in the best place in town: €80–100

➡ Dinner in a very good restaurant: €40

➡ Train/bus/taxi: €20

➡ Postojna Cave entry: €26

Opening Hours

Opening hours can vary throughout the year. We've provided high-season opening hours.

Banks 8.30am–12.30pm and 2pm–5pm Monday to Friday

Bars 11am–midnight Sunday to Thursday, to 1am or 2am Friday and Saturday

Restaurants 11am–10pm daily

Shops 8am–7pm Monday to Friday, to 1pm Saturday

Arriving in Slovenia

Jože Pučnik Airport (Ljubljana) Buses (€4.10) run to Ljubljana's main bus station hourly on weekdays (two hourly on weekends). Shuttle (€9) and taxi services (€35 to €40) will transfer you to the city centre in around half an hour.

Ljubljana train & bus stations Located next to each other 500m north of the Old Town and an easy walk away. Served by public buses 2, 5, 9, 12, 18, 25 and 27. Taxis within the city should cost no more than €8.

Getting Around

Transport in Slovenia is reasonably priced, quick and efficient. For national bus timetables, head to Avtobusna Postaja Ljubljana (www.ap-ljubljana.si); for train timetables: Slovenian Railways (www.slo-zeleznice.si).

Bus Generally efficient and good value but very crowded on Friday afternoons and severely restricted on Sundays and holidays.

Car A great way to explore the countryside, with rental firms everywhere.

Train Cheaper but usually slower than buses (with the exception of intercity high-speed services). Getting from A to B sometimes requires returning to Ljubljana.

For much more on **getting around**, see p269

What's New

Eat 'Local'

When it comes to food, Slovenia has remarkable regional diversity, and restaurants everywhere put the emphasis on using local ingredients. Kobarid's Hiša Franko sets the gold standard of a countrywide trend. (p122)

Wine Roads

Slovenia is an ideal destination for pairing winery visits with hikes and cycling trips, and all the main wine-making areas now have dedicated 'wine routes'. Goriška Brda features many small, family-owned wineries. (p146)

Sustainability

A buzzword everywhere, a mantra in Slovenia. The commitment extends to food at amazing Monstera Bistro, which employs minimal-waste, whole-animal practices. (p71)

Ziplines

Move over canyoning, ziplines are the hot new adventure sport. The Planica Zipline glides over the towering ski-jump centre near Kranjska Gora (p113), while the Zipline Dolinka takes you through a harrowing valley. (p92)

Bear Watching

The number of operators offering bear-watching tours has expanded, and the Green Karst has emerged as one of Europe's best wildlife-watching opportunities. (p138)

e-bikes

Electric-powered bicycles are a nuisance in Ljubljana, but in the open air around Bled, they make climbs accessible to people of all fitness levels. 3glav Adventures can lead a tour. (p92)

Craft Beer

Slovenes have embraced the mania for hoppy, fruity IPAs with the same zest they have for buckwheat groats. Find craft beers in bars everywhere. Big names include HumanFish, Pelican and Bevog.

Burgers

What pairs better with craft beer than burgers? The worldwide burger craze is here too, and done better than most places. Ljubljana is the epicentre, but Bohinj's Foksner remains king. (p107)

A Fountain of Beer

Beer lovers should make the hop over to Žalec to sip from the Green Gold Beer Fountain, the world's first fountain given over, yep, to beer. (p202)

Roman Frescoes

The discovery of an intact Roman villa and surviving frescoes in the cellar of the Celje Regional Museum is one of the most exciting archaeological finds in years. (p199)

For more recommendations and reviews, see lonelyplanet.com/slovenia

If You Like...

Dramatic Scenery

For such a small country, Slovenia packs an amazing amount of diversity and stunning natural beauty. Snowcapped Alps; long, green valleys; and lakes and rivers so blue they almost hurt your eyes.

Vršič Pass This curving WWI-era highway crosses the Alps at an elevation of 1611m as it runs from near Kranjska Gora to Bovec. (p115)

Velika Planina High-altitude Alpine pasture land that offers some of the best mountain photo ops we've ever seen. (p194)

Soča Valley Hair-raisingly steep verdant valleys and deep gorges cut through by impossibly blue water. (p116)

Lake Bohinj Bled's lesser-known (but larger) sister lake is no wallflower. It's an emerald-green mountain paradise with a quieter, more rustic feel and a glimpse of Mt Triglav. (p102)

Logarska Dolina The 'pearl of the Alpine region' offers caves, springs, rock towers and waterfalls – as well as rare fauna such as mountain eagles. (p195)

Škocjan Caves Dramatic scenery of a different sort – all of the melodrama here is below the ground. (p139)

Historic Towns

Slovenia's most attractive cities and towns are the kind of places where you feel you can walk through the past (be it Roman times, the Middle Ages or the communist era).

Ljubljana Roman Emona flanks a medieval core ringed with art nouveau creations and a communist hinterland of pre-fabs. (p46)

Ptuj One of the oldest towns in Slovenia, this former metropolis from the Middle Ages boasts a symphony of red-tiled roofs. (p209)

Škofja Loka The 'Bishop's Meadow' is a perfectly preserved medieval town with an intact square and a spooky hilltop castle. (p83)

Kropa This one-horse, former iron-working town is a surviving living museum of the country's once-mighty industrial tradition. (p89)

Piran It's hard to imagine a more romantic spot anywhere than this little Venetian port jutting out into the Adriatic. (p153)

Radovljica A colourful main square of 16th-century townhouses and the delightful Beekeeping Museum. (p86)

Castles & Churches

Slovenia had so many hilltop fortresses in the Middle Ages, it was known as the 'country of castles'. It is also blessed with some of the most beautiful houses of worship in Central Europe.

Predjama Castle Could easily be called 'pre-drama' for its dramatic perch tucked high inside a cliffside cave. (p134)

Ljubljana Castle For history, look no further than the capital's hilltop fortress that's been around since at least the 12th century. (p48)

Old Castle Celje There's not much inside this 13th-century fortress but it evokes the past like few others and the views are commanding. (p199)

Church of St John the Baptist Gazing out at Bohinj, this tiny church of unknown age is awash in delightful 15th- and 16th-century frescoes. (p102)

Church of the Holy Trinity You'll never forget the macabre 15th-century Dance of Death fresco at this church by the coast. (p143)

Basilica of the Patroness Mary Only named a basilica in 2010, this hilltop church contains a stunningly carved altar. (p216)

Walks & Hikes

Slovenia is crossed by thousands of kilometres of hiking trails, many passing through points of considerable natural beauty or paired to teach the lessons of the country's moving history.

Climbing Mt Triglav The ultimate Slovenian hike involves a trek to the top of Mt 'Three Heads'; at 2864m, it's a point of considerable national pride, especially for those who reach the top! (p108)

Trail of Remembrance This trail wends its way 34km around the capital along the boundary where German barbed wire once enclosed the city during WWII. (p64)

Alpe-Adria-Trail Six stages of this stunning transnational trail pass through Slovenia and through varying regions filled with mountains, lakes, rivers and vineyards. (p120)

Kobarid Historical Trail This 5km-long trail starting from Kobarid is the prettiest open-air museum of the atrocities committed during wartime that you're ever likely to see. (p121)

Jeruzalem-Ljutomer Wine Road Walk or cycle this lovely trail that begins at Ormož and continues for 18km north to Ljutomer, passing many wine cellars and restaurants en route. (p217)

Lake Bled If you're looking for something easy and relaxing, a two-hour circuit around lovely Lake Bled is just the ticket. (p90)

Top: Slovenian cheese

Bottom: Ice-climbing, Julian Alps (p81)

Food

Slovenia is in the midst of a slow-food, organic-food, local-food revolution that prizes original recipes and fresh, quality ingredients. The country's excellent wine is sorely underrated.

Odprta Kuhna This weekly food festival in Ljubljana's main market square allows you to taste your way round Slovenia. (p69)

Slovenian Coast Slovenia's tiny seacoast is big on seafood. Piran, in particular, is filled with excellent places to sample the spoils. (p147)

Groats If Slovenian cooking has a signature side, it would have to be stick-to-your-ribs barley or buckwheat groats. (p35)

Pršut Air-dried, thinly sliced ham similar to Italian prosciutto but maybe even airier and more flavourful. (p34)

Cream Cake Cafes and sweetshops around Lake Bled pride themselves on the quality of their *kremšnita:* a dollop of vanilla custard sandwiched between layers of flaky pastry and topped with whipped cream. (p36)

Carniolan Sausage Spicy, filling, delicious *Kranjska klobasa* hails from the Julian Alps and is so good it's won protection from the EU. (p34)

Wine, Brandy & Beer

Karst Wine Region An underrated wine region known for its Teran dark reds and Mediterranean malvasia whites. (p141)

Vipava Valley Many of the best reds in Slovenia are produced here, especially merlots. (p142)

Goriška Brda Small, family-run wineries in a wonderful setting of rolling hills and fortified villages. (p146)

Metlika Wine Area The hills north of Metlika are home to Bela Krajina's most important wine districts. (p177)

Žganje Classic brandy distilled from a variety of fruits – from plums and pears to cherries and blueberries. (p40)

Jeruzalem Ormož Winery Along the scenic Jeruzalem-Ljutomer Wine Road, try the peppery pinot grigio and spicy-sweet traminec. (p217)

Green Gold Beer Fountain The world's first beer fountain dispenses glasses of beer deep in the heart of hop-growing country. (p202)

Outdoor Activities

Slovenia is an active destination. And while hiking and biking are still the most popular ways to relax, there are lots of chances to swim, boat, raft or jump out of a plane.

Rafting the Soča The signature Slovenian outdoor adventure involves a breathtaking float down one of Europe's fastest and most beautiful rivers. (p117)

Adrenaline Sports A growing number of operators, particularly at Bovec, Bled and Bohinj – offer the chance to try ballooning, canyoning and paragliding, among other instant rushes. (p92)

Caving Slovenia has dozens of caves, and some are extraordinary: Škocjan has walls that run 100m high, while Postojna's caverns are vast and bejewelled. (p30)

Skiing The Julian Alps offers myriad chances to hit the slopes. Kranjska Gora is the centre of the country's ski universe, but is just one of several popular resorts. (p29)

Hiking Mt Triglav Slovenia's only national park, Triglav National Park, covers a huge swath of Slovenian turf in the northwest. It's a world of rivers, streams, waterfalls and hiking trails. (p108)

Viewing Brown Bears Go looking for brown bears in the beautiful forests of Lož Valley east of Postojna. (p138)

Spas & Thermal Baths

Slovenia counts upwards of 15 thermal spa resorts, most of them in the eastern part of the country, in Dolenjska and Prekmurje. They are excellent places not just for 'taking the cure' but for relaxing and meeting people.

Dolenjske Toplice Cosy and wooded resort town with all the mod cons, dating back to the 17th century. (p169)

Terme Olimia Enormous spa complex on the Croatian border with a great fortress looming above it. (p204)

Lepa Vida Thalasso Spa Luxury spa overlooking the salt pans of Sečovlje, where the Slovenian coast meets Croatia. (p162)

Terme Catez A 'Summer Thermal Riviera', packed with family-friendly fun and hugely popular on weekends. (p186)

Rogaška Riviera Located in Slovenia's oldest and largest spa town, a veritable 'cure factory' with a fin-de-siècle feel. (p207)

Month by Month

January

This is for the most part a quiet month after the holidays, though skiing is generally very good and it's the time of one of the most important sport events in the year.

☆ Women's World Cup Slalom & Giant Slalom Competition

One of the world's major international ski events held only for women – the coveted Zlata Lisica (Golden Fox) trophy – takes place on the Maribor Pohorje ski grounds for four days in late January/early February. (p225)

February

A cold and snowy month keeps things busy on the ski slopes near Kranjska Gora. Many of the country's best festivals are connected to Shrove Tuesday and Lent (February and early March) in the run-up to Easter.

☆ Kurentovanje

Ptuj marks Shrovetide with Kurentovanje, a rite of spring and fertility. Festivities are spread over 11 days in February, culminating in the Kurent parades on the weekend before Shrove Tuesday. (p211)

☆ Laufarija

A folkloric pre-Lenten carnival in Cerkno on the Sunday and Tuesday before Ash Wednesday. This ancient carnival sees masked participants chasing and executing the Pust, representing winter and the old year. (p128)

March

Still plenty of good skiing in the higher elevations; elsewhere the country is relatively quiet.

☆ Men's Slalom & Giant Slalom Vitranc Cup Competition

The number-one downhill ski event of the year – the Vitranc Cup – takes place at Kranjska Gora in early March. (p113)

April

Flowers bloom and trees blossom in lower elevations. Depending on the winter, there's skiing at higher elevations. The Vršič Pass opens to cars by late April.

☆ Spring Horticultural Fair, Volčji Potok

Slovenia's largest flower and gardening show takes place at an arboretum in Volčji Potok, near Kamnik, in late April. (p191)

May

Hit the Alpine valleys for a breakout of mountain wildflowers. Expect sunshine and warm daytime temperatures. It's too cold yet to swim in the Adriatic, but days are ideal for a portside promenade.

☆ International Wildflower Festival

Held over two weeks, this flower fest celebrates Bohinj's botanical riches and includes guided walks and tours and birdwatching. (p106)

June

June can be gloriously sunny or occasionally rainy. It's the best month for white-water rafting, as rivers swell after the spring thaw and temps warm up enough to make the idea palatable.

✦ Idrija Lace Festival

This celebration of all things lacy includes a gala opening, and lace-making exhibitions, as well as live music. (p125)

✦ Lent Festival

A two-week extravaganza of folklore and culture in Maribor's Old Town. (p222)

July

Mostly warm and sunny, July is a big month for festivals. Nearly every village and town has something going on. Trekkers, watch out for freak storms in higher elevations.

✦ Festival Bled

A fortnight of concerts (primarily classical, but also jazz and other genres) in beautiful venues around Lake Bled. (p94)

✦ Ljubljana Festival

The nation's premier festival of classical entertainment (music, theatre and dance) held in July and August. (p65)

August

The traditional summer holiday month for Europeans finds resorts like Piran and Portorož filled to the brim. Campgrounds are packed, and the waters of Lakes Bohinj and Bled warm up enough to swim.

✦ Festival Radovljica

One of the most important festivals of early classical music in Europe is staged over two weeks in August. (p88)

✦ Pisana Loka

This arts festival (the name means 'Colourful Loka') stages music and theatre, film and children's events over 10 days in late August. (p85)

September

Autumn chill comes to the mountains. Swimming winds down on the Adriatic coast and resorts like Bled and Bohinj hold their last big shindigs. Mushroom-hunting shifts into high gear.

✦ Cows' Ball

Zany weekend of folk dance, music, eating and drinking in Bohinj to mark the return of the cows from their high pastures in mid-September. (p106)

✦ Slovenian Film Festival

A pivotal event in the Slovenian cinema world, this three-day festival in Portorož in late September sees screenings and awards. (p160)

October

Coastal areas quiet down and the action shifts to cities like Ljubljana, where the cultural season is in full swing.

✦ City of Women

Ljubljana's 10-day international festival, Mesto Žensk, focusing on contemporary arts and culture created by women. (p66)

November

The solemn holiday of All Saints' Day (1 November) sets the tone for the rest of this grey, chilly month. On this day, Slovenes bring candles and red lanterns to the cemetery to remember the departed.

✦ St Martin's Day

Nationwide celebration to mark the day (11 November) when *mošt* (must; fermenting grape juice) officially becomes new wine.

December

Christmas (25 December) is the high point. Ski season starts.

☆ Christmas Concerts

Held throughout Slovenia; the most famous are in Postojna Cave, where you can also attend the Live Christmas Crib, a re-enactment of the Nativity. (p131)

Itineraries

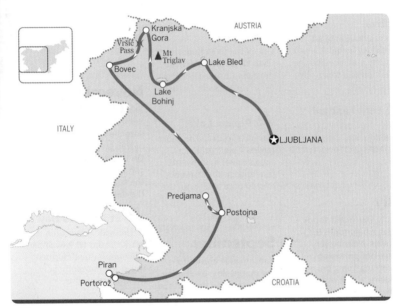

1 WEEK Essential Slovenia

This route is ideal for first-time visitors wanting to experience the highlights of the Alpine and coastal regions.

Begin in the capital, **Ljubljana**, allowing at least two nights for the sights, restaurants and beautiful riverside setting. Next, head north to **Lake Bled**, overnighting to allow time for lakeside ambles and taking a *pletna* (gondola) to Bled Island. **Lake Bohinj**, 26km southwest of Lake Bled, makes for a more rustic base and has views to **Mt Triglav**.

From here, travel northward to **Kranjska Gora**, the skiing capital and a good hiking base. It's the northern terminus of the spectacular **Vršič Pass**, a high-altitude roadway (open May to October) that zigzags for 50km down to the white-water rafting capital of **Bovec**. The next day continue on to the amazing cave at **Postojna**. An easy side trip is **Predjama**, where an impregnable castle in a cliffside cave defies description.

You're close to the coastal resorts of Piran and Portorož. For romance, choose **Piran**; for sun and fun, **Portorož**.

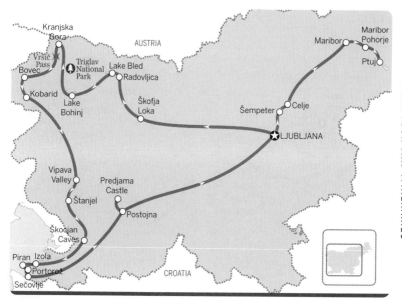

Slovenia in Depth

With two weeks to explore Slovenia, you'll be able to experience the best of the country's mountains and coast, plus get a good look at the country's untrampled east.

Allow a couple of nights in **Ljubljana**, then head north, stopping at one or both of the historic towns of **Škofja Loka** or **Radovljica**, to **Lake Bled**. Overnight and explore the lake and Bled Island, or stay a bit longer for adventure, such as rafting or canyoning. To the southwest, picturesque **Lake Bohinj** is an excellent base for exploring **Triglav National Park** or even climbing Mt Triglav itself.

Next head north to ski-capital **Kranjska Gora** to start your climb up and then down to the Soča Valley via the **Vršič Pass**. After 50km of hairpin turns you'll arrive at the country's white-water rafting capital of **Bovec**. Overnight here – especially if you plan to do any adventure sports – or in nearby **Kobarid**, a pretty town with a Mediterranean feel, an amazing WWI history and some of Slovenia's best restaurants.

Continue southward through Nova Gorica to the **Vipava Valley** and on to the Karst region. Little towns here, like **Štanjel** to the west, are rich in olives, ruby-red Teran wine, *pršut* (dry-cured ham) and red-tiled roofs.

Further south, following the main Hwy E70 to the coast near Divača, is the awe-inspiring **Škocjan Caves**, part of an immense system of limestone caves. From here, go coastal. **Piran** is the most romantic spot on the Adriatic, but **Izola** has some good food and **Portorož** can be more fun. Nearby is **Sečovlje** and its famous salt pans.

The return journey to Ljubljana passes through **Postojna**, another amazing cave, with a side trip to **Predjama Castle**. Avoid the capital altogether and continue driving along Hwy E57 to Celje, stopping to visit the awesome Roman necropolis at **Šempeter**. **Celje** is worth an afternoon for its wonderful castle and rich museums, but **Maribor**, Slovenia's second-largest city and regional centre, awaits. The surrounding highlands, the **Maribor Pohorje**, rate a look, but by now you might just want to spend some downtime along the Drava in Maribor's atmospheric Lent district.

Finish your journey in **Ptuj**, a charming town with a delightful castle and some excellent accommodation.

Mountain Majesty

What Slovenia has in spades is mountains. Active travellers can head for the hills near Kamnik, climb the dizzying heights of the Julian Alps and then descend into the adventure land of the Soča Valley.

Begin in **Ljubljana**, to stock up on hiking gear and regional maps, then make your way to **Kamnik** and the picturesque, high-altitude pastureland of **Velika Planina**. Heading back towards Kranj, continue north to impossibly cute **Radovljica**. Overnight here or a few kilometres north at **Lake Bled**.

Use Bled or nearby **Lake Bohinj** for forays into **Triglav National Park**. Both are popular approaches for scaling **Mt Triglav**. Proceed northward to **Kranjska Gora** and the heart-stopping **Vršič Pass** (closed in winter). The road down deposits you in the **Soča Valley**. Following the Soča River will bring you to the activities centre of **Bovec** and the WWI battlegrounds around **Kobarid**. From here, head through Tolmin to the sleepy town of **Cerkno**, famous for its pre-Lenten carnival. Route 210 is a sinuous mountain road through the Škofja Loka Hills, a region of steep slopes, valleys and ravines, to the charming town of **Škofja Loka** and back to Ljubljana.

Wine & Spas

Eastern and southern Slovenia are known for both their wines and spas. This tour includes the best of each.

From **Ljubljana** drive southeast to the delightful spa town of **Dolenjske Toplice**. **Otočec** and its stunning castle is not far away. Further east, **Brežice** draws visitors to its Terme Čatež spa complex and the wonderful **Bizeljsko-Sremič wine district**, known for its medium-dry whites and reds and for *repnice* – caves for storing wine.

Head north on route 219 to **Podčetrtek** and another inviting spa, Terme Olimia. From here it's a short distance through the Haloze Hills to atmospheric **Rogaška Slatina**, Slovenia's oldest and largest spa, a veritable 'cure factory' with a dozen hotels and far more treatments.

Head north to the charming town of **Ptuj** and its nearby Terme Ptuj spa, then go east to Ormož for the **Jeruzalem-Ljutomer district**, home to some of the country's best whites. Walk or hike the wine trail here.

The region's biggest city and cultural hub, **Maribor**, is not very far away. Who could possibly resist seeing the world's oldest (and still productive) grapevine dating back more than three centuries?

Rafting on the Soča River (p117)

Plan Your Trip
Outdoor Slovenia

Slovenia is blessed with a magnificent natural environment of mountains, lakes and rivers that lend a breathtaking backdrop to any activity. Popular pursuits include hiking, skiing and mountain biking, but there's also a world of more intrepid activities – from white-water rafting and caving to horse riding and canyoning.

The Best ...

Hiking & Climbing
Triglav National Park (p108) While the entire country is criss-crossed by trails, Slovenia's national park is the undisputed centre of hiking and climbing. There are trails to suit all levels of ability.

Skiing
Kranjska Gora (p111) While the slopes are suited mainly to beginners and intermediates, this is Slovenia's best-known and most popular ski resort, easily accessible from western and northern Europe.

Cycling
Lake Bohinj (p102) The villages to the north of Lake Bohinj are ideal for exploring on a leisurely ride, and the higher-altitude terrain nearby offers opportunities for cyclists seeking adrenaline.

Kayaking & Rafting
Bovec (p116) The Soča River, with its flow, froth and green colour, seems designed by nature to offer rafting experiences that excite the body and the senses.

Caves
Škocjan Caves (p139) For many travellers the sight of these immense and dramatic caverns is the highlight of their trip.

Hiking & Walking

Hiking is a national pastime. The country has an excellent system of well-marked trails that run to a total length of more than 9000km. Most trails are marked by a red circle with a white centre, with periodic updater signs along the way indicating distances and walking times. In addition, most regional tourist offices and bookshops stock a comprehensive selection of hiking maps.

The most popular areas for hikes include the Julian Alps and the Kamnik-Savinja Alps in the northwest, as well as the Pohorje Massif in the northeast, but there are wonderful trails in all of the country's regions. Some of the best of these are linked with less obviously salubrious activities, such as wine tasting.

Many trails can also be cycled, with the notable exception being most of the trails in Triglav National Park.

Great Slovenian Hikes

Slovenian Mountain Trail This trail runs for 500km from Maribor to Ankaran on the coast via the Pohorje Massif, the Kamnik-Savinja Alps, the Julian Alps, and the Cerkno and Idrija Hills. It was opened back in 1953 and was the first such national trail in Europe.

Walk of Peace (Pot Miru; www.potmiru.si) This 320km-long route connects the outdoor museums and the most important remains and memorials of the Isonzo Front of the Upper Soča Region.

Sub-Alpine Trail (Predalpska pot) This 470km-long trail covers Slovenia's hill country – from Cerkno and Idrija to Posavje via the Karst – and is for less-ambitious, but equally keen, walkers and hikers.

Jeruzalem-Ljutomer wine road A great *vinska cesta* (wine road) in eastern Slovenia, this route begins at Ormož and continues for 18km north to Ljutomer, via the beautiful hilltop village of Jeruzalem. There are many wine cellars along the way, and it can also be biked.

Haloze Mountain Path This lovely wine-oriented 12km-long footpath takes in the gentle landscape of the Haloze Hills wine region. It is accessible from near Štatenberg.

Major European Trails

E6 European Hiking Trail This 350km trail runs from the Baltic to the Adriatic seas and enters Slovenia at Radlje ob Dravi in northeastern Slovenia. It continues on to a point south of Snežnik in southern Slovenia. Budget 20 days end to end.

E7 European Hiking Trail This 600km trail connects the Atlantic with the Black Sea. It crosses into western Slovenia at Robič and runs along the Soča Valley. From here, it continues through the southern part of the country eastward to Bistrica ob Sotli, before exiting into Croatia. Takes about 30 days to hike end to end.

Via Alpina (www.via-alpina.com) Slovenia has joined Austria, Germany, Liechtenstein, Switzerland, Italy, France and Monaco to develop this system of five long trails that follow the entire arc of the Alps from Trieste to Monaco. Two of the trails pass through northern Slovenia:

the 14-stage Red Trail (220km) and the 10-stage Purple Trail (120km).

Alpe-Adria-Trail (www.alpe-adria-trail.com) This 700km through Austria, Italy and Slovenia, enters Slovenia at the Jepca mountain pass on the Austrian border and continues for 145km, exiting at Milje above Trieste.

Skiing

Skiing rivals hiking as the most popular recreational pursuit in Slovenia, and many Slovenes even believe the sport was invented here. Today an estimated 300,000 people – some 15% of the population – ski regularly. Just about everyone takes to the slopes or trails in season, and you can too on the more than three-dozen ski grounds and resorts of varying sizes listed in the Slovenian Tourist Board's useful *Ski Resorts in Slovenia*.

Most of Slovenia's ski areas are small and relatively unchallenging compared to the Alpine resorts of France, Switzerland and Italy, but they do have the attraction of lower prices and easy access. For more details, as well as the latest weather and snow reports, check out the Ski Resort Info website (www.skiresort.info) or **Snow Telephone** (Snežni Telefon; ☎01-620 36 14; www.snezni-telefon.si).

Julian Alps

Kranjska Gora (p112) (800m to 1215m) Kranjska Gora has some 20km of pistes, but the skiing here is fairly straightforward and suited mostly to beginners and intermediates. Nevertheless, for foreign visitors, it is probably Slovenia's best-known and most popular ski resort, being easily accessible from Austria and Italy.

Vogel (p104) (570m to 1800m) Above shimmering Lake Bohinj, Vogel offers dazzling views of Mt Triglav and reliable snow cover on around 22km of slopes.

Eastern Slovenia

Krvavec (p194) (1450m to 1970m) In the hills northeast of Kranj, Krvavec is one of the best-equipped ski areas in the country, with 30km of pistes and 40km of trails. In addition you'll find a number of ski (Alpine and telemark) and snowboard schools, equipment rental, a ski shop,

---

HIKING RESOURCES

➡ The Ljubljana-based Alpine Association of Slovenia (p259) is the fount of all information on hikes and treks. The organisation is a good first stop for basic info and arranging mountain guides. It also publishes hiking maps and maintains an up-to-date list of mountain huts, refuges and bivouacs throughout Slovenia on its website.

➡ The Slovenian Tourist Board (www.slovenia.info) publishes the excellent *Hiking in Slovenia* brochure with more than 30 suggested itineraries.

➡ *The Julian Alps of Slovenia* (Cicerone) by Justi Carey and Roy Clark features 58 walking routes and short treks. The same pair's *Trekking in Slovenia: The Slovene High Level Route* (Cicerone) includes 500km of mountain and upland trail walking. *Long Distance Trails*, published by the Slovenian Tourist Board and the Alpine Association of Slovenia, features several walks and hikes.

---

and some good restaurants and bars. As it's only an hour's drive from Ljubljana, it's best avoided at the weekends.

Maribor Pohorje (p225) (330m to 1350m) In the hills south of Maribor, this is the biggest downhill skiing area, with 42km of linked pistes and 27km of cross-country trails suitable for skiers of all levels. It offers a ski and snowboard school, equipment rental and floodlit night skiing, as well as being a good starting point for ski touring through the forested hills of the Pohorje.

Cycling & Mountain Biking

Slovenia is an excellent cycling destination, both for road and off-road riding. Ljubljana is a bike-friendly big city, with marked cycling paths, an active bike-riding population, and several bike-riding outfits, including an innovative rent-as-you-go cycling scheme called Bicike(lj) (p80). Around the

BIKE RENTALS & REPAIR

Rent bikes at TICs, adventure-travel agencies and many hotels. Rates depend on the make and quality of the bike, but expect to pay anywhere from €2 to €4 per hour and €12 to €18 per day for a good-quality mountain bike. Cheaper rates can sometimes be negotiated for longer rentals. Some places also offer electronic bikes (e-bikes) for rent. These are a lot of fun and can be lifesavers for helping inexperienced cyclists climb high hills. Expect to pay €30 to €60 per day to hire an e-bike, depending on the make and quality.

Bike-repair shops are thin on the ground, though big cities and towns will usually have a few. Bring spare tubes and repair kits with you on the trail. Local TICs can advise on the nearest repair place. In a pinch, bike-rental outfits or adventure-travel agencies may be able to help out.

country, you'll find trails suited both to casual and experienced riders. Some ski resorts reopen in summer as downhill-cycling adrenaline parks.

Great Regions for Rides

You'll find good cycling all around the country. Mountain bikers and trail riders will want to focus on the Julian Alps and Soča Valley areas, particularly around Bovec, Lake Bohinj and Kranjska Gora. The 13km-long Radovna cycling trail (p93), that starts northwest of Bled, is the only dedicated cycling path that takes you to the centre of the national park. Bled-based 3glav Adventures (p92) can lead a tour and also rents e-bikes that make the steep climbs like child's play.

The TICs at Lake Bohinj and Kranjska Gora are particularly bike savvy, offering guided tours and helpful cycling maps that mark out regional routes that go from family-friendly to downright crazy.

For real thrill seekers, the Bike Park Kranjska Gora (p113) whisks cyclists up some steep hills on a ski lift where they can then hurtle downward at breakneck speeds. Another popular adrenaline destination is Logarska Dolina and the surrounding Upper Savinja Valley in eastern Slovenia. Buy a copy of the *Upper Savinja Valley Cycling Map* (€3).

Slower, more scenic rides can be found in the Krka Valley in Dolenjska. Slovenia's many dedicated 'wine routes' also often make for great cycling trips.

Kayaking, Rafting & Canyoning

The country's centre for kayaking and rafting is the Soča River at Bovec (p116). The Soča is famed as one of Europe's best white-water rafting rivers and is one of only half-a-dozen water channels in the European Alps whose upper waters are still unspoiled.

The Soča is where to give canyoning a go. It's a sport that has grown by leaps and bounds in recent years and will have you descending through gorges, jumping over and sliding down waterfalls, swimming in rock pools and abseiling/rappelling. It's been described as being in one huge, natural water park. Operators at Lake Bled can set you up for the day.

Other rafting centres include the Krka and Kolpa Rivers in southern Slovenia, the Sava River at Bohinj, the Savinja River at Logarska Dolina and the Drava River near Dravograd in northeastern Slovenia.

Caving

It's hardly surprising that the country that gave the world the word 'karst' is riddled with caves – around 7500 have been recorded and described. The main potholing regions in Slovenia are the Karst around Postojna and the Julian Alps, and there are about 20 caves open to visitors.

Some caves, such as Škocjan (p139) and Postojna (p131), can be visited easily on a guided tour, others are demanding undertakings requiring more pre-planning. At Križna Cave (p138), you actually take a subterranean boat ride. This is Slovenia's only tourist cave without electric lighting – visitors are given lamps (and boots) for the visit. It's a special thrill for kids.

Mountaineering & Rock Climbing

Climbing mountains is a national mania, and indeed Slovenes are expected to summit the country's highest peak, Mt Triglav (2864m), in Triglav National Park (p108) at least once in their lives. It's a relatively demanding climb that's possible to do on your own (p96), but is better with the help of a guide. There are plenty of other, smaller mountains, like Viševnik (2050m) near Bled, that offer almost all of the views but don't necessarily demand all of the skills. Adventure outfits in both Bled and Lake Bohinj can help.

Scaling Rock Faces

The principal Alpine climbing areas in Slovenia include Mt Triglav's magnificent north face – where routes range from the classic 'Slovene Route' (Slovenski Pot; Grade II/III; 750m) to the modern 'Sphinx Face' (Obraz Sfinge; Grade IX+/X; 140m),

with a crux 6m roof – as well as the impressive northern buttresses of Prisank overlooking the Vršič Pass.

Another promising place for climbers is located in the coastal region, near the village of Osp, northeast of Koper. The four main climbing crags around Osp range in difficulty from intermediate to challenging.

Sport climbing *(športno plezanje)* is popular in Slovenia as well. The revised *Slovenija Športnoplezalni Vodnik* (Sport Climbing Guide to Slovenia; Sidarta) by climber Janez Skok et al covers 92 crags, with good topos and descriptions in English.

Birdwatching & Wildlife Spotting

Slovenia offers some of the most rewarding birding in Central Europe. Some 376 species have been sighted here, 219 of which are breeders. The Ljubljana Marsh, south of Ljubljana, Lake Cerknica, in southern Slovenia, and the Sečovlje salt pans near Portorož on the coast are especially good for sighting waterbirds and waders, as is the Drava River and its reservoirs in northeast Slovenia.

Slovenia slides in under the radar in terms of wildlife spotting, but the Green Karst region in southwestern Slovenia, particularly the Lož Valley, (p138) has emerged as one of the best places to spot

---

BEDDING DOWN ON HIGH

➡ The Alpine Association of Slovenia (p259) lists around 180 mountain huts throughout the country and these are ranked according to category.

➡ A bivouac is the most basic hut in the mountains of Slovenia, providing shelter only.

➡ A refuge has refreshments, and sometimes accommodation, but usually no running water.

➡ A *koča* (hut) or *dom* (house) can be a simple cottage or a fairly grand establishment.

➡ A bed for the night costs €21 to €27 in a Category I hut, the most remote hut, depending on the number of beds in the room, and €16 to €22 in a Category II hut, defined as being within an hour's walk of motor transport. Category III huts are allowed to set their own prices but usually cost less than Category I huts.

➡ There are around 50 mountain huts in the Julian Alps, most of them open at least between June and September; some huts at lower altitudes are open year-round.

IN SEARCH OF ADVENTURE

In recent years, Slovenia has become a mecca for high-altitude 'adventure sports' of all kinds, like paragliding, hot-air ballooning and, most recently, ziplining. The Julian Alps offers the best chances for paragliding, and adventure-travel agencies in Bled, Lake Bohinj and Bovec can help arrange jumps. The TIC (p78) in Ljubljana can organise hot-air balloon flights.

Ziplining, where you sail over a valley, blissfully gliding along a wire, is gaining in popularity and two outfitters now offer breathtaking sails high over scenic Alpine vistas:

Planica Zipline (p113) Operators claim this wire over the towering Planica Ski-Jump Centre is the world's steepest zipline.

Zipline Dolinka (p92) Breathless travel along five zipline cables through the stunning Sava Dolinka valley.

Every town in Slovenia seems to have an airstrip or an aerodrome, complete with an *aeroklub* whose enthusiastic members can take you 'flight-seeing'. The Ljubljana-based **Aeronautical Association of Slovenia** (Letalska Zveza Slovenije; ☑01-422 33 33; www.lzs-zveza.si; Tržaška cesta 2) has a list.

live bear. Several outfitters can help you observe the animals in their natural habitats from April to September. Most tours involve a drive into the forest, followed by a short walk to an observation hide. When looking for bears, keep an eye out for lynx and wolves, which also reside in local forests.

Horse Riding

Slovenia is a nation of horse riders. The world's most famous horse – the Lipizzaner of Spanish Riding School fame in Vienna – was first bred at Lipica and the Lipica Stud Farm (p142) is still the best place for serious riders to improve their skills. For a simpler day out on the horses, the Mrcina Ranč (p104) in Studor near Lake Bohinj offers a range of guided tours on horseback, many of which are suitable for children.

Fishing

Slovenia's mountain streams are teeming with brown and rainbow trout and grayling, and its lakes and more-sluggish rivers are home to pike, perch, carp, chub and other fish. The best rivers for angling are the Soča, the Krka, the Kolpa, the Sava Bohinjka near Bohinj, and the Unica in southern Slovenia.

Fishing is not cheap in Slovenia – a permit at the more popular rivers will cost €60 to €150 for two or three days. Catch-and-release permits are cheaper. You can usually buy short-term fishing permits at local TICs. The season runs from March/April to November.

Jesprenj (barley soup)

Plan Your Trip

Eat & Drink Like a Local

Slovenia has emerged as a full-on foodie destination. For such a small country, it boasts an incredibly diverse range of cuisines. Indeed, the Slovenian Tourist Board (www.slovenia.info) has identified two dozen culinary micro-regions and has encouraged restaurants and local authorities to highlight their own specialities through festivals and on menus. Everywhere the emphasis is on farm-fresh and sustainability.

Best Places to Eat

Hiša Franko (p122) Provenance is everything at this award-winner near Kobarid.

Castle Restaurant (p100) Hard to fault the superb location of Bled's in-castle restaurant.

Monstera Bistro (p71) Concept bistro of star TV chef Bine Volčič delivers 'best-meal-of-the-trip' quality.

Pri Mari (p158) Stylishly rustic restaurant serves inventive Mediterranean dishes.

Restavracija Mak (p223) Owner-chef David Vračko guides a multi-course food experience.

Gostilna Grabar (p215) Good eating dressed up with a dash of foams-crumbs-purées frippery.

The Slovenian Kitchen

Squeezed between four different culinary regions – Austria to the north, Hungary to the east, the Balkans to the south and Italy to the west – Slovenia has adopted and modified the cooking styles of its neighbours, while adding in the fresh vegetables, herbs and grains it grows on its own in abundance. The result is diversity and invention. On menus you're likely to see foods and ingredients, such as buckwheat, barley soup and horse, that you may have never encountered before. The default response, of course, is always 'YOLO': you only live once.

PUMPKIN-SEED OIL

Eastern Slovenia's distinctive *bučno olje* (pumpkin-seed oil) is not just an excellent condiment on salads but can also be poured over vanilla ice cream and sprinkled with green pumpkin seeds or cracked walnuts.

Start with a Soup

In keeping with the Central European tradition, most Slovenian meals start with soup *(juha)* – year-round but especially in winter. There are countless different varieties. As a starter, this is usually chicken/beef broth with little egg noodles *(kokošja/goveja juha z rezanci)* or mushroom soup *(gobova juha)*, often made from hand-picked mushrooms. More substantial varieties, which can also serve as a small meal to save money, include *jesprenj* (barley soup); *jota* (a thick potage of beans), sauerkraut or sour turnip, sometimes potatoes, and smoked pork or sausage; and *obara*, a stew often made with chicken or veal.

Breaking Bread

Nothing is more Slovenian than bread *(kruh)*, and it is generally excellent, especially wholewheat bread *(kmečki temni kruh)*. Real treats are the braided loaves made for weddings and around Christmas (not dissimilar to Jewish challah) and 'mottled bread' *(pisan kruh)* in which three types of dough (usually buckwheat, wheat and corn) are rolled up together and baked.

In 'Pršut' of Excellence

There's one culinary delicacy in Slovenia that practically justifies the cost of the trip alone. *Pršut* is air-dried, thinly sliced ham from the Karst region that's related to Italian prosciutto, though in our opinion is somehow airier and even more flavourful. Look for it in the western regions of the country. It works well as a starter and pairs beautifully with a plate of hard cheese and a glass of dark-red Teran wine.

Pršut is certainly not the only processed meat that pairs beautifully with a local wine or beer. Slovenia is replete with sausages and salamis. These include the ubiquitous (and delicious) Carniolan sausage *(Kranjska klobasa),* which hails originally from the Julian Alps region but can be found around the country. It's a large, round sausage that's seasoned with garlic and pepper. When served with a side of potato salad or pickled turnip, it makes for a filling meal in itself. Klobasarna (p69) in Ljubljana, as the name might indicate, has built an entire (successful) business around it. In season, salami made from

BORROWING FROM THE NEIGHBOURS

Culinary anthropologists looking over Slovenian menus would obviously notice the many subtle but undeniable influences that Slovenia's neighbours have had in shaping the national cuisine (or is it cuisines?).

From Austria & Hungary

From Austria, there's sausage (klobasa), strudel (zavitek or štrudelj) filled with fruit, nuts and/or curd cheese (skuta), and, of course, Wiener schnitzel (dunajski zrezek).

Hungary has contributed golaž (goulash), paprikaš (piquant chicken or beef 'stew') and palačinka (pancake filled with jam or nuts and topped with chocolate).

From Italy & the Balkans

The ravioli-like žlikrofi (pasta stuffed with potatoes, onion and spiced pork), njoki (potato dumplings) and rižota (risotto) have some clear Italian origins.

From Croatia and the rest of the Balkans come such popular grills as čevapčiči (spicy meatballs of beef or pork), pljeskavica (meat patties) and Ljubljana's number-one street food: burek (flaky pastry stuffed with meat or cheese).

game (divjačinska salama) rivals pršut for our devotion.

Bring in the Buckwheat

There's something about the taste of buckwheat (ajda) that's so earthy and satisfying, it's a mystery that more cuisines around the world don't make better use of it. Thankfully, buckwheat's appeal is not lost on cooks around Slovenia, who've built starters and whole main courses around this neglected, grainlike plant. Hardcore buckwheat fans should just go for the groats (žganci), unadorned and filling. They make for an excellent side or even modest main course. Groats here can also be made from barley (ječmen) and corn (koruza).

Beyond simple groats and starters, more ambitious local cooks have built up an entire buckwheat culinary repertoire. A real rib sticker is buckwheat porridge (ajdovi žganci z ocvirki), usually flavoured with the addition of pork crackling or scratchings (ocvirki). Our personal favourite would have to be buckwheat 'fritters' or dumplings (ajdovi krapi) stuffed with cottage cheese. The Gostilna Psnak (p109), tucked away within Triglav National Park, has perfected the art of the 'ajda'.

Horse, Turkey & Trout

Most Slovenian meals revolve around some kind of meat (meso) as the main course, and as elsewhere in Europe rest assured you'll find plenty of dishes built on common meats like pork (svinjina), beef (govedina) and chicken (piščanec). For Slovenian cooks, though, there's no reason to stop there when there are so many other possibilities to be sampled. During hunting season, usually from September to December, look on menus for game (divjačina) dishes, such as deer (srna), boar (merjasec) and pheasant (fazan). Turkey (puran) is as common in some areas as chicken, and can be delicious grilled. Even horsemeat (konj) finds its way onto the Slovenian table. For some, a visit to Ljubljana would not be complete without a stopover at Hot Horse (p71), where you can sample, gulp, a 'horse-burger'.

With their small Adriatic coast and Alpine rivers teeming with freshwater fish (riba), Slovenes are naturally big fans of fish and seafood, even far from the coast. When travelling through the Alps, look out for trout (postrv), particularly the variety from the Soča River, which can be superb. Ljubljana's fish market (p69), in the city centre below the Plečnik Colonnade, has open-air fish stands where you can buy a fresh and filling plate of calamari for as low as €7. The coastal port of Piran has half a dozen excellent seafood restaurants of its own.

Sweet Tooth

Slovenian cuisine boasts several calorific desserts. These are some of the favourites:

Prekmurska gibanica (pastry with cottage cheese, apples, poppyseed and walnuts)

Potica A national institution, Potica is a kind of nut roll (although it's often made with savoury fillings as well) eaten after a meal or at teatime.

Prekmurska gibanica Made from Slovenia's easternmost province, is this rich concoction of pastry filled with poppyseeds, walnuts, apples and cottage cheese and topped with cream.

Blejska kremna rezina Also known as 'Bled cream cake' or even *kremšnita* – a layer of vanilla custard topped with whipped cream and sandwiched between layers of flaky pastry.

Strudel *(zavitek* or *štrudelj)* Filled with fruit, nuts and/or curd cheese *(skuta).*

Street Food

The most popular street food in Slovenia is a Balkan import called *burek* – flaky pastry sometimes stuffed with meat but more often cheese or even apple – that is a cousin of Turkish *börek*. It's sold at outdoor stalls or kiosks and is very cheap and filling.

Other cheap snacks available are *čevapčiči* (spicy meatballs of beef or pork), *pljeskavica* (spicy meat patties), *ražnjiči* (shish kebab) and pizza (which sometimes appears spelled in Slovene as *pica).*

How to Eat

When to Eat

On the whole, Slovenes are not big eaters of breakfast *(zajtrk),* preferring a cup of coffee at home or on the way to work. Instead, many people eat a light meal called *malica* (literally, snack) at around 10.30am.

Lunch *(kosilo)* is traditionally the main meal in the countryside, and it's eaten at noon if *malica* has been skipped. Sometimes it is eaten much later, such as in the middle of the afternoon.

Dinner *(večerja)* – supper, really – is less substantial when eaten at home, often just sliced meats and cheese on a platter and salad.

Where to Eat

Slovenia covers the entire eating spectrum, from fancy sit-down places to street kiosks and food trucks. Most restaurants will have an English menu.

Restavracija A classic restaurant where you sit down and are served by a waiter.

Gostilna (Gostišče) These are rustic inns, with waiters too, and can be fancy or modest.

Samopostrežna restavracija A self-service place, where you order from a counter and carry your food on a tray.

Krčma More like taverns, with an emphasis on drinking rather than eating, though often serves snacks.

Slaščičarna The place for sweets and ice cream, along with coffee and milkshakes.

Going Meatless & Other Dietary Needs

Slovenes love their veggies, though surprisingly for a country that places such high value on foods that are farm-fresh and locally grown, there are not many dedicated vegetarian or vegan restaurants. Even a relatively large city like Ljubljana suffers from a dearth of these types of places. Vegetarian and vegan diners need not despair, though, as menus everywhere feature plenty of meatless options, and fresh fruit and veg markets abound.

Vegetarian Survival Kit

In practice, vegetarians normally have to tough it out by selecting meatless entries at standard restaurants and inns. The good news is that many restaurants will specially designate suitable entrees on menus with a sign or a symbol.

Štruklji are dumplings made with cheese and often flavoured with chives or tarragon. These are widely available, as are dishes like mushroom risotto *(gobova rižota)* and fried cheese *(ocvrti sir)*. Slovenes enjoy fresh *solata* (salad) and you can get one anywhere, even in a countryside *gostilna*. In season (usually late summer and autumn) the whole country indulges in *jurčki* (wild boletus mushrooms or ceps) in soups or salads or served grilled.

Options improve considerably for self-caterers. Fresh produce, cheeses and breads are widely available everywhere. Ljubljana's Central Market (p69) is a veg picnicker's dream.

Food Allergies & Intolerances

The situation is similar for diners with special food requirements, allergies or intolerances. The EU has mandated that restaurants display any possible food allergies alongside dishes on menus, though compliance with this law remains spotty.

In theory, at least, waiters should be informed of potential allergy risks. The best bet remains to ask before ordering.

THE YEAR IN FOOD

Spring (Apr–May)

The true harbingers of the spring cycle are dandelion greens and lamb's lettuce. Then comes asparagus from Istria, just ahead of the first strawberries and cherries from Goriška Brda.

Summer (Jun–Aug)

The bounty continues with raspberries and blueberries and then stone fruits like apricots. Next are pears and apples from Kozjansko and the start of the nut harvest. In the east, lots of goulash is stewed in outdoor cauldrons.

Autumn (Sep–Nov)

Folk engage in the national sport – mushroom gathering – and chestnut stalls arrive in Ljubljana. St Martin's Day (11 November) is when winemakers' fermenting grape juice officially becomes wine.

Winter (Dec–Mar)

Persimmons, olives and root vegetables arrive in the markets. It's time for hearty soups like *jota* and *ričet* and mulled wine (made with white wine here too). Christmas wouldn't be complete without *potica* (nut roll).

SLOVENIAN COOKBOOKS

Slovenian Cookery: Over 100 Classic Dishes by Slavko Adamlje and *Flavors of Slovenia: Food and Wine from Central Europe's Hidden Gem* by Heike Milhench are practical, though increasingly hard-to-find guides to making Slovenian dishes.

The Food & Cooking of Slovenia by ethnographer Janez Bogataj is a richly illustrated and instructive tome that divides Slovenia into two-dozen culinary regions – introducing dozens of dishes – and takes the reader along for the ride.

You'll find some excellent recipes from around Slovenia in English at www.slovenia.si/visit/cuisine/recipes.

Slovenian Wine

Slovenia is a badly underrated wine *(vino)* destination, but in fact wine has been made here since the arrival of the Celts in the 5th century BC (and the wine has only gotten much better since then!).

Slovenes usually drink wine with meals or socially at home. As elsewhere in Central Europe, a bottle or a glass of mineral water is ordered along with the wine when eating. It's a different story in summer, when people enjoy a *brizganec* or *špricer* (spritzer or wine cooler) of red or white wine mixed with mineral water. Wine comes in 0.75L bottles or is ordered by the deci (decilitre; 0.1L). A normal glass of wine is about *dva* deci (0.2L).

Wine-Making Regions & Varietals

Slovenia counts three major wine-growing regions, each with their own respective strengths and traditional varietals. Two regions, Podravje and Posavje, lie towards the eastern part of the country, while a third, Primorska, is in the west.

Podravje

Podravje (literally 'on the Drava'), encompassing the far-eastern Prekmurje and Štajerska Slovenija (Slovenian Styria) districts, is known best for quality whites, such as Welschriesling (Laški Rizling), Riesling (Renski Rizling), a true German Riesling, pinot blanc (Beli Pinot), Gewürztraminer (Traminec) and Furmint (Šipon).

Posavje

Posavje ('on the Sava') runs roughly through the southeast of the country across the Sava River into Dolenjska and Bela Krajina, and includes the Bizeljsko-Sremič, Dolenjska and Bela Krajina (Metlika) districts. This region produces both whites and reds, but its most famous wine is *Cviček,* a distinctly Slovenian dry light red – almost a rosé – with a low (8.5% to 10%) alcohol content.

Other popular varietals include the traditional dark-red Metlika black (Metliška Črnina), the white muscatel (Rumeni Muškat) and an Austrian red, Blaufränkisch.

Primorska

The Primorska (coastal) wine region, which encompasses the districts of Slovenska Istra (Slovenia Istria), Kras (Karst), Vipavska Dolina (Vipava Valley) and the celebrated Goriška Brda (Gorica Hills), excels at reds. The most famous of these is Teran, a ruby-red, peppery wine with high acidity made from Slovenian Refošk (Refosco) grapes in the Karst region.

Other wines from this region are malvasia (Malvazija), a yellowish white from Slovenian Istria that is light and dry, and red merlots, especially the ones from the Vipava Valley and Goriška Brda. A relatively recent phenomenon from the Vipava Valley is so-called 'orange' wine, a white wine with an orange tinge due to contact with the colouring pigments of red grape skins.

Popular Wine Pairings

Pairing food with wine is as great an obsession in Slovenia as it is in other wine-producing countries. Most people know that *pršut* with black olives, hard cheese and a glass of Teran is a near-perfect match, but what's less appreciated is the wonderful synergy other wines from the Karst, including red rebula, enjoy with these foodstuffs.

With heavier and/or spicier meat dishes, such as goulash and salami, try Cviček. Malvazija, a yellowish white from the coast, is good with fish, as is Laški Rizling. And with sweet food such as strudel and

DECIPHERING THE WINE LABEL

Before you plunk down your euros to buy a bottle of wine, it's helpful to know exactly what you are getting. Slovenian wines follow a carefully scripted formula for letting customers know what's in the bottle, but the system is not always transparent if you don't speak Slovene.

What Place, What Grape?

On a Slovenian wine label, the first word usually identifies where the wine is from and the second specifies the grape variety: Vipavski merlot, Mariborski traminec etc.

But this may not always be the case, and some wines bear names according to their places of origin, such as Jeruzalemčan, Bizeljčan or Haložan.

'Appellation d'Origine Contrôlée'

Slovenia's version of appellation d'origine contrôlée (AOC) is zaščiteno geografsko poreklo (ZGP), a trademark protection that guarantees provenance and sets the limits to three quality levels.

Some 9% or so is designated *vrhunsko vino* (premium wine), around 54% is *kakovostno vino* (quality wine) and 27% is *deželno vino* (regional wine), not dissimilar to French *vin du pays*. The last 10% are wines classified as *priznano tradicionalno poimenovanje* (recognised traditional designation) such as Cviček, Teran, Metliška Črnina, Belokranjec and Bizeljčan.

Very roughly, anything costing more than about €8 in the shops is a serious bottle of Slovenian wine; pay more than €12 and you'll be getting something very fine indeed.

Specialities & Sparkling Wines

One excellent Slovenian sparkling wine that employs the demanding *méthode classique* is Zlata Radgonska Penina from Gornja Radgona in Slovenian Styria, which is based on chardonnay and Beli Pinot. Kraška Penina, a sparkling Teran, is unique.

Late-harvest dessert wines include Rumeni Muškat from Bela Krajina and Slovenian Istria.

---

potica, it's got to be a glass of late-harvest Rumeni Muškat.

Hops & Beer

Eastern Slovenia is a major hops-growing region and beer *(pivo)* is popular, especially with younger people. The local hops *(Štajerska hmelj)* grown in the Savinja Valley are used locally and also exported to brewers around the world. They have been described as having the flavour of lemongrass.

Beer is traditionally served in a pub *(pivnica),* though it's almost always possible to grab a beer in any restaurant, inn or cafe. Draught beer *(točeno pivo)* is ordered as *veliko pivo* ('large beer'; 0.5L) or *malo pivo* ('small beer'; 0.3L). Many places now offer craft beers, sometimes on tap but usually in bottles.

The Big Players

Slovenia has two major commercial brewers, both of which are owned by the Laško brewery in the town of that name south of Celje. Laško produces the country's two most popular brands: Zlatorog and Union (which is brewed in Ljubljana). Both brands are standard pilsners, with a light golden colour and a hoppy, almost bitter taste. Of the two, Zlatorog is the more popular. Union is generally seen as the working-class beer – the right choice for a bender, when just about anything will do.

Laško also makes a popular, sweetish dark beer *(temno pivo)* called, appropriately enough, Laško Dark. It's frequently available on tap in bars and pubs. Union makes a very popular, low-alcohol (2.5%) shandy called Radler, flavoured with orange, lemon or grapefruit and available in cans and bottles.

Slovenian brandies: *borovnica* (made from blueberries) and *medica* (made from honey)

Craft Beer Revolution

Just like beer aficionados around the world, Slovenes have enthusiastically embraced the craft beer movement, and alongside the more common Laško offerings like Zlatorog and Union, at many pubs you'll find a bewildering menu of India Pale Ales (IPAs) and American Pale Ales (APAs), as well as other ales, brown ales, stouts and porters (and we're leaving out many others). These are often made by small, independent breweries you're likely never to have heard of. To help you decide, bar menus normally include a description of the beer and its alcohol content. Note craft beers tend to be much stronger than traditional pilsner-style beers.

Many of these new Slovenian beers are excellent. Some of the most highly regarded names to watch for include HumanFish, based in Vrhnika, Pelicon in Ajdovščina, Reservoir Dogs in Nova Gorica, and Bevog, which is actually run out of Austria. The Ljubljana TIC (p265) organises a two-tour tour of Ljubljana's best places to sample craft beers. For a more-DIY tour in the capital, check out the craft beer offerings at Pritličje (p72), Klub Daktari (p72) and Patrick's Irish Pub (p74).

That's the Spirit(s)

Wine and beer are fine for daily tipples, but special occasions often call for something a tad stronger. That's where *žganje*, a general term for strong brandy distilled from fruits, comes in. One of Slovenia's best brandies is Pleterska Hruška (also called *viljamovka*), a pear-based concoction made by the Carthusian monks at the Pleterje monastery (p184) near Kostanjevica na Krki in Dolenjska. For firewater with other fruits or flavourings, look out for the following:

Borovnica Made from forest blueberries.

Slivovka Made with plums.

Češnjevec Made with cherries.

Sadjevec Made with mixed fruit.

Brinjevec Made with juniper.

Medeno žganje Fruit brandy flavoured with honey.

Plan Your Trip

Travel with Children

Slovenia is prime family-holiday territory, especially in July and August when Europeans hit the road and celebrate the summer break. Water parks, caves, swimmable lakes and walking trails designed for little legs are just part of the story – many businesses go out of their way to make families welcome.

Slovenia for Kids

If you're travelling with kids, you're in for a pretty easy ride. Slovenia gets a big tick for its friendly locals, accessible nature, unique attractions and short travel distances. Get your kids involved in your travel plans – if they've helped to work out where you're going and they've heard plans of dancing white horses, train rides through caves, or dragons on bridges, they'll have plenty to look forward to in Slovenia.

Sights & Activities

Make a point of stopping by the local TICs – everywhere has attractions where kids are king, and there will be recommendations on sights, activities and how to spend a rainy day.

Newer museums are interactive (some have a dedicated kids' section), and there are parks, playgrounds and swimming pools, plus year-round water parks. Many attractions allow free admission for young kids (up to about seven years) and half-price (or substantially discounted) admission for those up to about 15. Discounted family tickets are usually available.

In the great outdoors, there are loads of family activities. Kids will enjoy paddling on a lake at Bled or Bohinj, swimming in

Best Regions for Kids

Ljubljana
The capital's attractions include a bridge guarded by dragons, a castle reached by funicular, a zoo, the House of Experiments and a mega water park.

The Julian Alps
Prime spot for outdoor, active pursuits. For younger kids, there are cable cars up to the mountaintops, lakes to swim in and leisurely boat rides. Teens will enjoy rafting, camping, cycling and 'glamping' in the open air.

Southwestern Slovenia
Kids won't soon forget descents into two enormous, awe-inspiring caves, plus castles, dancing horses and the usual seaside activities.

Southeastern Slovenia
Castles, gentle forest walks and cycling, water parks and white-water rafting rides suitable for the whole family.

Eastern Slovenia
Castles, forest trails, massive water parks and uncrowded ski areas.

the Adriatic, taking a cable car up a mountain at Vogel or Velika Planina, or riding a train through a cave at mighty Postojna.

Sleeping & Eating

In peak season (July and August) campgrounds are hives of activity, and many organise activity programs for juniors; some are attached to water parks. Campgrounds often have bungalows for rent, while 'glamping' (upscale camping) brings creature comforts to the great outdoors – and with options ranging from log cabins to treehouses and safari tents, it's a fun way to amuse the kids.

Most hostels are geared more towards young backpackers, but others are set up for, and welcoming to, families. Rooms may sleep up to six (in bunks); there will invariably be kitchen and lounge facilities.

On the whole, restaurants welcome children. Many will have a highchair and a children's menu, or serve the kind of food kids will eat (like pizza and chicken). Self-catering is a breeze if you stay somewhere with kitchen facilities – larger supermarkets stock all you'll need (including baby items), but may have shorter opening hours than you might expect.

Children's Highlights

Castles

Ljubljana Castle (p48) Ride the funicular to the castle, and poke around up top among the ruins. Older kids will like the 'Time Machine' tours.

Bled Castle (p90) A cool mountaintop fortress with tip-top views. Halloween celebrations here are awesome.

Predjama Castle (p134) A castle in a cave with history that involves a toilet – it's every kid's dream.

Old Castle Celje (p199) The largest fortress in Slovenia, perched on a high hill, is straight out of a fairy tale.

Water Parks

Atlantis (p61) Multiple pools in the capital.

Terme Čatež (p186) Near Brežice, with watery activities and a campground bursting with family fun.

Terme Ptuj (p213) Out east, with indoor and outdoor pools and lots of water slides.

Balnea Wellness Centre (p169) Ahoy! At Dolenjske Toplice, the Lagoon at this spa centre has an open-air pool with a pirate ship.

Terme Olimia (p204) At Podčetrtek, with an abundance of slides, pools and activities, plus a child-care club.

Natural Wonders

Vintgar Gorge (p101) Near Bled, this is an easy path (1.6km each way) through fabulous nature, on a wooden walkway.

Postojna Cave (p131) Stalagmites, stalactites, a train ride through a cave, eyeless human fish. If your kid likes science projects, this is paradise.

Savica Waterfall (p102) Magnificent waterfall that cuts deep into a gorge. The long hike out to the falls is more suited to older children and teens.

Križna Cave (p138) What fun! You get boots and a lamp, and set out on a boat ride across a lake inside a cave.

Fresh-Air Fun

Bled (p90) For lake swimming, rowboats, bike rides and the *kremšnita* cream cake.

Bohinj (p102) More lake swimming, boat rides, horse riding, and a cable-car ride up Vogel.

Bovec (p116) Family river rafting is perfect; the older/braver can try canyoning and kayaking.

Kranjska Gora (p111) Winter skiing is facility-laden; summertime sees hiking and cycling.

Portorož (p159) The most active city on the coast, with lots of seaside activities.

Planning

The best time for families to visit Slovenia is between May and September, when you're likely to get good weather and attractions are in full swing. On the downside, facilities crowd up once local schools close for summer holidays from late June to early September.

All car-rental firms in Slovenia have children's safety seats for hire. Hotels will also usually be able to handle special requests, like cots and cribs, but it's always better to arrange these things in advance.

Regions at a Glance

Ljubljana

Entertainment
Architecture
Food

Thriving Culture

Ljubljana has a thriving cultural scene year-round, with something for everyone. Come summer, nearly every weekend brings a festival or an event, and buzzing riverside cafes lend the feeling of a perpetual street party.

Elegant Edifices

Ljubljana may be Europe's greenest city but it's also home to some of its finest architecture. You can't miss the work of architect and designer extraordinaire Jože Plečnik, whose bridges and baubles, pylons and pyramids are both playful and elegant.

Gastronomic Delights

Food has become an obsession in the capital in recent years, with locally sourced ingredients topping most shopping lists. Take a gastronomic tour of Slovenia without leaving town by grazing through the city's weekly Open Kitchen food festival.

p46

Lake Bled & The Julian Alps

Scenery
Hiking
Activities

Mountain Vistas

The Vršič Pass, Lakes Bled and Bohinj, Alpine peaks – if you're seeking awe-inspiring natural beauty and Instagram-worthy vistas, you've come to the right place.

Hiking Heaven

Go easy with lakeside trails, or amp it up with hikes through gorges, over Alpine pastures or to spectacular waterfalls. If you're feeling ambitious, the mother of all Slovenian hikes is a Mt Triglav ascent.

River Antics

The Soča Valley is one of Slovenia's best (and most beautiful) outdoor playgrounds. The Soča River's aquamarine waters are made for rafting, kayaking and canyoning, the trails for hiking and biking – or you can paraglide above it all.

p81

Southwestern Slovenia

Caves
Coast
Food & Wine

Underground Splendour

Tours of monumental Postojna and Škocjan caves reveal the surprising Slovenia hidden below the surface – vast, ancient and extraordinary.

Coastal Gems

Slovenia's 47km-long coast is rich in history, Venetian architecture, seafood, resorts and popular swimming spots. The jewel in the crown is perfectly poised Piran.

Fruits & Wine

Tour the vineyards of Goriška Brda and the Vipava Valley, tasting olive oils and stone fruits as well as the excellent indigenous wine varieties, and stop off at Idrija for some *žlikrofi* (potato-filled dumplings).

p129

Southeastern Slovenia & the Krka Valley

Castles
Scenery
Activities

Treasure-Laden Castles

Castles dazzle with five-star accommodation at Otočec, a glorious riverside perch at Žužemberk, stories of witch trials at Ribnica, and breathtaking frescoes in Brežice.

Slow Travel, Scenic Vistas

Rolling green hills, meandering rivers, church spires, forested slopes and fields filled with grapevines and fruit trees. It's as idyllic and tranquil as it sounds. Take a breather, smell the roses, taste the wines.

Aquatic Fun

Dolenjske Toplice and Čatež ob Savi, near Brežice, have thermal-water spas and water parks. The winding Krka and Kolpa Rivers offer rafting and kayaking and delightful riverside camping, hiking and biking possibilities.

p163

Eastern Slovenia

Architecture
Wine & Beer
Activities

Historic Towns

Ptuj's cobblestoned core is a harmonious mishmash of Gothic, Renaissance and baroque. Maribor's Old Town merges contemporary cafe culture with ornate facades; Celje's Roman heritage can be glimpsed in the ongoing excavations.

Hopfields & Vineyards

From the hopfields surrounding Žalek to the rolling, vineyard-striped hills along the Jeruzalem–Ljutomer wine road, the countryside has a long tradition of producing fine tipples. Test the results at a rural winery or the world's first beer fountain.

Hiking & Skiing

Hike or mountain bike through the lush green valley of Logarska Dolina or up to Velika Planina or the Maribor Pohorje highlands, where, if you wait until winter, you can explore the same slopes on skis or a snowboard.

p190

On the
Road

Ljubljana

♪01 / POP 279,750 / ELEV 297M

Best Places to Eat

➜ Strelec (p68)

➜ Monstera Bistro (p71)

➜ Pop's Place (p68)

➜ Gostilna Dela (p70)

➜ Ek Bistro (p71)

Best Places to Stay

➜ Vander Urbani Resort (p66)

➜ Adora Hotel (p66)

➜ Hostel Vrba (p68)

➜ Cubo (p67)

➜ Celica Hostel (p67)

Why Go?

Slovenia's capital and largest city is one of Europe's greenest and most liveable capitals; it was the European Commission's Green Capital of Europe in 2016. Car traffic is restricted in the centre, leaving the leafy banks of the emerald-green Ljubljanica River, which flows through the city's heart, free for pedestrians and cyclists. In summer, cafes set up terrace seating along the river; it almost feels like a nightly street party.

Slovenia's master of early-modern, minimalist design, Jože Plečnik, graced Ljubljana with beautiful bridges and buildings as well as dozens of urban design elements such as pillars, pyramids and lamp posts, which exist solely to make the city even prettier. Attractive cities are often described as 'jewel boxes', and here the name really fits. Some 50,000 students support an active clubbing scene, and Ljubljana's museums and restaurants are among the best in the country.

When to Go
Ljubljana

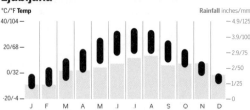

Apr & May Sunny days, blossoms, and cafe terraces on the banks of the Ljubljanica.

Jul & Aug Street theatre, happenings every week, and the lively Ljubljana Festival.

Sep & Oct Warm temperatures during the day, and an autumn cultural program.

Ljubljana Highlights

❶ Ljubljana Castle (p48) Riding the funicular to the castle for an overview of the city's past and present.

❷ Slovenska Hiša (p72) Spending an evening at an outside table at a riverside cafe.

❸ Central Market (p69) Indulging in some fresh fruits, vegetables, meats, cheeses and (of course) delicious fish.

❹ National & University Library (p57) Appreciating the masterwork of genius of Slovenian architect Jože Plečnik.

❺ Stari Trg (p53) Marvelling at the quaintness of this picturesque lane in the centre of a modern capital.

❻ Metelkova Mesto (p74) Drinking and dancing in hideously beautiful spaces at this student-occupied squat.

❼ Breg (p57) Taking in the natural beauty of the river from the redesigned embankment all the way south to **Špica**.

History

Ljubljana began life in the 1st century AD as a smallish Roman city of 5000 inhabitants. The city, called Emona, thrived as a strategic crossroad on the routes linking Upper Pannonia in the south with the Roman colonies at Noricum and Aquileia to the north and west. Remnants of the old Roman walls, dwellings and early churches can still be seen throughout Ljubljana and new discoveries are constantly being made.

Emona was sacked and destroyed by the Huns, Ostrogoths and Langobards (Lombards) from the mid-5th century; by the end of the next century tribes of early Slavs began to settle here.

First mentioned in writing as 'Laibach' in 1144, Ljubljana changed hands frequently in the Middle Ages. The last and most momentous change came in 1335, when the Habsburgs became the town's new rulers, a position they would retain almost without interruption until the end of WWI in 1918.

The town and its hilltop castle were able to repel the Turks in the late 15th century, but a devastating earthquake in 1511 reduced much of medieval Ljubljana to a pile of rubble. This led to a period of frantic construction in the 17th and 18th centuries that provided the city with many of its pale-coloured baroque churches and mansions – and the nickname Bela Ljubljana (White Ljubljana).

When Napoleon established his Illyrian Provinces in 1809 in a bid to cut Habsburg Austria's access to the Adriatic, he made Ljubljana the capital (though Austrian rule was restored just four years later). In 1821 Ljubljana walked onto the world stage when the four members of the Holy Alliance (Austria, Prussia, Russia and Naples) met at the Congress of Laibach to discuss measures to suppress the democratic revolutionary and national movements in Italy.

Railways linked Ljubljana with Vienna and Trieste in 1849 and 1857, stimulating economic development of the town. But in 1895 another, more powerful earthquake struck, forcing the city to rebuild once again. To Ljubljana's great benefit, secessionist and art nouveau styles were all the rage in Central Europe at the time, and many of the wonderful buildings erected then still stand.

During WWII Ljubljana was occupied by the Italians and then the Germans, who encircled the city with a barbed-wire fence creating, in effect, an urban concentration camp. Ljubljana became the capital of the Socialist Republic of Slovenia within Yugoslavia in 1945 and remained the capital after Slovenia's independence in 1991.

◉ Sights

The easiest way to see Ljubljana is on foot. The oldest part of town, with the most important historical buildings and sights (including Ljubljana Castle) lies on the right (east) bank of the Ljubljanica River. Center, which has the lion's share of the city's museums and galleries, is on the left (west) side of the river.

◉ Castle Hill

Begin an exploration of the city by making the trek up to Castle Hill (Grajska Planota) to poke around grand Ljubljana Castle. The castle area offers a couple of worthwhile exhibitions, and the castle watchtower affords amazing views over the city.

★ **Ljubljana Castle** CASTLE
(Ljubljanski Grad; Map p54; ☑ 01-306 42 93; www.ljubljanskigrad.si; Grajska Planota 1; adult/child incl funicular & castle attractions €10/7, incl castle attractions only €7.50/5.20; ⊙ castle 9am-11pm Jun-Sep, to 9pm Apr, May & Oct, 10am-8pm Jan-Mar & Nov, to 10pm Dec) Crowning a 375m-high hill east of the Old Town, this castle is an architectural mishmash, with most of it dating from the early 16th century when it was largely rebuilt after a devastating earthquake. It's free to ramble around the castle grounds, but you'll have to pay to enter the Watchtower and the Chapel of St George, and to see the worthwhile Slovenian History Exhibition, visit the Puppet Theatre and take the Time Machine tour.

There are several ways to access the castle, with the easiest being a 70m-long **funicular** (☑ 01-306 42 00; Krekov trg; adult/child €4/3 return, €2.20/1.50 one-way; ⊙ 10am-6pm) that leaves from the Old Town not far from the market on Vodnikov trg. There's also an hourly tourist train that departs from south of the Ljubljana TIC (p78). There are three main walking routes: Študentovska ulica, which runs south from Ciril Metodov trg; steep Reber ulica from Stari trg (p53); and Ulica na Grad from Gornji trg (p53).

You can explore the castle's various attractions at your own pace, or join one of the highly recommended 90-minute **Time Machine tours** (Časovni Stroj; ☑ 01-232 99 94; www.ljubljanskigrad.si/en/castle-experiences/guided-tours/time-machine; castle admission incl Time

LJUBLJANA IN ...

One Day
Take the funicular up to Ljubljana Castle to get the lay of the land. Come down and explore the Central Market (p69). After a quick lunch at the Fish Market (p69) or Gostilna Dela (p70) and a coffee at Magda (p72), explore the Old Town, walking through the three contiguous squares – Mestni trg (p53), Stari trg (p53) and Gornji trg (p53) – before crossing over St James Bridge. Walk north along Vegova ulica to Kongresni trg (p58) and Prešernov trg. Plan your evening over a fortifying libation at one of the cafes along the Ljubljanica such as Slovenska Hiša (p72), then head to atmospheric Druga Violina (p68) for excellent local dishes before hitting Metelkova Mesto (p74) for some alternative culture.

Two Days
On your second day, check out the city's excellent museums and galleries – the National Museum of Slovenia (p59) for history and icons, the Museum of Modern Art (p59) for the best in contemporary works – then stroll or cycle on a Ljubljana Bike (p79) or Bicike(lj) (p80) through Park Tivoli, stopping for an oh-so-local horse burger at Hot Horse (p71). In the evening, take in a performance at the Križanke (p75) or Cankarjev Dom (p75). Otherwise, dine at fancy Monstera (p71) or casual Pop's Place (p68) and then head out for a drop at Wine Bar Šuklje (p73) or music at Kino Šiška (p75).

Machine tour €10/7; ☺ tours 11am, 1pm & 5pm daily Jul-Sep, noon daily May-Jun, noon Sat & Sun Oct-Apr), led by costumed guides.

The castle's 19th-century watchtower is located on the southwestern side of the castle courtyard. The climb to the top, via a double wrought-iron staircase (95 steps from the museum level) and a walk along the ramparts, is worth the effort for the views down into the Old Town and across the river to Center. Within the watchtower, there is a 12-minute video tour of Ljubljana and its history in several languages.

Situated below the watchtower down a small flight of stairs, the remarkable Chapel of St George (Kapela Sv Jurija) is one of the oldest surviving remnants of the castle, dating from 1489. It is covered in frescoes and the coats of arms of the Dukes of Carniola.

The interesting and well-presented interactive Slovenian History Exhibition (Razstava Slovenska Zgodovina) looks at the country through the ages, running from the very earliest Roman times, through the Middle Ages, the 19th century, WWI and WWII, and ending with socialist Yugoslavia and independence.

Also worth a look, the Museum of Puppetry (Lutkovni Muzej) explores the world of puppetry, from the manufacture of marionettes and glove puppets to the staging of the shows themselves. It's very interactive and lots of fun.

The Ljubljana Castle Information Centre (☎ 01-306 42 93; Grajska Planota 1; ☺10am-6pm Jan-Mar & Nov, 9am-8pm Apr-May & Oct, 9am-9pm Jun-Sep, 10am-7pm Dec) can advise on tours and events that might be on during your visit.

◉ Prešernov Trg & Around

★ Triple Bridge
BRIDGE

(Tromostovje; Map p54) Running south from Prešernov trg to the Old Town is the much celebrated Triple Bridge, originally called Špital (Hospital) Bridge. When it was built as a single span in 1842 it was nothing spectacular, but between 1929 and 1932 superstar architect Jože Plečnik added the two pedestrian side bridges, furnished all three with stone balustrades and lamps, and forced a name change. Stairways on each of the side bridges lead down to the poplar-lined terraces along the Ljubljanica River.

Prešernov Trg
SQUARE

(Prešeren Sq; Map p54) The centrepiece of Ljubljana's wonderful architectural aesthetic is this marvellous square, a public space of understated elegance that serves not only as the link between the Center district and the Old Town but also as the city's favourite meeting point. Taking pride of place is the Prešeren monument (1905), erected in honour of Slovenia's greatest poet, France Prešeren (1800–49).

Ljubljana

35

19

Kino Šiška
(1.5km)

6

Celovška c

Tivolska c

22

GoOpti

Pivovarniška ul

Dvoržakova ul

36 60

Vošnjakova ul

Kersnikova ul

Slovenska c

Cigaletova ul

Pražakova ul

30

Gosposvetska c

29 44

Trdinova ul

20

54

Miklošičeva c

4

Park
Tivoli

Jakopičevo sprehajališče

Puharjeva ul

Argentinski
Park 32

Tavčarjeva ul

Miklošičev
Park

24

8

Štefanova ul

Trg
Ajdovščina 37

Dalmatinova ul

Cesta 27 Aprila

Gostilna Čad
(800m)

Cesta v Rožno dolino

Tobačna

7

Cankarjeva c

Slovenska c

9

Tomšičeva ul

Trg
Narodnih
Herojev

Prešernov
trg

Šubičeva ul

Veselova
ul

Prešernova c

Park Sveta
Evropa

15   50   17

3

Erjavčeva c

Kongresni
trg

Castle
Hill

Aeronautical
Association
of Slovenia

Trg Mladinskih
Delovnih
Brigad

49

Rimska c

41

Slovenska c

Tržaška c

43

Aškerčeva c

Snežniška ul

Lestikova ul

Zoisova c

See Central Ljubljana Map (p54)

Bičevje ul

Jamova c

Lepi pot

Groharjevac

14   13

Mirje

Murnikova ul

Krakovska ul

Vrtna ul

Krakovski nasip

Žabjak ul

Hrenova ul

Vozarski pot

Zvonarska

Emonska c

39

27

Cimpermanova

Barjanska c

Bibharieva ul

18

Gradaška ul

Eipprova ul

46   59   38

Grudnovo nabrežje

Trnovski pristan

34

Kolezijska ul

Karunova ul

11

Trnovska ul

56

Švabičeva ul

Mencingerjeva

Kopališka

Kolezijska ul

Zelena pot

Devinska

Zihertova ul

Mlivka

Jeranova

Opekarska c

Rezljanska

Gerbičeva

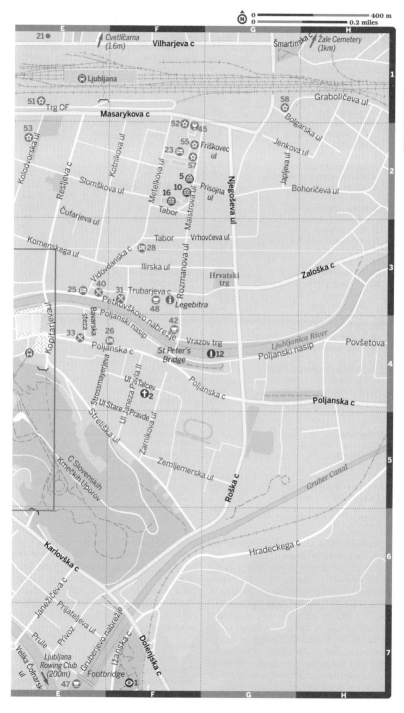

0   400 m
0   0.2 miles

21
Cvetličarna
(1.6m)
Vilharjeva c
Šmartinska c
Žale Cemetery
(1km)

Ljubljana

51 Trg OF
Graboličeva ul
58
Bolgarska ul
Masarykova c
52 45
Jenkova ul
53
Kolodvorska ul
Resljeva c
Kotnikova ul
55 Friškovec ul
23
57
Japljeva ul
Slomškova ul
Metelkova ul
5
10
Prisojna ul
Bohoričeva ul
Čufarjeva ul
16
Tabor
Maistrova ul
Njegoševa ul
Komenskega ul
Tabor
Vrhovčeva ul
28
Vidovdanska c
Ilirska ul
Rozmanova ul
Hrvatski trg
Zaloška c
25
40
31 Trubarjeva c
Legebitra
48
Petkovškovo nabrežje
42
33
26
Bavarska steza
Poljanski nasip
Vrazov trg
Ljubljanica River
Poljanska c
St Peter's Bridge
12
Poljanski nasip
Povšetova
Strossmayerjeva ul
Ul Janeza Pavla II
2
Poljanska c
Poljanska c
Ul Stare Pravde
Zarnikova ul
Ul Janeza Pavla II
Streliška ul
Zemljemerska ul
Roška c
Gruber Canal
C Slovenskih Kmečkih Uporov
Karlovška c
Hradeckega c
Janežičeva c
Prijateljeva ul
Privoz
Prule
Gruberjevo nabrežje
Ižanska c
Dolenjska c
Velika Čolnarska ul
Ljubljana Rowing Club
(200m)
Footbridge
47
1

Ljubljana

Immediately south of the statue is the city's architectural poster-child, the small but much acclaimed Triple Bridge (p49). To the east of the monument, at No 5 is the Italianate **Central Pharmacy** (Centralna Lekarna; ☑ 01-230 61 00; ⊙ 7.30am-7.30pm Mon-Fri, 8am-3pm Sat), an erstwhile cafe frequented by intellectuals in the 19th century. To the north sits the Franciscan Church of the Annunciation, and on the corner of Trubarjeva cesta and Miklošičeva cesta, the delightful secessionist **Palača Urbanc** building (1903), which now houses a fancy department store.

Diagonally across the square at No 1 is another secessionist gem: the **Hauptmann House** (⊙ Closed to the public). Two doors down at Wolfova ulica 4 you'll see a terracotta figure peeking out from a window. The figure is Julija Primič, a love interest of Prešeren's, though the union was apparently never consummated.

Franciscan Church of the Annunciation CHURCH

(Frančiškanska cerkev Marijinega oznanjenja; Map p54; ☑ 01-242 93 00; www.marijino-oznanjenje. si; Prešernov trg 4; ⊙ 6.40am-noon & 3-8pm)

FREE The 17th-century salmon-pink Franciscan Church of the Annunciation stands on the northern side of Prešernov trg. The interior has six side altars and an enormous choir stall. The main altar was designed by the Italian sculptor Francesco Robba (1698–1757). To the left of the main altar is a glass-fronted coffin with the spooky remains of St Deodatus.

Miklošičeva Cesta ARCHITECTURE
(Map p54) This 650m-long thoroughfare links Prešernov trg with the train and bus stations; the southern end boasts a splendid array of secessionist buildings and a fine park.

Buildings along the stretch include the 1908 **People's Loan Bank** (⊘ Not open to the public) at No 4, the one-time **Cooperative Bank** (⊘ Not open to the public) at No 8, and, just opposite, the Grand Hotel Union (p66), the grande dame of Ljubljana hotels, built in 1905. About 150m to the north is **Miklošičev Park**, laid out by Slovenian urban planner Maks Fabiani in 1902. Many of the buildings facing it are art nouveau masterpieces.

◉ Old Town

Ljubljana's Old Town (Staro Mesto) occupies a narrow swath of land along the right (eastern) bank of the Ljubljanica River. This is the city's oldest and most important historical quarter. It's comprised of three contiguous long squares that include **Mestni trg** (Town Sq; Map p54), **Stari trg** (Old Sq) and **Gornji trg** (Upper Sq) as you move south and east. It's an architectural gold mine, with a large portion of the buildings baroque and some townhouses along Stari trg and Gornji trg retaining their medieval layout.

Town Hall HISTORIC BUILDING
(Mestna Hiša; Map p54; ☑ 01-306 30 00; Mestni trg 1; tours €5; ⊘ 8am-5pm Mon-Fri) **FREE** The seat of the city government and sometimes referred to as the Magistrat or Rotovž, the town hall was erected in the late 15th century and rebuilt in 1718. The Gothic courtyard inside, arcaded on three levels, is where theatrical performances once took place; it contains some lovely graffiti. One-hour guided tours are offered in English on Saturdays at 1pm. Tours must be booked in advance through the Ljubljana TIC (p78).

If you look above the south portal leading to a second courtyard you'll see a relief map of Ljubljana as it appeared in the second half of the 17th century.

Cobblers' Bridge BRIDGE
(Čevljarski Most; Map p54) In the midst of the Old Town, a small street running west from Stari trg called Pod Trančo (Below Tranča) leads to this evocatively named footbridge. During the Middle Ages this was a place of trade, and a tolled gateway led to the town. Craftspeople worked and lived on bridges (in this case 16 shoemakers) to catch the traffic and avoid paying town taxes – a medieval version of duty-free.

Church of St Florian CHURCH
(Cerkev Sv Florijana; Map p54; Gornji trg; ⊘ 7am-6pm) Built in 1672, this church was dedicated to the patron saint of fires after a serious blaze destroyed much of the Old Town. Architect Jože Plečnik was involved in the church's reconstruction in 1933 and 1934.

Church of St James CHURCH
(Cerkev Sv Jakoba; Map p54; ☑ 01-252 17 27; Gornji trg 18; ⊘ 7am-8pm) The Church of St James, built in 1615, houses Italian sculptor Francesco Robba's main altar (1732), though far more interesting is the one in the church's Chapel of St Francis Xavier to the left, with statues of a 'White Queen' and a 'Black King'.

LJUBLJANA SIGHTS

LJUBLJANA'S DRAGONS

Ljubljana's town hall is topped with a golden dragon, which is a symbol of Ljubljana but not an ancient one, as many people assume. Just before the turn of the 20th century a wily mayor named Ivan Hribar apparently persuaded the authorities in Vienna that Ljubljana needed a new crossing over the Ljubljanica, and he submitted plans for a 'Jubilee Bridge' to mark 50 years of the reign of Franz Joseph. The result was the much-loved Dragon Bridge (p56), which stands northeast of the Old Town, just beyond Vodnikov trg. City folk joke that the winged bronze dragons supposedly wag their tails whenever a virgin crosses the bridge.

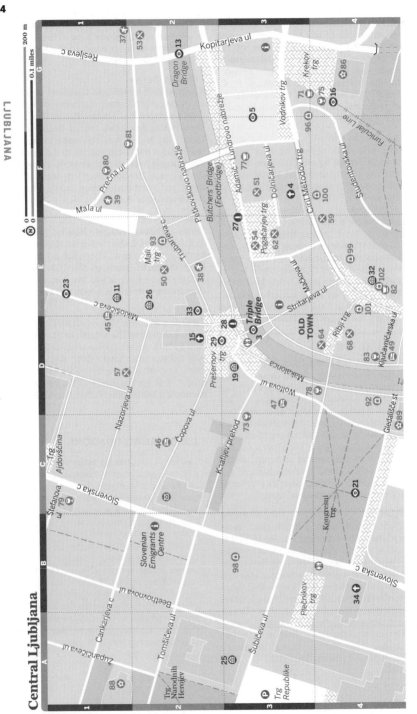

Central Ljubljana

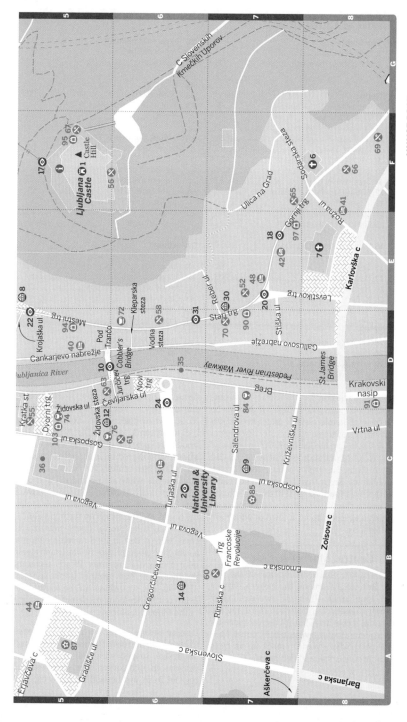

Central Ljubljana

Botanical Garden GARDENS
(Botanični Vrt; Map p50; ☑01-427 12 80; www.bo tanicni-vrt.si; Ižanska cesta 15; garden free, tropical glasshouse adult/child €2.80/1.30; ⊙7am-8pm Jul & Aug, to 7pm Apr-Jun, Sep & Oct, to 5pm Nov-Mar) **FREE** About 800m southeast of the Old Town along Karlovška cesta and over the Ljubljanica River, this 2.5-hectare botanical garden was founded in 1810 as a sanctuary of native flora. It contains 4500 species of plants and trees, about a third of which are indigenous.

⊙ Central Market & East

The market area extends east of the Triple Bridge (p49) along the eastern edge of the Ljubljanica River, following Adamič-Lundrovo nabrežje. There are not many traditional sights here, but it's a great place for a stroll and to pay a visit to the Central Market (p69), where you can stock up on fresh local produce, fish and deli items.

Cathedral of St Nicholas CHURCH
(Stolna Cerkev Sv Nikolaja; Map p54; ☑01-234 26 90; www.lj-stolnica.rkc.si; Dolničarjeva ulica 1; ⊙10am-noon & 3-6pm) **FREE** A church has stood here since the 13th century, but the existing twin-towered building dates from the start of the 18th century. Inside it's a vision of pink marble, white stucco and gilt and contains a panoply of baroque frescoes. Have a look at the magnificent carved choir stalls, the organ and the angels on the main altar.

Two stunning bronze doors, now blackened, were added in 1996 to commemorate a visit by Pope John Paul II. The (main) west door facing the Bishop's Palace recounts the history of 1250 years of Christianity in Slovenia. The six bishops on the south door fronting Ciril Metodov trg depict the history of the Ljubljana diocese.

Dragon Bridge BRIDGE
(Zmajski Most; Map p54) The much-loved Dragon Bridge, topped with four scary-looking dragons on each corner, stands northeast of the Old Town, just beyond Vodnikov trg. The

Eating

50	Ajdovo Zrno	E2
51	Covered Market	F3
52	Druga Violina	E7
53	Falafel	G2
54	Fish Market	E3
55	Gelateria Romantika	C5
56	Gostilna na Gradu	F5
57	Hood Burger Center	D1
58	Julija	D6
59	Klobasarna	E4
60	Le Petit Café	B7
61	Monstera Bistro	C6
62	Odprta Kuhna	E3
63	Paninoteka	D5
64	Pop's Place	D4
65	Repete	F7
66	Špajza	F8
67	Strelec	F5
68	TaBar	D4
69	Taverna Tatjana	F8
70	Vino & Ribe	D7

Drinking & Nightlife

71	Cafe Čokl	G3
72	Čajna Hiša	D6
73	Cutty Sark Pub	C3
74	Dvorni Bar	C5
75	Klub Daktari	G4
76	Kolibri	C5
77	Magda	F3

78	Makalonca	D4
79	Nebotičnik	C1
80	Patrick's Irish Pub	F1
81	Postaja Centralna	F2
82	Pritličje	E4
83	Slovenska Hiša	D4
84	Wine Bar Šuklje	D7

Entertainment

85	Križanke	C7
86	Ljubljana Puppet Theatre	G4
87	National Drama Theatre	A5
88	Opera Ballet Ljubljana	A1
89	Slovenia Philharmonic Hall	C4

Shopping

90	3 Muhe	D7
91	Annapurna	D8
92	Antikvariat Alef	D4
93	Carniola Antiqua	E2
94	Galerija Idrijske Čipke	D5
95	Galerija Rustika	F5
96	Kraševka	G3
97	Lina	E7
98	Mladinska Knjiga	B3
99	Oliviers & Co.	E4
100	Trgovina IKA	F4
101	Trubarjev Antikvariat	E4
102	Vinoteka Movia	E4
103	Wine Point Dvor	C5

bridge was built in Viennese secession (art nouveau) style and dates from 1900–01.

Church of St Joseph CHURCH
(Cerkev sv Jožefa; Map p50; ☎ 01-438 39 80; www.svjozef.si; Ulica Janeza Pavla II 13; ⊙ 8am-6pm, English mass 10am Sun) **FREE** The Jesuit Church of St Joseph was built in neo-Romanesque style by the architect Anzelm Werner in 1913, then later extended and rebuilt by local architect Jože Plečnik, including the addition of the austere altar in 1941. The church offers weekly Catholic services in English.

⊙ Center

This large district on the left bank of the Ljubljanica is the nerve centre of modern Ljubljana. It is filled with shops, commercial offices, government departments and embassies. Center is divided into several distinct neighbourhoods centred on squares.

Novi Trg SQUARE
(New Sq; Map p54) South of Cobblers' Bridge (p53), this was a walled settlement of fisherfolk outside the town administration in the Middle Ages. Remnants include the very narrow street to the north called Židovska ulica and its offshoot Židovska steza (Jewish Lane), once the site of a medieval synagogue. Breg, the city's port when the Ljubljanica River was still navigable commercially this far inland, runs south from the square and is entirely pedestrianised.

**★ National &
University Library** ARCHITECTURE
(Narodna in Univerzitetna Knjižnica, NUK; Map p54; ☎ 01-200 12 09; www.nuk.uni-lj.si; Turjaška ulica 1; ⊙ 8am-8pm Mon-Fri, 9am-2pm Sat) **FREE** This library is architect Jože Plečnik's masterpiece, completed in 1941. To appreciate this great man's philosophy, enter through the main door (note the horse-head doorknobs) on Turjaška ulica – you'll find yourself in near darkness, entombed in black marble. As you ascend the steps, you'll emerge into a colonnade suffused with light – the light of knowledge, according to the architect's plans.

The **Main Reading Room** (Velika Čitalnica), open to nonstudents only by group tour

JOŽE PLEČNIK, ARCHITECT EXTRAORDINAIRE

Few architects anywhere in the world have had as great an impact on the city of their birth as Jože Plečnik. His work is eclectic, inspired, unique – and found everywhere in the capital.

Born in Ljubljana in 1872, Plečnik was educated at the College of Arts in Graz and studied under the architect Otto Wagner in Vienna. From 1911 he spent a decade in Prague teaching and later helping to renovate Prague Castle.

Plečnik's work in his hometown began in 1921. Almost single-handedly, he transformed the city, adding elements of classical Greek and Roman architecture with Byzantine, Islamic, ancient Egyptian and folkloric motifs to its baroque and secessionist faces. The list of his creations and renovations is endless – from the National & University Library (p57) and the colonnaded Central Market (p69) to the magnificent cemetery at Žale (p61), where you can see his own simple, modernist headstone.

Plečnik was also a city planner and designer. Not only did he redesign the banks of the Ljubljanica River, including Triple Bridge (p49) and the monumental lock (Map p50) downstream, and entire streets such as Zoisova cesta and Park Tivoli, but he also set his sights elsewhere – on monumental stairways (Kranj) and public buildings (Kamnik). An intensely religious man, Plečnik designed many furnishings and liturgical objects – chalices, candlesticks, lanterns – for churches throughout Slovenia, such as Škofja Loka's Church of St James (p83). One of Plečnik's designs that was never realised was an extravagant parliament, complete with an enormous cone-shaped structure, to be built on Castle Hill after WWII.

Plečnik's eclecticism and individuality alienated him from the mainstream of modern architecture during his lifetime, and he was relatively unknown (much less appreciated) outside Eastern and Central Europe when he died in 1957. Today he is hailed as a forerunner of postmodernism.

(adult/child €5/3) in July and August, has huge glass walls and some stunning lamps, also designed by Plečnik.

City Museum of Ljubljana
MUSEUM

(Mestni Muzej Ljubljana; Map p54; ☑ 01-241 25 00; www.mgml.si; Gosposka ulica 15; adult/child €6/4; ☉ 10am-6pm Tue, Wed & Fri-Sun, to 9pm Thu) The excellent city museum, established in 1935, focuses on Ljubljana's history, culture and politics via imaginative multimedia and interactive displays. The reconstructed street that once linked the eastern gates of the Roman colony of Emona (today's Ljubljana) to the Ljubljanica River and the collection of well-preserved classical artefacts in the basement treasury are worth a visit in themselves. So too are the models of buildings that the celebrated architect Jože Plečnik never got around to erecting.

Ursuline Church of the Holy Trinity
CHURCH

(Uršulinska Cerkev Sv Trojice; Map p54; ☑ 01-252 48 64; http://zupnija-lj-sv-trojica.rkc.si; Slovenska cesta 21; ☉ 6-7.30am, 9-11am & 5-7pm) This church, which faces Kongresni trg (Congress Sq) from across Slovenska cesta and dates from 1726, is the most beautiful baroque building in the city. It contains a multicoloured altar by Italian sculptor Francesco Robba made of African marble.

Early Christian Centre Archaeological Park
HISTORIC SITE

(Zgodnjekrščansko Arheološki Park; Map p50; ☑ 01-241 25 00; www.mgml.si; Erjavčeva cesta 18; adult/child €2/1; ☉ 10am-6pm Apr-Oct) Behind the Cankarjev Dom (p75) centre is this important site, with the remains of an early Christian church portico with mosaics from the 4th century, a total-immersion baptistery and a hypocaust system. Opposite and to the west of the Cankarjev Dom are the remains of a Roman wall (Map p50; Erjavčeva cesta) dating from 14–15 AD. The city's northern gate is closer to Kongresni trg.

Parliament Building
HISTORIC BUILDING

(Parlament; Map p54; ☑ 01-478 97 88; www.dz-rs. si; Šubičeva ulica 4; ☉ tours by prior arrangement) FREE The parliament building at the northeast corner of Trg Republike, built between 1954 and 1959 by Vinko Glanz, is no beauty-pageant winner on the outside, but the mammoth portal festooned with bronze sculptures is noteworthy. If you time it right, it's worth booking a guided tour via the website to see the inside, especially the period-piece mural by Slavko Pengov.

Museum Area

Four of Ljubljana's most important museums are located in this area, which is only a short distance to the northwest of **Trg Republike** (Republic Sq; Map p50).

National Museum of Slovenia   MUSEUM
(Narodni Muzej Slovenije; Map p50; ☑01-241 44 00; www.nms.si; Prešernova cesta 20; adult/student €6/4, with National Museum of Slovenia–Metelkova or Slovenian Museum of Natural History €8.50/6, lapidarium free; ☉10am-6pm, to 8pm Thu) Housed in a grand building from 1888 – the same building as the Slovenian Museum of Natural History (p60) – highlights include the highly embossed *Vače situla* – a Celtic pail from the 6th century BC that was unearthed in a town east of Ljubljana. There's also a Stone Age bone flute (p125) discovered near Cerkno in western Slovenia in 1995. You'll find examples of Roman jewellery found in 6th-century Slavic graves, as well as a glass-enclosed Roman lapidarium outside to the north.

Check out the ceiling fresco in the foyer of the main building, which features an allegorical image of the ancient Slovenian province of Carniola surrounded by important Slovenes from the past, and the statues of the Muses and Fates relaxing on the stairway banisters. Note the entry to both this museum and the Slovenian Museum of Natural History are on the eastern side of the building, facing a park.

Museum of Modern Art   MUSEUM
(MG, Moderna Galerija; Map p50; ☑01-241 68 34; www.mg-lj.si; Cankarjeva cesta 15; adult/student €5/2.50, with Museum of Contemporary Art Metelkova €7.50; ☉10am-6pm Tue-Sun, to 8pm Thu Jul & Aug) This gallery houses the very best in modern Slovenian art. Keep an eye out for works by painters Tone Kralj *(Family)*, the expressionist France Mihelič *(The Quintet)* and the surrealist Stane Kregar *(Hunter at Daybreak)* as well as sculptors including Jakob Savinšek *(Protest)*. The museum also owns works by the influential 1980s and 1990s multimedia group Neue Slowenische Kunst (NSK; *Suitcase for Spiritual Use: Baptism under Triglav*) and the artists' cooperative Irwin *(Capital)*.

National Gallery of Slovenia   MUSEUM
(Map p50 ; ☑01-241 54 18; www.ng-slo.si; Prešernova cesta 24; adult/child €7/3, 1st Sun of month free; ☉10am-6pm Tue, Wed & Fri-Sun, to 8pm Thu) Slovenia's foremost assembly of fine art is housed over two floors in an old building (1896) and a modern wing. It exhibits copies of medieval frescoes and wonderful Gothic statuary as well as Slovenian landscapes from the 17th to 19th centuries (check out works by Romantic painters Pavel Künl and Marko Pernhart). Other noteworthies: impressionists Jurij Šubic *(Before the Hunt)* and Rihard Jakopič *(Birches in Autumn)*, the pointillist Ivan Grohar *(Larch)* and Slovenia's most celebrated female painter, Ivana Kobilca *(Summer)*.

The bronzes by Franc Berneker and Alojz Gangl are exceptional. In the entrance vestibule stands the original Robba Fountain,

---

A CITY OF GALLERIES

Ljubljana is awash with galleries, both public and commercial; head straight to a few of the best to get a taste of contemporary Slovenian art culture.

City Art Gallery (Mestna Galerija; Map p54; ☑01-241 17 70; https://mgml.si/sl/mestna-galerija; Mestni trg 5; ☉11am-7pm Tue, Wed, Fri & Sat, to 9pm Thu, to 3pm Sun) Easy-to-miss Old Town gallery with rotating displays of modern and contemporary painting, sculpture, graphic art and photography. There's a small gift shop on street level.

Equrna Gallery (Galerija Equrna; Map p54; ☑01-252 71 23; www.equrna.si; Gregorčičeva ulica 3; ☉noon-7pm Mon-Fri) Arguably the most innovative modern gallery in town thanks to the discerning owner/curator.

Škuc Gallery (Galerija Škuc; Map p54; ☑01-251 65 40; www.galerijaskuc.si; Stari trg 21; ☉noon-7pm Tue-Sun) Cutting-edge contemporary art gallery with a studenty vibe in the heart of the Old Town.

DESSA Architectural Gallery (Map p54; ☑01-251 60 10; www.dessa.si; Židovska steza 4; ☉noon-6pm Tue-Fri) Small gallery spotlighting contemporary Slovenian and international architecture and architects.

which was moved here from Mestni trg (p53) in the Old Town in 2008.

Slovenian Museum of Natural History
MUSEUM

(Prirodoslovni Muzej Slovenije; Map p50; ☑01-241 09 40; www.pms-lj.si; Prešernova cesta 20; adult/student €4/3, with National Museum of Slovenia €8.50/6, 1st Sun of month free; ☑10am-6pm Fri-Wed, to 8pm Thu; ℗) This museum shares the same building as the National Museum of Slovenia (p59), and contains reassembled mammoth and whale skeletons, stuffed birds, reptiles and mammals. The mineral collections amassed by the philanthropic Baron Žiga Zois in the early 19th century and the display on Slovenia's unique salamander *Proteus anguinus* are worth the visit. Note the entrance to both museums is on the eastern side of the building, facing the park.

◉ Trubarjeva Cesta & Tabor

North of Castle Hill across the Ljubljanica River, the bustling street lined with waterholes and eateries gives way to leafy, residential Tabor, home to three world-class museums and Metelkova Mesto (p74), Ljubljana's centre of alternative culture.

Slovenian Ethnographic Museum
MUSEUM

(Slovenski Etnografski Muzej; Map p50; ☑01-300 87 45; www.etno-muzej.si; Metelkova ulica 2; adult/child €4.50/2.50, 1st Sun of month free; ☑10am-6pm Tue-Sun) Housed in the 1886 Belgian Barracks on the southern edge of Metelkova, this museum has a permanent collection on the 2nd and 3rd floors. There's traditional Slovenian trades and handicrafts – everything from beekeeping and blacksmithing to glass-painting and pottery making – and some excellent exhibits directed at children.

Museum of Contemporary Art Metelkova
GALLERY

(MSUM, Muzej Sodobne Umetnosti Metelkova; Map p50; ☑01-241 68 00; www.mg-lj.si; Maistrova ulica 3; adult/student €5/2.50, with Museum of Modern Art €7.50; ☑10am-6pm Tue-Sun, to 8pm Thu Jul & Aug) This gallery, housed in a sleekly redesigned block building, picks up the thread from its sister institution, the Museum of Modern Art (p59), with Eastern European (mostly ex-Yugoslav) works from the 1960s till today. Plenty of obscure material here, but just as much of it is challenging and thought-provoking.

National Museum of Slovenia – Metelkova
MUSEUM

(Narodni Muzej Slovenije – Metelkova; Map p50; ☑01-230 70 30; www.nms.si; Maistrova ulica 1; adult/student €6/4, with National Museum of Slovenia €8.50/6, 1st Sun of month free; ☑10am-6pm Tue-Sun) This modern building in what is now becoming known as the Museum Quarter contains a bizarre assortment of mostly applied art and objets d'art (furniture, icons, paintings, sporting goods etc) that are tenuously linked through themes (Seating & Lighting). It's a rich collection spread over two very large floors.

◉ Park Tivoli & Around

Laid out in 1813, this 510-hectare park is Ljubljana's leafy playground and the perfect spot for a walk or bike ride. One of the highlights is the Jakopičevo sprehajališče, the monumental 'Jakopič Promenade', designed by local architect Jože Plečnik in the 1920s and '30s.

International Centre of Graphic Arts
MUSEUM

(Mednarodni Grafični Likovni Center; Map p50; ☑01-241 38 00; www.mglc-lj.si; Pod Turnom 3; adult/senior & student €5/3; ☑10am-6pm Tue-Sun) This museum and gallery dedicated to the graphic arts regularly hosts rotating exhibitions and is home to the International Biennial of Graphic Arts every odd-numbered year. The centre is located in the 17th-century Tivoli Mansion (Grad Tivoli) and has a delightful terrace cafe with views over the park.

Museum of Contemporary History of Slovenia
MUSEUM

(Muzej Novejše Zgodovine Slovenije; Map p50; ☑01-300 96 10; www.muzej-nz.si; Celovška cesta 23; adult/student €4.50/2.50, 1st Sun of month free; ☑10am-6pm Tue-Sat) This museum, housed in the 18th-century Cekin Mansion (Grad Cekinov), traces the history of Slovenia in the 20th century through multimedia and artefacts. Note the contrast between the sober earnestness of the communist-era rooms and the exuberant, logo-mad commercialism of the industrial exhibits. The sections focusing on Ljubljana under occupation during WWII are very effective. The gloriously baroque Ceremonial Hall (Viteška Dvorana) on the 1st floor is how the whole mansion once looked. Cutting-edge special exhibits too.

LJUBLJANA FOR CHILDREN

Ljubljana, for a big city, is reasonably child-friendly. Public buses normally have space to hold prams. Pavements are smooth and corners often have dropped kerbs for easy navigation. Public toilets with baby-change facilities are still the exception and not the norm, though these are becoming more common.

Park Tivoli, with a couple of children's playgrounds, **swimming pools** (Map p50; ✏ 01-431 51 55; www.sport-ljubljana.si; Celovška cesta 25; pool adult/child Mon-Fri €7.50/5.50, Sat & Sun €8.50/7.50; ☺ 6am-2pm Mon, 6am-2pm & 6pm-10pm Tue-Fri, 10am-8pm Sat & Sun Sep-Jun) and a **zoo** (Živalski Vrt Ljubljana; ✏ 01-244 21 82; www.zoo-ljubljana.si; Večna pot 70; adult/child €8/5.50; ☺ 9am-7pm Apr-Aug, to 6pm Sep, to 5pm Mar & Oct, to 4pm Nov-Feb; ▣ 18 Večna pot), is an excellent place to take the kids, as are the two water parks, **Laguna** (✏ 01-589 01 41; www.laguna.si; Dunajska cesta 270; day pass adult/child Mon-Fri €15/10, Sat & Sun €16/12; ☺ 9am-8pm May-Sep; ▣ 6, 8 or 11 to Ježica) and **Atlantis** (✏ 01-585 21 00; www. atlantis-vodnomesto.si; BTC City, Šmartinska cesta 152; day pass adult/child Mon-Fri €16.10/13.60, Sat & Sun €18.50/16; ☺ 9am-8pm Sun-Thu, to 9pm Fri & Sat; ▣ 27 to BTC Emporium).

In the warmer months the **Mini Summer for Children International Festival** (www.mini-teater.si; ☺ late-Jun–Aug) stages puppet shows from around the world for kids. Also, check out the year-round program at the Ljubljana Puppet Theatre (p76).

The best museums for children, with handouts, hands-on exhibits and trails to follow, are the Natural History Museum, the City Museum (p58) and the Ethnographic Museum. The **House of Experiments** (Hiša Eksperimentov; Map p54; ✏ 01-300 68 88; www.he.si; Trubarjeva cesta 39; €6; ☺ 4pm-8pm Wed, 11am-7pm Sat & Sun), a hands-on science centre with inventive exhibits and a science adventure show, is also a super place for kids.

Mala Ulica (Little Street; Map p54; ✏ 01-306 27 00; www.malaulica.si; Prečna ulica 7; family/child €4/2; ☺ 10am-7pm Mon-Fri, to 6pm Sat & Sun), billed as a 'public living room' for parents and preschool children, has workshops, crafts, puppet shows and more.

The Ljubljana TIC (p78) website is a good source of info for events suitable for children.

Union Experience   MUSEUM
(Union doživetje; Map p50; ✏ 041 303 050; www. union-experience.si; Union Brewery, Celovška cesta 22; adult/child €14/11; ☺ tours noon, 2pm, 4pm & 6pm Mon-Fri, 2pm, 4pm & 6pm Sat; ▣ 1, 3 or 5 to Tivoli) This museum at the Union Brewery offers various displays of brewing, a film and a tasting. Walk here from Center.

☺ Krakovo & Trnovo

These two attractive districts south of Center are Ljubljana's oldest suburbs; they have a number of interesting buildings and historical sites. The neighbourhood around Krakovska ulica, with its two-storey cottages, was once called the Montmartre of Ljubljana because of all the artists living there.

The **Roman wall** (Map p50; Mirje ulica) running along Mirje from Barjanska cesta dates from about AD 15; the archway topped with a **pyramid** (cnr Murnikova ulica & Mirje ulica) is an addition by local architect Jože Plečnik. Spanning the picturesque canal called Gradaščica to the south is little **Trnovo**

Bridge, designed in 1932 by Plečnik, who added five of his trademark pyramids.

Plečnik House   MUSEUM
(Hiša Plečnik; Map p50; ✏ 01-241 25 06; www.mgml. si; Karunova ulica 4-6; adult/child €6/4; ☺ 10am-6pm Tue-Sun) This small house in Trnovo is where local architect Jože Plečnik lived and worked for almost 40 years. There's an excellent introduction by hourly guided tour to this almost ascetically religious man's life, inspiration and work.

☺ Žale & Beyond

Žale Cemetery   CEMETERY
(Pokopališče Žale; ✏ 01-420 17 00; www.zale.si; Med Hmeljniki 2; ☺ 7am-9pm Apr-Sep, to 7pm Oct-Mar; ▣ 2, 7 or 22 to Žale) **FREE** This cemetery, some 2km northeast of Tabor, is Ljubljana's answer to Père Lachaise in Paris or London's Highgate. It is 'home' to a number of distinguished Slovenes, including architect Jože Plečnik, but is best known for the ornamental gates, chapels and colonnades at the complex's entrance designed by Plečnik

MATEJ KASTELIC/KASTO80/500PX ©

1. Ljubljana Castle (p48)
Ride the funicular up to the castle for panoramic views of the city.

2. Dragon Bridge (p56)
This much-loved bridge is guarded by four dragons standing on each corner.

3. National & University Library (p57)
Bask in the glorious architecture of Jože Plečnik's masterwork.

MATEJ KASTELIC/KASTO80/500PX ©

SLOVENIAN HERITAGE

If you are searching for your Slovenian roots, check first with the *mestna občina* (municipal government office) or *občina* (county office); they usually have birth and death certificates going back a century. Vital records beyond the 100-year limit are kept at the **Archives of the Republic of Slovenia** (Arhiv Republike Slovenije; ☎ 01-241 42 00; www.arhiv.gov.si; Gruber Palace, Zvezdarska ulica 1; ◷ 8am-2pm Mon-Fri, to 3pm in winter). Ethnic Slovenes living abroad might be interested in contacting the **Slovenian Emigrants Centre** (Slovenska Izseljenska Matica; Map p54; ☎ 01-241 02 80; www.zdruzenje-sim.si; 2nd fl, Cankarjeva cesta 1; ◷ by appointment).

himself in 1940. There are also the graves of Austrian, Italian and German soldiers from both world wars and a small Jewish section.

Plečnik's modest grave marker is located in the main part of the cemetery, area A, in section 6. To find it, walk past the yellow church at the front of the cemetery, and turn left at the end of the first section.

Museum of Architecture & Design   MUSEUM
(Muzej za arhitekturo in oblikovanje; ☎ 01-548 42 80; www.mao.si; Fužine Castle, Pot na Fužine 2; adult/child €3.50/2, 1st Sun of month free; ◷ 10am-6pm Tue-Sun; ☐ 20 or 22 to Fužine) This museum, housed in the stunningly preserved 16th-century Fužine Castle (worth the visit alone) about 5.5km east of the centre, preserves some 150,000 items from architects, designers and photographers and hosts temporary themed exhibitions.

🏃 Activities

Ballooning

The Ljubljana TIC organises **hot-air balloon rides** (☎ 01-306 45 83; www.visitljubljana.com/en/visitors/tours-and-trips/balloon-adventure; adult/child €170/119; ◷ 6am Apr-Oct) with stunning views of the city, Ljubljana Marsh and the Julian Alps. Departure is from the Slovenian Tourist Information Centre (p78); times vary. You'll get one to 1½ hours in the air.

Boating & Rafting

Skok Sport   WATER SPORTS
(☎ 01-512 44 02; www.skok-sport.si; Marinovševa cesta 8; ◷ 8am-1pm & 3-8pm May-Oct; ☐ 8 to Brod) In Šentvid, 9km northwest of Center, this place organises combination cycling and rafting trips on the nearby Sava lasting 2½ to three hours and costing €40. It can also arrange kayak and canoe excursions on the Ljubljanica and runs a kayaking school. Rental kayaks for half/full day start at €7/10.

Ljubljana Rowing Club   BOATING
(Veslaški Klub Ljubljana; ☎ 01-283 87 12; www.vesl-klub-ljubljanica.si; Velika Čolnarska ulica 20; per hour €6-8; ◷ 11am-10pm mid-May–Sep) This club in Trnovo has dinghies and larger rowing boats for hire on the Ljubljanica River.

Walking & Hiking

Popular with walkers and joggers, the marked **Trail of Remembrance** (Pot Spominov) runs for 34km around Ljubljana where German barbed wire once completely enclosed the city during WWII. The easiest places to reach the trail are from the AMZS headquarters (p269; take bus 6, 8 or 11 to the AMZS stop), or from Trg Komandanta Staneta just northwest of the LPP (p80) central office (take bus 1 to the Remiza stop). You can also join it from the northwestern side of Žale Cemetery (p61; take bus 19 to the Nove Žale stop), or south of Trnovo (take bus 9 to the Veliki Štradon stop).

Tours

The Ljubljana TIC (p78) offers a number of guided tours of the city, organised around modes of transport (including bike, kayak, Segway, or stand-up paddleboard) or around themes such as food and drink, including a highly recommended tour of craft beer joints. See the website for the current list.

LjubljanaNjam   TOURS
(☎ 041 878 959; www.ljubljananjam.si; 3-4hr tours €55-65) Among the best of several companies offering food walking tours in Ljubljana. The name 'LjubljanaNjam' translates roughly as 'Ljubljana Yum', and epicure Iva Gruden will have you eating out of bakers' hands, nibbling goat cheese in the market, scoffing Carniola sausage and slurping fairtrade espresso. Also runs tours focused on wines and craft beers.

Ljubljana Free Tour   WALKING
(Map p54; ☎ 040 604 476; www.ljubljanafreetour.com; Prešernov trg; donation expected;

⊙ 11am year-round & also 3pm May-Oct) Highly recommendable 'free' city tour (the name is a misnomer because you are expected to tip). Groups meet up in Prešernov trg (p49); tours last about 2½ hours and cover most of the major sights (except the castle). Check the website for fixed-price themed tours on the communist era and medieval Ljubljana (both €10).

CurioCity
TOURS
(☑ 051 640 750; www.curiocity.si; tours €30-50) This unusual outfit organises a number of personal tours – from those scouting out the best selfie locations to expeditions in search of dragons – but the most innovative is 'From Ljubljana with Love', which introduces you to the people and stories behind six socially responsible businesses, from secondhand shops and fair-trade cafes to restaurants supporting those with learning disabilities.

Barka Ljubljanica
BOATING
(Ljubljanica Boat; Map p54; ☑ 041 386 945; www.barka-ljubljanica.si; Breg 2; adult/child €10/free; ⊙ sailings hourly 10am-8pm May-Oct, 11am-8pm Nov-Jan) There are more and more boat tours up and down the river in Ljubljana but only the creatively named Barka Ljubljanica (Ljubljanica Boat) sails a wooden vessel. It's 10m long and carries up to 48 people plus crew on a 45-minute tour. Board it on the west bank of the river, just down from Novi trg (p57).

🎊 Festivals & Events

Druga Godba
MUSIC
(Another Story; https://drugagodba.si; ⊙ May) This festival of alternative and world music takes place in the Križanke (p75).

Ljubljana Pride
LGBT
(www.ljubljanapride.org; ⊙ Jun) Annual gay pride parade and festival, with a week of conferences, movies, performances and discussions at venues around town. See the website for calendar.

Ljubljanska Vinska Pot
WINE
(Ljubljana Wine Route; www.ljubljanskavinskapot.si; ⊙ Jun) Held on a Saturday in June, this event brings winemakers from around the country to central Ljubljana, where visitors spend the day wandering around and tasting the offerings.

Ana Desetnica International Street Theatre Festival
THEATRE
(www.anamonro.si/ana-desetnica; ⊙ Jun-Jul) Organised by the Ana Monró Theatre in late June/early July, this festival is not to be missed.

Ljubljana Festival
MUSIC
(www.ljubljanafestival.si; ⊙ Jul-Aug) The number-one event on Ljubljana's social calendar is the Ljubljana Festival, a celebration from early July to late August of music, opera, theatre and dance held at venues throughout the city, but principally in the open-air theatre (p75) at the Križanke.

RACE AGAINST THE CLOCK: LJUBLJANA'S ESCAPE GAMES

In the last few years, Ljubljana has picked up on the emerging trend of live escape games, in which teams of between two and 12 people willingly lock themselves in a set of rooms in order to spend an hour or so working through numerous riddles that will eventually unlock the door back to freedom.

Each game has a distinct theme and story and involves not only the solving of puzzles but, crucially, the ability to identify the puzzles in the first place. Some tips for first-timers: try all of your ideas; search everywhere; and request extra clues from your captors!

Escape Room Enigmarium (Map p50; ☑ 031 334 488; www.escape-room.si; Trdinova ulica 8; 2-5 players €60; ⊙ 9.30am-10pm) Ljubljana's first – and some would say best – escape game has several different themes to choose from, including the Classroom of Doom and – our favourite – the Escape Igloo, based on a really icy one set up in Kranjska Gora in winter. Teams of two to five players can test their puzzling skills to riddle their way free in 60 minutes.

Key Escape Room (Map p54; ☑ 030 232 323; www.thekey.si; Obrežna steza 2; 2-3/4-5/10-12 players €50/60/100; ⊙ 10.30am-9pm) The central Key has two escape rooms – one named after Da Vinci and the other after Sherlock Holmes. You're really stretching your detective, scientific and artistic skills to the limit here and in this case you must get out of both locked rooms in just 70 minutes. Riddle-dee-dee.

Trnfest MUSIC

(www.kud.si; ☉ Aug) An international festival of alternative arts and culture and a favourite annual event of many *Ljubljančani* (local people), Trnfest takes place at the KUD France Prešeren (p75) in Trnovo and at other venues through the month of August.

International Ljubljana Marathon SPORTS

(www.ljubljanskimaraton.si; ☉ Oct) This major sporting event takes place on the last Sunday in October.

Mesto Žensk CULTURAL

(City of Women; www.cityofwomen.org; ☉ Oct) Held in the first half of October in venues throughout Ljubljana, this festival showcases all forms of artistic expression by women.

🛌 Sleeping

Accommodation prices in Ljubljana are the highest in the country. For tighter budgets, there is a growing number of high-quality modern hostels, some with private singles and doubles. The **Ljubljana TIC** website (www.visitljubljana.com) maintains a comprehensive list of hotels, apartments and other sleeping options, including private rooms (single/double/triple from €35/55/80). A few of these are in the centre but most require a bus trip north to Bežigrad or beyond.

🛌 Prešernov Trg & Around

Hotel Emonec HOTEL **$$**

(Map p54; ☑ 01-200 15 20; www.hotel-emonec. com; Wolfova ulica 12; s/d/tr from €65/75/95; 🅿 ❄ @ 🛜) After a complete revamping, the decor remains simple and functionally modern at this 54-room hotel. Everything is spotless and you can't beat the central location. Air-con costs extra but fans are free. There's a small in-house spa with fitness and sauna, and an in-house self-service laundry.

Grand Hotel Union HOTEL **$$$**

(Map p54; ☑ 01-308 12 70; www.gh-union.si; Miklošičeva cesta 1; s €100-150, d €120-200, ste €180-240; 🅿 ❄ @ 🛜) The 194-room Grand Hotel Union, the art nouveau southern wing of a two-part hostelry, was built in 1905 and remains one of the most desirable addresses in town. It has glorious public areas and guests can use the indoor pool and fitness centre of the adjacent 133-room Grand Union Business Hotel, in the hotel's renovated modern wing.

🛌 Old Town

Ad Hoc Hostel HOSTEL **$**

(Map p54; ☑ 051 268 288; www.adhoc-hostel.com; Cankarjevo nabrežje 27; dm €17.50-21, d €40-66; ❄ @ 🛜) This very well-situated, efficiently run 106-bed hostel on the Ljubljanica has brightly painted, airy dorms with four to eight metal bunks and eight doubles. Room Nos 104 and 106 overlook the river. There are also several apartments. Great kitchen too.

Hotel Galleria BOUTIQUE HOTEL **$$**

(Map p54; ☑ 01-421 35 60; www.hotelgalleria.eu; Gornji trg 3; s €70-110, d €90-130; ❄ @ 🛜) This attractive boutique hotel has been cobbled together from several Old Town townhouses. There are 16 spacious rooms and a multi-tiered back garden. The decor is kitsch with a smirk and there are fabulous touches everywhere. Among our favourite rooms are the enormous No 8, with views of the **Hercules Fountain** (Map p54; Levstikov trg), and No 13, with glimpses of Ljubljana Castle.

★ Adora Hotel HOTEL **$$$**

(Map p54; ☑ 082 057 240; www.adorahotel.si; Rožna ulica 7; s €115, d €125-155, apt €135-165; 🅿 ❄ @ 🛜) This small hotel below Gornji trg is a welcome addition to accommodation in the Old Town. The 10 rooms are small but fully equipped, with lovely hardwood floors and tasteful furnishings. The breakfast room looks out onto a small garden, bikes are free for guests' use and the staff is overwhelmingly friendly and helpful.

★ Vander Urbani Resort BOUTIQUE HOTEL **$$$**

(Map p54; ☑ 01-200 90 00; www.vanderhotel. com; Krojaška ulica 6-8; r €130-210; ❄ @ 🛜 ❄) This stunning boutique hotel in the heart of Ljubljana's Old Town is formed from four 17th-century buildings. But history stops there, for this hostelry – with 16 rooms over three floors – is as modern as tomorrow. Designed by the trendsetting Sadar Vuga architectural firm, the rooms are not huge but each is unique and makes use of natural materials.

One of the best rooms in the hotel is No 36, with views of the Ljubljanica and a large bathroom with a shower and tub. The rooftop terrace boasts an infinity pool and heart-stopping views of Ljubljana Castle and the Old Town.

Allegro Hotel   BOUTIQUE HOTEL **$$$**
(Map p54; ☑ 059 119 620; www.allegrohotel.si;
Gornji trg 6; s €80-100, d €100-120; P ❄ @ 🛜)
This 17-room historical boutique hotel in the
Old Town is a symphony of designer chic
with rooms that give on to Gornji trg (p53)
and a charming back courtyard. Room Nos
2 and 3 have a balcony, No 15 a small terrace
and No 12 at the top sleeps four.

🛏 Central Market & East

Hostel 24 Center   HOSTEL **$**
(Map p50; ☑ 040 780 036; https://hostel24.si/
center; Poljanska cesta 15; dm €16-20, d €50-58;
❄ @ 🛜) One of three hostels in a chain, this
one is just east of the central market (p69)
and Dragon Bridge (p56) on a street that
seems to be gaining momentum (and a few
bars and restaurants). Hostel 24 offers dorm
accommodation in six- to 12-bed rooms, as
well as several private apartments for two to
four people.

There's a great kitchen and lounge, plus
an in-house bakery.

🛏 Center

Hostel Tresor   HOSTEL **$**
(Map p54; ☑ 01-200 90 60; www.hostel-tresor.
si; Čopova ulica 38; dm €12-20, d €58; ❄ @ 🛜)
This 28-room hostel in the heart of Center is
housed in a secessionist-style former bank,
and the money theme continues right into
rooms named after currencies and finan-
cial aphorisms on the walls. Dorms have
between four and 10 beds but are spacious.
The communal areas (we love the atrium)
are stunning; breakfast is in the vaults.

Slamič B&B   B&B **$$**
(Map p50; ☑ 01-433 82 33; www.slamic.si; Ker-
snikova ulica 1; s €65-75, d €95-110, ste from €135;
P ❄ 🛜) It's slightly away from the action
but Slamič, a B&B above a famous cafe and
teahouse, offers 17 bright, refurbished rooms
with en-suite facilities and large comfortable
beds. Choice rooms include those looking on
to a back garden, and the one just off an enormous terrace used by the KavaČaj (Coffee
Tea), a gem of a cafe on the ground floor.

Cubo   BOUTIQUE HOTEL **$$$**
(Map p54; ☑ 01-425 60 00; www.hotelcubo.com;
Slovenska cesta 15; s/d €120/140; ❄ @ 🛜) The
stylish 26-room Cubo has raised the bar
of Ljubljana accommodation. The overall
design is minimalist, with an emphasis on
neutral tones of grey, beige and charcoal.
Some of the high-quality materials used in
the furnishings are unusual: check out the
silver thread in the guestroom drapes that
cost a king's ransom and the bedside lamps
made with silkworm cocoons.

City Hotel Ljubljana   HOTEL **$$$**
(Map p50; ☑ 01-239 00 00; www.cityhotel.
si; Dalmatinova ulica 15; s €80-110, d €100-140;
P ❄ @ 🛜) An attractive high-rise hotel offering 202 clean, basic rooms and a central
location. Rooms vary from 'economy' to
'comfort', with the latter larger and air-
conditioned. It's an odd place – primary colours splashed hither and yon, a kind of circus
make-up feel, trees and books in the lobby,
but it all works and, frankly, we love it here.

**Antiq Palace
Hotel & Spa**   BOUTIQUE HOTEL **$$$**
(Map p54; ☑ 040 638 163, 083 896 700; www.antiq
palace.com; Gosposka ulica 10; s/d €180/210;
❄ @ 🛜) The city's most luxurious sleeping
option, the Antiq Palace occupies a 16th-
century townhouse, about a block from the
river. Accommodation is in 18 individually
designed rooms and suites, some stretching
to 250 sq metres in size and with jacuzzi.
Many retain their original features (hard-
wood floors, floor-to-ceiling windows) and
are furnished in an eclectic manner with
quirky rococo touches.

🛏 Trubarjeva Cesta & Tabor

Celica Hostel   HOSTEL **$**
(Map p50; ☑ 01-230 97 00; www.hostelcelica.com;
Metelkova ulica 8; dm €18-26, s/d cell €58/62;
@ 🛜) This stylishly revamped former pris-
on (1882) in Metelkova (p74) has 20 'cells',
designed by different artists and architects
and complete with original bars. There are
nine rooms and apartments with three to
seven beds and a packed, popular 12-bed
dorm. The ground floor is home to a cafe
and restaurant (set lunch around €7). Bikes
cost €3/6 for a half/full day.

H2O Hostel   HOSTEL **$**
(Map p50; ☑ 041 662 266; www.h2ohostel.com;
Petkovškovo nabrežje 47; dm €17-22, d €36-58, q
€68-88; @ 🛜) One of our favourite hostels
in Ljubljana, this seven-room place wraps
around a tiny courtyard bordering the Lju-
bljanica River. One room has views of the
castle. Private doubles are available and
guests have access to a common kitchen.

Hotel Park Urban & Green   HOTEL **$$$**
(Map p50; ☎01-300 25 00; www.hotelpark.si; Tabor 9; s €110-120, d €130-140; P❄@🛜) 🚲 This tower-block hotel, in a leafy residential area just north of the centre, has undergone a thorough makeover and offers clean, decent-value accommodation. Rooms are divided into 'standard' and 'superior', though there's little difference between the two aside from more-modern furniture. The hotel prides itself on sustainability, waste reduction and promotion of cycling and electric vehicles.

🛏 Krakovo & Trnovo

★Hostel Vrba   HOSTEL **$**
(Map p50; ☎064 133 555; www.hostelvrba.si; Gradaška ulica 10; dm €22-30, d €65-75; @🛜) Definitely one of our favourite budget digs in Ljubljana, this nine-room hostel on the Gradiščica Canal is just opposite the bars and restaurants of delightful Trnovo. There are three twin doubles, dorms with four to eight beds (including a popular all-female dorm), hardwood floors, and an always warm welcome. Free bikes in summer.

🛏 Žale & Beyond

Ljubljana Resort   CAMPGROUND **$**
(☎01-589 01 30; www.ljubljanaresort.si; Dunajska cesta 270; adult €10-15, child €7-9.50, hotel s €60-70, d €75-85; P❄@🚗; 🚌6, 8 or 11 to Ježica) This attractive 6-hectare campground-cum-resort 4km north of the centre has the facilities to match the grandiose name. Along with a 60-room hotel and 12 stationary mobile homes (€100 to €140), there's the Laguna (p61) water park next door, which is half-price for guests. Note that not all hotel rooms have air-conditioning.

🍴 Eating

Ljubljana has Slovenia's best selection of restaurants. Although prices tend to be higher here than elsewhere, it is still possible to eat well at moderate cost; even the more expensive restaurants usually offer an excellent-value three-course *dnevno kosilo* (set lunch) for around €10.

🍴 Castle Hill

Gostilna na Gradu   SLOVENIAN **$$**
(Inn at the Castle; Map p54; ☎031 301 777; www.nagradu.si; Grajska planota 1; mains €12-18; ⏰10am-midnight Mon-Sat, noon-6pm Sun; 🛜)

Right within the Ljubljana Castle (p48) complex, Na Gradu is much too stylish to be just a *gostilna* (inn-like restaurant). The award-winning chefs use only Slovenian-sourced breads, cheeses and meats, and age-old recipes to prepare a meal to remember. If you really want to taste your way across the country, try the five-course gourmet tasting menu for €42.20.

★Strelec   SLOVENIAN **$$$**
(Archer; Map p54; ☎031 687 648; www.kaval-group.si/strelec.asp; Grajska Planota 1; mains €15-30; ⏰noon-10pm Mon-Sat; 🛜) This is haute cuisine from on high –the Archer's Tower of Ljubljana Castle (p48), no less – with a menu that traces the city's history chosen by ethnologist Janez Bogataj and prepared by Igor Jagodic, recognised as one of the top chefs in Slovenia. Tasting menus are priced from €32 to €77 for between three and nine courses.

🍴 Old Town

★Pop's Place   BURGERS **$**
(Map p54; ☎059 042 856; www.facebook.com/popsplaceburgerbar; Cankarjevo nabrežje 3; burgers €8-10; ⏰noon-midnight; 🛜) Centrally located craft-beer and burger bar that's evolved into a must-visit. The burgers, with locally sourced beef and brioche-style buns, are excellent, as are the beers and cocktails. The dining area feels festive, with an open kitchen behind the bar and communal tables out front for diners to rub elbows and compare burgers. Avoid traditional meal times: Pop's gets busy.

Druga Violina   SLOVENIAN **$**
(Map p54; ☎082 052 506; www.facebook.com/drugaviolina; Stari trg 21; mains €6-10; ⏰8am-midnight; 🛜) Just opposite the Academy of Music, the 'Second Fiddle' is an extremely pleasant and affordable place for a meal in the Old Town. There are lots of Slovenian dishes, including *ajdova kaša z jurčki* (buckwheat groats with ceps) and *obara* (a thick stew of chicken and vegetables), on the menu. It's a social enterprise designed to help those with disabilities.

Vino & Ribe   MEDITERRANEAN **$**
(Wine & Fish; Map p54; ☎082 055 283; www.facebook.com/vinoinribe; Stari trg 28; mains €8-12; ⏰noon-10pm) This unsuspecting spot along Stari trg, looking something like a diner, focuses on a couple of things (hint: they're in the name) and does them very well. Order

TO MARKET, TO MARKET

The **Central Market** (Centralna Tržnica; Map p54; Vodnikov trg; ⊙ open-air market 6am-6pm Mon-Fri, to 4pm Sat summer, to 4pm Mon-Sat winter) is Ljubljana's larder and worth a trip both to stock up on provisions or just have a good snoop (and sniff) around. Go first to the vast open-air market (Tržnica na Prostem) just across the Triple Bridge to the southeast of Prešernov trg on Vodnikov trg. Here you'll find a daily farmers market (except Sunday). In the next neighbouring square – Pogačarjev trg – there are always stalls selling everything from foraged wild mushrooms and forest berries to honey and homemade cheeses.

On Friday, in summer, this is the venue for **Odprta Kuhna** (Open Kitchen; www.odprta kuhna.si; Pogačarjev trg; mains €8-15; ⊙ 10am-9pm Fri mid-Mar–Oct, up to 11pm in summer), a weekly food fair with local and international specialities cooked on-site from restaurants around the city and beyond. The **covered market** (Pokrita Tržnica; Map p54; Pogačarjev trg 2; ⊙ 7am-3pm Mon-Sat) nearby also sells meats and cheeses, and there's also a **fish market** (Ribarnica; Map p54; Adamič-Lundrovo nabrežje 1; ⊙ 7am-4pm Mon-Fri, to 2pm Sat) below the **Plečnik Colonnade** (Map p54) FREE. You'll find open-air fish stands selling fried calamari for as low as €7.

at the counter from a small menu of grilled fish, fried fish, sardines, fried potatoes and carafes of house wine. No atmosphere to speak of, but no need with food this good.

Repete SLOVENIAN $
(Map p54; ☑ 059 015 934; www.facebook.com/repetegt; Gornji trg 23; mains €7-12; ⊙ 8am-1am Mon-Fri, 10am-1am Sat, to 5pm Sun; 🕿 ☑) Subtitled 'Jazz & Okrepčila' (Jazz & Snacks), this is where you come to get both. There's locally sourced vegetarian fare only midweek, with carnivorous offerings emerging at the weekend (some serious burgers here). It's a tiny place, with sleek and minimalist decor, but warm and cosy. Jazz concerts at 8pm on Thursday.

Klobasarna SLOVENIAN $
(Map p54; ☑ 051 605 017; www.klobasarna.si; Ciril Metodov trg 15; dishes €3.50-6; ⊙ 10am-9pm Mon-Sat, to 3pm Sun) This hole-in-the-wall eatery in the Old Town specialises in that most Slovenian of dishes, *Kranjska klobasa*, an EU-protected fatty sausage. Buy 'em by the half/whole with a bit of cabbage, bread and mustard on the side. If you're really hungry, add *jota* (a hearty soup of beans and pickled turnip) or *ričet* (a thick barley stew).

Špajza SLOVENIAN $$
(Map p54; ☑ 01-425 30 94; www.spajza-restaurant.si; Gornji trg 28; mains €18-24; ⊙ noon-11pm Mon-Sat, to 10pm Sun; 🕿) The 'Pantry' attracts as much with its homey decor as with its Slovenian cuisine, executed with a modern touch. Several rooms in an ancient townhouse filled with rough-hewn tables and

chairs, wooden floors and nostalgic bric-a-brac lead to a small garden. Expect less common meats on the menu: rabbit, lamb and *žrebičkov z jurčki* (colt with ceps; €24).

TaBar TAPAS $$
(Map p54; ☑ 031 764 063; www.tabar.si; Ribji trg 6; tapas €4-10, 2-/4-lunch menu €12/16; ⊙ noon-midnight Mon-Sat; 🕿) Seriously inventive (and borderless) tapas and an excellent wine list, in sleek postmodern surrounds. Check the website for the current list of cold and warm dishes, which change from week to week. Good-value lunch specials through the week.

Julija MEDITERRANEAN $$
(Map p54; ☑ 01-425 64 63; http://julijarestaurant.com; Stari trg 9; mains €10-20; ⊙ 11.30am-midnight; 🕿) Arguably the best of several restaurants standing side by side on touristy Stari trg. The menu revolves around risottos and pastas, with plenty of tempting meat and fish options. The atmosphere is casual, though the relatively formal baroque setting makes Julija a solid choice for a fancy meal or a date. The three-course set lunches (around €9) are good value.

Taverna Tatjana SEAFOOD $$
(Map p54; ☑ 01-421 00 87; www.taverna-tatjana.si; Gornji trg 38; mains €10-25; ⊙ 5pm-midnight Mon-Sat; 🕿) This charming little tavern on the far end of Gornji trg specialises in fish and seafood (though there's some beef and foal on the menu too). It's housed in several vaulted rooms of an atmospheric old townhouse with wooden ceiling beams, and the fish is fresher than a spring shower.

✗ Central Market & East

Gostilna Dela INTERNATIONAL $

(Map p50; ☑ 059 925 446; www.facebook.com/
gostilnadela; Poljanska cesta 7; mains €5-7; ⊙ 8am-
4pm Mon-Fri; ☞🖉) This delightful bistro
serves tasty homestyle cuisine, only much
better. From the soups and the meat and
vegetarian main courses to the shop-made
štruklji (dumplings), it's all memorable. The
breakfast omelettes stretch off the plate.
What's more, 'Dela' (Work) is helping to
create job opportunities for local youth otherwise excluded from the working world.
Breakfast and lunch only.

✗ Center

Gelateria Romantika ICE CREAM $

(Map p54; ☑ 040 978 566; www.gelateria-
romantika.si; Dvorni trg 1; 2 scoops around €2.50;
⊙ 10am-11pm Mon-Thu, to midnight Fri & Sat, to
9pm Sun Apr-Sep, 10pm Mon-Thu, noon-11pm Fri &
Sat, 10am-9pm Sun Oct & Nov, Jan-Mar, 4.30-11pm
Dec) Some might say this isn't just Ljubljana's best ice cream, but some of the best in
the world. We'll let you decide, but the diverse flavour combinations (pumpkin-seed
oil, cucumber, bilberry) are a welcome
change from the standard chocolate and
vanilla, and you'll be back for more. Occasionally closes for breaks outside of the main
April–September season.

Figovec SLOVENIAN $

(Slovenska Hiša; Map p50; ☑ 01-426 44 10; www.
facebook.com/figovec; Gosposvetska cesta 1; mains
€10-15; ⊙ 8am-11pm Mon-Sat, from 9am Sun; ☞)
The unfussy interior of plain wooden tables,
white-brick walls and traditional floor tiles
complement simple but delicious Slovenian dishes from around the country, including big plates of sausages and sauerkraut,
roast pork and buckwheat groats. Excellent selection of domestic wines and craft
beers. The staff is knowledgeable and can
help you make your selection. Reservations
recommended.

Zbornica BURGERS $

(Map p50; ☑ 040 583 355; www.zbornicabar.com;
Rimska cesta 13; mains €6-8; ⊙ 8am-10pm Mon-
Fri, from 10am Sat; ☞) This student-friendly
joint calls itself a burger bar, but it's more
than that; it also serves delicious good-
value Balkan-style grilled meats, salads and
pastas. The service is quick and the setting
informal, making it a better choice for lunch
than dinner. To find it, walk around the side
of the building and enter from the back
through the park.

Hood Burger Center BURGERS $

(Map p54; ☑ 040 540 411; www.hoodburger.si; Nazorjeva ulica 4; burger & fries €8; ⊙ 11am-midnight
Mon-Fri, from noon Sat & Sun; ☞) These delicious burgers, sourced from Slovenian beef,
and fries, coleslaw, shakes and craft beers
are a big step up from international fast-
food chains. Tell the person at the counter
how you want your burger cooked and find a
table. An easy, convenient option for a quick
lunch or dinner. Gluten-free buns available.

Mala Terasa INTERNATIONAL $

(Map p50; ☑ 031 303 777; www.malaterasa.com;
Trg Ajdovščina 1; lunch €7-9; ⊙ 11am-5pm Mon-
Fri; ☞🖉) This student-oriented terrace
in Center is a solid choice for a quick and
cheap lunch. Line up at the counter and order from a small menu of sandwiches, salads, burgers and chicken dishes; there are
also several vegetarian options. Everything
is fresh and there's usually a daily good-
value lunch option.

Burek Olimpija FAST FOOD $

(Map p50; ☑ 031 386 687; www.facebook.com/
burekolimpija; Slovenska cesta 58; pies from €2;
⊙ 24h; 🖉) A pre- or post-drinking culinary
tradition is to snag one of these greasy (but
delicious) filo-dough pies, stuffed with meat
or cheese, for takeaway. Olimpija, conveniently, is open round the clock.

Paninoteka SANDWICHES $

(Map p54; ☑ 040 349 329; www.facebook.com/
Paninoteka.Restaurant; Jurčičev trg 3; soups &
toasted sandwiches €4-15; ⊙ 8am-11pm Mon-Fri,
from 9am Sat & Sun; ☞) A handy central spot
for a quick lunch, breakfast (€5 to €7), coffee or beer. Paninoteka is best known for its
healthy sandwich creations, though it also
offers more ambitious pastas and hot meals.
Sit inside or out on the terrace, with a view
toward the Cobblers' Bridge (p53).

Le Petit Café CAFE $$

(Map p54; ☑ 01-251 25 75; www.lepetit.si; Trg Fran-
coske Revolucije 4; mains €8-18; ⊙ 7.30am-mid-
night; ☞) Just opposite the Križanke (p75),
this pleasant, boho place offers great cof-
fee and a wide range of breakfast goodies,
lunches and light meals, plus an excellent
restaurant on the 1st floor with a provin-
cial-style decor and menu.

★**Monstera Bistro** SLOVENIAN **$$$**
(Map p54; ☑040 431 123; http://monsterabistro.
si; Gosposka ulica 9; three-course lunch €19, seven-
course tasting menu €55; ⊘11.30am-5pm Mon-
Wed, to 11pm Thu-Sat; 🕿🍴) 🍴 The concept
bistro of star TV chef Bine Volčič delivers
'best-meal-of-the-trip' quality using local-
ly sourced, seasonal ingredients and ze-
ro-waste food-prep concepts. Most diners
opt for the three-course lunch (starter, main
course, dessert), though the multi-course
dinners are consistently good. The light-
infused dining room, with white-brick walls
and light woods, feels dressy without being
overly formal. Book in advance.

JB Restavracija SLOVENIAN **$$$**
(Map p50; ☑01-430 70 70; www.jb-slo.com; Mik-
lošičeva cesta 17; mains €25-35; ⊘noon-10pm
Mon-Fri, 6-11pm Sat; 🕿) Old-world charm, a hybrid menu featuring Slovenian, French and
Mediterranean dishes, a top-notch wine list
and very stylish decor have made this restaurant one of the most popular in town for
a fancy meal. Feast your way through one of
chef Janez Bratovž' tasting menus of meat/
fish/traditional Slovenian for €45/50/60.

⚙ Trubarjeva Cesta & Tabor

★**Ek Bistro** INTERNATIONAL **$**
(Map p50; ☑041 937 534; www.facebook.com/ekl
jubljana; Petkovškovo nabrežje 65; breakfasts €8-
10; ⊘8am-8pm Mon-Thu, to 9pm Fri & Sat, to 3pm
Sun; 🕿🍴) Ljubljana's top spot for brunch,
meaning in this case big slices of avocado
toast on homemade bread, bowls of muesli
and yoghurt, and eggs Benedict on fresh-
baked English muffins. Wash it down with a
glass of freshly squeezed something or a flat
white. The fresh-cut flowers on the tables
look great against the distressed brick walls.

Skuhna INTERNATIONAL **$**
(Map p50; ☑041 339 978; www.facebook.com/
Skuhna; Trubarjeva cesta 56; set menu €6-11;
⊘11.30am-6pm Mon-Wed, to 10pm Thu & Fri, noon-
10pm Sat) This unique eatery is the work of
Slovenian nonprofit organisations that are
helping the city's migrant community to in-
tegrate. A half-dozen chefs from countries as
diverse as Sri Lanka, Tunisia and Colombia
take turns cooking every day, and the result
is a cornucopia of authentic world cuisine.
Choicest tables are in the kitchen.

Falafel MIDDLE EASTERN **$**
(Map p54; ☑041 640 166; www.falafel.si; Trubarjeva cesta 40; sandwiches €5-8; ⊘9am-midnight

Mon-Sat, 11am-10pm Sun; 🕿) Authentic Middle
Eastern food, such as falafel and hummus,
served up to go or eat-in at a few tables and
chairs scattered about. Perfect choice for
a quick meal on the run or the late-night
munchies.

Ajdovo Zrno VEGAN **$**
(Map p54; ☑041 832 446; www.ajdovozrno.si;
Trubarjeva cesta 7; mains €4-6, set lunch €7.50;
⊘8am-5pm Mon-Fri; 🕿🍴) 'Buckwheat Grain'
serves soups, lots of different salads, and
baked vegetarian and vegan dishes. It also
has terrific freshly squeezed juices. Enter
from Mali trg.

⚙ Park Tivoli & Around

Hot Horse BURGERS **$**
(Map p50; ☑01-521 14 27; www.facebook.com/Hot
Horse; Park Tivoli, Celovška cesta 25; small/large
burger €3/6; ⊘9am-midnight Sun-Thu, to 2am Fri
& Sat) This little place in the city's biggest
park supplies *Ljubljančani* (local people)
with one of their favourite treats: horseflesh.
It's a little place – a kiosk, really – just down
the hill from the Museum of Contemporary
History (p60), but it's open until late and
popular among merrymakers and party-
goers. Choose from a menu of horse burgers,
hot dogs, steaks and wraps.

Gostilna Čad BALKAN **$$**
(Pod Rožnikom; ☑01-251 34 46; www.gostilna-cad.
si; Cesta na Rožnik 18; mains €7-18; ⊘11am-11pm;
🕿; 🚌18) This place under Rožnik Hill, just
downwind from the zoo (p61) in Park Tivoli,
serves southern-Slav-style grills, including
pljeskavica (spicy meat patties) with *ajvar*
(roasted red peppers, tomatoes and egg-
plant cooked into a purée) and starters such
as *prebranac* (onions and beans cooked in
an earthenware pot). At 120-plus years, it's
the oldest show in town and phenomenally
popular.

⚙ Krakovo & Trnovo

Gostilna Jakob Franc SLOVENIAN **$$**
(Map p50; ☑051 616 000; www.facebook.com/
gostilnaJakobFranc; Trnovski pristan 4a; mains €8-
20; ⊘11am-11pm Mon-Sat, to 4pm Sun; 🕿) This
small place in Trnovo is great for lunch,
particularly if you're in the mood for pork.
Jakob Franc is a Slovenian wunderkind
who's taken concepts such as farm-fresh and
whole-animal and applied them to local pig
varieties. The results are satisfying dishes
including the smoked pork neck on buck-

wheat porridge with mushrooms. The wine list is excellent.

Pri Škofu
SLOVENIAN $$

(Map p50; 01-426 45 08; Rečna ulica 8; mains €10-22; 10am-11pm Tue-Fri, noon-11pm Sat & Sun;) Run by women, this wonderful little place south of the centre in tranquil Krakovo serves some of the best-prepared local dishes and salads in Ljubljana, with an ever-changing menu. Start with the soup of the day (€4) and for dessert try the traditional cherry-and-cheese dumpling. Weekday set lunches (€9) are good value.

Manna
SLOVENIAN $$$

(Map p50; 059 922 308; www.restaurant-manna. com; Eipprova ulica 1a; mains €18-49; 11am-midnight Mon-Sat, to 9pm Sun;) Splashed across the front of this canalside restaurant in Trnovo is the slogan *'Manna: Božanske Jedi na Zemlji'* (Manna: Heavenly Dishes on Earth). Its divine contemporary Slovenian cuisine includes delicacies such as cold smoked trout and tiny traditional dumplings *(žlikrofi)* of bear meat from Kočevje. For mains there's plenty of fish from the Adriatic and a scrumptious roast lamb dish.

Drinking & Nightlife

Ljubljana offers a dizzying array of drinking options, whether your tipple is beer, wine and spirits or tea and coffee. In summer, the banks of the Ljubljanica River transform into one long terrace and serve as the perfect spot for supping, sipping and people-watching.

Prešernov Trg & Around

Makalonca
COCKTAIL BAR

(Map p54; 01-620 94 36; Hribarjevo nabrežje 19; 8am-3am;) Why sit on the embankment when you can sit *below* it? This striking cafe and cocktail bar with a 100m-long terrace within the columns of the Ljubljanica embankment is the perfect place to nurse a drink and watch the river roll by. It even has tables floating *in* the river.

Cutty Sark Pub
PUB

(Map p54; 051 686 209; www.cuttysarkpub.si; Knafljev prehod 1; 8am-1am Mon-Wed, to 3am Thu-Sat, 9am-1am Sun;) A pleasant and well-stocked pub with colourful bright-yellow windows and a long history. Set in the courtyard behind Wolfova ulica 6, the ivy-covered Cutty Sark is a congenial place for a *pivo*

(beer) or glass of *vino* (wine). Happy hour is from 4pm to 6pm.

Old Town

★ Slovenska Hiša
COCKTAIL BAR

(Slovenian House; Map p54; 083 899 811; www. slovenskahisa.si; Cankarjevo nabrežje 13; 8am-1am Sun-Thu, to 3am Fri & Sat;) Our favourite boozer along the river is so cute it's almost twee. Choose from artisanal coffees, wines, lemonades, cocktails and spirits, featuring ingredients sourced only in Slovenia. Order one of the inventive meat and cheese plates (€4 to €7) to soak up the alcohol.

Pritličje
CAFE

(Ground Floor; Map p54; 082 058 742; www. pritlicje.si; Mestni trg 2; 9am-1am Sun-Wed, to 3am Thu-Sat;) The ultra-inclusive 'Ground Floor' offers something for everyone: cafe, bar, live music, cultural centre and comic-book shop. Events are scheduled almost nightly and the location next to the Town Hall (p53), with good views across Mestni trg (p53), couldn't be more perfect.

Čajna Hiša
TEAHOUSE

(Tea House; Map p54; 01-252 70 10; www.cha.si; Stari trg 3; 8am-10pm Mon-Fri, to 3pm Sat;) This elegant and centrally located teahouse takes its teas very seriously. Also serves light meals (lunch €10) and there's a tea shop next door.

Central Market & East

★ Magda
CAFE

(Map p54; 01-620 26 10; https://barmagda.si; Pogačarjev trg 1; 7am-1am Mon-Sat, from 10am Sun;) It's hard to put a finger on what makes Magda so special. Maybe it's the expertly prepared espresso (just €1 a cup purchased at the bar) or the unique 'tapas-style' breakfast menu, where you choose from local meats and cheeses, or the craft gins and local homemade brandies on offer. It's a great choice to start or end the day.

★ Klub Daktari
BAR

(Map p54; 064 166 212; www.daktari.si; Krekov trg 7; 7.30am-1am Mon-Fri, 8am-1am Sat, 9am-midnight Sun;) This rabbit warren of a watering hole at the foot of the funicular to Ljubljana Castle is so chilled there's practically frost on the windows. The decor is retro-distressed, with shelves full of old books and a piano in the corner. More a cultural centre than a club, Daktari hosts live music and an eclectic mix of other cultural events.

Cafe Čokl
CAFE

(Map p54; ☑ 041 837 556; http://cafecokl.si; Krekov trg 8; ⊘ 7am-11pm Mon-Fri, 9am-11pm Sat, 9am-8pm Sun; 🛜) This fair-trade place at the foot of the lower funicular station (p48) takes its java very seriously indeed – roasting it in-house and featuring daily special recommendations on a chalkboard outside. Serves a mean cup of coffee.

Center

⭐ Wine Bar Šuklje
WINE BAR

(Map p54; ☑ 040 654 575; www.winebar.suklje.com; Breg 10; ⊘ 9am-midnight Mon-Sat, to 4pm Sun; 🛜) This central upscale tasting room is the perfect choice for sampling wines from around Slovenia. The owner is a winemaker and has a knowledgeable palate for assembling tasting flights plus meat and cheese plates to space the tastings. It also sells bottles from the family winery in the southeastern region of Bela Krajina and from select wineries around the country.

Kolibri
COCKTAIL BAR

(Map p54; ☑ 031 336 087; Židovska steza 2; ⊘ 7pm-1am; 🛜) Exquisitely crafted cocktails in a cozy nook on a hidden corner. The bartenders clearly take pride in their work, and there's live piano music on Fridays and Saturdays.

Dvorni Bar
WINE BAR

(Map p54; ☑ 01-251 12 57; www.dvornibar.net; Dvorni trg 2; ⊘ 9am-1am) This large L-shaped venue just up from the Ljubljanica on the river's west bank is a bit of a Dr Jekyll and Mr Hyde affair – it's a delightful cafe and tapas bar, and also one of the best wine bars in town come evening. It stocks more than 100 varieties and has monthly wine tastings.

Nebotičnik
CLUB

(Map p54; ☑ 040 233 078; www.neboticnik.si; 11th fl, Štefanova ulica 1; ⊘ 9am-1am Sun-Wed, to 3am Thu-Sat; 🛜) This upscale club does double duty: by day, it's an elegant cafe with a breathtaking terrace atop Ljubljana's famed art deco Skyscraper (1933) offering spectacular 360-degree views; by night, it's a flashy club and lounge for the city's beautiful party people.

Žmauc
PUB

(Map p50; ☑ 01-251 03 24; www.facebook.com/barzmauc; Rimska cesta 21; ⊘ 7.30am-1am Mon-Fri, from 10am Sat, from 6pm Sun; 🛜) Žmauc is the best place to slum it in Ljubljana, with a smallish bar inside packed day and night. The décor is great – check out the manga comic-strip scenes and figures scurrying up the walls. There's a pretty garden terrace for summer evening drinking, but try to arrive early to snag a table.

STA Café
CAFE

(Map p50; www.stapotovanja.com/sta/sta-travel-cafe; 1st fl, Trg Ajdovščina 1; ⊘ 8am-midnight Mon-Sat; 🛜) Good coffee, great wi-fi and friendly staff. Find the flight of stairs that runs off busy Slovenska cesta and climb one flight to find a big, welcoming terrace. It's associated with the student travel agency (p78) of the same name and occasionally hosts talks or travel.

Trubarjeva Cesta & Tabor

Kavarna Rog
CAFE

(Map p50; ☑ 070 170 282; www.kavarna-rog.si; Petkovškovo nabrežje 67; ⊘ 7am-midnight; 🛜) A great neighbourhood find in the quiet area along the Ljubljanica River, east of the centre. The early opening hours are convenient for wake-up coffees and a hearty breakfast. There are sidewalk seats overlooking the river and a highly polished interior that makes an ideal backdrop for evening cocktails.

Postaja Centralna
COCKTAIL BAR

(Central Station; Map p54; ☑ 059 190 400; www.facebook.com/centralnapostajaljubljana; Trubarjeva cesta 23; ⊘ 8am-1am Mon-Thu, to 3am Fri & Sat; 🛜) This classy place tries – and largely succeeds – at being just about everything to everyone. It's a slightly louche cocktail bar, with street-art tags on the walls and lots of dazzling neon, a club with DJs at the weekend, a cafe with its own homemade fruit teas and a restaurant with burgers.

Kavarna SEM
CAFE

(Map p50; ☑ 041 729 619; www.facebook.com/kavarnaSEM; Metelkova ulica 2; ⊘ 7am-1am Sun-Tue, to 2am Wed & Thu, to 3am Fri & Sat; 🛜) This delightful cafe attached to the Slovenian Ethnographic Museum (p60) is all glass and modern art with views of the attached pottery workshop. Live swing music on Tuesday and salsa on Friday.

LJUBLJANA'S STUDENT SQUATS

For a scruffier alternative to trendy clubs, head for one of the city's two 'squats' – student-occupied spaces that provide both low-cost housing to residents and handy places for hanging out, drinking and taking in some music or theatre.

The best-known and best-established of these is **Metelkova Mesto** (Metelkova Town; Map p50; www.metelkovamesto.org; Masarykova cesta 24), converted from an army garrison into a free-living commune by squatters in the 1990s. In this two-courtyard block, a dozen idiosyncratic venues hide behind brightly tagged doorways, coming to life generally after midnight daily in summer and on Fridays and Saturdays during the rest of the year. The quality of the acts and performances varies with the night, though there's usually a little of something for everyone.

To explore Metelkova Mesto, enter the complex's main gate on Masarykova cesta. The building to the immediate right houses **Gala Hala** (☑ 01-431 70 63; www.galahala.com; tickets €3-10), with live bands and club nights, and **Channel Zero** (www.ch0.org; tickets from €3; ☺ hours variable; ☎), with dub and hardcore. Easy to miss in the first building to the left is Q Cultural Centre (p76), which includes Klub Tiffany (p76) for gay men and Klub Monokel (p76) for lesbians. Due south are a couple of other popular venues. **Klub Gromka** (www.klubgromka.org; ☺ hours variable) hosts folk concerts, improv, theatre and lectures. Just nearby is **Galerija Alkatraz** (Alkatraz Gallery; ☑ 01-434 03 45; http:// galerijalkatraz.org; ☺ 11am-3pm, 4-8pm Mon-Thu, 3pm-11pm Fri) 🆓, with a great exhibition space, and **Menza pri Koritu** (☑ 01-434 03 45; www.menzaprikoritu.com; tickets from €4), under the creepy ET-like figures, with performances and concerts. If you're staying at Celica Hostel (p67), all of this is just around the corner.

Ljubljana's second squat, **Tovarna Rog** (Map p50; https://tovarna.org; Trubarjeva cesta 72; ☺ varies according to program), is not nearly as well known or well organised, though depending on the night can also be a rewarding stopover. Rog was originally a bicycle factory that was occupied by squatters in 2006. Unlike Metelkova Mesto, there are few if any established clubs here. Instead, walk through the gate toward the eastern end of Trubarjeva cesta and listen for some music or ask anyone around if anything's going on during your visit.

Patrick's Irish Pub　　　　　IRISH PUB

(Map p54; ☑ 01-230 17 68; www.irishpub-ljubljana. si; Prečna ulica 6; ☺ 5pm-1am Tue-Sat, to midnight Sun & Mon; ☎) This excellent local version of an Irish pub is popular with both expats and locals. There's decent bar food, such as chicken wings and burgers, and a solid line-up of local beers and imports. It's a reliable spot to watch broadcasts of big live sports events.

🍸 Park Tivoli & Around

Klub Cirkus　　　　　CLUB

(Map p50; ☑ 041 777 747; www.cirkusklub.si; Trg Mladinskih Delovnih Brigad 7; admission from €5; ☺ 10pm-5am Wed-Sat; ☎) Located in the former Kinoklub Vič arthouse cinema, this is one of the most popular clubs in town and is within easy walking distance of the centre. Lots of themed nights and DJs; opens on Tuesdays and Thursdays for special events and parties.

🍸 Krakovo & Trnovo

Šank Pub Anika　　　　　PUB

(Map p50; ☑ 040 671 483; Eipprova ulica 19; ☺ 7am-1am Mon-Fri, 8am-1am Sat & Sun; ☎) Down in studenty Trnovo, the Šank is one of a number of inviting bars and cafes along this stretch of Eipprova ulica. This raggedy little place, with a brick ceiling and wooden floor, is a relaxed option and has a great choice of craft beers, including Bervog's Ond smoked porter and its Baja oatmeal stout.

Špica　　　　　CAFE

(Map p50; ☑ 051 368 658; www.kaval-group.si/ spica_caffe.asp; Gruberjevo nabrežje; ☺ 8am-11pm Mon-Thu, to midnight Fri & Sat, 9am-10pm Sun; ☎) This cafe-bar at the Špica, the point of land well south of the Old Town where the Ljubljanica River splits before entering the city, is tailor-made for a relaxing sundowner after jumping ship from any of the boats that moor at the pier here. It's opposite the Botanical Garden (p56).

☆ Entertainment

Ljubljana in Your Pocket (www.inyourpocket.com/ljubljana), which comes out every couple of months, is an excellent English-language source for what's on in the capital. Buy tickets for shows and events at the venue's box office, online through **Eventim** (Map p50; ☑ 090 55 77; www.eventim.si; Trg Osvobodilne Fronte 6; ⊘ 5am-10pm), or at the Ljubljana TIC (p78). Expect to pay €10 to €20 for tickets to live acts.

Live Music

★ Kino Šiška   LIVE MUSIC
(☑ 030 310 110, box office 01-500 30 00; www.kinosiska.si; Trg Prekomorskih brigad 3; ⊘ box office 3-8pm Mon-Fri, pub 8am-midnight, events 8pm-2am; 🛜; 🚍 1, 3, 5, 8, 22, 25) This renovated old movie theatre now houses an urban cultural centre, hosting mainly indie, rock and alternative bands from around Slovenia and the rest of Europe. Buy tickets at the box office or at Eventim offices around town.

Cvetličarna   LIVE MUSIC
(☑ 040 689 559; www.cvetlicarna.info; Kranjčeva ulica 20; ⊘ 9pm-4am Fri & Sat, other times according to event; 🚍 13, 20) Cavernous concert hall hosting live acts and DJs most weekends, as well as a variety of other types of performances, including comedy, on some weeknights. Check the website for an up-to-date calendar of events.

Sax Pub   JAZZ
(Map p50; ☑ 040 168 804; www.facebook.com/saxpublj; Eipprova ulica 7; ⊘ 9am-1am; 🛜) Nearly three decades in Trnovo and decorated with colourful murals and graffiti outside, the tiny and convivial Sax has live jazz as well as blues and folk at 8pm on Thursday year-round. Canned stuff rules at other times.

Orto Bar   LIVE MUSIC
(Map p50; ☑ 01-232 16 74; www.orto-bar.com; Graboličeva ulica 1; ⊘ 9pm-5am Thu-Sat) A popular bar and live music venue for late-night drinking and dancing amid a crowd of leather-clad partygoers. It's just a 300m stroll northeast from Metelkova; enter from Bolgarska ulica. Note the program takes a hiatus in summer during July and August.

Classical Music & Opera

Križanke   PERFORMING ARTS
(Map p54; ☑ 01-241 60 00, box office 01-241 60 26; www.ljubljanafestival.si; Trg Francoske Revolucije 1-2; ⊘ box office 10am-8pm Mon-Fri, to 2pm Sat May-Sep, noon-5pm Mon-Fri, 10am-2pm Sat

Oct-Apr, 1hr before performance) The open-air theatre seating more than 1200 spectators at this sprawling 18th-century monastery, remodelled by local architect Jože Plečnik in the 1950s, hosts the events of the summer Ljubljana Festival (p65). The smaller Knights Hall (Viteška Dvorana) is the venue for chamber concerts.

Slovenia Philharmonic Hall   CLASSICAL MUSIC
(Slovenska Filharmonija; Map p54; ☑ 01-241 08 00; www.filharmonija.si; Kongresni trg 10; tickets €8-16; ⊘ box office 11am-1pm & 3-6pm Mon-Fri) Home to the Slovenian Philharmonic founded in 1701, this small but atmospheric venue at the southeast corner of Kongresni trg (p58) also stages concerts and hosts performances of the Slovenian Chamber Choir (Slovenski Komorni Zbor). Haydn, Beethoven and Brahms were honorary Philharmonic members, and Gustav Mahler was resident conductor for a season (1881–82).

Opera Ballet Ljubljana   OPERA
(Map p54; ☑ 01-241 59 00, box office 01-241 59 59; www.opera.si; Župančičeva ulica 1; ⊘ box office 10am-1pm & 2-6pm Mon-Fri, 10am-1pm Sat, 1hr before performance) Home to the Slovenian National Opera and Ballet companies, this historical neo-Renaissance theatre has been restored to its former glory. Enter from Cankarjeva cesta.

Cankarjev Dom   CLASSICAL MUSIC
(Map p50; ☑ 01-241 71 00, box office 01-241 72 99; www.cd-cc.si; Prešernova cesta 10; ⊘ box office 11am-1pm & 3-8pm Mon-Fri, 11am-1pm Sat, 1hr before performance) Ljubljana's premier cultural and conference centre has two large auditoriums (the Gallus Hall is said to have perfect acoustics) and a dozen smaller performance spaces offering a remarkable smorgasbord of performance arts.

Theatre

National Drama Theatre   THEATRE
(Narodno Gledališče Drama; Map p54; ☑ 01-252 14 62, box office 01-252 15 11; www.en.drama.si; Erjavčeva cesta 1; ⊘ box office 11am-8pm Mon-Fri, 6-8pm Sat, 1hr before performance) Built as a German-language theatre in 1911, this wonderful art nouveau building is home to the national theatre company. Performances are in Slovene.

KUD France Prešeren   THEATRE
(Map p50; ☑ 051 657 852, 01-283 22 88; www.kudfp.si; Karunova ulica 14; ⊘ 10am-1am Mon-Sat, from 2pm Sun) This 'noninstitutional culture and

LJUBLJANA SHOPPING

LGBT+ LJUBLJANA

Ljubljana may not be the most queer-friendly city in Central Europe, but there are a few decent options. For general information and advice, contact the **Q Cultural Centre** (Kulturni Center Q; Map p50; ☑ 01-430 35 35; www.kulturnicenterq.org; Metelkova Mesto, Masarykova cesta 24). The website for **Legebitra** (Map p50; ☑ 01-430 51 44; https://legebi tra.si; Trubarjeva cesta 76a, Ljubljana; ⊙ noon-4pm Mon, to 6pm Tue & Fri, to 9pm Wed & Thu), a rights group for the LGBTQ+ community and individuals, has a few listings for club or cafe meet-ups.

Klub Tiffany (Map p50; www.kulturnicenterq.org; Metelkova Mesto, Masarykova cesta 24; ⊙ 11pm-5am Fri & Sat) Part of the Q Cultural Centre, this Metelkova Mesto (p74) club is considered the city's best LGBTQ+ party venue. It also hosts workshops, lectures and cultural activities.

Klub Monokel (Map p50; www.klubmonokel.com; Metelkova Mesto, Masarykova cesta 24; ⊙ 11pm-5am Fri) Lesbian club situated in the Metelkova Mesto (p74) complex.

Roza Klub (Map p50; http://klub-k4.si; Kersnikova ulica 4; ⊙ 10pm-6am Sat & Sun) A popular spot for both gays and lesbians is this on-again, off-again weekend disco at **Klub K4** (Map p50; ☑ 031 424 111; www.klub-k4.si; Kersnikova ulica 4; ⊙ 11pm-6am Fri & Sat; ☎). The music takes no risks, but the crowd is lively. See the website for dates and details.

arts society' in Trnovo stages concerts as well as performances, literary events, exhibitions, workshops etc on most nights. Trnfest (p66) takes place here in August.

Ljubljana Puppet Theatre PUPPET THEATRE (Lutkovno Gledališče Ljubljana; Map p54; ☑ box office 01-300 09 82; www.lgl.si; Krekov trg 2; tickets €5; ⊙ box office 9am-7pm Mon-Fri, to 1pm Sat, 1hr before performance) The Ljubljana Puppet Theatre stages its own shows throughout the year and hosts Lutke, the International Puppet Festival (Mednarodni Lutkovni Festival), every even-numbered year in September.

Cinema

Kinodvor CINEMA (Map p50; ☑ box office 01-239 22 17; www.kinod vor.org; Kolodvorska ulica 13; tickets adult/student €5.30/3.80; ⊙ cinema varies by event; cafe 10am-midnight) The 'Court Cinema' screens both contemporary art films as well as films on general release. There's also a small cafe with a terrace from April to November.

Kinoteka CINEMA (Map p50; ☑ 01-434 25 10; www.kinoteka.si; Miklošičeva cesta 28; tickets adult/student €4/2; ⊙ varies by event) The Kinoteka shows archival art and classic films in their original language usually with Slovene subtitles. Films normally start at 8pm or 9.30pm. Check the website.

Shopping

Ljubljana has plenty on offer in the way of folk art, antiques, music, wine, food and, increasingly, fashion. If you want everything under one roof, head for **BTC City** (☑ 01-585 22 22; www.btc-city.com; Šmartinska cesta 152; ⊙ 9am-9pm Mon-Sat; 🚌 2, 7, 12, 24, 27) or **City Park** (☑ 01-587 30 50; www.citypark.si; Šmartinska cesta 152g; ⊙ 9am-9pm Mon-Sat, to 3pm Sun; 🚌 2, 7, 12, 24, 27), sprawling malls side by side with hundreds of shops in Moste, northeast of Center.

Castle Area

Galerija Rustika ARTS & CRAFTS (Map p54; ☑ 01-251 17 18; www.galerijarustika.si; Ljubljana Castle, Grajska planota 1; ⊙ 10am-6pm) This attractive gallery and shop, with wooden floors and a really 'rustic' feel, is good for folk art. Conveniently located in Ljubljana Castle (p48).

Old Town

⭐**Vinoteka Movia** DRINKS (Map p54; ☑ 051 304 590; www.movia.si; Mestni trg 2; ⊙ noon-midnight Mon-Sat) As much a wine shop as a wine bar, this is always our first port of call when buying a bottle. Although Movia is its own label, the knowledgeable staff here will advise you on and sell you wine from other vintners.

3 Muhe
ARTS & CRAFTS

(3 Flies; Map p54; ☑ 01-421 07 15; www.3muhe.
si; Stari trg 30; ⊙ 10am-7.30pm Mon-Fri, to 2pm
Sat) Only fair-trade products make it to the
shelves of this socially conscious enterprise,
be it coffee from Uganda, spices from Sri
Lanka, baskets from Ghana or stemware
from Guatemala. You'll feel good just walking in.

Lina
FASHION & ACCESSORIES

(Map p54; ☑ 01-421 08 92; www.svila-lina.net;
Gornji trg 14; ⊙ 10am-1pm & 3-7pm Mon-Fri, to 1pm
Sat) Dušanka Herman's scrumptious painted silk accessories include unevenly cut ties
and scarves for men and daringly coloured
dresses for women. Just try to leave without
buying something.

Galerija Idrijske Čipke
GIFTS & SOUVENIRS

(Idrija Lace Gallery; Map p54; ☑ 01-425 00 51;
www.idrija-lace.com; Mestni trg 17; ⊙ 10am-7pm
Mon-Fri, to 2pm Sat) If Idrija in Primorska is
not on your itinerary but you hanker for
some of the fine lace for which that town is
renowned, visit this shop. It has a large collection of curtains, tablecloths and bed linen
on sale, as well as smaller items including
handkerchiefs, doilies and even a Christmas
tree ornament in the shape of a dragon.

Trubarjev Antikvariat
BOOKS

(Map p54; ☑ 01-244 26 83; Mestni trg 25; ⊙ 9am-
7pm Mon-Fri, 8.30am-1.30pm Sat) Come here for
antiquarian and secondhand books. There's
a good selection of antique maps upstairs.

Oliviers & Co
FOOD & DRINKS

(Map p54; ☑ 083 837 816; www.oliviers-co.si; Ciril
Metodov trg 20; ⊙ 10am-7pm Mon-Fri, 9am-6pm
Sat, 10am-4pm Sun) Part of a French chain,
this shop has gone totally local and sells
the finest oils from around the country,
including olive oil from Slovenian Istria,
the unusual spruce oil *(smrekovo olje)* and
the finest of both cold-pressed and roasted
pumpkin-seed oil *(bučno olje)* from Kocbek.

🏠 Central Market & East

★ Kraševka
FOOD & DRINKS

(Map p54; ☑ 01-232 14 45; www.krasevka.si; Vodnikov trg 4; ⊙ 9am-7pm Mon-Fri, to 3pm Sat) This
fantastic delicatessen with more than 300
products from farms (mostly) in the Karst
stocks *pršut* (dry, cured ham) in all its var-

iations and cheeses, as well as wines and
spirits, oils and vinegars, and honeys and
marmalades.

Trgovina IKA
GIFTS & SOUVENIRS

(Map p54; ☑ 01-232 17 43; www.trgovina-ika.si; Ciril
Metodov trg 13; ⊙ 9am-7.30pm Mon-Fri, to 6pm Sat,
10am-2pm Sun) This gift shop-cum-art gallery-
cum-fashion designer opposite the cathedral and Central Market sells handmade
items that put a modern spin on traditional
forms and motifs. More than 100 designers
have clothing, jewellery, porcelain etc on
sale here.

🏠 Center

Antikvariat Alef
BOOKS

(Map p54; ☑ 01-320 57 54; www.antikvariatalef.
si; Hribarjevo nabrežje 13; ⊙ 9am-1pm & 3.30-7pm
Mon-Fri) This pleasingly jumbled, old-school
bookstore advertises itself as a shop 'for
readers'. There's mainly used books on the
shelves, with some titles in English, including author John Bills' very funny *An Illustrated History of Slavic Misery*.

Wine Point Dvor
WINE

(Map p54; ☑ 01-251 36 44; www.kozelj.si; Dvorni
trg 2; ⊙ 11am-8pm Mon-Fri, 10am-2pm Sat) Just
up from the Dvorni Bar (p73), this small
but perfectly formed and independently run
shop has a large selection of wine as well as
fruit brandies.

Mladinska Knjiga
BOOKS

(Map p54; ☑ 01-241 46 84; www.mladinska.com;
1st fl, Slovenska cesta 29; ⊙ 8am-8pm Mon-Fri,
9am-2pm Sat) 'MK' is the city's biggest and
best-stocked bookshop, with lots of guidebooks, maps, pictorials, fiction and newspapers and periodicals in English. There's
a **branch** (Map p50; ☑ 01-234 27 80; http://en.
mladinska.com; Miklošičeva cesta 40; ⊙ 7am-7pm
Mon-Fri) on Miklošičeva cesta.

🏠 Trubarjeva Cesta & Tabor

Carniola Antiqua
ANTIQUES

(Map p54; ☑ 01-231 63 97; www.facebook.com/
CarniolaAntiqua; Trubarjeva cesta 9; ⊙ 4-6pm
Mon, 10am-1pm & 4-6pm Tue-Thu, 10am-1pm Fri &
Sat) With a large selection of items from the
1950s and '60s, this long-established shop
is among the best and most helpful antique
galleries in town.

Krakovo & Trnovo

Annapurna SPORTS & OUTDOORS
(Map p54; ☑01-426 34 28; www.annapurna.si;
Krakovski nasip 4; ☺9am-7pm Mon-Fri, to 1pm Sat)
If you've forgotten your sleeping bag, ski
poles, hiking boots, climbing gear or ruck-
sack, this shop in Krakovo can supply you
with all of it – and more. Very helpful and
knowledgeable staff.

❶ Information

DISCOUNT CARDS

The **Ljubljana Card** (www.visitljubljana.com/
en/ljubljana-card; per 24/48/72hr adult
€27/34/39, child aged 6-14 €16/20/23), available from the tourist office for 24/48/72 hours,
offers free admission to 19 attractions, walking
and boat tours, unlimited travel on city buses
and internet access.

INTERNET ACCESS

Many cafes and restaurants provide free wi-fi
for customers, and **WiFreeLjubljana** (www.
wifreeljubljana.si) offers visitors one hour of free
internet access a day. Most hostels and some
hotels have a public computer for guests to surf
the internet. The Slovenian Tourist Information
Centre has computers on hand to check email.

LEFT LUGGAGE

Left Luggage in Bus Station (Trg Osvobodilne
Fronte 4; per day €3; ☺5am-10.30pm Mon-Sat,
5.30am-10.30pm Sun) Window No 3.

Left Luggage in Train Station (Trg Osvobodilne Fronte 6; per day €3; ☺24hr) Coin lockers
on platform 1.

MEDICAL SERVICES

Barsos Medical Centre (☑01-242 07 00;
http://barsos.si; Gregorčičeva ulica 11; ☺8am-
8pm Mon-Fri) Private clinic, with prices starting
at around €50 per consultation.

Central Pharmacy (p52) Central option for
pharmaceutical goods; in an Italianate building
that was once a cafe frequented by intellectuals
in the 19th century.

Community Health Centre (Zdravstveni Dom
Ljubljana; ☑01-522 84 08, 01-472 37 00;
www.zd-lj.si/en; Metelkova ulica 9; ☺7.30am-
7pm Mon-Fri, 8am-4pm Sat) Ljubljana For
non-emergencies.

University Medical Centre Ljubljana (Univer-
zitetni Klinični Center Ljubljana; ☑information
01-522 50 50; www.kclj.si; Zaloška cesta 7;
☺24hr) University medical clinic with 24-hour
accident and emergency service.

MONEY

ATMs are everywhere, including several outside
the Ljubljana TIC. Full-service banks are all
around the centre; they're the best places to
exchange cash.

Abanka (☑01-300 15 00; www.abanka.si; Slovenska cesta 50; ☺8.30am-5pm Mon-Fri)

Nova Ljubljanska Banka (NLB; ☑01-477 20
00; www.nlb.si; Trg Republike 2; ☺8am-6pm
Mon-Fri)

POST

Main Post Office (Map p54; Slovenska cesta
32; ☺8am-7pm Mon-Fri, to noon Sat) Holds
poste restante for 30 days and changes money.

Post Office Branch (Map p50; Pražakova
ulica 3; ☺8am-6pm Mon-Fri, to noon Sat) Just
southwest of the bus and train stations.

TOURIST INFORMATION

Ljubljana Tourist Information Centre (TIC;
Map p54; ☑01-306 12 15; www.visitljubljana.
com; Adamič-Lundrovo nabrežje 2; ☺8am-9pm
Jun-Sep, to 7pm Oct-May) Knowledgeable and
enthusiastic staff dispense information, maps
and useful literature and help with accommodation. Offers a range of interesting city
and regional tours and maintains an excellent
website.

Slovenian Tourist Information Centre (STIC;
Map p54; ☑01-306 45 76; www.slovenia.info;
Krekov trg 10; ☺8am-9pm daily Jun-Sep, 8am-
7pm Mon-Fri, 9am-5pm Sat & Sun Oct-May; 🐦)
Good source of information for travel to the
rest of Slovenia, with internet and bicycle rental
also available.

TRAVEL AGENCIES

STA Travel (☑lodging 01-439 16 90, travel
tickets 041 612 711; www.sta-lj.com; 1st fl, Trg
Ajdovščina 1; ☺8am-5pm Mon-Fri) Discount
airfares for students.

USEFUL WEBSITES

Alongside the websites of the Slovenian Tourist
Information Centre (www.slovenia.info) and
the Ljubljana Tourist Information Centre (www.
visitljubljana.com), these additional sites provide helpful information on upcoming events
and more:

City of Ljubljana (www.ljubljana.si) Comprehensive city hall information portal on every
aspect of life and tourism.

In Your Pocket (www.inyourpocket.com/
ljubljana) Insider info on the capital updated
bimonthly.

Slovenia Times (www.sloveniatimes.com)
News in English.

ⓘ Getting There & Away

BUS

Buses to destinations both within Slovenia and abroad leave from the **bus station** (Avtobusna Postaja Ljubljana; Map p50; ☑ 01-234 46 00; www.ap-ljubljana.si; Trg Osvobodilne Fronte 4; ⏱ 5am-10.30pm Mon-Fri, 5am-10pm Sat, 5.30am-10.30pm Sun) just next to the train station. The station website has an excellent time-table for checking departure times and prices. At the station, you'll find multilingual informa-tion phones and a touchscreen computer next to the ticket windows. There's another touchscreen computer outside. You do not usually have to buy your ticket in advance; just pay as you board the bus. But for long-distance trips on Fridays, just before the school break and public holidays, you run the risk of not getting a seat. To be safe, book the day before and reserve a seat.

You can reach virtually anywhere in the coun-try by bus – as close as Kamnik (€3.10, 50 min-utes, 25km, every half hour) or as far away as Murska Sobota (€16, three hours, 200km, one or two a day). Some sample one-way fares (return fares are usually double) from the capital:

Bled €7.80, 1½hrs, 57km, hourly
Bohinj €9.80, 2hrs, 91km, hourly
Koper €11.10, 2½hrs, 122km, 5 daily with more in season
Maribor €11.40, 2-3hrs, 141km, 2-4 daily
Novo Mesto €7.20, 1hr, 72km, up to 7 daily
Piran €12, 3hrs, 140km, up to 7 daily
Postojna €6 1hr, 53km, up to 24 daily

CAR & MOTORCYCLE

Most of the big international car-hire firms have offices in Ljubljana and at the airport. You can rent locally on the spot or often snag a better deal renting in advance over the company website. The Slovenian Automobile Association, AMZS (p269), provides emergency roadside service.
Atet Rent a Car (☑ 01-320 82 30; www.atet.si; Devova ulica 6a; ⏱ 8am-6pm Mon-Fri, to 1pm Sat & Sun)
Avis (☑ 01-421 73 40; www.avis.si; Miklošičeva cesta 3; ⏱ 8am-4pm Mon-Fri, to noon Sat & Sun)
Central Rent (☑ 24hr support 040 216 660, rental 059 014 550; www.centralrent.si; Slov-enska cesta 36; ⏱ 9am-4pm Mon-Fri, 8am-1pm Sat) Offers some of the best car-rental deals in town.
Europcar (☑ 031 382 052; www.europcar.si; City Hotel Ljubljana, Dalmatinova ulica 15; ⏱ 8am-6pm Mon-Fri, to noon Sat & Sun)
Hertz (☑ 01-434 01 47; www.hertz.si; Trdinova ulica 9; ⏱ 7am-7pm Mon-Fri, 8am to noon Sat & Sun)

TRAIN

Domestic and international trains arrive at and depart from central Ljubljana's **train station** (Železniška Postaja; ☑ 01-291 33 32; www.slo-zeleznice.si; Trg Osvobodilne Fronte 6; ⏱ 5am-10pm), where you'll find a separate information centre on the way to the platforms. The website has an excellent timetable with departure times and prices. Buy domestic tickets from windows No 1 to 8 and international ones from either window No 9 or the information centre.

The following are one-way, 2nd-class domestic fares, travel times, distances and frequencies from Ljubljana. Return fares are double the price, and there's a surcharge of €1.80 on domestic InterCity (IC) and EuroCity (EC) train tickets.

Bled €6.60, 55min, 51km, up to 21 daily
Koper €9.60, 2½hrs, 153km, up to 4 daily, with more in summer
Maribor €9.60, 1¾hrs, 156km, up to 25 daily
Murska Sobota €13, 3¼hrs, 216km, up to 5 daily
Novo Mesto €6.60, 1½hrs, 75km, up to 14 daily

ⓘ Getting Around

TO & FROM THE AIRPORT

The cheapest way to **Jože Pučnik Airport** (Aero-drom Ljubljana; ☑ 04-206 19 81; www.lju-air port.si; Zgornji Brnik 130a, Brnik) is by public bus (€4.10, 50 minutes, 27km) from **stop No 28** (Map p50; €4.10 one way; ⏱ 5.20am-8.10pm) at the bus station. These run at 5.20am and hourly from 6.10am to 8.10pm Monday to Friday; at the weekend there's a bus at 6.10am and then one every two hours from 9.10am to 7.10pm. Buy tickets from the driver.

Two airport shuttle services that get con-sistently good reviews are **GoOpti** (Map p50; ☑ 01-320 45 30; www.goopti.com; Trg Osvo-bodilne Fronte 4; €9 one way) and **Markun Shuttle** (☑ reservations 041 792 865; www.prevozi-markun.com; €9 one way), which will transfer you from Brnik (where the airport is) to central Ljubljana in half an hour. Book by phone or online.

A taxi from the airport to Ljubljana will cost from €35 to €45.

BICYCLE

Ljubljana is a pleasure for cyclists, and there are bike lanes and special traffic lights everywhere.
Ljubljana Bike (☑ 01-306 45 76; www.visitljubljana.si; Krekov trg 10; per 2hr/day €2/8; ⏱ 8am-7pm Mon-Fri, 9am-5pm Sat & Sun Apr, May & Oct, 8am-9pm Jun-Sep) rents two-wheelers in two-hour or full-day incre-ments from April through October from the Slovenian Tourist Information Centre.

For short rides, you can hire bicycles as needed from **38 Bicike(lj)** (www.bicikelj.si; subscription weekly/yearly €1/3, plus hourly rate; ⊘ 24hr) stations with 300 bikes located around the city. To rent a bike requires pre-registration and subscription over the company website plus a valid credit or debit card. After registering simply submit your card or the public transport authority's Urbana card plus a PIN. The first hour of the rental is free, the second hour costs €1, the third hour €2, and each additional hour €4. Bikes must be returned within 24 hours.

CAR & MOTORCYCLE

The centre is walkable and many streets are off limits to motor vehicle traffic, so you're best advised to stow your car on arrival and walk or take public transport as needed to get around. Parking in Ljubljana is tight, especially on workdays. Most parking in the centre is metered (€0.70 to €1.20 per hour, from 8am to 7pm Monday to Friday, and 8am to 1pm Saturday). There are enclosed car parks throughout the city, and their locations are indicated on most maps. Parking rates normally start at €.60 to €2.40 per hour; expect to pay a day rate from around €25.

PUBLIC TRANSPORT

Ljubljana's city buses, many of them running on methane, operate every five to 15 minutes from 5am (6am on Sunday) to around 10.30pm. There are also a half-dozen night buses. A flat fare of €1.20 (good for 90 minutes of unlimited travel, including transfers) is paid with a stored-value magnetic Urbana card, which can be purchased at newsstands, tourist offices and the public-transport authority's **Information Centre** (☑ 01-430 51 74; www.lpp.si/en; Slovenska cesta 56; ⊘ 6.30am-7pm Mon-Fri) for €2; credit can then be added (from €1 to €50).

Run by the LPP (Ljubljana city bus network), **Kavalir** (☑ 031 666 332, 031 666 331; www.ljubljana.si; ⊘ 8am-8pm) is a transport service that will pick you up and drop you off anywhere in the pedestrianised Old Town free of charge. All you have to do is call (and wait – there are only three of the golf-cart-like vehicles available April to October and just one the rest of the year).

TAXI

Metered taxis can be hailed on the street or hired from ranks, (eg near the train station), at the Ljubljana TIC (p78) on Stritarjeva ulica, in front of the Grand Hotel Union; p66). Flagfall is around €1 and the per-kilometre charge ranges from €0.90 to €1.70, depending on the company and whether you call ahead (cheaper) or hail a taxi on the street. Uber does not operate in Slovenia (as of research time).

Laguna Taxi (☑ 01-511 23 14, 080 12 33; www.taxi-laguna.com) Reliable radio taxi with English-speaking operators.

Lake Bled & the Julian Alps

Best Places to Eat

➡ Hiša Franko (p122)

➡ Finefood – Penzion Berc (p100)

➡ Foksner (p107)

➡ Štrud'l (p107)

➡ Restaurant Lazar (p122)

Best Places to Stay

➡ Design Rooms Pr' Gavedarjo (p113)

➡ Dobra Vila (p119)

➡ Nebesa (p122)

➡ Vila Park (p106)

➡ Linhart Hotel (p88)

Why Go?

This is the Slovenia of tourist posters: mountain peaks, postcard-perfect lakes and blue-green rivers. Prepare to be charmed by Lake Bled (with an island and a castle!) and surprised by Lake Bohinj (how does Bled score all that attention when down the road is Bohinj?). The lofty peak of Mt Triglav, at the centre of a national park of the same name, may dazzle you enough to prompt an ascent.

On the other side of the breathtaking Vršič Pass, but still within the confines of Triglav National Park, rivers don't come much more scenic than the Soča (*so*-cha). This aquamarine-coloured watercourse threads through the Soča Valley (Dolina Soče) from its source in the Julian Alps and gives rise to a smorgasbord of gorges, waterfalls and rapids of blue-green water washing over white rock. Loads of activities get travellers up close to the natural splendour from busy centres such as Bovec and Kobarid.

When to Go
Bled

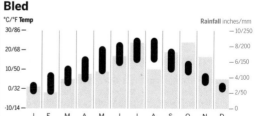

May & Jun River rafting, waterfalls and wildflowers at their peak.

Jul & Aug Swimming season is short and sweet (and draws the crowds) at Lakes Bled and Bohinj.

Dec–Apr Decent skiing conditions can last through to spring.

Lake Bled & the Julian Alps Highlights

1 Lake Bled (p90) Enjoying this unforgettable lake from every angle: a shoreline walk, a swim, a gondola ride, or from the castle terrace.

2 Mt Triglav (p108) Climbing Slovenia's highest peak and proclaiming yourself Slovene.

3 Soča River (p116) Marvelling over the exquisite green waters, while rafting or kayaking.

4 Vršič Pass (p115) Driving or cycling over this hair-raising (and spine-tingling) mountain pass.

5 Lake Bohinj (p102) Swimming in, kayaking on or walking around Slovenia's 'other' unforgettable lake.

6 Franja Partisan Hospital (p127) Wondering about the resilience of the human spirit at this poignant museum.

7 Kanin Cable Car (p117) Riding the gondolas up to Slovenia's highest ski centre, either to ski or simply admire the view.

Škofja Loka

📍 04 / POP 11,830 / ELEV 348M

Škofja Loka (Bishop's Meadow), just 26km from Ljubljana, is among the most beautiful and oldest settlements in Slovenia. Its evocative Old Town has been protected as a historical monument since 1987. It can be explored as a day trip from the capital or as an overnight stay (though book accommodation in advance since there's just a handful of lodging options). When the castle and other old buildings are illuminated on weekend nights, Škofja Loka takes on the appearance of a fairy tale. It's also an excellent springboard for walking in the Škofja Loka Hills to the west.

◉ Sights

★ Loka Museum   MUSEUM

(Loški muzej; 📞 04-517 04 00; www.loski-muzej. si; Grajska pot 13; adult/child €5/3; ⊘ 10am-6pm Tue-Sun May-Oct, to 5pm Nov-Apr) The town's premier sight is the commanding Loka castle, overlooking the settlement from a grassy hill west of Mestni trg. It dates from the 13th century and was extensively renovated after an earthquake in 1511. Today the castle houses the Loka Museum, which boasts an excellent ethnographic collection spread over two-dozen galleries on two floors. Exhibits run the gamut from taxidermied animals to church frescoes by way of local painters, lace-making traditions and WWII partisans; English labelling can be patchy for some exhibits.

In the garden, you'll find a typical peasant house from nearby Puštal dating from the 16th century. Don't miss the four spectacular golden altars in the castle chapel. These date from the 17th century and were taken from a church destroyed during WWII in Dražgoše, northwest of Škofja Loka.

Two paths lead up to the castle from the Old Town; one starts just opposite Kavarna Homan, the other next to Martin House. A longer walking trail, the Three Castles Path, begins at the castle and travels a circular, forested path for about 5km (two hours), past the ruins of the Krancelj Tower and the Old Castle. The TIC has a brochure with map.

★ Mestni Trg   SQUARE

(Town Square) The group of pastel-hued 16th-century burghers' houses on this main square have earned the town the nickname 'Colourful Loka'. Almost every one is of historical and architectural importance, but arguably the most impressive is Homan House (Homanova Hiša), dating from 1511 with graffiti and bits of frescoes of St Christopher and of a soldier.

Another building to look out for is the former Town Hall (Stari Rotovž), remarkable for its three-storey Gothic courtyard and the 17th-century frescoes on its facade. Further south, 17th-century Martin House (Martinova Hiša) leans on part of the Old Town wall. It has a wooden 1st floor, a late-Gothic portal and a vaulted entrance hall.

★ Capuchin Bridge   HISTORIC SITE

(Kapucinski Most) The tiny Capuchin Bridge (sometimes called the Stone Bridge) leading from the Capuchin monastery is one of the symbols of the town. It originally dates from the 14th century and is an excellent vantage point for the Old Town and the castle as well as the river. To capture the bridge in its full photogenic glory, cross the footbridge over the river just to the east.

Parish Church of St James   CHURCH

(Župnijska Cerkev Sv Jakoba; 📞 04-512 06 72; Cankarjev trg 14; ⊘ 7am-6pm) FREE The town's most important church dates back to the 13th century, with key features like the nave, the presbytery with star vaulting (1524) and the tall bell tower (1532) added over the next three centuries. The dozen or so distinctive ceiling lamps and the baptismal font were designed by Jože Plečnik.

Church of the Annunciation   CHURCH

(Cerkev Marijinega Oznanenja; 📞 04-513 16 14; www. zupnija-staraloka.si; Crngrob; ⊘ interior by appointment) FREE This small church in the village of Crngrob, 4km north of Škofja Loka, has one of the most treasured frescoes in Slovenia. Look for it on the outside wall under a 19th-century portico near the church entrance. Called Holy Sunday (Sveta Nedelja) and produced in 1460, the fresco explains in pictures what good Christians do on Sunday (pray, go to Mass, help the sick) and what they don't do (gamble, drink or fight).

Spodnji Trg   SQUARE

(Lower Square) The large square to the east of Mestni trg was where the poorer folk lived in the Middle Ages. The 16th-century Granary (Kašča) at the square's northern end, is where the town's grain stores, collected as taxes, were once kept. Over two floors in the granary house you'll find France Mihelič Gallery (Galerija Franceta Miheliča; 📞 04-517 04 00; www.loski-muzej.si; €2; ⊘ by appointment),

Škofja Loka

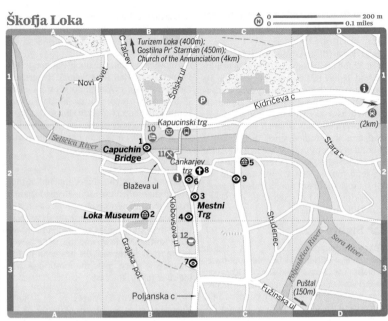

Škofja Loka

which displays the works of the eponymous artist born in nearby Virmaše in 1907.

🏃 Activities

Škofja Loka is an underrated destination for awe-inspiring walks, hikes and cycling trips. If you catch a hot day, head for a popular swimming spot on the river, just a short walk from the Old Town. From December to March, there's also pretty good skiing nearby.

Hiking & Walking

The **Škofja Loka Hills**, a region of steep slopes, deep valleys and ravines, is an excellent area for walks or hikes, and there are

several huts with accommodation in the area. If you're serious about exploring, buy a copy of the map and guide for cyclists, hikers and drivers entitled *Škofjeloško, Idrijsko in Cerkljansko Hribovje (Škofja Loka, Idrija and Cerkno Hills;* €12 from the TIC).

One of the more rewarding trips is to **Lubnik**, a 1025m peak northwest of the Old Town, which can be reached on foot in two hours via Vincarje (a difficult route), or via the castle ruins near Gabrovo. A shorter option (40 minutes) is from the village of Breznica. A mountain hut near the summit, **Dom na Lubniku** (☑ 04-512 05 01, 031 655 556; www.pd-skofjaloka.com; Lubnik; per person €25), has four rooms (12 beds) plus a restaurant and a terrace with great views.

A hike to 1562m **Blegoš**, further west, would be more demanding, but it takes only about three hours from Javorje, a village accessible by bus from Škofja Loka. With your own wheels, drive to the village of Črni Kal and you can reach it within an hour. There is an excellent mountain hut in the area: **Koča na Blegošu** (📞 051 614 587; www.pd-skofjaloka. com; per person €20; ⊙ Tue-Sun May-Oct), at 1391m, with 61 beds (in rooms and dorms), restaurants and good family facilities.

Swimming

In the summer heat, join the locals at the town's pretty riverside swimming area. It's in Puštal, about a 10-minute walk southeast of the Old Town (signposted from Fužinska ulica). There's a summertime cafe-bar here, as well as the wooden 'Devil's Footbridge'.

🎊 Festivals & Events

⭐ Škofja Loka Passion Play   RELIGIOUS

(www.pasijon.si; ⊙ late Mar/Apr) The staging of the Škofja Loka Passion Play is the biggest outdoor theatre production in Slovenia – it involves as many as 800 actors and 80 horses (and hundreds of volunteers). It's staged every six years (the next is set for 2021 – the event's 300th anniversary) and is held throughout the Old Town in the three weeks prior to Easter.

Pisana Loka   MUSIC

(www.pisanaloka.si; ⊙ Aug-Sep) This arts festival (the name means 'Colourful Loka') stages music and theatre performances, film screenings and children's events over 10 days in late August. Event locations include the various town squares and the castle.

🛏 Sleeping

Škofja Loka suffers from a shortage of sleeping options, and it's best to book as soon as you know your travel dates. On the plus side, the lack of big hotels keeps the tour buses to a minimum. In a pinch, the TIC (p86) is happy to help find a room and maintains a list of private rooms online.

Kavarna Vahtnca   PENSION $

(📞 04-512 14 79; www.vahtnca.si; Mestni trg 31; s/d €30/48; 🛜) This modern cafe in the heart of Škofja Loka's Old Town has two compact, simply furnished but good-value rooms upstairs that put you in the centre of the action.

Turizem Loka   PENSION $$

(📞 04-515 09 86; www.loka.si; Stara Loka 8a, Stara Loka; s/d/apt from €40/60/85; 🅿 ❄ @ 🛜) A 10-minute walk from the bus station is the small village of Stara Loka, where you'll find this very comfortable pension (and a nearby neighbour, Gostilna Pr' Starman). On offer are bright, spotless rooms and family-sized apartments, plus a good breakfast spread. With advance notice, you can arrange pickup from the train station.

Hotel Garni Paleta   HOTEL $$

(📞 041 874 427; www.hotel-skofjaloka.si; Kapucinski trg 17; d/q €70/120; 🅿 ❄ 🛜) Welcoming Igor and Irene run this upbeat place next door to an art-supplies shop (thus the name), just by Capuchin Bridge. There are six no-frills rooms – three rooms have a set of bunks, suitable for families. Rooms 1, 3, 5 and 6 have views of the river and the castle; there are discounts for stays longer than one night.

🍴 Eating

The number of restaurants in Škofja Loka is small, but the level of quality is high. Danilo (p86), 6km east of Škofja Loka, is ranked among Slovenia's best restaurants, though you'll need to reserve ahead to get a table here.

Jesharna   ITALIAN $

(📞 04-512 25 61; www.facebook.com/jesharna; Blaževa ulica 10; pizza & pasta €8-10; ⊙ 11am-11pm Mon-Thu, to midnight Fri, noon-midnight Sat, noon-10pm Sun; 🛜 🌿) This welcoming pizzeria and spaghetti house serves the town's best pizza, good salads and pasta dishes that are so big they could easily be shared. It also makes a point of catering to vegetarian and gluten-free eaters. It's directly across the bridge from the bus station, with steps down to its riverside terrace.

Gostilna Pr' Starman   SLOVENIAN $$

(📞 04-512 64 90; www.gostilnastarman.si; Stara Loka 22, Stara Loka; mains €8-18; ⊙ 7am-10pm Mon-Thu, to midnight Fri & Sat; 🛜) This popular *gostilna* (inn-like restaurant) is about 1.5km from the bus station (a 15-minute walk) in the charming village of Stara Loka. It serves authentic traditional Slovenian cooking in an informal tavern setting; prepare for stomach-expanding portions of steaks, pork cutlet and homemade sausage. There's an alfresco terrace too.

Gostilna Kašča   SLOVENIAN $$

(📞 04-512 43 00; www.gostilna-kasca.si; Spodnji trg 1; mains €10-18; ⊙ 11am-11pm Mon-Sat; 🛜)

This attractive (and huge) pub and wine bar in the cellar of the town's 16th-century granary is Škofja Loka's most upscale dining option, and the perfect venue for a big meal out. The menu is strong on traditional Slovenian food and there's also an appealing range of pizzas.

★**Danilo**   SLOVENIAN $$$
(🗐04-515 34 44; www.danilogostilna.si; Reteče 48; degustation €55; ⏰noon-3.30pm & 7-10pm Wed-Fri, noon-10pm Sat, to 4pm Sun; 🎧) Winning praise from influential French restaurant guide Gault Millau, this traditional, family-run *gostilna* serves some of the region's best food. It adheres to Slow Food principles and has a knockout wine list; eight courses for €55 is the deal – and it's wonderful value. It's in the village of Reteče, about 6km east of Škofja Loka; book ahead.

🍷 Drinking & Nightlife

Kavarna Vahtnca   CAFE
(🗐04-512 14 79; www.vahtnca.si; Mestni trg 31; ⏰8am-10pm Mon-Thu, to midnight Fri & Sat, 9am-10pm Sun; 🎧) With a tiered back terrace peeking up at the castle, and tables on the main square, this attractive modern cafe in the heart of the Old Town is an appealing place to refuel. The cafe rents rooms on the upper floor.

Kavarna Homan   CAFE
(🗐04-512 30 47; www.kavarnahoman.si; Mestni trg 2; ⏰8am-10pm Sun-Thu, to 11pm Fri & Sat; 🎧) This ground-floor cafe in historical Homan House is always busy, especially in the warm weather when tables are set out on Mestni trg under the giant linden tree. Homemade ice cream and cakes, too.

ℹ️ Information

Post Office (🗐04-517 02 10; Kapucinski trg 14; ⏰8am-6pm Mon-Fri, to noon Sat)

SKB Banka (Kapucinski trg 4; ⏰8.30am-noon & 2-5pm Mon-Fri)

Tourist Information Centre – Old Town (TIC; 🗐04-512 02 68; www.visitskofjaloka.si; Mestni trg 42; ⏰8.30am-7.30pm Mon-Fri, 9am-5pm Sat & Sun Jun-Sep, 8.30am-7pm Mon-Fri, to 12.30pm Sat Oct-May) Excellent source of general information. Has books and maps on the area; sells decent souvenirs.

Tourist Information Centre (TIC; 🗐04-517 06 00; www.visitskofjaloka.si; Kidričeva cesta 1a; ⏰8am-6pm May, Jun & Sep, to 8pm Jul & Aug, to 4pm Mon-Sat Oct-Apr) A roadside office, as you enter the town centre.

ℹ️ Getting There & Away

BUS
Škofja Loka is well served by regional buses at the **bus station** (Avtobusna Postaja; 🗐04-517 03 00; Kapucinski trg 13). Count on at least hourly buses weekdays to/from Ljubljana (€3.10, 36 minutes, 25km). There are fewer departures at the weekend.

To travel on to Lakes Bled or Bohinj or to Kranjska Gora, take one of the frequent buses to Kranj (€2.30, 24 minutes) and change there.

TRAIN
Škofja Loka can be reached by up to 17 trains a day from Ljubljana (€1.85, 25 minutes, 20km).

Some 15 services go north to Jesenice via Kranj, Radovljica and Lesce-Bled. Several of these cross the border for Villach, 87km to the north in Austria.

The train station is 2.5km northeast of the Old Town.

Radovljica

🗐04 / POP 5922 / ELEV 490M
The town of Radovljica (sometimes shortened to Radol'ca) is filled with impossibly cute, historic buildings and blessed with scenic views of the Alps, including Triglav. It was settled by the early Slavs, and by the 14th century had grown into an important market town centred on a large rectangular square, today's Linhartov trg, and fortified with high stone walls. Much of the original architecture, amazingly, is still standing and looks remarkably unchanged from those early days.

Radovljica has just a couple of places to stay, so it's advisable to book in advance or turn to the TIC to snag a private room. It's an easy day trip from Bled, just 7km away.

◉ Sights

★**Linhartov Trg**   SQUARE
Radovljica's colourful main square is the town's leading attraction, lined with houses from the 16th and 17th centuries. Look especially for **Thurn Manor**, a baroque palace that is home to museums and a school of music, and **Koman House** (Komanova Hiša), identified by a baroque painting of St Florian on its facade. **Mali House** (Malijeva Hiša) has a barely visible picture of St George slaying the dragon. Vidič House (p89) has a corner projection and is painted in red, yellow, green and blue.

★**Beekeeping Museum** MUSEUM
(Čebelarski Muzej; ☑04-532 05 20; www.mro.si; Linhartov trg 1; adult/child €3/2; ⊙10am-6pm Tue-Sun May-Oct, 8am-3pm Tue, Thu & Fri, 10am-noon & 3-5pm Wed, Sat & Sun Mar, Apr, Nov & Dec, 8am-3pm Tue-Fri Jan & Feb) More interesting than it sounds, this apiculture museum takes a closer look at the long tradition of beekeeping in Slovenia. The museum's collection of illustrated beehive panels from the 18th and 19th centuries, a folk art unique to Slovenia, is the largest in the country, and there are some rather astounding beehives in improbable shapes: (life-sized) people, a miniature mansion, even a lion. You can also observe a live beehive in action, filled with a family of indigenous Carniolan bees.

Bees are still kept in Slovenia for their honey and wax but much more lucrative are such by-products as pollen, propolis and royal jelly.

The somewhat esoteric **municipal museum** (Mestni muzej; ☑04-532 05 20; www.mro.si; Linhartov trg 1; adult/child €3/2; ⊙10am-6pm Tue-Sun May-Oct, 8am-3pm Tue, Thu & Fri, 10am-noon & 3-5pm Wed, Sat & Sun Mar, Apr, Nov & Dec, 8am-3pm Tue-Fri Jan & Feb) shares the building with the beekeeping museum (open the same hours; combined ticket adult/child €5/3). It tells the history of the town, especially as it relates to the life of Anton Tomaž Linhart (1756–95). Linhart was Slovenia's first dramatist and historian, and was born in Radovljica.

Parish Church of St Peter CHURCH
(Župnijska Cerkev Sv Petra; Linhartov trg; ⊙7am-8pm) At the end of Linhartov trg is the Gothic Parish Church of St Peter, a hall church modelled after the one in Kranj. The three portals are flamboyant Gothic, and the sculptures inside were done by Angelo Pozzo in 1713. The building with the arcaded courtyard south of the church is the **rectory** (župnišče), where exhibitions are sometimes held.

Šivec House MUSEUM
(Šivčeva Hiša; ☑04-532 05 23; www.muzeji-radovljica.si; Linhartov trg 22; adult/child €3/2; ⊙10am-1pm & 5-8pm Tue-Sun May-Oct, shorter hours Nov-Apr) Possibly the most important house on Linhartov trg is 16th-century Šivec House, which is an interesting hybrid: Renaissance on the outside and Gothic within. On the ground floor is a vaulted hall, which now serves as a **gallery** (changing exhibitions). On the 1st floor are three restored rooms, including a **'black kitchen'** and a wood-panelled, beam-ceilinged, late-Gothic

Radovljica

drawing room used as a wedding hall. Our favourite feature is the 2nd-floor collection of children's book illustrations by celebrated Slovenian artists.

⭐ Festivals & Events

Chocolate Festival FOOD & DRINK
(www.festival-cokolade.si; ⊙mid-Apr) Who can resist a chocolate festival? Radovljica takes its 'honestly sweet' slogan seriously over this weekend in mid-April, with cooking demonstrations, tastings and kids' workshops.

THE BOARDS & THE BEES

Radovljica is known throughout Slovenia as a centre for beekeeping, an integral part of Slovenian agriculture since the 16th century. Slovenes were at the forefront in developing early ways to improve beekeeping techniques, including the invention of what became known as the *kranjič* hive, with removable boxes that resembled a chest of drawers. This created multiple hives and solved an early problem of damaging an entire hive when the honeycomb was removed. It also led to the development of one of Slovenia's most important forms of folk art.

The *kranjič* hives are constructed with front boards above the entrance, and enterprising beekeepers soon began the practice of painting and decorating these panels with religious and other motifs. Radovljica's Beekeeping Museum (p87) has an extensive collection on display, and some of the artwork is nothing short of phenomenal.

Festival Radovljica   MUSIC
(www.festival-radovljica.si; ⊘ Aug) The biggest event of the year is the two-week Festival Radovljica, one of the most important festivals of early classical music in Europe. Culture and music blend nicely in the town's historic setting.

🛏 Sleeping

Vidic House   HOSTEL $
(Vidičeva Hiša; ☑ 031 810 767; www.vidichouse.com; Linhartov trg 3; per person €25; 🕾) This 400-year-old historic townhouse on the main square offers accommodation in four large, homely apartments, with postcard views over Linhartov trg. There's a kitchen in each apartment, and access to a laundry, plus a cool cafe downstairs. Breakfast costs €4.

Camping Šobec   CAMPGROUND $
(☑ 04-535 37 00; www.sobec.si; Šobčeva cesta 25, Lesce; sites per person €11-19, bungalows per 2/6 people €157/180; ⊘ May-Sep; 🅿🕾) The largest and quite possibly the best-equipped campground in Slovenia is in Lesce, about 2.5km northwest of Radovljica. Situated on a small lake near a bend of the Sava Dolinka River, the camping resort offers no end of summer activities and recreation facilities: beach, playgrounds, bike hire, swimming, fishing, guided walks. The bungalows (really timber chalets) are top quality.

★ Linhart Hotel   HOTEL $$
(☑ 059 187 547; www.linharthotel.com; Linhartov trg 17; r €70-90, ste €110; 🅿🕾) Opened in 2017, the Linhart goes for a toned-down version of elegance, occupying a sensitively restored 17th-century townhouse on central Linhartov trg. Many of the original features, including the stone staircase leading to the rooms, arched ceilings and exposed wood beams have been preserved. The rooms are simply furnished but exude real quality. The family that owns the property couldn't be friendlier.

Gostilna Lectar   PENSION $$
(☑ 04-537 48 00; www.lectar.com; Linhartov trg 2; s/d €75/110; 🌢🕾) This delightful B&B on the main square has nine individually decorated rooms done up in folk motifs – painted headboards and room signs made of *lect* (gingerbread) – that could have ended up kitsch but instead feel like those in a village farmhouse from the 19th century, but with modern creature comforts. Note: prices are reduced outside August.

Vila Podvin   GUESTHOUSE $$$
(☑ 083 843 470; www.vilapodvin.si; Mošnje 1; s/d/ste €100/150/190; 🅿🌢🕾) Not content with wowing diners with fabulous food, Vila Podvin also has a handful of modern rooms and suites on offer, in the former stables of the Grad Podvin estate (3km east of Linhartov trg). Rooms are on the pricier side, but the setting is lovely and the hospitality warm.

🍴 Eating

Gostilna Avguštin   SLOVENIAN $$
(☑ 04-531 41 63; www.gostilna-avgustin.si; Linhartov trg 15; mains €10-18; ⊘ 9am-10pm) The huge portions match the big welcome at this delightful central restaurant (the name is often anglicised to Augustin). It serves excellent Slovenian dishes to order. Don't miss the cellar dining room, which was once part of a prison (and may have seen an execution or two), and the wonderful back terrace with views of Triglav.

Gostilna Lectar   SLOVENIAN $$
(☑ 04-537 48 00; www.lectar.com; Linhartov trg 2; mains €12-20; ⊘ 11am-10pm; 🕾) Take your time to peruse the huge, multilingual menu of local specialities here. Some items may not immediately appeal (eg pickled beef tongue,

THE FORMER FORGING VILLAGE OF KROPA

In the early years of the Industrial Revolution, the towns and villages around Radovljica grew wealthy through forging and metal working. The custom still lives on in the pretty hillside village of Kropa (population 840), 13km southeast of Radovljica.

Kropa has been a 'workhorse' for centuries, mining iron ore and hammering out the nails and decorative wrought iron that can still be seen in many parts of Slovenia. Today the village has turned its attention to screws – the German-owned Novi Plamen factory is based here – but artisans continue their work, clanging away in the workshop on the village's single street. The work of their forebears is evident in weather vanes, shutters and ornamental street lamps shaped like birds and dragons.

Kropa's sleepy charm lies in the town's remote feel and the lovely, centuries-old former workers' housing that lines a fast-flowing mountain stream, the Kroparica, which runs right through the centre of town.

The main sight is the **Iron Forging Museum** (Kovaški Muzej; ☑04-533 72 00; www.mro.si; Kropa 10; adult/child €3/2; ☺10am-6pm Tue-Sun May-Oct, reduced hours Nov-Apr), which traces the history of iron mining and forging in Kropa and nearby Kamna Gorica from the 14th to the early 20th centuries. Just across the street from the museum, pop in to the **UKO Kropa forgers' workshop** (☑04-533 73 00; www.uko.si; Kropa 7a; ☺8am-3pm Mon-Fri), which exhibits and sells all manner of articles made of wrought iron – from lamps and doorknobs to garden gates.

Kropa is not exactly awash with dining and lodging options, though don't miss a chance to try the traditional Slovenian cooking at **Gostilna Pr' Kovač** (At the Smith's; ☑04-533 63 20; Kropa 30; mains €9-15; ☺10am-11pm Tue-Sun).

If you don't have your own car, the best way to get here is by bus from Radovljica. Up to 10 buses a day run between the towns (€2.30, 20 minutes, 13km), but not on weekends.

---

sausage in hog's grease), while others boast of a long family pedigree and almost demand to be sampled: the homemade *štruklji* (cheese dumplings) and *žlikrofi* (ravioli of cheese, bacon and chives), for example, and the Lectar strudel.

★ **Vila Podvin** SLOVENIAN $$$
(☑083 843 470; www.vilapodvin.si; Mošnje 1; mains €22-32; ☺noon-10pm Tue-Sat, to 5pm Sun; 🛜) Winning plaudits from diners local and foreign, this elegant establishment is 3km east of Linhartov trg, on the 14th-century Grad Podvin Estate. Kitchen creativity combines with quality local produce and some time-honoured techniques to produce plates that match the beauty of the setting. Lunch is great value (three courses for €18), as is the chef's tasting menu (four/six courses €40/60).

🍷 Drinking & Nightlife

Vidic House CAFE
(Vidičeva Hiša; ☑04-029 63 62; www.vidichouse.com; Linhartov trg 3; coffee €2; ☺9am-10pm; 🛜) Arguably the most charming of several cafes along historic Linhartov trg, Vidic House specialises in coffee, cakes and ice cream. The cute vaulted interior is jammed with found items.

Vinoteka Sodček WINE BAR
(☑041 678 408; www.vinoteka-sodcek.si; Linhartov trg 8; ☺9am-9pm Mon-Sat; 🛜) We applaud the deal at this wine bar: for €15 you can enjoy five tastes of Slovenian wines, served with *pršut* (air-dried ham from the Karst), plus local cheese and olive oil.

❶ Information

Post Office (Kranjska cesta 1; ☺8am-7pm Mon-Fri, to noon Sat) Also has an ATM.

SKB Banka (Gorenjska cesta 10; ☺8am-noon & 2-5pm Mon-Fri) Full service bank and ATM within easy walking distance of the Old Town.

Tourist Information Centre (TIC; ☑04-531 51 12; www.radolca.si; Linhartov trg 9; ☺9am-7pm Jun-Sep, to 4pm Oct-May; 🛜) Centrally located, helps book rooms, sells good local hiking and cycling maps, rents bikes, and has a computer on hand for gratis surfing. The office also sells local souvenirs.

❶ Getting There & Away

BUS

The **bus station** (Kranjska cesta) is 300m northwest of Linhartov trg. There's a timetable posted on a board outside the station, or check bus schedule info online at www.alpetour.si.

Roughly half-hourly services depart for Bled (€1.80, 14 minutes, 7km) from around 5am to 11pm (hourly on weekends). Services to Ljubljana are also frequent, running half-hourly or hourly from 5am to 9pm (€5.60, one hour, 50km). There are also regular buses to Lake Bohinj (€4.70, 50 minutes, 36km) and Kranjska Gora (€5.20, 53 minutes, 41km).

TRAIN

The train station is 100m below the Old Town on Cesta Svoboda. International trains use the nearby station at Lesce-Bled.

Radovljica is on a main rail line linking Ljubljana (€4.28, one hour, 48km) with Jesenice (€1.95, 17 minutes, 16km) via Škofja Loka, Kranj and Lesce-Bled. At least 10 trains a day pass through the town in each direction.

Lake Bled

📝 04 / POP 5100 / ELEV 481M

Yes, it's every bit as lovely in real life. With its bluish-green lake, picture-postcard church on an islet, a medieval castle clinging to a rocky cliff and some of the highest peaks of the Julian Alps and the Karavanke as backdrops, Bled is Slovenia's most popular resort, drawing everyone from honeymooners lured by the over-the-top romantic setting to backpackers, who come for the hiking, biking, water-sports and canyoning possibilities.

That said, Bled can be overpriced and swarming with tourists in July and August. But as is the case with many popular destinations around the world, people come in droves – and will continue to do so – because the place is so special.

History

Bled was the site of a Hallstatt settlement in the early Iron Age, but as it was far from the main trade routes, the Romans gave it short shrift. From the 7th century the early Slavs came in waves, establishing themselves at Pristava below the castle, on the tiny island and at a dozen other sites around the lake. Around the turn of the first millennium, the German Emperor Henry II presented Bled Castle and its lands to the Bishops of Brixen in South Tyrol, who retained secular control of the area until the early 19th century when the Habsburgs took it over.

Bled's beauty and its warm waters were well known to medieval pilgrims who came to pray at the island church; the place made it into print in 1689 when Janez Vajkard Valvasor described the lake's thermal springs in *The Glory of the Duchy of Carniola*. But Bled's wealth was not fully appreciated at that time, and in the late 18th century the keeper of the castle seriously considered draining Lake Bled and using the clay to make bricks.

Fortunately, along came a Swiss doctor named Arnold Rikli, who saw the lake's full potential. In 1855 he opened baths where the casino now stands, taking advantage of the springs, the clean air and the mountain light. With the opening of the railway from Ljubljana to Tarvisio (Trbiž) in 1870, more and more guests came to Bled and the resort was a favourite of wealthy Europeans from the turn of the century right up to WWII. In fact, under the Kingdom of Serbs, Croats and Slovenes, Bled was the summer residence of the Yugoslav royal family (and later of Tito).

◎ Sights

★ **Lake Bled** LAKE
(Blejsko jezero; Map p91) Bled's greatest attraction is its exquisite blue-green lake, measuring just 2km by 1.4km. The lake is lovely to behold from almost any vantage point, and makes a beautiful backdrop for the 6km walk along the shore. Mild thermal springs warm the water to a swimmable 22°C (72°F) from June through August. The lake is naturally the focus of the entire town: you can rent rowboats, splash around on stand-up paddle boards or simply snap countless photos.

★ **Bled Castle** CASTLE
(Blejski Grad; Map p91; 📝 04-572 97 82; www. blejski-grad.si; Grajska cesta 25; adult/child €11/5; ⊙ 8am-9pm Jun-Aug, to 8pm Apr-May & Sep-Oct, to 6pm Nov-Mar) Perched atop a steep cliff more than 100m above the lake, Bled Castle is how most people imagine a medieval fortress to be, with towers, ramparts, moats and a terrace offering magnificent views. The castle houses a museum collection that traces the lake's history from earliest times to the development of Bled as a resort in the 19th century.

The castle, built on two levels, dates back to the early 11th century, although most of what stands here now is from the 16th century. For 800 years it was the seat of the Bishops of Brixen. Among the museum holdings, there's a large collection of armour and weapons, and jewellery found at the early Slav burial pits at Pristava. The smallish 16th-century Gothic chapel contains paintings of castle donor Henry II and his wife Kunigunda on either side of the main altar.

Lake Bled

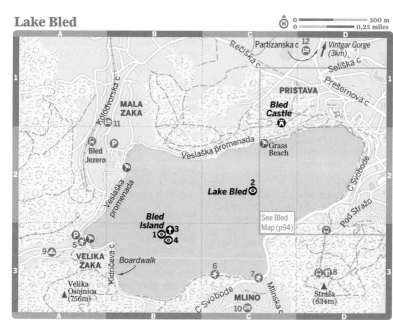

You can reach the castle on foot via one of three trails signposted 'Grad'. The first trail starts from the car park behind the Bledec Hostel; the second is a tortuous path up from the Castle Lido swimming area; and the third starts just north of the Parish Church of St Martin.

★ **Bled Island** ISLAND
(Blejski Otok; Map p91; www.blejskiotok.si; ⊙9am-7pm) Tiny, tear-shaped Bled Island beckons from the shore. There's the Church of the Assumption and a small museum, the **Provost's House** (☑04-576 79 78; www.blejskiotok. si; adult/child €6/1, incl with admission to Church of the Assumption; ⊙9am-7pm May-Sep, to 6pm Apr & Oct, to 4pm Nov-Mar), but the real thrill is the ride out by *pletna* (gondola). The *pletna* will set you down on the south side at the monumental **South Staircase** (Južno Stopnišče), built in 1655. The staircase comprises 99 steps – a local tradition is for the husband to carry his new bride up them.

There is no charge to visit the island, except for what you pay to travel there (eg the gondola ride or hire of a rowboat); you are free to wander and visit the cafe and souvenir store. However, there is an admission charge to enter the church.

Lake Bled

Church of the Assumption CHURCH
(Cerkev Marijinega Vnebovzetja; Map p91; ☑04-576 79 79; www.blejskiotok.si; Bled Island; adult/child €6/1; ⊙9am-7pm May-Sep, to 6pm Apr & Oct, to 4pm Nov-Mar) The baroque Church of the Assumption dates from the 17th century, though there's been a church here since the 9th century. Go inside to see some fresco fragments from the 15th century, a large gold altar and part of the apse of a

pre-Romanesque chapel. The 15th-century **belfry** contains a 'wishing bell' you can ring to ask a special favour.

🏃 Activities

Horse-Drawn Carriages TOURS
(Map p94; www.fijaker-bled.si; Cesta Svobode) A romantic way to experience Bled is to take a horse-drawn carriage *(fijaker)* from a stand on Cesta Svobode, 200m north of the TIC. A spin around the lake costs €50, and it's the same price to the castle (an extra 30 minutes inside costs €60 total).

Tourist Train TOURS
(Map p94; adult/child €5/3; ⊙9am-9pm Jun-Sep, 10am-5pm Sat & Sun May & Oct) This easy, family-friendly 45-minute twirl around the lake departs from just south of the TIC up to 20 times a day in season, making stops at a number of convenient places (Mlino, the campground, the Castle Lido).

Adventure Sports
Several local outfits organise a wide range of outdoor activities in and around Bled, including trekking, mountaineering, rock climbing, ski touring, cross-country skiing, mountain biking, rafting, kayaking, canyoning, horse riding, paragliding and ballooning.

There's a cluster of agencies around the bus station, and accommodation providers (especially hostels) can often book you onto their own (or affiliated) tours and activities.

★3glav Adventures ADVENTURE SPORTS
(Map p94; ☑041 683 184; www.3glav.com; Ljubljanska cesta 1; ⊙9am-noon & 4-7pm mid-Apr-Oct) Bled's number-one adventure-sport specialist. It's most popular trip is the Emerald River Adventure (from €80), an 11-hour hiking and swimming foray into Triglav National Park and along the Soča River that covers a sightseeing loop of the region (from Bled over the Vršič Pass and down the Soča Valley, with optional rafting trip). Book by phone or via the website.

There are loads more options. A two-day guided ascent of Mt Triglav costs €245. If you don't fancy scaling mountains, a half-day of scenic hiking or mountain biking in the national park is €65.

On the water, a 2½-hour rafting trip down the mild Sava Bohinjka River costs €35; on the Soča is €45 (but the latter trip starts from near Bovec). Popular canyoning trips cost €65.

The menu extends to paragliding, ballooning, diving, kayaking and horse riding – see the website for details. It also rents high-quality mountain bikes (€20 per day) and electric bikes (from €60 per day).

Mamut ADVENTURE SPORTS
(Map p94; ☑040 121 900; www.slovenija.eu.com; Cesta Svobode 4; ⊙8am-7pm May-Sep) Offers a full menu of outdoor activities (rafting, canyoning, hiking, paragliding etc), plus rental of bikes and SUP boards. It also offers guided trips to Vintgar Gorge (€4 per person) as well as convenient transfers to Ljubljana city centre (€9 per person) and to Jože Pučnik Airport (€12 per person).

Life Adventures ADVENTURE SPORTS
(Map p94; ☑040 508 853; www.lifeadventures.si; Grajska cesta 10; ⊙8am-7pm May-Sep) Offers a wide range of adventure activities, including a demanding but fun full day of canyoning from €148 and three hours of snorkelling in the Soča River gorge (from €68). Can help arrange self-guided itineraries for Slovenia and Croatia (walking, cycling, driving, activity-based), and has comprehensive winter options: backcountry skiing, snowshoeing, ice climbing, sledding etc in the Julian Alps.

Zipline Dolinka ADVENTURE SPORTS
(Map p94; ☑031 845 900; www.zipline-dolinka.si; Grajska cesta 16; per person €65; ⊙8am-6pm May-Sep) This attraction opened in 2018 and involves breathless travel along five zipline cables, with an overall length of 2.4km, through the stunning Sava Dolinka valley. The price includes equipment rental as well as transfer to and from the zipline centre. Book in person or online.

Ballooning

Balonarski Center Barje BALLOONING
(Map p94; ☑041 664 545; www.ballooning-bled.com; flights €190) Hot-air ballooning offers an incredible vantage point for taking in Bled's breathtaking early-morning peace and beauty (weather permitting, of course). Grega, the owner and balloon pilot, has flown all over the world and is trained as a meteorologist. Book directly or via 3glav Adventures. Trips usually meet at the Bled bus station.

Boating & Water-sports
Lake Bled is open to rowboats (motorboats are banned); there are also plenty of summertime stand-up paddleboarders (SUP) on the water. Rental agencies (9am to 7pm May through September) are in various locations,

including at the waterfront below the **Vila Bled hotel** (Map p91); the **Castle Lido** (Map p94); the beach in front of **Camping Bled** (Map p91); and the lido by **Grand Hotel Toplice** (Map p94; Cesta Svobode 12). Rowboats generally cost €20 to €25 per hour and SUPs €10.

Gondola Ride   BOATING

(Pletna; Map p91; ☑ 041 427 155; www.bled.si; per person return €14; ⊙ 8am-9pm Mon-Sat, to 6pm Sun Jul & Aug, 8am-7pm Mon-Sat, 11am-5pm Sun Apr-Jun, Sep & Oct, 8am-6pm Mon-Sat, to 1pm Sun Nov-Mar) Riding a piloted gondola (known as a *pletna*) out to Bled Island is the archetypal tourist experience. There is a convenient jetty just below the **TIC** and another in **Mlino** on the south shore. You get about half an hour to explore the island. In all, the trip to the island and back takes about 1¼ hours.

Cycling

The 6km-long perimeter path around the lake is suitable for cycling, though the trail is narrow in places and often overflowing with pedestrians. It takes around 45 minutes at a leisurely pace.

There are some excellent mountain-bike trails in the hills surrounding Bled, including the beautiful 13km-long **Radovna cycling path** (Krnica; ⊙ 24h) FREE that starts in the village Krnica, about 6km from Bled, and runs through Triglav National Park. Pick up a cycling map at the TIC or organise the trip through one of the adventure-sports companies in town.

Fishing

Fishing is allowed on Lake Bled, provided you have a permit. The surrounding lakes and streams are rich with all manner of river fish.

Slovenia Fly Fishing   FISHING

(Map p94; ☑ 04-163 31 47; www.faunabled.com; Cesta Svobode 12; ⊙ 8am-noon & 3-7pm Mon-Fri, 8am-noon Sat, 8-10am Sun) One-stop shopping for all your fishing needs, including guiding (on request), advice, map and gear rental. Sells fishing permits valid for a day on the lake (€30) and licences required for fishing the various local rivers. Enter through the Panorama Restaurant.

Golf

Royal Bled Golf   GOLF

(☑ 01-200 99 01; www.golfbled.com; Vrba 37a, Lesce; 9/18 holes €45/80) The 18-hole, par-72 Bled Golf Course, 3km east of the lake near Lesce, is Slovenia's best course and, with its dramatic mountain backdrop, one of the most beautiful in Europe. You can rent clubs and carts; bookings advised.

Hiking

There are many short and easy, signposted hikes around Bled (numbered signs correspond to numbered routes on local hiking and cycling maps; good maps are available in town for around €6).

One of the best trails is No 6 from the southwest corner of the lake. There, a steep forested path takes about 45 minutes to reach **Mala Osojnica** (685m), and another 20-minute walk leads to the top of **Velika Osojnica** (756m). The view from the top – over the lake, island and castle, with the peaks of the Karavanke in the background – is stunning, especially towards sunset. This peak is a photographer's favourite.

Skiing

Straža Bled Ski Centre   SKIING

(Map p91; ☑ 04-578 05 30; www.straza-bled.si; day pass adult/child €17/9; ⊙ mid-Dec–mid-Mar) Beginners and families will be content with the tiny (6-hectare) ski centre close to town. A chairlift takes you up the hill to the 634m summit in three minutes; you'll be down the short slope in no time. Equipment is available for hire on-site.

Outside of winter, Straža is transformed into a family-friendly adventure area: there's a 520m **summer toboggan** run down the slope, and Pustolovski Park (www.pustolovski-park-bled.si), an 'adrenaline park' of ropes courses, at the summit. Both activities are pricey, though, with the chairlift and one toboggan ride costing €9/6 per adult/child; two hours at Pustolovski Park costs €22/10 per adult/child.

Swimming

Bled's warmish (22°C/72°F at source) and crystal-clear water – it rates a Blue Flag (a voluntary and independent eco-label awarded to beaches around the world for their cleanliness and water quality) – makes it suitable for swimming all summer, and there are decent beaches around the lake, including a popular one near the campground (rich in activity options) and a lovely grass one on the northern side.

The public swimming areas are excellent, and there are a couple of private beaches too, including a refined one at the **Grand Hotel Toplice** (Map p94; ☑ 04-579 16 00; Cesta

Bled

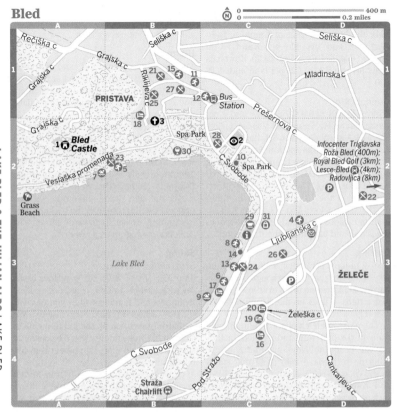

Svobode 12; admission €15, hotel guests free; ⊙9am-7pm Jun-Sep).

Castle Lido
SWIMMING
(Grajsko Kopališče; Map p94; ☑04-578 05 28; www.kopalisce-bled.si; Veslaška promenada 11; day pass adult/child €8/6; ⊙9am-8pm Jul-Aug, to 7pm Jun) The popular grass beach below the castle offers lake swimming behind protected enclosures as well as water slides and other family-friendly amusements. You can rent lockers, deckchairs and umbrellas. Note that it's normally closed on rainy days. There are slightly cheaper tickets if you arrive after 5pm.

✵ Festivals & Events

A number of special events take place during summer in Bled, including summertime concerts at the **Festival Hall** (Festivalna Dvorana; Map p94; ☑04-572 97 70; www.kongresni-center-bled.si; Cesta Svobode 11; ⊙hours vary by event) and the **Parish Church of St Martin** (Farna Cerkev Sv Martina; Map p94; Riklijeva cesta; ⊙8am-7pm) FREE, or theatrical performances at Bled Castle. There are frequent live music performances at lakeside venues like the Park Cafe terrace. You may like to track down the pop-up open-air yoga classes. See more details on www.bled.si/events.

Festival Bled
MUSIC
(www.festivalbled.com; ⊙Jul) A fortnight of concerts in beautiful venues (primarily classical music, but also jazz and other genres). Includes masterclasses with accomplished musicians, and an international viola and violin competition.

Okarina Etno Festival
MUSIC
(www.festival-okarina.si; ⊙late Jul-Aug) A festival chock-full of great international folk and world music artists, with free concerts by the lake (and ticketed gigs in the castle).

Bled

⊙ Top Sights
1 Bled Castle.. A2

⊙ Sights
2 Festival Hall C2
3 Parish Church of St Martin................... B2

⊙ Activities, Courses & Tours
4 3glav Adventures.................................. D3
  Balonarski Center Barje............... (see 12)
5 Boat Rental Castle Lido B2
6 Boat Rental Grand Hotel Toplice.......... C3
7 Castle Lido A2
8 Gondolas TIC... C3
9 Grand Hotel Toplice Lido...................... C3
10 Horse-Drawn Carriages C2
11 Life Adventures..................................... B1
12 Mamut.. C1
13 Slovenia Fly Fishing............................. C3
14 Tourist Train C3
15 Zipline Dolinka...................................... B1

🛏 Sleeping
16 Garni Hotel Berc.................................... C4

17 Grand Hotel Toplice C3
18 Old Parish House.................................... B1
19 Penzion Berc.. C4
20 Penzion Mayer....................................... C3

✕ Eating
  Castle Restaurant ....(see 1)
  Finefood – Penzion Berc ....(see 19)
21 Gostilna Murka...................................... B1
22 Gostilna Union Bled............................... D2
23 Grajska Plaža B2
24 Ostarija Peglez'n................................... C3
25 Pizzeria Rustika B1
26 Public & Vegan Kitchen C3
27 Slaščičarna Zima................................... B1
28 Špica C2

🍷 Drinking & Nightlife
29 Park Restaurant & Cafe......................... C3
  Pub Bled ....(see 24)
30 Vila Prešeren... B2

🛍 Shopping
31 Zakladi Slovenije................................... C3

🛏 Sleeping

Bled has a wide range of accommodation, but book well in advance if you're travelling in July or August.

Private rooms and apartments are offered by many homes in the area. Both Kompas and the TIC have lists.

Prices indicated are for peak season (July and August); there may be discounts in quieter periods – hotel websites list all prices. If you're driving, ask about parking at or near your accommodation.

★ Jazz Hostel & Apartments
HOSTEL, GUESTHOUSE $

(Map p91; ☏ 040 634 555; www.jazzbled.com; Prešernova cesta 68; dm €35, d €80, without bathroom €60, apt d/q €90/100; P @ 🛜) If you don't mind being a little way (a short walk) from the action, this is a first-class budget choice. Guests rave about Jazz, mainly thanks to Jani, the superbly friendly owner who runs a sparkling, well-kitted-out complex. There are dorms (bunk-free, and with underbed storage) and colourful en-suite rooms, plus family-sized apartments with a full kitchen. Book well in advance.

Camping Bled
CAMPGROUND $

(Map p91; ☏ 04-575 20 00; www.sava-camping. com; Kidričeva cesta 10c; sites from €23, glamping huts from €90; P @ 🛜) Bled's hugely popular, amenity-laden campground is in a rural valley at the western end of the lake, about 4km from the bus station. There's a rich array of family-friendly activities available, and a restaurant and a store on-site.

★ Old Parish House
GUESTHOUSE $$

(Stari Farovž; Map p94; ☏ 045 767 979; www.blej skiotok.si; Riklijeva cesta 22; s/d from €80/120; P 🛜) In a privileged position, the Old Parish House belonging to the Parish Church of St Martin has been transformed into a simple, welcoming guesthouse, with timber beams, hardwood floors and neutral, minimalist style. Pros include car parking, lake views and waking to church bells.

Penzion Mayer
PENSION $$

(Map p94; ☏ 04-576 57 40; www.mayer-sp.si; Želeška cesta 7; s/d €65/90, apt from €130; P 🛜) This flower-bedecked, 12-room inn in a renovated 19th-century house sits in a lovely garden in a quiet location above the lake. The larger apartment is in a delightful wooden cabin and the in-house restaurant (primarily for guests) is excellent.

Garni Hotel Berc
HOTEL $$

(Map p94; ☏ 04-576 56 58; www.berc-sp.si; Pod Stražo 13; s/d €70/90; ⊙ Apr-Oct; P 🛜) Not to be confused with Penzion Berc across the road, this charming 15-room hotel is reminiscent of a Swiss chalet, with a cosy

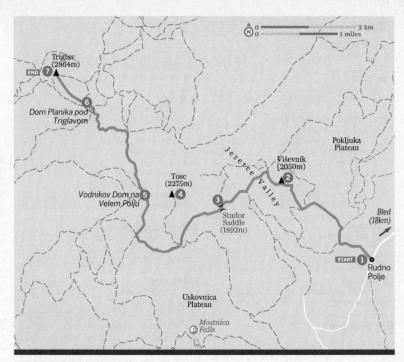

🏃 Walking Tour
Summiting Mt Triglav from Lake Bled

START RUDNO POLJE
END RUDNO POLJE
LENGTH 26KM; TWO DAYS

The shortest (and considered the easiest, though still challenging) ascent of Mt Triglav starts from **1 Rudno Polje** (1347m) on the Pokljuka Plateau, in a remote area 18km west of Bled. An experienced climber could do this in under 12 hours out and back, but most mortals choose to stay overnight.

If you have your own wheels, the trailhead is accessible to motor vehicles and there are parking spots for you to leave the car overnight. Otherwise, you'll have to arrange a drop-off and pickup from someone in Bled. If you're climbing with a guide or have arranged through an adventure agency, these details will be sorted out for you.

The route follows a well-marked trail under **2 Višsevnik** (2050m), considered to be the most popular of Slovenia's 2000m peaks because of the views. The trail heads northwest and then bends sharply south before passing over the **3 Studor Saddle** (1892m). From

here, the path contours around the slopes of towering **4 Tosc** (2275m).

Around three hours of hiking from the Studor Saddle brings you to the welcome sight of the **5 Vodnikov Dom na Velem Polju** mountain hut, at 1817m. The hut has around 60 beds and a restaurant. You can sleep here or continue on for another two hours, heading north and west, to the **6 Dom Planika pod Triglavom**, at 2401m, which offers another chance to bed down or grab a bite to eat. Always pre-book a bed in advance, since neither hut has emergency overflow in case all the beds are taken.

From this hut, it's 1½ hours of steep climbing and scrambling along the summit ridge, grabbing hold of metal spikes and grips, to the **7 top of Triglav**.

The descent follows the same path in the reverse direction. The way down is easier and quicker than the climb, though trickier in part due to loose rocks or potentially wet (and slippery) paths. Provided you've reached the summit in the early morning, you'll be back on the ground in Rudno Polje by the late afternoon.

traditional feel and lots of pine wood in its simple, appealing rooms. It's one of a great pocket of guesthouses in a quiet location above the lake. Free bikes are a bonus.

★ **Garden Village Bled** RESORT **$$$**
(Map p91; ☑ 083 899 220; www.gardenvillagebled.com; Cesta Gorenjskega odreda 16; pier tent €130, treehouse €320, glamping tent €370; ⊘ Apr-Oct; P @ 🛜 ☲) Garden Village embraces and executes the eco-resort concept with aplomb, taking glamping to a whole new level and delivering lashings of wow factor. Accommodation ranges from small two-person tents (with shared bathroom) on piers over a trout-filled stream, to family-sized treehouses and large safari-style tents. Plus there are beautiful grounds, a natural swimming pool and an organic restaurant.

Hotel Triglav Bled BOUTIQUE HOTEL **$$$**
(Map p91; ☑ 04-575 26 10; www.hoteltriglavbled.si; Kolodvorska cesta 33; s/d/ste from €140/160/300; P ✳ @ 🛜 ☲) Elegant 22-room hotel resides in a restored inn dating from 1906 and enjoys delightful panoramas from an out-of-the-way location on a hill above the northern lakeshore – close to Bled Jezero train station. Its dining room has an esteemed reputation to match the views, while rooms feature hardwood floors, oriental carpets and antiques. There's a wine cellar and a wellness area.

Penzion Berc PENSION **$$$**
(Map p94; ☑ 04-574 18 38; www.penzion-berc.si; Želeška cesta 15; r €160-190; P 🛜) Rooms at this snug pension are in demand, and it's not hard to see why: a quiet position a few minutes' walk from town, a delightful 19th-century farmhouse aesthetic and a garden that's home to a great restaurant. There's also the chance to arrange small-group sightseeing trips.

Grand Hotel Toplice HOTEL **$$$**
(Map p94; ☑ 04-579 10 00; www.hotel-toplice.com; Cesta Svobode 12; d with/without view €250/200, ste €350; P ✳ @ 🛜 ☲) With a history that goes back to the 19th century, the 87-room Toplice is Bled's 'olde-worlde' five-star hotel, with attractive public areas and superb views of the lake. It's one of only two Slovenian members of Small Luxury Hotels of the World. Features include a wellness area and an indoor pool, a terrace bar and a restaurant, and a private lakeside lido (p93).

🍴 Eating

For all of its natural splendour, Lake Bled is not a culinary paradise. While there are a few notable exceptions, many places, regrettably, appear content to push out overpriced, generic food to the mass of visitors. Bled Castle (p100) has a magnificent restaurant, though advance booking is required.

Pizzeria Rustika PIZZA **$**
(Map p94; ☑ 04-576 89 00; www.pizzeria-rustika.com; Riklijeva cesta 13; pizza €8-11; ⊘ noon-11pm) The best pizza in town is conveniently located on the same hill as many of Bled's hostels. A cool terrace, ample topping options, and home delivery offered too.

Slaščičarna Zima CAFE **$**
(Map p94; ☑ 04-574 16 16; www.smon.si; Grajska cesta 3; kremna rezina €3; ⊘ 7.30am-9pm) Bled's culinary speciality is the delicious *kremna rezina*, also known as the *kremšnita*: a layer of vanilla custard topped with whipped cream and sandwiched between two layers of flaky pastry. While Šmon patisserie may not be its place of birth, it remains the best place in which to try it – retro decor and all.

Public & Vegan Kitchen VEGETARIAN **$**
(Map p94; ☑ 070 270 712; www.facebook.com/PublicBarVeganKitchen; Ljubljanska cesta 4; mains €6-10; ⊘ noon-9pm; 🛜 ⟋) The decent vegetarian cooking here, mostly salads and veggie burgers, won't have you screaming Michelin star, but nevertheless fills a big gap in the market for non-meat alternatives. Lots of gluten-free options on the menu as well. Find it towards the top and back of the Bled Shopping Centre (keep climbing the stairs until you see it).

Grajska Plaža SLOVENIAN **$$**
(Castle Beach Restaurant; Map p94; ☑ 031 813 886; www.grajska-plaza.com; Veslaška promenada 11; mains €8-20; ⊘ 9am-11pm May–mid-Oct; 🛜) Even the locals say that dining here feels like a summer holiday. It's built on a terrace over the Castle Lido and has a relaxed vibe, helpful service and an easy all-day menu that stretches from morning coffee to end-of-day cocktails. Meal options like grilled trout or octopus salad are generous and tasty.

Gostilna Murka SLOVENIAN **$$**
(Map p94; ☑ 04-574 33 40; www.gostilna-murka.com; Riklijeva cesta 9; mains €10-20; ⊘ 10am-10pm Mon-Fri, noon-11pm Sat & Sun; 🛜) This traditional restaurant set within a large,

98

1. Wild Ibex, Julian Alps (p81)
Slovenia's mountains and lush green valleys teem with wildlife

2. Vogel cable car (p102)
The glorious setting and panoramic views make this cablecar a beautiful trip, whether in summer or ski season.

3. Tolmin Gorges (p123)
Scenic river gorges in the south of Triglav National Park (p108).

4. Lake Bohinj (p102)
Sparkling blue-green water, surrounged by idyllic villages and hiking and cycling trails.

leafy garden may at first appear a bit theme-park-ish – but this is one of the first places locals recommend and the food is authentic (lots of old-school national dishes). Offers good-value lunch specials for around €6 (but you'll have to ask the server).

Ostarija Peglez'n SEAFOOD $$
(Map p94; ☑ 04-574 42 18; Cesta Svobode 19; mains €9-23; ☺ 11am-11pm; ☎) Fish is the main game at the lovely, central 'Iron Inn'. Enjoy the cute retro decor with lots of antiques and curios, and choose from a tempting menu of trout from local rivers, John Dory from the Adriatic coast, and a host of calamari, seafood pasta and fish soup options. Meaty mains and veggie options also offered. Book in advance.

Špica INTERNATIONAL $$
(Map p94; ☑ 04-574 30 27; www.restavracija-spica.si; Cesta Svobode 9; mains €11-18; ☺ 9am-midnight; ☎) If you don't mind the occasional tour bus filing through, this is a reliable standby for good grilled meats, pastas, burgers and the odd Mexican dish. There's a big terrace for dining in the sunshine and a more secluded terrace towards the back. Unusual for Bled, it serves big breakfasts (€9 to €10) from 9am until noon.

Gostilna Union Bled GRILL $$
(Map p94; ☑ 04-578 01 50; www.union-bled.com; Ljubljanska cesta 9; mains €12-17; ☺ 6-11pm; ☎) In a resort not particularly known for its excellent food, this outdoor grill serves very good and reasonably priced steaks, chops and fish dishes. The shady terrace at the back is a big plus, as is the location – about 200m east of the lake and well away from the tourist-bus hustle and bustle.

★ Castle Restaurant SLOVENIAN $$$
(Map p94; ☑ advance booking 04-620 34 44; www.jezersek.si/en/bled-castle-restaurant; Grajska cesta 61; mains €20-40, tasting menu from €50; ☺ 10.30am-10pm; ☎) It's hard to fault the superb location of the castle's restaurant, with a terrace and views straight from a postcard. What a relief the food is as good as it is: smoked trout, roast pork, poached fish. Note advance booking by phone is compulsory for dinner and only the multi-course tasting menu is available.

★ Finefood – Penzion Berc SLOVENIAN $$$
(Map p94; ☑ 04-574 18 38; www.penzion-berc.si; Želeška cesta 15; mains €18-40; ☺ 5-11pm May-Oct; ☎) In a magical garden setting, Penzion Berc sets up a summertime restaurant, with

local produce served fresh from its open kitchen. Try sea bass with asparagus soufflé, homemade pasta with fresh black truffle, deer entrecote or Black Angus steak. Fine-food's reputation for high-class flavour and atmosphere is well known: book ahead.

☕ Drinking & Nightlife

Pub Bled PUB
(Map p94; ☑ 04-574 26 22; Cesta Svobode 19; ☺ 9am-1am Sun-Thu, to 3am Fri & Sat; ☎) The pick of the town's pubs, this convivial place sits above the Ostarija Peglez'n restaurant and has great cocktails and, on some nights, a DJ.

Vila Prešeren BAR
(Map p94; ☑ 04-575 25 10; www.sportina-turizem.si; Veslaška promenada 14; ☺ 7am-midnight Mon-Thu, to 1am Fri-Sun; ☎) A consummate all-rounder, this glamorous cafe-bar-restaurant-guesthouse sits in pole position on the lakeside promenade, with a huge terrace that's designed for people (and lake) watching. It morphs from coffees to cocktails and has a crowd-pleasing menu that helpfully flags dishes that bring you a taste of Bled, Slovenia or 'Ex Yu' (Yugoslavian).

Park Restaurant & Cafe CAFE
(Map p94; ☑ 04-579 18 18; www.sava-hotels-resorts.com; Cesta Svobode 15; ☺ 9am-9pm Tue-Sun; ☎) The Park Cafe has a huge terrace and a commanding position over the lake's eastern end – it's a good spot for coffee and *kremna rezina* (€3.50). The cafe is said to be the place where the cake was first created – as well as the original recipe, you can now try variants with fruit or chocolate.

🛍 Shopping

Zakladi Slovenije GIFTS & SOUVENIRS
(Slovenia's Treasures; Map p94; ☑ 083 824 180; Cesta Svobode 15; ☺ 9am-9pm) The perfect spot to pick up that last-minute gift or souvenir – whether it be a bottle of wine, a T-shirt or locally made cheese, honey or chocolate.

❶ Information

Good online sources of info include Turizem Bled (www.bled.si) and In Your Pocket (www.inyourpocket.com/bled).

MONEY

Gorenjska Banka (☑ 04-208 46 76; Cesta Svobode 15; ☺ 8am-7pm Mon-Sat)

POST

Post Office (Map p94; Ljubljanska cesta 10; ☺ 8am-7pm Mon-Fri, to noon Sat)

VINTGAR GORGE

One of the easiest and most satisfying half-day trips from Bled is to **Vintgar Gorge** (Soteska Vintgar; ☑ 031 344 053; www.vintgar.si; adult/child €5/2.50; ☺8am-7pm late Apr-Oct), some 4km to the northwest of Bled village.

The highlight is a 1600m **wooden walkway** through the gorge, built in 1893 and continually rebuilt since. It criss-crosses the swirling Radovna River four times over rapids, waterfalls and pools before reaching 16m-high **Šum Waterfall**.

The entire walk is spectacular, although it can get pretty wet and slippery. There are little snack bars at the beginning and the end of the walkway; the path to view Šum Waterfall is behind the kiosk at the walkway's end.

It's an easy walk to the gorge from Bled. Head northwest on Prešernova cesta then north on Partizanska cesta to Cesta Vintgar. This will take you to **Podhom**, where signs show the way to the gorge entrance. To return, you can either retrace your steps or, from Šum Waterfall, walk eastward over **Hom** (834m) to the ancient pilgrimage **Church of St Catherine** (signed 'Katarina Bled'), which retains some 15th-century fortifications. From there it's due south through **Zasip** to Bled. Count on about three hours all in.

In July and August, a **tourist bus** (☑ 04-201 32 10; www.alpetour.si; one way €2.50) leaves Bled bus station daily at 8.30am, 9.30am and 10.30am and heads for Vintgar Gorge, stopping at several points, including Bled Castle, along the way, and arriving about 40 minutes later. There's regular return service at approximately the same intervals.

LAKE BLED & THE JULIAN ALPS LAKE BLED

TOURIST INFORMATION

Infocenter Triglavska Roža Bled (☑ 04-578 02 05; www.tnp.si; Ljubljanska cesta 27; ☺8am-6pm mid-Apr–mid-Oct, to 4pm mid-Oct–mid-Apr; ☏) An excellent info centre for Bled and the entire region, with maps, guides and displays on Triglav National Park. Free exhibitions, plus an on-site cafe and a gift shop. Worth a stop.

Tourist Information Centre (Map p94; ☑ 04-574 11 22; www.bled.si; Cesta Svobode 10; ☺8am-9pm Mon-Sat, 9am-5pm Sun Jul & Aug, reduced hours Sep-Jun; ☏) Occupies a small office behind the casino at Cesta Svobode 10; sells maps and souvenirs, rents bikes and has internet access. It's open year-round: outside high season until at least 6pm Monday to Friday, to 3pm Sunday.

TRAVEL AGENCIES

Kompas (☑ 04-572 75 01; www.kompas-bled.si; Bled Shopping Centre, Ljubljanska cesta 4; ☺8am-7pm Mon-Sat) Helpful, full-service travel agency offering sightseeing tours to Bohinj, Radovljica and Ljubljana (among other destinations), plus airport transfers and transport, guiding, and bike and ski rental. Also arranges good-value accommodation in private homes and apartments throughout the region.

❶ Getting There & Away

BUS

Bled is well connected by bus; the **bus station** (Map p94; Cesta Svobode 4) is a hub of activity at the lake's northeast. **Alpetour** (☑ 04-201 32 10; www.alpetour.si) runs most of the bus connections in the Julian Alps region, so check its website for schedules.

Popular services:

Kranjska Gora (€4.70, 50 minutes, 40km, up to 12 daily) Note: these buses depart from Lesce-Bled train station, not from Bled.

Lake Bohinj (€3.60, 37 minutes, 29km, up to 12 daily)

Lesce-Bled train station (€1.30, nine minutes, 5km, up to five an hour)

Ljubljana (€7.80, 70 to 80 minutes, 57km, up to 15 daily)

Radovljica (€1.80, 14 minutes, 7km, at least half-hourly)

TRAIN

Bled has two train stations, though neither one is close to the town centre:

Lesce-Bled station Four kilometres east of Bled township on the road to Radovljica. It's on the rail line linking Ljubljana with Jesenice and Austria. Trains to/from Ljubljana (€5.20 to €7, 40 minutes to one hour, 51km, up to 20 daily) travel via Škofja Loka, Kranj and Radovljica. Buses connect the station with Bled.

Bled Jezero station On Kolodvorska cesta northwest of the lake. Trains to Bohinjska Bistrica (€1.85, 20 minutes, 18km, seven daily), from where you can catch a bus to Lake Bohinj, use this smaller station. You can travel on this line further south to Most na Soči and Nova Gorica.

Lake Bohinj

04 / POP 5100 / ELEV 542M

Many visitors to Slovenia say they've never seen a more beautiful lake than Bled...that is, until they've seen the blue-green waters of Lake Bohinj, 26km to the southwest. Admittedly, Bohinj lacks Bled's glamour, but it's less crowded and in many ways more authentic. It's an ideal summer holiday destination. People come primarily to chill out or to swim in the crystal-clear water, with leisurely cycling and walking trails to occupy them as well as outdoor pursuits like kayaking, hiking and horse riding.

Note there's no actual town called Bohinj; the name refers to the region. At the lake, Ribčev Laz is the main hub, where you can find everything of a practical nature. Ukanc is a smaller hamlet on the lake's southwest shore. To the northeast is a string of idyllic villages: Stara Fužina, Studor and Srednja Vas. The largest town is Bohinjska Bistrica, 6km east of the lake.

◉ Sights

★ **Church of St John the Baptist**   CHURCH
(Cerkev Sv Janeza Krstnika; 04-574 60 10; Ribčev Laz 56; church & bell tower €4, church only €2.50; 10am-4pm Jun-Aug, group bookings only May & Sep) This postcard-worthy church and bell tower, at the head of the lake and beside the stone bridge, dates back at least 700 years and is what every medieval church should be: small, surrounded by natural beauty, and full of exquisite frescoes. The nave is Romanesque, but the Gothic presbytery dates from about 1440. Many walls and ceilings are covered with 15th- and 16th-century frescoes.

★ **Savica Waterfall**   WATERFALL
(Slap Savica; 04-574 60 10; www.bohinj.si; Ukanc; adult/child €3/1.50; 8am-8pm Jul & Aug, 9am-7pm Apr-Jun, to 5pm Sep-Nov) The magnificent Savica Waterfall, which cuts deep into a gorge 78m below, is 4km from Ukanc and can be reached by a walking path from there in 1½ hours. By car, you can continue past Ukanc via a sealed road to a car park beside the Savica restaurant, from where it's a 25-minute walk up more than 500 steps and over rapids and streams to the falls. Wear decent shoes for the slippery path.

Vogel   MOUNTAIN
(04-572 97 12; www.vogel.si; cable car return adult/child €20/10; cable car 8am-7pm) The glorious setting and spectacular panoramas make it worth a trip up Vogel – during winter, when it's a popular ski resort (p104), but also in its 'green season', when walks and photo ops abound. The cable car runs every 30 minutes or so from its base near Ukanc – the base station is at 569m, the top station at 1535m.

Alpine Dairy Farming Museum   MUSEUM
(Planšarski Muzej; 04-577 01 56; www.bohinj.si; Stara Fužina 181; adult/child €3.50/2.50; 10am-7pm Tue-Sun Jul & Aug, 11am-6pm Tue-Sun May, 10am-noon & 4-6pm Tue-Sun Sep, Oct & Jan-Apr) This museum in Stara Fužina, 1.5km north of Ribčev Laz, has a small collection related to Alpine dairy farming – look for it behind Gostilna Mihovc. The four rooms of the museum – once a cheese dairy itself – contain a mock-up of a mid-19th-century herder's cottage, old photographs, cheese presses, wooden butter moulds, copper vats, enormous snowshoes and sledges, and wonderful hand-carved shepherds' crooks.

Oplen House   MUSEUM
(Oplenova Hiša; 04-572 35 22; www.bohinj.si; Studor 16; adult/child €3.50/2.50; 10am-7pm Tue-Sun Jul & Aug, 11am-6pm Tue-Sun May, 10am-noon & 4-6pm Tue-Sun Sep, Oct & Jan-Apr) The hamlet of Studor, about 3.5km from Ribčev Laz, is home to Oplen House – a typical old peasant's cottage with a chimney-less 'black kitchen' that has been turned into a museum focusing on the domestic life of peasants in the Bohinj area.

Studor's real claims to fame are its many *toplarji*, the photogenic, double-linked hayracks with barns or storage areas at the top. Look for the ones at the entrance to the village; they date from the 18th and 19th centuries.

🏃 Activities

Lake Bohinj is filled with activities of all sorts, from active pursuits like canyoning and paragliding from Vogel to more sedate pastimes like hiking, cycling and horse riding. The TIC in Ribčev Laz maintains a list of tour operators and equipment-rental outfits, and can help arrange trips and tours.

Adventure Sports

PAC Sports   ADVENTURE SPORTS
(Perfect Adventure Choice; 04-572 34 61; www.pac.si; Hostel Pod Voglom, Ribčev Laz 60; 8am-10pm Jun-Sep, to 8pm Oct-May) Popular sports and adventure company, based in Hostel Pod Voglom, 2km west of Ribčev Laz; also has a summertime lakeside kiosk at Camp

Lake Bohinj

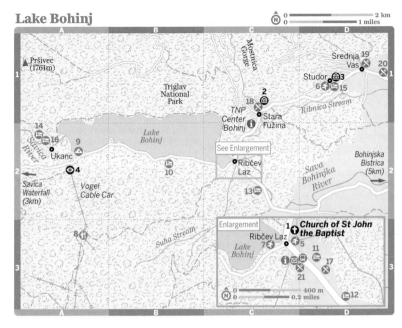

Lake Bohinj

◎ Top Sights

1 Church of St John the
   Baptist..C3

◎ Sights

2 Alpine Dairy Farming
   Museum..C1
3 Oplen House...D1
4 Vogel...A2

⊕ Activities, Courses & Tours

5 Alpinsport..C3
6 Mrcina Ranč..D1
  PAC Sports....................................(see 10)
7 Tourist Boat - Ribčev Laz.....................C3
8 Vogel Ski Centre.................................A3

⊜ Sleeping

9 Camp Zlatorog.....................................A2
10 Hostel Pod Voglom.............................B2
11 Hotel Bohinj..D3
12 Hotel Gasperin....................................D3
13 Hotel Kristal...C2
14 Pension Stare......................................A2
15 Rustic House 13...................................D1
16 Vila Park..A2

⊗ Eating

17 Foksner...D3
18 Gostilna Mihovc...................................C1
19 Gostilna Pri Hrvatu.............................D1
20 Gostilna Rupa......................................D1
21 Mercator...D3

Zlatorog (p106). Rents bikes, canoes, SUPs and kayaks, and operates guided canyoning, rafting and caving trips. In winter, it rents sleds and offers ice climbing and snowshoeing.

Alpinsport   ADVENTURE SPORTS
(☑ 04-572 34 86; www.alpinsport.si; Ribčev Laz 53; ⊙10am-6pm) Rents equipment: canoes, kayaks, SUPs and bikes in summer, skis and snowboards in winter. It also operates guided rafting and canyoning trips. Its base is opposite Hotel Jezero in Ribčev Laz.

Boating

Summertime boating is popular on the lake. Both Alpinsport and PAC Sports rent kayaks, canoes and SUP boards (you're looking at €9 to €12 per hour, with hourly prices decreasing the longer you rent).

Both companies also offer guided rafting and canoeing trips on Lake Bohinj and along the Sava Bohinjka River – PAC Sports has the most options in this category. Prices start at around €35 per person, including equipment, guide and transfers. Expect relatively mild rapids in June and a slower pace by August.

Tourist Boat – Ribčev Laz BOATING
(Turistična Ladja; ☑ 041 353 064; www.tourist-boat.eu; Ribčev Laz; adult/child one-way €9/6.50, return €10.50/7.50; ☺ May-Sep) An easy family-friendly sail from Ribčev Laz to Camp Zlatorog in Ukanc (and back). It's worth checking the timetable online – boats depart Ribčev Laz at 80-minute intervals from 10.50am to 5.30pm.

Cycling

Lake Bohinj is perfect for cyclists of all skill sets – in fine weather, cycling is the best way to get around. There's a well-marked 9km asphalt cycling route running along the Sava Bohinjka River from the village of Stara Fužina to Bohinjska Bistrica (and eventually on to Bled – another 20km). Find the signposted trailhead 300m north of Ribčev Laz on the right just after you enter Stara Fužina. The country road that leads from Ribčev Laz to the villages of Stara Fužina, Studor and Srednja Vas has relatively light traffic and is also suitable for cycling.

From the TIC in Ribčev Laz, pick up the free *Cycling Routes* map, which illustrates routes and their difficulty level. You can rent bikes from many hotels, the TIC, and from both Alpinsport (p103) and PAC Sports (p102) – half-/whole day around €12/16.

Fishing

Lake Bohinj is home to lake trout and char, and the jade-coloured Sava Bohinjka River, which starts at the stone bridge in front of the church in Ribčev Laz, is rich in brown trout and grayling. You can buy fishing licences (lake €25, river as far as Bitnje catch/catch and release €60/42) valid for a day from the TICs and some hotels. The season runs from March/April to November.

The **International Fly Fishing Festival** (www.bohinj.si/ribolov; ☺ Sep-Oct) in the autumn draws anglers from around the world.

Hiking

Lake Bohinj is an ideal destination for hiking and walking. A good easy walk around the lake (12km) from Ribčev Laz should take between three and four hours. Otherwise you could just do parts of it by following the hunters' trail in the forest above the south shore of the lake to Ukanc and taking the bus back, or walking along the more tranquil northern shore under the cliffs of Pršivec (1761m).

The **Zlatorog Fairy Trail** (Zlatorogova pravljična pot) is especially suited for kids and families. The signposted, 2km circular trail starts in Ukanc. Each post along the trail is marked by a different Slovenian fairy-tale figure. The trail is open from May to November. The TICs have more details.

Another excellent hike is the two-hour walk north from Stara Fužina through the Mostnica Gorge to the **Mostnica Waterfalls** (Mostniški Slapovi), which rival Savica Waterfall after heavy rain.

For recreational hikers, a recommended map is the *Bohinj Hiking Trails* map, outlining 22 marked trails and a handful of cycling routes (€6 from the TICs).

There are several day hikes and longer treks that set out from Vogel. Experienced hikers might try the ascent up to Vogel (1922m) from the cable car's upper station. Bring a map and a compass. The whole trip should take about four hours.

Horse Riding

Mrcina Ranč HORSE RIDING
(☑ 041 790 297; www.ranc-mrcina.com; Studor; 1/4hr from €25/60) Pretty Mrcina Ranč in Studor offers a range of guided tours on horseback through unspoiled countryside. Tours can last from one to seven hours; in spring and autumn overnight trips are possible. Tours are on sturdy Icelandic horses; kids can be catered to. Bookings required.

Skiing

Vogel Ski Centre SKIING
(☑ 04-572 97 12; www.vogel.si; day pass adult/child €32/16; ☺ mid-Dec–Mar) Vogel Ski Centre lies 1540m above the lake's southwestern corner and is accessible by cable car from Ukanc. With skiing up to 1800m, the season can be long, sometimes from late November to April. Vogel has 22km of ski runs.

Swimming

Lake Bohinj's chilly waters warm to a swimmable 22°C (72°F) in July and August. Swimming is not restricted and you can enter the water from any point on shore, though there are decent, small beaches on both the northern and southern shores. Some beaches on the northern shore are reserved for naturists.

Aquapark Bohinj WATER PARK
(Vodni Park Bohinj; ☑ 082 004 080; www.vodni-park-bohinj.si; Triglavska cesta 17, Bohinjska Bistrica; pools adult/child 3hr €14/10; ☺ 9am-9pm) This water park is open year-round and overflows with indoor and outdoor pools, slides and play areas, as well as saunas, steam rooms, salt rooms, and fitness and wellness

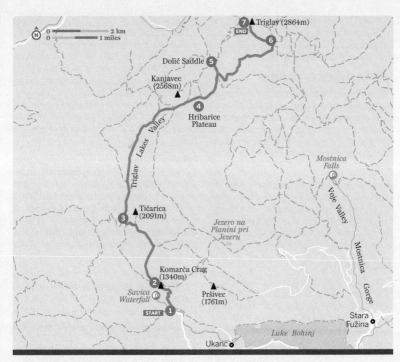

🏃 Walking Tour
Summiting Mt Triglav from Lake Bohinj

START SAVICA WATERFALL
END SAVICA WATERFALL
LENGTH 34KM; THREE DAYS

Approaches to Mt Triglav from Lake Bohinj are longer and involve more ascent than those in the north, but are more gently graded. They are more often used for descent. This option starts from near the **1 Savica Waterfall**, just west of the hamlet of Ukanc at the western end of Lake Bohinj. It's one of the loveliest routes, with vistas of the fantastic Triglav Lakes Valley.

The path immediately heads northwest from the falls as it zigzags up the steep and tricky **2 Komarča Crag** (1340m). A helmet is recommended due to the risk of falling stones. Four hours north of Savica is **3 Koča pri Triglavskih Jezerih** (1685m), at the southern end of the Triglav Lakes Valley, which has lots of beds and a large dining room. This is where you'll spend the first night. For a good view over the valley, provided you still have enough energy, you can

climb to Tičarica (2091m) to the northeast in about an hour.

On the second day, hike north along a ridge overlooking the Triglav Lakes Valley, and then follow the trail northeast to the **4 Hribarice Plateau** (2358m). From here, descend to the Dolič Saddle (2164m) and into the awaiting arms of the **5 Koča na Doliču** hut, at 2151m, for a meal and a second overnight. You could also carry on to **6 Dom Planika pod Triglavom**, about two hours to the northeast and on the way to the summit, but this hut is often packed. Unless you've already reserved a room, it's best to stay where you are. From the Dom Planika pod Triglavom, it's another 1½ hours of steep climbing to the **7 summit of Triglav**.

The descent follows the same path in the reverse direction. Provided you've reached the summit in the morning, you should be able to make your way back to the Koča pri Triglavskih Jezerih hut by late afternoon. On the third day, it's a relatively quick but tricky climb down to the Savica Waterfall and Lake Bohinj.

centres. If you're travelling with kids, it can be a lifesaver in winter or a rainy-day treat in summer. It's located in Bohinjska Bistrica, next to the Bohinj ECO Hotel.

✪✪ Festivals & Events

International Wildflower Festival BOTANICAL
(www.bohinj.si/alpskocvetje; ⊙late May-early Jun) Held over two weeks, this festival celebrates Bohinj's botanical riches and includes guided walks and tours, birdwatching, traditional craft markets and concerts.

Cows' Ball CULTURAL
(Kravji Bal; www.bohinj-info.com; ⊙mid-Sep) The Cows' Ball is a wacky weekend of folk dance, music, eating and drinking to mark the return of the cows from their high pastures to the valleys. It shares the weekend celebrations with a cheese and wine festival.

🛏 Sleeping

From May through September, many houses in Stara Fužina, Studor and Srednja Vas, north of Ribčev Laz, offer private accommodation. Look for the signs 'sobe' or 'apartma', indicating the owners have a room to let.

The TICs can also arrange accommodation in the region: private rooms (€20 to €30 per person), plus apartments and holiday houses. Apartments for two/six in summer start at €50/120. The website www.bohinj.si has more details.

Camp Zlatorog CAMPGROUND $
(☎059 923 648; www.camp-bohinj.si; Ukanc 5; per person €11-15.50; ⊙May-Sep; P🐾) This tree-filled campground can accommodate up to 750 guests and sits photogenically on the lake's southwestern corner, 5km from Ribčev Laz. Prices vary according to site location, with the most expensive (and desirable) sites right on the lake. Facilities are very good – including a restaurant, a laundry and water-sport rentals – and the tourist boat docks here. Tents can be hired.

Hostel Pod Voglom HOSTEL $
(☎04-572 34 61; www.hostel-podvoglom.com; Ribčev Laz 60; dm €16-19, r per person €23-29; P@🐾) Bohinj's lively, well-run hostel, 1.5km west of Ribčev Laz on the road to Ukanc, is a hive of activity – and a hub for activities. There are big grounds, and 130 beds in two buildings: the 'hostel' building has rooms and dorms (maximum four beds), all with shared facilities; rooms in the annexe have private bathrooms.

Hotel Bohinj HOTEL $$
(☎059 113 354; www.hotelbohinj.si; Ribčev Laz 45; s/d €70/90; P@🐾) This Alpine lodge has arguably seen better days but nevertheless offers very good value and is more than likely to have a free room. Simply furnished rooms are large and clean. Many have balconies. Ask for a room overlooking the mountains at the back. The staff is young and eager to please. There's a small garden terrace at the front for coffee.

Pension Stare PENSION $$
(☎040 558 669; www.bohinj-hotel.com; Ukanc 128; s/d €60/90; P🐾) This sweet 10-room pension is on the Savica River in Ukanc, surrounded by a large, peaceful garden. If you really want to get away from it all without having to climb mountains, this is your place. Rooms are no-frills; there's a half-board option too.

Hotel Gasperin HOTEL $$
(☎041 540 805; www.gasperin-bohinj.com; Ribčev Laz 36a; d €80-110; P❄@🐾) This spotless chalet-style hotel is 350m southeast of the Ribčev Laz TIC and run by a friendly British-Slovenian couple who offer loads of local info and insight (including bike hire). Most of the 24 rooms and apartments have balconies; apartments have cooking facilities. The (cheaper) upper-storey rooms can get hot in summer, but each has air-con.

Hotel Kristal HOTEL $$
(☎04-577 82 00; www.hotel-kristal-slovenia.com; Ribčev Laz 4a; half-board per person €50-80; P🐾) There's a great energy at Kristal, thanks in large part to the super-friendly management, walls filled with original artwork, and an Ayurvedic wellness centre and yoga room (plus appealing massage pavilion in the garden). Add some simple, classy guestrooms and a quality restaurant and you can't go wrong. It's about 800m from the lakeshore.

★ Vila Park BOUTIQUE HOTEL $$$
(☎04-572 3300; www.vila-park.si; Ukanc 129; d €100-120; P🐾) Vila Park creates a great first impression, with sunloungers set in expansive riverside grounds, and balconies overflowing with flowers. The interior is equally impressive, with eight elegant rooms plus a handsome lounge and dining area. Note: it's a kid-free zone.

Rustic House 13 PENSION $$$
(Hiša 13; ☎031 466 707; www.studor13.si; Studor 13; ste €160; P🐾) 🖉 Cosy Rustic House

gives you a delightful taste of village life. It's owned by an Australian-Slovenian couple and houses two super suites that each sleep up to four and are rented as an entire unit. Prices drop in May and September. There's a shared kitchen and a lounge – admire Andy's photos of the surrounds (he also offers photography tours).

Bohinj ECO Hotel
HOTEL $$$

(Bohinj Park Hotel; ☑ 082 004 140; www.bohinj-eco-hotel.si; Triglavska cesta 17, Bohinjska Bistrica; per person from €88; P ✳ @ 🛜 🛝) 🏊 We might not have chosen this modern, high-rise at first glance – located in Bohinjska Bistrica it's 6km from Lake Bohinj. But it's a green, eco-minded hotel, it has an excellent in-house restaurant (named 2864, after Triglav's height), there's bowling and a small cinema, and Aquapark Bohinj (p104) is at the back door and included in the price of some rooms.

🍴 Eating & Drinking

Many of the better restaurants are spread out to the north and east of Ribčev Laz, which will require a modest hike, or car or bike to reach. There's a **Mercator** (☑ 04-572 95 32; Ribčev Laz 49; ⊙ 7am-7pm Mon-Sat, to noon Sun) supermarket next to the TIC in Ribčev Laz.

★ Foksner
BURGERS $

(www.facebook.com/foksner; Ribčev Laz 49; burgers €7-10; ⊙ 4-10pm; 🛜) Easily a candidate for the best burger joint in Slovenia, and centrally located, within easy walking distance of the TIC in Ribčev Laz. The burgers are grilled on the deck and served with a side of potato wedges and a locally brewed craft beer or a decent domestic wine. Simple food done very well. Dinner only.

★ Štrud'l
SLOVENIAN $

(☑ 041 541 877; www.facebook.com/gostilnica.trgo-vinica.strudl; Triglavska cesta 23, Bohinjska Bistrica; mains €6-12; ⊙ 8am-10pm; 🛜) This modern take on traditional farmhouse cooking is a must for foodies keen to sample local specialities. Overlook the incongruous location in the centre of Bohinjska Bistrica, and enjoy dishes like *ričet s klobaso* (barley porridge with sausage and beans).

Gostilna Mihovc
SLOVENIAN $

(☑ 04-021 61 06; www.gostilna-mihovc.si; Stara Fužina 118; mains €8-15; ⊙ 9am-11pm) This place in Stara Fužina is popular – not least for its homemade brandy. Try the *pasulj* (bean soup) with sausage (€7) or the beef *golač*

(goulash; €7). Live music on Friday and Saturday evenings. In summer book in advance to secure a garden table.

Gostilna Pri Hrvatu
SLOVENIAN $$

(☑ 031 234 300; Srednja Vas 76; mains €10-18; ⊙ 10am-11pm Wed-Mon) Get an eyeful of mountain views from the sweet creek-side terrace of this relaxed inn in Srednja Vas. Flavourful homemade dishes include buckwheat dumplings, polenta with porcini, local chamois in piquant sauce, and grilled trout.

Gostilna Rupa
SLOVENIAN $$

(☑ 04-572 34 01; www.gostilna-rupa.si; Srednja Vas 87; mains €8-20; ⊙ 11am-9pm) If you're under your own steam, head for this country-style restaurant at the eastern edge of Srednja Vas. Among the excellent home-cooked dishes are *ajdova krapi* (crescent-shaped dumplings made from buckwheat and cheese), various types of local *klobasa* (sausage) and Bohinj trout.

ℹ Information

MONEY

There's an ATM in Ribčev Laz next to the TIC. There's a **Gorenjska Banka** (Trg Svobode 2b, Bohinjska Bistrica; ⊙ 8-11.30am & 2-5pm Mon-Fri) branch next to the post office in Bohinjska Bistrica.

POST

Bohinjska Bistrica Post Office (☑ 04-572 96 41; Trg Svobode 2, Bohinjska Bistrica; ⊙ 8am-6pm Mon-Fri, to noon Sat)

Ribčev Laz Post Office (Ribčev Laz 46a; ⊙ 8am-6pm Mon, to 5pm Tue-Fri, to 11am Sat)

TOURIST INFORMATION

There are two main TICs in the Bohinj area. The office in **Ribčev Laz** (TIC; ☑ 04-574 60 10; www.bohinj-info.com; Ribčev Laz 48; ⊙ 8am-8pm Mon-Sat, to 6pm Sun Jul & Aug, 9am-5pm Mon-Sat, to 3pm Sun Nov & Dec, 8am-7pm Mon-Sat, 9am-3pm Sun Jan, Feb, May, Jun, Sep & Oct; 🛜) is closer to the lake and handier for most visitors than the office in **Bohinjska Bistrica** (LD TURIZEM; ☑ 04-574 76 00; www.ld-turizem.si; Mencingerjeva ulica 10, Bohinjska Bistrica; ⊙ 8am-7pm Mon-Sat, to 1pm Sun Jul & Aug, 9am-noon & 2-6pm Mon-Fri, 9am-1pm Sat, to noon Sun Sep-Jun; 🛜). Both have a wealth of free material, sell souvenirs and local food products, book rooms in private homes, and offer free internet.

Both offices sell the **Bohinj Guest Card** (www.bohinj.si; adult/family €15/20), which entitles the holder to free parking in the lake area and free bus rides, along with discounts at local businesses.

The **national park centre** (☑ 04-578 02 45; www.tnp.si; Stara Fužina 38; ☺ 8am-6pm Jul & Aug, 9am-5pm Apr-Jun, Sep & Oct) in Stara Fužina is well worth a stop.

⊙ Getting There & Away

BUS

The easiest way to get to Lake Bohinj is by **bus** (Ribčev Laz) – services run frequently from Ljubljana, via Bled and Bohinjska Bistrica. **Alpetour** (☑ information 04-201 32 10; www.alpetour.si) is the major bus operator for the region.

Services from Lake Bohinj (departing from Ribčev Laz, near the TIC):

Bled (€3.60, 40 minutes, 29km, up to 12 daily)

Bohinjska Bistrica (€1.80, eight minutes, 7km, up to 20 daily)

Ljubljana (€9.80, two hours, 86km, up to nine daily)

TRAIN

Bohinjska Bistrica station is the closest you can get to the lake by train.

Several trains daily make the run to Bohinjska Bistrica from Ljubljana (€7.30, two hours, six daily), though this route requires a change in Jesenice. There are also trains between Bled's small Bled Jezero station and Bohinjska Bistrica (€1.85, 20 minutes, 18km, seven daily).

From Bohinjska Bistrica, passenger trains to Nova Gorica (€5.80, 1¼ hours, 61km, up to eight daily) make use of a century-old, 6.3km tunnel under the mountains that provides the only direct option for reaching the Soča Valley.

⊙ Getting Around

In July and August there is a bus loop linking Bohinjska Bistrica with the lake via the villages of Stara Fužina, Studor and Srednja Vas, and another loop from Ribčev Laz west to Ukanc, the Vogel cable car and Savica Waterfall (sample fare: Ribčev Laz to Savica €1.80). A timetable is posted at the bus stops, or ask at the TICs.

It's generally necessary to pay for car parking in popular spots around the lake (€2.50 per hour). Buy a Bohinj Guest Card (which includes parking and local buses) if you plan to stay a few days. Or better – leave your car at your accommodation and walk or cycle.

Triglav National Park

☑ 04, 05 / ELEV UP TO 2864M

Triglav National Park (Triglavski Narodni Park; commonly abbreviated as TNP), with an area of 840 sq km (over 4% of Slovenian territory), is one of the largest national reserves in Europe. It is a pristine, visually spectacular world of rocky mountains – the centrepiece of which is Mt Triglav (2864m), the country's highest peak – as well as river gorges, ravines, lakes, canyons, caves, rivers, waterfalls, forests and Alpine meadows.

History

Although Slovenia counts three large regional parks and 44 smaller country (or 'landscape') parks, TNP is the country's only gazetted national park, and it includes almost all of the Alps lying within Slovenia. The idea of a park was first mooted in 1908 and realised in 1924, when 1600 hectares of the Triglav Lakes Valley were put under temporary protection. The area was renamed Triglav National Park in 1961 and expanded 20 years later to include most of the eastern Julian Alps.

Today the park stretches from Kranjska Gora in the north to Tolmin in the south and from the Italian border in the west almost to Bled in the east.

⊙ Sights & Activities

★ Mt Triglav   MOUNTAIN

The 2864m limestone peak called Triglav (Three Heads) has been a source of inspiration and an object of devotion for Slovenes for more than a millennium – it even appears on the country's flag. The early Slavs believed the mountain to be the home of a three-headed deity who ruled the sky, the earth and the underworld.

No one managed to reach the summit until 1778, when an Austrian mountaineer and his three Slovenian guides climbed it from Bohinj. For Slovenes under the Habsburgs in the 19th century, the 'pilgrimage' to Triglav became, in effect, a confirmation of one's ethnic identity, and this tradition continues to this day: a Slovene is expected to climb Triglav at least once in his or her life.

Pokljuka Plateau   NATURE RESERVE

Close to Bled, the forests and meadows of the Pokljuka Plateau offer plenty of walking trails and winter-sports facilities. While Vintgar Gorge (p101) gets all the limelight, the 2km-long Pokljuka Gorge (Pokljuška Soteška) is also impressive, and sees far fewer visitors. Access is possible by bus from Bled to Krnica. Note that Pokljuka is the favoured departure point for ascents of Triglav.

🛏 Sleeping

There are a few hotels, private rooms and campgrounds in the towns within TNP or on its periphery. The Triglav National Park website (www.tnp.si) lists apartments and

CLIMBING MT TRIGLAV

Patriotic locals – and curious tourists – are naturally drawn to Triglav's 2864m-high peak. And despite the fact that on a fine summer's day hundreds of people will reach the summit, Triglav is not for the unfit or faint-hearted. In fact, its popularity is one of the main sources of danger. On the final approach to the top, there are often scores of people clambering along a rocky, knife-edge ridge in both directions, trying to pass each other.

If you are relatively fit and confident, have a good head for heights, and have the right equipment, then by all means go for it. However, we *strongly* recommend hiring a guide, even if you have some mountain-climbing experience. A local guide will know the trails and conditions, and can prove invaluable in helping to arrange sleeping space in mountain huts and trailhead transport. Guides can be hired through activity operators in Bled or Bohinj (p92), or via the TNP info centres or the Alpine Association of Slovenia (p259).

The prime time to climb is from June (or when the snow melts) to mid-October (or before the snow comes); the best months are August and September. Most people allow two days for the trip: one day up and one down.

It bears stressing: never underestimate the extremes of mountain weather. The list of items to take reflects common sense: quality boots, warm clothes, hat, gloves, rain gear, sun protection, map, compass, whistle, head torch, first-aid kit, and emergency food and drink.

Huts are operated by different Alpine clubs, but a comprehensive list is published on the website of the Alpine Association of Slovenia, with contact details and access information. Expect to pay around €25 for a bed. It's always a good idea to book your bed in advance.

There are many ways to reach the peak, with the most popular approaches coming from the south, either starting from Pokljuka, near Bled, or from near Lake Bohinj. You can also climb Mt Triglav from the north and the east (Mojstrana and the Vrata Valley). All of the approaches offer varying degrees of difficulty (differing in altitude and length of ascent) and have their pros and cons.

LAKE BLED & THE JULIAN ALPS TRIGLAV NATIONAL PARK

mountain huts for rent. Away from the towns, accommodation is limited mainly to mountain huts situated along the trails. The Alpine Association of Slovenia (p259) maintains a comprehensive list on its website. Always book in advance. Expect to pay around €25 for a bed.

✖ Eating

Away from the towns, places to eat in the national park are few and far between. Bring food and drink in with you for the trail, though in a pinch you can usually find food at a mountain hut, provided it is open.

Gostilna Psnak　　　　　　SLOVENIAN **$**
(✆04-589 11 52; www.facebook.com/psnak.radovna; Zgornja Radovna 18; mains €8-12; ☺11am-8pm Tue-Sun) Lunch or dinner at this traditional inn within the confines of Triglav National Park, about 15km northwest of Bled, is a just reward for cycling the Radovna bike trail. Enjoy the sausages, sauerkraut, and cottage-cheese-stuffed buckwheat dumplings *(ajdovi krapi)*, all washed down with beer. Eat in or, during nice weather, under the trees with the mountains in the distance.

❶ Orientation

It's easy to enjoy TNP from one of countless hubs – the biggest include Bled, Bohinj, Kranjska Gora, Bovec and Kobarid. One of the most spectacular – and easy – trips to get you to the heart of TNP is to follow the paved road over the Vršič Pass.

These hubs offer natural features you can visit (waterfalls, gorges etc), and activities that grant you access to the park's natural beauty: hiking, mountain biking, skiing, fishing, rafting, swimming. Marked trails in the park lead to countless peaks and summits besides Mt Triglav, but it's not only about climbing mountains. There are easy hikes through beautiful valleys, forests and meadows, too.

❶ Information

Information centres Regular TICs have loads of information, brochures and maps, and there are dedicated TNP info centres at Bled (p101), Stara Fužina in Bohinj and Trenta (p116) on the Vršič Pass. These info centres have great displays on park flora and fauna and are well worth a stop. They have a good program of activities in summer (including guided walks), and can put you in touch with mountain guides.

Julian Alps & Triglav National Park

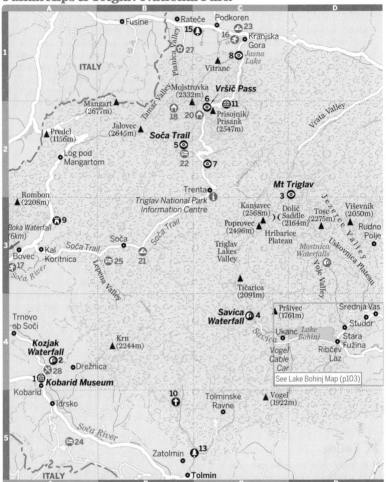

Websites and apps Good starting points are www.tnp.si and www.hiking-trail.net. There is a free app named 'Julius Guide' with coverage of TNP.

Maps Several hiking maps are available from TICs. Two good options: the laminated 1:50,000-scale *Triglavski Narodni Park* (€9.10; buy online from shop.pzs.si) from the Alpine Association of Slovenia (PZS), and Kartografija's widely available 1:50,000-scale *Triglavski Narodni Park* (€8; www.kartografija.si).

Books *The Julian Alps of Slovenia* (Cicerone; www.cicerone.co.uk) by Justi Carey and Roy Clark outlines 58 mountain walks and short treks. Includes high-mountain routes.

🛈 Getting There & Away

BUS

Alpetour (☎ 04-201 31 30; www.alpetour.si) buses link the major towns around Triglav National Park. From here, it's possible to hike or bike into the park itself. From late June through August, Alpetour also runs buses in both directions over the Vršič Pass, connecting Kranskja Gora and Bovec (€7, one hour 40 minutes, 46km) via Trenta. Check the website for timetables; there are at least two departures daily. Buses stop at most of the major landmarks and accommodation on the route.

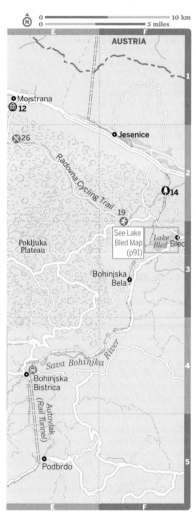

Kranjska Gora

04 / POP 1491 / ELEV 806M

Nestling in the Sava Dolinka Valley some 40km northwest of Bled, Kranjska Gora (Carniolan Mountain) is among Slovenia's largest and best-equipped ski resorts. It's at its most perfect under a blanket of snow, but its surroundings – nudging both the Austrian and Italian borders – are wonderful to explore at other times, too. There are endless possibilities for hiking, cycling and mountaineering in Triglav National Park, which is right on the town's doorstep to the south, and few travellers will be unimpressed by a trip over the Vršič Pass, the gateway to the Soča Valley.

◉ Sights

Slovenian Alpine Museum MUSEUM
(Slovenski Planinski Muzej; ☑083 806 730; www. planinskimuzej.si; Triglavska cesta 49, Mojstrana; adult/child €6/3.60; ⊙9am-7pm Jun–mid-Sep, to 5pm mid-Sep–May) This modern, interactive museum dedicated to mountain exploration is a great rainy-day activity, especially for kids. There are movies showing off the beauty of the peaks, lots of climbing gear and even an escape room. The museum is located in Mojstrana, about 15km south of Kranjska Gora. It's the traditional starting point for the northern approaches to Mt Triglav.

Liznjek House MUSEUM
(Liznjekova Domačija; ☑04-588 19 99; www.gmj. si; Borovška cesta 63; adult/child €2.50/1.70; ⊙10am-6pm Tue-Sat, to 5pm Sun) The endearing 17th-century Liznjek House contains a good collection of traditional household objects and furnishings peculiar to this area. Among the various exhibits are some excellent examples of trousseau chests covered in folk paintings, some 19th-century icons painted on glass and a collection of linen tablecloths (the valley was famed for its flax and for its weaving).

Jasna Lake LAKE
(Jezero Jasna) Jasna Lake lies just south of Kranjska Gora, and if you're heading over the Vršič Pass it's the first spot of interest. It's a small, blue glacial lake with white sand around its rim and the little Pišnica River flowing alongside. Standing guard is a bronze statue of Zlatorog. The lake is a popular recreation area; there's a pocket of accommodation on the hill above.

CAR & MOTORCYCLE
The Vršič Pass, a high-altitude, 50km road that connects Kranjska Gora with Bovec, runs through Triglav National Park and is open most years from May to October. Outside of the pass, vehicle traffic through the park is highly restricted.

TRAIN
Trains service several towns along or near the periphery of the national park, including Bled, Bohinjska Bistrica, Jesenice and Most na Soči.

Julian Alps & Triglav National Park

Zelenci   NATURE RESERVE
(⊙ 24h) FREE About 5km west of Kranjska Gora, signed just off the main road, is this idyllic nature reserve and wetlands. It's the perfect leg-stretcher, with a short path to a turquoise-coloured lake that is the source of the Sava River. You can easily walk here in about an hour on a path from Kranjska Gora via Podkoren following the signs towards Rateče.

Church of the
Assumption of Virgin Mary   CHURCH
(Župnijska cerkev Marijinega vnebovzetja; ☏ 04-588 11 03; Borovška cesta 76; ⊙ hours vary) Kranjska Gora's late-Gothic church, at the centre of town, lends a dignified element to what is, in effect, a ski resort. The church's design dates from 1510 and the Gothic influence can be seen clearly in the ribbed vaulting. The doors are normally open daily from 9am to 6pm, though you can only enter the interior during Mass (times posted by the door).

🏃 Activities

Skiing
Skiing is Kranjska Gora's bread and butter and the resort can get very crowded in January and February. The season usually lasts from mid-December through March.

There are a number of ski schools and ski-rental outlets – a good source of information is the website www.kranjska-gora.si.

Kranjska Gora Ski Centre   SKIING
(RTC Žičnice; ☏ 04-580 94 00; www.kr-gora.si; Borovška cesta 103a; day pass adult/child €34/22; ⊙ Dec-Mar) Kranjska Gora's main ski area is just five minutes' walk from the town centre. The slopes of Vitranc mountain run for several kilometres west to Podkoren and Planica, making effectively one big piste. All up, there are 18 slopes of varying technical difficulty, at altitudes of 800m to 1215m. There's also 40km of cross-country trails, and a fun park for snowboarders.

ASK Kranjska Gora Ski School   SKIING
(☏ 04-588 53 02; www.ask-kg.com; Borovška cesta 99a; ⊙ 9am-4pm Mon-Sat, 10am-6pm Sun mid-Dec–mid-Mar, 9am-3pm Mon-Fri mid-Mar–mid-Dec) The leading ski school in town offers a wide selection of instruction in Alpine skiing and snowboarding. Offers several instruction packages, some combined with ski passes. See the website for details.

Hiking
The area around Kranjska Gora and into Triglav National Park is excellent for hikes and walks, ranging from the very easy to the difficult. Before heading out, buy the 1:30,000-scale *Kranjska Gora* hiking map published by LTO Kranjska Gora and available at the TIC for €6.50 – it details 20 walking routes and 15 cycling tracks.

There's a well-marked trail from Planica to the Category II, 50-bed mountain hut, **Planinski dom Tamar** (Dom v Tamarju; ☏ 04-587 60 55; www.en.pzs.si; per person €10-20), at

1108m in the Tamar Valley – reserve ahead. The one-hour walk here from the Planica Ski-Jump Centre is spectacular, and lies in the shadow of Mojstrovka (2332m) to the east and Jalovec (2645m) to the south. From the hut, the Vršič Pass is about three hours away on foot.

Cycling & Adventure Sports

In recent years, Kranjska Gora has evolved into one of the country's leading centres for mountain biking and Alpine downhilling, the kind of extreme riding where you take your bike up on a chairlift and race downhill.

There are plenty of easier, family-friendly rides as well. The 1:30,000-scale *Kranjska Gora* map (€6.50) marks out 15 cycling routes of varying difficulty. Most of the ski-rental outfits hire out bikes in summer; expect to pay €10 to €20 for full-day rental.

Bike Park Kranjska Gora　MOUNTAIN BIKING
(☑ 041 706 786; www.bike-park.si; Borovška cesta 107; day pass €26, bike rental per day €55; ☉ 9am-5pm daily Jun-Aug, Fri-Sun May, Sep & Oct) On the central slopes of Vitranc, this park is a mecca for mountain bikers – a chairlift takes you up the hill and you descend on trails of varying difficulty. The park offers rental of bikes and protective gear, plus guided and shuttle tours into the surrounding mountains.

Planica Zipline　ADVENTURE SPORTS
(☑ 041 828 151; www.planica-zipline.si; Planica Nordic Centre, Rateče; individual/tandem €25/40; ☉ by appointment only from 11am & 1.30pm daily Jul & Aug, Sat & Sun only Jun & Sep) The operators claim this is the world's steepest zipline, and with a path that glides over the towering Planica Ski-Jump Centre, who are we to argue. The descent runs 566m and takes under a minute. The altitude differential is about 200m. Note: it's mandatory to prebook your spot via the website. The location is 6km west of Kranjska Gora.

✯✯ Festivals & Events

Vitranc Cup　SPORTS
(www.pokal-vitranc.com; ☉ Mar) The number-one downhill ski event of the year for men – the Vitranc Cup – takes place at Kranjska Gora in early March.

🛏 Sleeping

Accommodation demand (and prices) peak from December to March and in midsummer. There are a number of large chain hotels but these are generally pricey and un-inspiring; there are some real gems in the smaller, family-run places, though.

The TIC books private rooms (€20 to €30 per person) and apartments (for two €40 to €60, for four €70 to €100), with prices depending on size, quality and time of year.

Natura Eco Camp　CAMPGROUND $
(☑ 064 121 966; www.naturaecocamp.si; sites per adult/child €15/10, safari tent €150, tree tent €80; ☉ Jun-Sep; 🅿 🛜) 🐾 This back-to-nature campground some 600m north of the highway (signposted) sits in a green glade and is as close to paradise as we've been for a while. Pitch a tent or stay in one of the safari tents or the unique tree tents (great teardrop pods suspended from branches, with mattresses on a platform inside).

To find it from town, head north of the town centre along Koroška cesta, cross the highway and the Sava, and keep walking north.

★ Design Rooms Pr' Gavedarjo　B&B $$
(☑ 031 479 087; www.prgavedarjo.si; Podkoren 72; s €60-80, d €80-150; 🅿 🛜) 🐾 There's a lot to love about this incarnation of a century-old homestead, especially the clever design that celebrates Slovenian heritage and melds old with new in each of its five guestrooms. Added bonus: its location on a pretty village square in Podkoren, 3km west of Kranjska Gora. This place is popular and you'll need to reserve weeks in advance.

Hotel Lipa　PENSION $$
(☑ 04-582 00 00; www.hotel-lipa.si; Koroška cesta 14; s €60-80, d €70-90; 🅿 🛜) Arguably the best hotel in terms of size (just 11 rooms), quality of the room furnishings, views out over the mountains and location – close to the town centre but far enough away to feel removed from the crowds. The restaurant is excellent, as are the buffet breakfasts. Find it just north of the TIC, beside the small bus station.

Hotel Kotnik　HOTEL $$
(☑ 041 671 980; www.hotel-kotnik.si; Borovška cesta 75; s €70-90, d €90-110; 🅿 🛜) This charming, bright-yellow, flower-adorned hotel sits plumb in the heart of town. It has 15 cosy rooms, friendly staff, a great restaurant and pizzeria downstairs, and bikes for hire (€17 per day).

Hotel Miklič　HOTEL $$$
(☑ 04-588 16 35; www.hotelmiklic.com; Vitranška ulica 13; s €80-110, d €120-160; 🅿 🛜) There's warm, personalised service at this pristine 17-room, family-run hotel south of the town

centre. Most of the rooms are large, with living space, and families are well accommodated (there's a kids' playroom). Half-board is possible at the high-quality on-site restaurant. The location is within comfortable walking distance of Jasna Lake.

Skipass Hotel   BOUTIQUE HOTEL **$$$**
(☑04-582 10 00; www.skipasshotel.si; Koroška ulica 14c; r €140-180; P✷🐕🛜) This is a stylish addition to the town's offerings: a 10-room boutique hotel with Scandi-chic, timber-lined rooms. It's run by Skipass Travel and has an excellent restaurant on-site. The more expensive rooms offer balconies and mountain views. Find it about 200m north of the town centre (north of the TIC) and next to the town's small bus station.

✖ Eating

Pick up picnic supplies at the **Mercator** (☑04-583 45 78; Borovška cesta 92; ⊙8am-7pm Mon-Sat, to 1pm Sun) supermarket, located west of the town centre, next to the post office.

Gostilna Pri Martinu   SLOVENIAN **$**
(☑04-582 03 00; Borovška cesta 61; mains €6-15; ⊙10am-11pm) Ask a local where to eat and they'll invariably suggest here: it's an atmospheric tavern-restaurant with a country farmhouse vibe, and you will certainly not leave hungry. Dishes are old-school (house specialities include roast pork, beef goulash, river trout, and sausage with sauerkraut) and the portions are huge.

★**Skipass**
Hotel Restaurant   INTERNATIONAL **$$**
(☑04-582 10 00; www.skipasshotel.si; Borovška cesta 14c; mains €15-21; ⊙5-10pm Mon-Fri, from 1pm Sat & Sun; 🛜) Easily the most upscale dining option in town. The geometric timber feature above the bar creates a fresh first impression and the menu follows its lead. It's an appealing combination of influences from across the nearby Italian and Austrian borders, the food given a local twist and sharp presentation. The three-/five-course chef's menu is €28/45.

Hotel Lipa Restaurant   SLOVENIAN **$$**
(☑04-582 00 00; www.hotel-lipa.si; Koroška cesta 14; mains €8-20; ⊙noon-11pm; 🛜🅿) The in-house restaurant of the Hotel Lipa offers excellent value, with a solid range of pastas and pizzas, plus excellent and affordable up-market main dishes (oven-baked octopus, beefsteak with black truffles). Still relatively

rare for Slovenia, it has vegan and gluten-free pizza options. Eat in or out on the terrace in nice weather.

🍺 Drinking & Nightlife

Vopa Pub   PUB
(☑041 502 908; Borovška cesta 92; ⊙7am-1am Sun-Thu, to 3am Fri & Sat; 🛜) This bar near the post office is practically the only place in town with a pulse after 10pm. The ground-floor pub operates year-round, while a club downstairs is the place to go during the ski season. Count on DJs and a pretty lively aprés-ski scene on weekends.

☆ Entertainment

Planica Ski-Jump Centre   SPECTATOR SPORT
(☑01-200 61 11; www.planica.si; Planica Nordic Centre, Rateče) The gorgeous Planica Valley, 6km west of Kranjska Gora, is renowned for ski jumping and its newly enlarged facilities host frequent competitions (open to spectators) – including the annual Ski Jumping World Cup held in mid-March. Check the website for ticketing info.

❶ Information

Post office (Borovška cesta 92; ⊙8am-6pm Mon-Fri, to noon Sat)

Skipass Travel (☑04-582 10 00; www.ski passtravel.si; Skipass Hotel, Borovška cesta 14c; ⊙7.30am-5pm Mon-Fri, to noon Sat & Sun; 🛜) A full-service travel agency that offers ski instruction and equipment rental, as well as airport transfers and special skiing excursions to nearby Italy and Austria. Based at Skipass Hotel.

Tourist Information Centre (TIC; ☑04-580 94 40; www.kranjska-gora.si; Kolodvorska ulica 1c; ⊙8am-8pm Jun-Sep, to 6pm Oct-May; 🛜) Well-stocked, central TIC, with a cafe and a computer for short-term use. Sells hiking and cycling maps.

❶ Getting There & Away

The closest train station is in Jesenice, 23km southeast of Kranjska Gora. Buses are your best option; these are mainly run by Alpetour (www.alpetour.si). The small **bus stop** (Avtobusna postaja; ☑04-201 32 15; www.alpetour.si; Koroška cesta) is located 200m north of the TIC.

Popular bus routes:

Bled (€6, 64 minutes, 43km) Only two direct services daily – however, there are hourly buses to Lesce-Bled train station (€4.70, 50 minutes, 40km).

Jesenice (€3.10, 28 minutes, 23km, hourly)

Ljubljana (€9, two hours, 91km, up to nine daily)

Vršič Pass Alpetour runs buses to Bovec (€7, one hour 40 minutes, 46km) via Trenta (€5, 70 minutes, 25km) from late June through August. Check the website for timetables; there are two departures daily.

In July and August (and weekends in September), a big red **tourist bus** (day ticket around €9) runs a loop through the villages of the Upper Sava Valley, from Mojstrana to Podkoren and Rateče, with brief stops for photos at Planica and Zelenci; the aim is a hop-on, hop-off bus but it doesn't quite run often enough. Still, if you are without your own wheels, it's worth investigating. Ask at the TIC for the schedule and map.

Vršič Pass

Just a couple of kilometres from Kranjska Gora is one of the road-engineering marvels of the 20th century: a breakneck, Alpine road that connects Kranjska Gora with Bovec, 50km to the southwest. The trip involves no fewer than 50 pulse-quickening hairpin turns and dramatic vistas as you cross the Vršič Pass at 1611m.

The road was commissioned during WWI by Germany and Austria-Hungary in their epic struggle with Italy. Much of the hard labour was done by Russian prisoners of war, and for that reason, the road from Kranjska Gora to the top of the pass is now called the Ruska cesta (Russian Road).

The road over the pass is usually open from May to October and is easiest to navigate by car, motorbike or bus (in summer, buses between Kranjska Gora and Bovec use this road). It is also possible – and increasingly popular – to cycle it.

◎ Sights

★ Vršič Pass   MOUNTAIN PASS
(Prelaz Vršič) Sitting at a view-enhanced elevation of 1611m, this mountain pass is about 13km southwest of Kranjska Gora, via a storied road that zigzags madly and passes numerous sites of interest as it climbs. From the pass itself, the peak-tastic views take in **Mojstrovka** (2332m) to the west and **Prisojnik/Prisank** (2547m) to the east; to the south the valley of the **Soča River** points the way to western Slovenia.

From Kranjska Gora, as the road reaches just over 1100m you come to the beautiful wooden Russian Chapel. From here the climb begins in earnest as the road meanders past a couple of huts and corkscrews up the next few kilometres to the pass itself.

From here, a hair-raising descent of about 10km ends just short of a **monument to Dr Julius Kugy** (1858–1944), a pioneer climber and writer whose books eulogise the beauty of the Julian Alps.

The road continues to the settlements of Trenta and Soča, 8km downstream. The activity hub of Bovec is 12km west of Soča. En route, the narrow **Lepena Valley** is well worth a detour, for accommodation, splendid vistas and a range of walks.

Alpinum Juliana   GARDENS
(☑ 01-241 09 40; www.pms-lj.si/juliana; Trenta; adult/child €3/2; ☉8.30am-6.30pm May-Sep) About 600 different plant species prosper in this botanical garden, established in 1926. Most of them are Alpine species, but because of the relatively low altitude, quite a few Karst species can also be found.

Russian Chapel   HISTORIC BUILDING
(Ruska kapelica; ☑ 04-580 94 40; www.kranjska-gora.si; Vršič Pass) This beautiful wooden Russian Orthodox chapel, at around 1100m approaching from Kranjska Gora, marks the spot where more than 300 Russian POWs perished in an avalanche in March 1916. The interior is often closed and the chapel is not open to the public, but if you do get a chance to peek inside you'll find a simple interior lit by candles. The location is a pretty place to take a break but the walk up to the church is steep.

Trenta   VILLAGE
The elongated mountain village of Trenta (elevation 620m) is the main settlement along the road over the Vršič Pass. The lower section, Spodnja Trenta (Lower Trenta), is home to the Triglav National Park Information Centre (p116). In the same building you'll find the **Trenta Museum** (☑ 05-388 93 30; adult/child €5/3.50; ☉9am-7pm Jul-Aug, 10am-6pm May, Jun, Sep & Oct, 10am-2pm Mon-Fri Jan-Apr, closed Nov-Dec), which focuses on the park's geology and natural history.

☆ Activities

★ Source of the Soča   WALKING
(Izvir Soče) From close to the monument to Dr Julius Kugy on the road over the Vršič Pass, a side road takes you about 1.3km to a simple mountain lodge (named Koča pri Izviru Soče, with beds and food), and from here you can take a 15-minute walk along the first part of the Soča Trail to the source of the Soča River.

Fed by an underground lake, the infant river bursts from a dark cave before dropping 15m to the rocky bed from where it begins its long journey to the Adriatic.

★ Soča Trail WALKING

(Soška Pot; www.soca-trenta.si) The Soča Trail extends 25km along the turquoise Soča River, from its source west as far as the edge of Triglav National Park at Kršovec. From here, a trail known as the **Bovec Walking Trail** continues to Bovec. All up, it's a marked, five-hour, easy walking trail, with scenic highlights including the footbridges that cross the river at several points.

🛏 Sleeping & Eating

Campgrounds abound, especially west of Trenta. There are also several mountain huts on or near the Vršič road, all of which offer beds and basic meals. Expect to pay €20 to €25 per person for a bunk. Most are open from May through September.

The number of quality eating options is limited along the pass, though hotels and guesthouses usually have restaurants. A better idea is to pack a lunch and enjoy it at one of several scenic-view stopovers on the way.

Camp Korita CAMPGROUND $

(☏ 051 645 677; www.camp-korita.com; Soča 38; site per adult/child €12.50/9, glamping per person €16-40; ☺ May-Sep; 🅿) A great riverside spot in Soča, Korita has a smorgasbord of camping choices: regular pitches, plus fab glamping options like wooden A-frame huts, or tents under wooden shelters. You can even choose a sleeping hammock strung between trees. There are more standard mattresses on the floor of the 'hostel', and a couple of old bungalows.

Tičarjev Dom na Vršiču HUT $

(☏ 04-586 60 70, 051 634 571; www.pdjesenice-drustvo.si; Trenta 85; per person €20-30; ☺ mid-May–mid-Sep; 🅿) This category-II cyclists' and hikers' haven has 60 beds and sits right on the pass itself at 1620m. It also has a popular restaurant serving basic meals.

★ Kekčeva Domačija GUESTHOUSE $$$

(Kekec Homestead; ☏ 041 413 087; www.kekceva-domacija.si; Trenta 76; per person €70; 🅿☒) The enchanting Kekčeva Domačija, off the main road and 700m past the source of the Soča, has rooms named after characters in the Kekec children's tales (the eponymous movie

was filmed nearby in 1951). It's a delightful spot, with fabulous food (€85 delivers half-board). There are lovely walks and views, and even a small rock pool for cooling off.

ℹ Information

Triglav National Park Information Centre (Dom Trenta; ☏ 05-388 93 30; www.tnp.si; Trenta; ☺ 9am-7pm Jul-Aug, 10am-6pm May, Jun, Sep & Oct, 10am-2pm Mon-Fri Jan-Apr, closed Nov-Dec) Displays, maps and information on the park, and the region. On-site is the Trenta Museum (p115). There's accommodation upstairs (apartments from €60), a simple restaurant next door and a grocery store across the road.

ℹ Getting There & Away

From late June through August, **Alpetour** (☏ 04-201 31 30; www.alpetour.si) runs buses in both directions over the pass, connecting Kranskja Gora and Bovec (€7, one hour 40 minutes, 46km) via Trenta. Check the website for timetables; there are at least two departures daily. Buses stop at most of the major landmarks and accommodation on the route.

SOČA VALLEY

The Soča Valley region (Posočje) stretches from Triglav National Park to Nova Gorica, including the outdoor activity centres of Bovec and Kobarid. Threading through it is the magically aquamarine Soča River. Most people come here for the rafting, hiking and skiing, though there are plenty of historical sights and locations, particularly relating to WWI, when millions of troops fought on the mountainous battlefront here; between the wars, the Soča Valley fell under Italian jurisdiction. Another big drawcard is the food – Kobarid is the epicentre of the region's growing culinary reputation.

Bovec

☏ 05 / POP 3150 / ELEV 456M

Soča Valley's de facto capital, Bovec offers plenty for adventure-sports enthusiasts. With the Julian Alps above, the Soča River below and Triglav National Park (p108) all around, you could spend a week here rafting, hiking, kayaking, mountain biking and, in winter, skiing, without ever doing the same thing twice. It's beautiful country and Bovec's a pleasant town in which to base yourself for these activities.

◉ Sights

★ Boka Waterfall
WATERFALL

(Slap Boka) With a sheer vertical drop of 106m (and a second drop of 30m), Boka is the highest waterfall in Slovenia – and it's especially stunning in the spring, when snowmelt gives it extra oomph. It's 5.5km southwest of Bovec – you can drive or cycle to the area and park by the bridge, then walk about 15 minutes to the viewpoint.

Kanin Cable Car
CABLE CAR

(☑ 05-917 93 01; www.kanin.si; adult €10-34, child €8-28; ⊙ hours vary) This cable car whisks you up to the Bovec Kanin Ski Centre in a number of stages. It's most often used as an access for winter skiing or summer activities, but it's equally rewarding for sightseers – the views from the top station and en route are sweepingly beautiful. In summer in particular, the last departure heading up the mountain can be as early as 2pm, so it's usually best to visit in the morning.

Kluže Fortress
CASTLE

(Trdnjava Kluže; ☑ 05-388 67 58; www.kluze.net; adult/student/child €3/2/1.50; ⊙ 9am-8pm Jul & Aug, 10am-5pm Sun-Fri, to 6pm Sat Jun & Sep, 10am-5pm Sat & Sun May & Oct) Built by the Austrians in 1882 on the site of a 17th-century fortress above a 70m ravine on the Koritnica River, Kluže Fortress is 4km northeast of Bovec. It was the site of an Austro-Hungarian garrison during WWI, right behind the front line of the Isonzo battlefield. Exhibitions outline its turbulent history. Even more dramatic is the upper fortress, Fort Hermann, built in 1900 halfway up Mt Rombon to the west.

🏃 Activities

Cycling

Ask the TIC for the *Biking Trails* pamphlet, which lists 16 trips of various degrees of difficulty. Most agencies rent mountain bikes from €15/20 for a half-/full day, and offer guided trips (from €30).

Hiking & Walking

The 1:25,000-scale *Bovec z Okolico* (*Bovec and Surrounds*; €7) map lists a number of walks, from two-hour strolls to the ascent of Mt Rombon (2208m), a good five hours one way. Other great areas to explore include Lepena, en route to Trenta; the spectacular Mangart Saddle (at 2072m, reached by Slovenia's highest road); and the Alpine valley of Loška Koritnica. Ask for more info at the TIC.

Closer to town, a number of trails begin and end in Bovec itself. Pick up the free *Hiking Trails in Bovec Land* from the TIC for more information.

Karst Spring (3km, two to three hours) A short trail but with a pretty spring, a waterfall and terrific views.

Great Soča Gorge (4.8km, two to three hours) Relatively easy loop from/to the centre of Bovec, passing the 15m-deep gorge and fine views en route

Soča River (7.6km, three to four hours) Valley-floor trail that begins and ends in Bovec, follows the crystalline river and passes through a couple of small villages.

Zapotok Waterfalls (7.9km, three to four hours) This trail begins and ends at Soča and passes a number of gorgeous waterfalls en route.

Goat Trails (13.4km, five to six hours) A more challenging route that climbs along old goat-herding paths and through forests for stunning views and small villages before returning to Bovec.

Skiing

Kanin Ski Centre
SKIING

(☑ 05-917 93 01; www.kanin.si) Bovec Kanin Ski Centre offers skiing up to 2300m, the highest in Slovenia, often with good spring skiing from November and December into early May. It's a cross-border ski resort, connected to Sella Nevea on the Italian side, and there are plenty of summer activities, including hiking, mountain biking and paragliding as well as a via ferrata.

Rafting & Kayaking

Rafting and kayaking on the beautiful Soča River (10% to 40% gradient; Grades I to VI) is a major draw. The season lasts from April to October, with the highest water levels in the spring. Almost every agency sells trips, and generally travels the same stretch of river (from Boka to Trnovo ob Soči). The stretch of river immediately southeast of Trnovo ob Soči is only for experienced rafters and paddlers.

Companies operate three rafting trips a day in high season. Children are welcome – generally from five years for rafting, eight years for other activities, but this may depend on water levels and weather conditions.

Rafting trips on the Soča over a distance of around 8km (1½ hours) cost around €40 to €50; longer trips may be possible when

BOVEC ADVENTURE-SPORTS AGENCIES

There are dozens of adrenaline-raising companies in Bovec; some specialise in one activity (often rafting), while others offer multiday packages so you can try various activities (rafting, canyoning, kayaking, paragliding, climbing, caving, ziplining). Some agencies offer winter sports too, like dog-sledding and snowshoeing.

Accommodation providers can often book you onto their own (or affiliated) tours and activities. Alternatively, if you choose a package from a sports company, they can usually arrange accommodation as part of the deal.

Central booking offices are generally open long hours in summer (usually 9am to 7pm).

Nature's Ways (☑ 031 200 651; www.econaturesways.com; Čezsoča) Right by the river around 2km from Bovec, this company runs all the usual Bovec activities, including canyoning, rafting, kayaking, ziplining, caving and mountain biking. Reducing plastic pollution is part of its mantra.

Soca Rider (☑ 041 596 104; www.socarider.com; Trg Golobarskih Žrtev 40) Does all of the usual trips, but distinguishes itself by making families and beginners a key part of its offering.

Bovec Rafting Team (☑ 041 338 308; www.bovec-rafting-team.com; Mala Vas 106) On-the-water specialists (rafting, minirafting, kayaking, hydrospeeding, canyoning). Prices start from €50/40 per adult/child for a three-hour rafting trip to €270 for a three-day rafting course. Also offers caving, paragliding and winter activities like snowshoeing and dog-sledding.

Aktivni Planet (☑ 040 639 433; www.aktivniplanet.si; Trg Golobarskih Žrtev 19) Professional outfit that offers multiday packages so you can try all its various activities (rafting, canyoning, kayaking, caving, ziplining, biking, hiking). Affiliated with Hostel Soča Rocks.

water levels are high. Prices include guiding, transport to/from the river, a neoprene suit, boots, life jacket, helmet and paddle. Wear a swimsuit; bring a towel.

Minirafting uses a smaller boat than a raft, carrying two or three people. The key difference: there is no guide in the boat (the guide accompanies you in a kayak). You navigate the waters on your own (with advice), making it good for more-experienced paddlers. Trips cost around €50.

Kayaking courses for beginners are on offer (from €60); guided kayak trips (around 8km) are also available (€50 to €60). Kayaks and canoes can be hired.

If you're experienced and prefer to DIY, a number of companies will rent you equipment and help with transport.

Canyoning & Hydrospeeding

Canyoning along the Soča, in which you descend through gorges, swim through pools, slide down rocks and jump over falls attached to a rope, costs around €50 for a two-hour trip through Bovec agencies. Longer, more-demanding canyons can be tackled for around €90.

Hydrospeeding (also known as riverboarding) is growing in popularity – this involves surfing the rapids with flippers on your feet, holding on to a flotation device. Expect to pay €40 to €50.

🛏 Sleeping

Bovec has some excellent accommodation, across a range of budgets. In addition to hotels and hostels, the TIC has dozens of private rooms and apartments (from €20 per person) on its lists. Don't discount the many scenic options along the road to Trenta towards the Vršič Pass, especially if you have a campervan.

⭐**Adrenaline Check**
Eco Place   CAMPGROUND $
(☑ 041 383 662; www.adrenaline-check.com; Podklopca 4; campsite per person €15, s/d tent from €40/50, safari tent €120-150; ☺May-Sep; P🐾) About 3km southwest of town, this fun, fabulous campground makes camping easy: hire a tent under a lean-to shelter that comes with mattresses and linen, or a big, furnished safari-style tent. Cars are left in a car park, and you walk through to a large, picturesque clearing (so it's not for campervans).

Hostel Soča Rocks   HOSTEL $
(☑ 041 317 777; www.hostelsocarocks.com; Mala Vas 120; dm €13-18, d €35-50; P@🐾) Hostel Soča Rocks is a new breed of hostel: colourful,

spotlessly clean and social, with a bar that never seems to quit. Dorms sleep a maximum of six; there are also a few doubles (all bathrooms shared). Cheap meals are served (including summertime barbecue dinners), and a full activity menu is offered: the hostel is affiliated with Aktivni Planet.

★**Hotel Sanje ob Soči**　　　　　HOTEL **$$**
(☏ 05-389 60 00; www.sanjeobsoci.com; Mala Vas 105a; s/d €80/110; [P] [🖭]) 'Dream on the Soča' is an architecturally striking hotel on the edge of town. Interiors are minimalist and colourful, and room sizes range from 'economy' on the ground floor to studios and family-sized apartments (named after the mountain you can see from the room's windows). There's friendly service, a sauna area, and a great breakfast spread (€12).

★**Pristava Lepena**　　　　　RESORT **$$$**
(☏ 041 671 981, 05-388 99 00; www.pristava-lepena.com; Lepena 2; r from €126; ⊙ mid-May–mid-Oct; [P][🖭][❄]) This positively idyllic 'hotel village' is set in an Alpine meadow above the Lepena Valley. It's a small collection of rustic houses and rooms, run by a charming Slovenian-Uruguayan couple. In a beautiful setting, there's a pool, a high-quality restaurant (open to all), a sauna and a tennis court, and fishing and horse-riding opportunities.

★**Dobra Vila**　　　　BOUTIQUE HOTEL **$$$**
(☏ 05-389 64 00; www.dobra-vila-bovec.si; Mala Vas 112; r €140-270; [P][✳][@][🛰]) This stunning 10-room boutique hotel is housed in an erstwhile telephone-exchange building dating from 1932. Peppered with art deco flourishes, interesting artefacts and objets d'art, it has its own library and a wine cellar, and a fabulous restaurant with a winter garden and an outdoor terrace.

Hotel Boka　　　　　HOTEL **$$$**
(☏ 05-384 55 12; www.hotel-boka.si; Žaga 156a; d €85-115, ste €175-220) Around 6km southwest of Bovec and just past the trailhead for Boka Waterfall, Hotel Boka has a privileged position with lovely views from some rooms and from its terrace bar, as well as from the nearby bridge. The rooms themselves are large and modern, but the colour scheme could do with a little freshening up.

✕ Eating & Drinking

You won't go hungry in Bovec, and there's a handful of good choices sprinkled around the town centre. That said, it lacks the choice of Kobarid or, a little further afield, the appealing local specialities of Idrija.

Gostilna Sovdat　　　　SLOVENIAN **$$**
(☏ 05-388 60 27; www.gostilna-sovdat.si; Trg Golobarskih Žrtev 24; mains €7-22; ⊙ 10am-10pm) Sovdat isn't strong on aesthetics and its outdoor terrace isn't as pretty as others in town, but the crowd of locals attests to its popularity and value. Lots on the menu falls under €10, including plentiful pastas and bumper burgers. You can go upmarket, too, with the likes of gnocchi in a truffle sauce or roast beef with Gorgonzola.

Martinov Hram　　　　SLOVENIAN **$$**
(☏ 05-388 62 14; www.martinov-hram.si; Trg Golobarskih Žrtev 27; mains €8-19; ⊙ 10am-10pm Tue-Fri, to midnight Sat & Sun) This traditional restaurant gets mixed reviews, but on a good day you'll enjoy well-prepared local specialities, including venison, Soča trout and mushroom dishes. The best place to enjoy them is from the street-front terrace, under the grapevines.

Dobra Vila Restaurant　　　SLOVENIAN **$$$**
(☏ 05-389 64 00; www.dobra-vila-bovec.si; Mala Vas 112; 4-/6-course set menu €45/60) Easily the best place to eat in town is the polished restaurant at Dobra Vila – preferably in the pretty garden in summer. A carefully constructed menu of local, seasonal ingredients is served to an appreciative crowd. Setting, service and food are first-class; bookings are essential.

★**Črno Ovca**　　　　　PUB
(www.facebook.com/crnaovca.bovec; Trg Golobarskih Žrtev 18; ⊙ 4pm-midnight Mon-Thu, 10am-3am Fri & Sat, to 11pm Sun) You may have to search for this tucked-away bar, but the Black Sheep is worth the hunt (hint: it's close to Hotel Kanin). Enjoy the relaxed atmosphere, occasional live music and the activities available (kids' playground, petanque, tennis courts for hire) – or just sit and drink in the mountain views.

ℹ Information

Post Office (Trg Golobarskih Žrtev 8; ⊙ 8am-6pm Mon-Fri, to noon Sat) Just northwest of the TIC.

Tourist Information Centre (TIC; ☏ 05-302 96 47; www.bovec.si; Trg Golobarskih Žrtev 22; ⊙ 8am-8pm Jul & Aug, 9am-7pm Jun & Sep, 8.30am-12.30pm & 1.30-5pm Mon-Fri, 9am-5pm Sat & Sun May, shorter hours Oct-Apr) The TIC is open year-round. Winter hours will depend on the reopening of the local ski centre

LONG-DISTANCE HIKING TRAILS

Two popular long-distance hiking trails range through the Soča Valley, from the Alps to the Adriatic, and it's easy for visitors to walk a stage or two: the Alpe-Adria-Trail and the Walk of Peace.

Alpe-Adria-Trail

The transnational Alpe-Adria-Trail (www.alpe-adria-trail.com) links existing paths in three countries, from the foot of the Grossglockner mountain (Austria's highest peak) through varying regions filled with mountains, lakes, rivers and vineyards, then on to Trieste and the Adriatic coast of Italy. The trail is about 700km in length, broken into stages that are roughly 20km long (each stage takes about six hours to walk). The route can be walked in either direction. Several stages pass through Slovenia:

Stage 23 Kranjska Gora to Trenta (19.4km, eight hours) This challenging trail is infinitely rewarding, beginning amid Alpine meadows, climbing through forests, past the salmon-coloured Russian Chapel to the glorious Vršič Pass (1611m) before the steep descent to Trenta.

Stage 24 Trenta to Bovec (21km, 6½ hours) A gentler stage after the exertions of the previous stage, although there's plenty of visual interest as you follow the Soča River down the valley, even including a thrilling crossing of a suspension bridge over the Kršovec Gorge.

Stage 25 Bovec to Drežnica (6km northeast of Kobarid; 22km, 7¼ hours) If you fell in love with the Soča River on Stage 24, you'll love today – the trail follows the river for most of the way, including passing the Boka Waterfall (p117), with mountain views the whole way.

Stage 26 Drežnica to Tolmin (22.1km, eight hours) The first 6km here climbs steeply from 547m to 1236m, but then it's downhill all the way. On the descent, you'll pass the quiet mountain village of Krn.

Stage 27 Tolmin to Tribil di Sopra (Italy; 18.9km, 7½ hours) The moderate trail leaves Slovenia and crosses into Italy after around 9km.

Full details are on the website, including route details, accommodation, and trip packages.

Walk of Peace

The 320km-long Walk of Peace (Pot Miru; www.potmiru.si) connects the outdoor museums and the most important remains and memorials of the Isonzo Front of the Upper Soča region. It was along this front (p140) that some of the most important and most devastating battles of WWI took place; more than 300,000 people lost their lives from 1915 to 1917. Along the way, you'll pass cemeteries, commemorative chapels and other monuments dedicated to keeping alive the memory of those times and those who were killed.

The oldest, best-known section of the walk ranges in five sections from Log pod Mangartom in the north to near Tolmin in the south; there's an excellent visitor centre (p122) in Kobarid where you can get information. Guiding is possible too, especially at the 15 outdoor museums that you'll pass along the way.

(p117) – expect long hours when the ski season is fully operating.

ℹ Getting There & Away

Popular bus routes:

Kobarid (€3.30, 30 minutes, 22km, five daily)
Ljubljana (€14, 3¾ hours, 151km, three daily)
Vršič Pass Busline **Alpetour** (☑ 04-532 04 45; www.alpetour.si) runs buses to Kranjska Gora (€7, 1¾ hours, 46km) via Trenta (€2.90, 30 minutes, 20km) from May through September. Check the website for timetables; there are five or six departures daily.

Kobarid

☑ 05 / POP 4143 / ELEV 231M

Charming Kobarid is quainter than nearby Bovec, and despite being surrounded by mountain peaks it feels more Mediterranean than Alpine, with an Italianate look (the border at Robič is only 9km to the west).

On the surface not a whole lot has changed since Ernest Hemingway described Kobarid (then Caporetto) in *A Farewell to Arms* (1929) as 'a little white town with a campanile in a valley', with 'a fine fountain in the square'. The bell in the tower still rings on the hour, but the fountain has sadly disappeared.

History

Kobarid was a military settlement during Roman times, was hotly contested in the Middle Ages and was hit by a devastating earthquake in 1976, but the world will always remember it as the site of the decisive battle of 1917 in which the combined forces of the Central Powers defeated the Italian Army.

⊙ Sights

The centre of town is Trg Svobode, dominated by the **Church of the Assumption** (Trg Svobode; ⊙ hours vary) and the bell tower made famous by Hemingway.

★**Kobarid Museum**   MUSEUM
(Kobariški Muzej; ☑ 05-389 00 00; www.kobariski-muzej.si; Gregorčičeva ulica 10; adult/child €6/2.50; ⊙ 9am-6pm Apr-Sep, 10am-5pm Oct-Mar) This museum is devoted almost entirely to the Soča Front and the 'war to end all wars'. Themed rooms describe powerfully the 29 months of fighting, and there's a 20-minute video (available in 10 languages) that gives context. There are many photos documenting the horrors of the front, military charts, diaries and maps, and two large relief displays showing the front lines and offensives through the Krn Mountains and the positions in the Upper Soča Valley.

★**Kozjak Waterfall**   WATERFALL
(Slap Kozjak) One of the region's loveliest short walking trails (approximately 30 minutes) leads to the photogenic, 15m-high Kozjak Waterfall, which gushes over a rocky ledge in a cavern-like amphitheatre, into a green pool below. Access the trail from various spots: from a footbridge from Kamp Lazar campground, or from a car park opposite Kamp Koren. Alternatively, it's part of the Kobarid Historical Trail.

🏃 Activities

Kobarid doesn't quite keep to the same frenetic pace as nearby Bovec, but it still has a handful of operators who can get you active (and usually rather wet). There's also good hiking in the area.

X Point   ADVENTURE SPORTS
(☑ 05-388 53 08; www.xpoint.si; Trg Svobode 6) Operates from its base at X Point Hostel, with the usual water-borne activities (rafting, kayaking etc) and mountain biking, and it's the place to come for tandem-paragliding.

Positive Sport   ADVENTURE SPORTS
(☑ 040 654 475; www.positive-sport.com; Trg Svobode 15) Offers rafting, canyoning, kayaking and mountain biking. Bookings can be made online, or at its office on the main square.

🎊 Festivals & Events

★**Drežnica Carnival**   CARNIVAL
On the Sunday before Lent, head for Drežnica, 6km northeast of Kobarid one of Slovenia's most cherished festivals. Unmarried young men and boys don handmade wooden masks, either Ta Lepi (the Pretty Ones) or Ta Grdi (the Ugly Ones). The former visit

---

KOBARID HISTORICAL TRAIL

The TIC (p122) offers a free brochure describing the 5km-long Kobarid Historical Trail.

From the Kobarid Museum walk to the north side of Trg Svobode and take the winding road lined with the Stations of the Cross to the **Italian Charnel House** (Italijanska Kostnica), which contains the bones of more than 7000 Italian soldiers killed on the Soča Front. It's topped by the 17th-century **Church of St Anthony**.

From here, a path leads north (bearing left) for just over 1km to the ancient fortified hill of **Tonocov Grad**, then descends through the remains of the **Italian Defence Line** (Italijanska Obrambna Črta), past cleared trenches, gun emplacements and observation posts, before crossing the Soča over a 52m footbridge. A path leads up a side valley that takes you to the foot of the beautiful Kozjak Waterfall. The return path leads over **Napoleon Bridge** (Napoleonov Most), a replica of a bridge built by the French in the early 19th century and destroyed in 1915, and finishes at a small **Cheese Museum** that explores the local cheese-making tradition, just a short walk from the trail's starting point.

every house in the village to wish the inhabitants well and receive gifts in return.

🛏 Sleeping

X Point Hostel
HOSTEL $

(☑ 05-388 53 08; www.xpoint.si; Trg Svobode 6; per person €16-20; 🛜) Above its town-centre activity base, X Point offers six small, neat hostel rooms, with shared bathrooms plus kitchen and laundry facilities.

Hemingway House
APARTMENT $$

(☑ 040 774 106; www.hemingwayhouseslovenia. com; Volaričeva ulica 10; apt €40-70; 🛜) A good-value option in the town centre, honouring Papa Hemingway and owned by Marie, a Canadian. The house has five apartments (each with a bathroom and a kitchen) over three floors – they sleep between two and five people, and share a lovely garden where breakfast (€5) can be served. In the rooms, we like the exposed wooden beams. Off-season and weekly rates too.

⭐ Hiša Franko
GUESTHOUSE $$$

(☑ 05-389 41 20; www.hisafranko.com; Staro Selo 1; r €120-150; 🅿🛜) This foodie favourite is in an old farmhouse 3km west of Kobarid in Staro Selo, halfway to the Italian border. Here 10 rooms ooze character, with rich colours and fabrics and interesting artworks. A handful of rooms have huge bathtubs; others have terraces. All partake in a sumptuous breakfast (€20 per person). And best of all: the acclaimed restaurant downstairs.

⭐ Nebesa
CHALET $$$

(☑ 05-384 46 20; www.nebesa.si; Livek 39; d €185-275; 🅿🛜) The name translates as 'Heaven', and it's fitting. These four heavenly mountain retreats sit at the top of a 7km winding road from Idrsko village (2km south of Kobarid) and enjoy stupendous views. Each sleeps two and is large and self-contained, with a kitchenette and a terrace; there's also a communal house with a kitchen and a wine cellar, plus saunas.

✖ Eating

⭐ Restaurant Lazar
SLOVENIAN $$

(☑ 05-388 53 33; www.lazar.si; Trnovo ob Soči 1b; mains €7-22; ⊗ 8am-10pm Apr-Oct, shorter hours Nov-Mar) Where do top locals chefs recommend for a casual meal? This fun, rustic outdoor restaurant-bar at the riverside Lazar holiday centre (camping and quality rooms also available). Its menu ranges from cheap, filling pancakes to Black Angus steaks, and

fire-roasted lamb and pork ribs. It's well placed for the walk to/from Kozjak Waterfall.

⭐ Hiša Franko
SLOVENIAN $$$

(☑ 05-389 41 20; www.hisafranko.com; Staro Selo 1; 6-/8-course set menu €125/150, wine pairing €50/75; ⊗ noon-4pm Mon, 5-11pm Wed-Fri, noon-4pm & 7-11pm Sat & Sun Jun-Sep, closed Mon Oct-May) Provenance is everything at this restaurant in Staro Selo, just west of town and one of the best in the country. Menus change with the seasons and showcase produce from Chef Ana's garden, plus berries, trout, mushrooms, cheese, meat and fish delivered by local farmers. The resulting dishes are innovative and delicious, and ably paired with top-notch wines. Service is first class.

Topli Val
SEAFOOD $$$

(☑ 05-389 9300; www.hotelhvala.si; Trg Svobode 1; mains €11-46; ⊗ noon-3pm & 6-10pm; 🍴) Seafood is the focus of the menu, and it's excellent, from the carpaccio of sea bass to the Soča trout and signature lobster with pasta. It's not exclusively aquatic – the 'mountains meet the sea' here: venison is also a speciality, and vegetarians will fare well. For dessert, try the *kobariški štruklji*.

ℹ Information

Tourist Information Centre (TIC; ☑ 05-380 04 90; www.soca-valley.com; Trg Svobode 16; ⊗ 9am-8pm Jul & Aug, 9am-1pm & 2-7pm Mon-Fri, 9am-1pm & 4-7pm Sat & Sun May, Jun & Sep, 9am-4pm Mon-Fri, 10am-4pm Sat Oct-Apr) Good local maps and brochures, plus information on Triglav National Park (p108).

Walk of Peace Visitor Centre (Pot Miru; ☑ 05-389 01 67; www.potmiru.si; Gregorčičeva ulica 8; ⊗ 9am-1pm & 2-7pm daily Jul-Aug, shorter hours rest of year) Based opposite the Kobarid Museum, this foundation provides information about the Walk of Peace (p120) long-distance trail and the various heritage sites of the Soča Front. There are maps and books, plus guiding services can be organised.

ℹ Getting There & Away

The closest train station is at Most na Soči (22km south, and good for trains to/from Bohinjska Bistrica and Bled Jezero).

Buses stop in front of the Cinca Marinca bar-cafe at Trg Svobode 10. Popular bus services from Kobarid include the following:

Bovec (€3.30, 30 minutes, 22km, five daily) In July and August, two of these services connect with buses over the Vršič Pass to Kranjska Gora.

Ljubljana (€12.20, 3¼ hours, 131km, four daily)

THE SCENIC GORGES OF TOLMIN

Tolmin (population 11,646), a town in the Soča Valley 16km southeast of Kobarid, is enjoying a growing reputation as a paragliding hot spot and as a summertime music-festival hub – annual metal, punk rock and reggae festivals are staged in July and August. We like Tolmin best for some of the natural attractions on its doorstep and a pretty stone-and-wood church.

Tolmin Gorges (Tolminska Korita; ☑ 05-380 04 80; www.soca-valley.com; adult/child €5/2.50 Sep-Jun, €6/3 Jul & Aug; ☉ 8.30am-7.30pm Jun-Aug, shorter hours Apr, May, Sep & Oct) A scenic river confluence is found here, at the southernmost entry point of Triglav National Park (p108). The ticket kiosk is a 2km walk northeast of Tolmin town (by road, follow the signs to Zatolmin), and the circular **walk** through the gorges formed by the Tolminka and Zadlaščica Rivers takes about an hour. A short detour off the main path leads to the much-photographed **Medvedova glava**, a wedged rock in the shape of a bear's head.

Most na Soči The name of this settlement 5km south of Tolmin literally means 'Bridge on the Soča River'. The village (population 430) sits, in fact, on a beautiful aquamarine lake – surprisingly, it's an artificial lake at the confluence of the Soča and Idrijca Rivers, created by a nearby hydroplant. It's a super-scenic place to pause for a lakeside walk or for some boating; rowboats and kayaks can be hired.

Memorial Church of the Holy Spirit (☑ 05-380 04 80; Javorca; adult/child €4/2; ☉ 10am-7pm mid-Jun–Aug, shorter hours rest of year) This fascinating stone-and-wood church, north of Tolmin, has a wonderful location that commands sweeping views down an Alpine valley. Decorated by Remigius Geyling, contemporary and friend of Gustav Klimt, it was built in the early 20th century to commemorate the fallen soldiers of the Austro-Hungarian Empire who died along the Soča Front; the 20 coats of arms that adorn the exterior reference 20 of the empire's provinces.

Most na Soči (€3.25, 50 minutes, 22km, five daily)
Tolmin (€2.90, 20 to 30 minutes, 18km, eight daily)

CENTRAL PRIMORSKA

If you're heading to the Soča Valley from Ljubljana (rather than through the Julian Alps), you'll pass through central Primorska, a land of steep slopes, deep valleys and innumerable ravines with plenty of good hiking. The region is dominated by the Cerkno and Idrija Hills, foothills of the Julian Alps. The towns here don't feature too high on traveller radars, but that, combined with some quirky attractions, may be a large part of their appeal.

Idrija

☑ 05 / POP 5860 / ELEV 325M

Idrija means three things: *žlikrofi,* lace and mercury. The women of Idrija have been taking care of the first two for centuries, while the men went underground to extract the

latter, making Idrija one of the richest towns in Europe during the Middle Ages. In 2012 Unesco granted World Heritage status to Idrija's mercury mine (together with a similar mine in Almadén, Spain). Aside from these rather disparate attractions, Idrija is a pretty provincial town that makes a fine base for this corner of the region.

History

The first mine opened at Idrija in 1500; within three centuries Idrija produced 13% of the world's quality mercury. Its uses ranged widely, from the extraction of gold and silver in the mines of the New World to treatments for syphilis. Miners faced many health hazards, but the relatively high wages attracted workers from all over the Habsburg Empire and because of the toxic effects of mercury, doctors and lawyers flocked as well.

The mines are no longer in operation, but their legacy remains: Idrija sits on 700km of shafts that descend 15 levels, and expensive measures continue to be taken to ensure the town doesn't sink.

Idrija

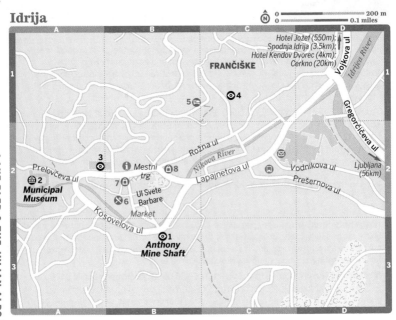

Idrija

◉ Top Sights

◉ Sights

⚑ Sleeping

✕ Eating

🛍 Shopping

◉ Sights

★ Municipal Museum

MUSEUM

(Mestni Muzej; ☎ 05-372 66 00; www.muzej-idrija-cerkno.si; Prelovčeva ulica 9; adult/child €5/3; ⊗ 9am-6pm) This award-winning museum is housed in the hilltop **Gewerkenegg Castle** (Prelovčeva ulica 9). The excellent collections, which deal with mercury, lace and local history (but, sadly, not *žlikrofi*) are exhibited in three wings centred on a beautiful courtyard, and an accompanying booklet guides visitors through the rooms.

Exhibits span rocks and fossils (and a bowl of mercury in room 3) to lifestyles of the miners and the growth of the town. Head down the steps of the Mercury Tower (room 7) to see the mining tools used, and also the lovely modern sculpture of mercury drops suspended in perspex.

Another highlight is the wing given over entirely to the bobbin lace *(klekljana čipka)* woven here. Check out the tablecloth that measures 3m by 1.8m. It was designed for Madame Tito and took 5000 hours to make.

The castle itself was built in the 1520s to serve as the administrative headquarters of the Idrija mine.

★ Anthony Mine Shaft

MINE

(Antonijev Rov; ☎ 05-377 11 42; www.cudhg-idrija.si; Kosovelova ulica 3; adult/child €10/5; ⊗ tour 10am, noon, 2pm, 3pm & 4pm daily Jul & Aug, 10am & 3pm Mon-Fri, 10am, 3pm & 4pm Sat & Sun Mar-May, Oct & Nov, 10am & 3pm Sat & Sun Dec-Feb) The mine is a 'living museum', allowing you to get a feel for the working conditions of mercury miners in Idrija. The entrance is the Anthony Shaft, built in 1500, which led to the first mine: 1.5km long, 600m wide and 400m deep. The tour covers about 1200m and lasts 1½ hours; it begins in the 'call room' of an 18th-century building where miners were selected each morning and assigned their duties.

Wild Lake NATURE RESERVE

(Divje Jezero) A 3km trail called **Pot ob Rakah** follows the Idrijca River Canal from the **Kamšt** (an 18th-century waterwheel used by the mines) to Wild Lake, a tiny, impossibly green lake fed by a deep karst spring. After heavy rains, water gushes up from the tunnel like a geyser and the lake appears to be boiling. With your own wheels, take the road out of town towards Ljubljana and turn at the sign to Idrijska Bela – it's 600m to the lake.

Miner's House NOTABLE BUILDING

(Rudarska Hiša; ☑ 05-372 66 00; www.muzej-idrija-cerkno.si; Bazoviška 4; adult/child €3/2; ☺ 9am-4pm by appointment) Laid out across the slopes encircling the valley are Idrija's distinctive miners' houses. Large wooden A-frames with cladding and dozens of windows, they usually had four storeys with living quarters for three or four families. You can visit a traditional miner's house above the town centre accompanied by a guide from the museum.

Idrija Lace School WORKSHOP, MUSEUM

(Čipkarska Šola Idrija; ☑ 05-373 45 70; www.cipkarskasola.si; Prelovčeva ulica 2; adult/child €2.50/free; ☺ 8am-3pm Mon-Sat Jul-Aug, 10am-1pm Mon-Fri Sep-Jun) The Idrija Lace School was founded in 1876 (it's the biggest and oldest lace school in the world), and continues to offer lace-making skills to younger generations. The showroom exhibits remarkable pieces made by students aged six to 15. There are also items for purchase, made locally.

★✿ Festivals & Events

Lace Festival CULTURAL

(Festival Idrijske Čipke; www.festivalidrijskecipke.si; ☺ mid-Jun) The big event in Idrija is the three-day Lace Festival in mid- to late June. This celebration of all things lacy includes a gala opening, lace-making exhibitions and live music.

🛏 Sleeping

Idrija's hotels are generally of a high standard, although there are few genuinely mid-range options. The TIC has a list of private rooms available from €20 per person.

Hostel Idrija HOSTEL $

(☑ 05-373 40 70; www.youth-hostel.si; Ulica IX Korpusa 17; dm/d from €11/26; ⓟ 🛜) Basic budget beds with shared bathroom, about 600m northeast of Mestni trg.

Na Kluk B&B B&B $$

(☑ 05-143 54 97; www.nakluk.si; Govejk 14c, Spodnja Idrija; s/d €40/70) Out along the quiet backroads east of Spodna Idrija, this lovely farmhouse has modern rooms all decked out in pine and wicker with tiled floors. Meals are available and the whole place has a real country warmth. You'll need your own wheels.

★ Na Kupčku Estate APARTMENT, COTTAGE $$$

(☑ 03-161 64 11; www.nakupcku.com; Čeokvnik 22; apt 1/2/3/4 people €105/115/125/135; ⓟ 🛜) Now here's something really special. Saša

LAKE BLED & THE JULIAN ALPS IDRIJA

STONE AGE MUSIC

Despite our preconceptions, our prehistoric forebears were a sophisticated bunch. In 1995 palaeontologists looking for Stone Age tools were directed to Divje Babe, a cave some 200m above the main road linking Cerkno with the Tolmin–Idrija highway. After careful digging they found a piece of cave bear femur measuring 10cm long and perforated with four aligned holes (two intact, two incomplete) at either end. It looked exactly like, well, a flute.

The flute was dated using electron spin resonance techniques and is believed to be around 43,000 years old. Although dubbed the 'Neanderthal flute' in Slovenia, some debate persists about whether or not it was made by that species or by Cro-Magnons – modern humans. (There is also conjecture that the punctures may simply have been made by a carnivore bite, but studies cast doubt on this theory.)

If it *is* a flute, Slovenia can claim the oldest known musical instrument on earth. And – in case you were wondering – it could play a tune (search for 'Neanderthal Bone Flute Music' on YouTube, in which a replica is played). It's on display at the National Museum of Slovenia (p59) in Ljubljana.

and Jure have built the most marvellous little escape in the forested hills, 9km from Idrija. The apartment, designed with impeccable taste, has fine views and you could easily spend a week or more here. They've also built a cottage from wood found on the property. Meals can be arranged.

★**Hotel Kendov Dvorec**　　　　　HOTEL **$$$**
(☑05-372 51 00; www.kendov-dvorec.com; Na Griču 2, Spodnja Idrija; s/d from €130/180; P🅟🛜) The most charming, romantic option in the area is this 'castle hotel' 4km north of Idrija. There are 11 rooms in a converted manor, the oldest part of which dates from the 14th century. Antique furniture, pretty gardens and dreamy views along the Idrijca Valley are central to the allure.

✖ Eating

There are few standout dining venues, but you're able to get your fill of *žlikrofi* everywhere.

Gostilna Pri Škafarju　　　　SLOVENIAN **$**
(☑05-377 32 40; www.skafar.si; Ulica Svete Barbare 9; mains €9-18; ⊙10am-4pm Mon-Thu, to 9pm Fri & Sat, 11am-8pm Sun) Pizza baked in a wood-burning tile stove is why many people come to this welcoming *gostilna,* but there are plenty of other items on the menu, such as a tasting plate of *žlikrofi* with various sauces (for two people; €20) and *štruklji* (pastries) of spinach and cheese.

★**Hotel Jožef**　　　　　　　SLOVENIAN **$$**
(☑082 004 250; www.hotel-jozef.si; Vojkova 9a; mains €8-20; ⊙noon-3pm & 6-10pm) The word among locals is that this hotel restaurant is the best place in town to try *žlikrofi,* cooked in the traditional way with mutton sauce.

Otherwise, the inventive menu includes a lovely red polenta starter, rabbit and even buffalo carpaccio.

🛍 Shopping

Idrija lace is among the finest in the world, and a small piece makes a great gift or souvenir. There are numerous shops across town.

Studio Koder　　　　　　ARTS & CRAFTS
(☑05-377 13 59; www.idrija-lace.si; Mestni trg 16; ⊙10am-noon & 4-7pm Mon-Fri, 10am-noon Sat) Of all the lace shops in town, we like the superior Studio Koder, a small, but stylish shop across from the TIC – the quality is unimpeachable, and there's no hard sell.

Vanda Lapajne　　　　　　ARTS & CRAFTS
(☑04-163 12 33; www.vanda-lapajne.si; Mestni trg 13; ⊙4-7pm Tue & Wed, 9am-noon Thu-Sat) An excellent lace shop that's been in the same family since 1875, Vanda Lapajne has the usual tablecloths and the like, but also some modern takes on the whole lace obsession with earrings, bracelets and handbags.

ⓘ Information

Post Office (Vodnikova ulica 1; ⊙8am-6pm Mon-Fri, to noon Sat)
Tourist Information Centre (TIC; ☑05-374 39 16; www.visit-idrija.si; Mestni trg 2; ⊙9am-7pm Mon-Fri, to 6pm Sat & Sun May-Sep, to 4pm Mon-Fri, 10am-3pm Sat & Sun Oct-Apr) Centrally placed; can help with info and accommodation.

ⓘ Getting There & Away

From the **bus station** (Lapaijnetova ulica), services include the following:

ŽLIKROFI: SLOVENIA'S TASTY PASTA POCKETS

Idrijski žlikrofi are pasta pockets not unlike small ravioli; they're made from egg-flour dough with a potato filling (with pork fat or lard, or smoked bacon, onion and herbs); in 2010 they were awarded a protected geographical status (the first Slovenian dish to get such recognition). One local legend holds that *žlikrofi* were first made on the occasion of Napoleon Bonaparte's visit to Idrija, and that his mistress made the dumplings for him in the shape of his hat. More seriously, the making of *žlikrofi* is a prescribed art form – to be recognised as the authentic article, they must be 3cm long and 2cm high; the imprint on top comes from the maker's finger and is considered his or her personal signature.

Traditionally they are eaten with *bakalca,* a meat sauce made with mutton, but they are also popular with Gorgonzola, mushrooms or pork. They can be served as a main dish, or as a side. You'll find them elsewhere in Slovenia, but they somehow taste better at the source.

Idrija's residents eat *žlikrofi* year-round, but they celebrate it with special gusto on the first Saturday in September with tastings at the city's restaurants and other events.

VOJSKO & NAŠRAJ: ALPINE MEADOWS & SLOW FOOD

If you have your own wheels and have time for a three-or-more-hour excursion, consider driving up to **Vojsko**, the highest village in the area and a 14km drive from Idrija. Lovely Alpine meadows and superlative views in every direction are the main attraction, quite apart from the quiet pleasures of visiting a non-touristy Slovenian mountain village. The TIC in Idrija has a brochure on Vojsko, with a map and directions on how to reach its Partisan cemetery. Vojsko is signposted on Idrija's western boundary – take Ulica Henrika Freyija, then follow the signs.

Continuing north of Vojsko, **NašRaj** (☑04-045 09 09; www.kmetijanasraj.net; Gorenja Trebuša 91; ⊙Fri-Sun Apr-Nov) is a fine add-on. Describing this place as a farm doesn't do it justice. This ecological farm, for want of a better word, sits almost 1000m above sea level around 20km from Idrija, and is a terrific place. Take a tour of the farm, learn about the organic philosophy behind it and enjoy a culinary experience of tastings – it's a member of the Slow Food international movement. Ring ahead for directions and to let them know you're coming. There's also accommodation if you love the place so much you can't bear to leave.

Bovec (€10.30, 2½ hours, two daily) Via Tolmin and Kobarid.

Cerkno (€3.25, 28 minutes, hourly)

Ljubljana (€6.90, 1¼ hours, roughly hourly)

Cerkno

☑05 / POP 4650 / ELEV 323M

A sleepy village in the broad Cerknica River Valley, Cerkno is close to a remarkable WWII Partisan hospital hidden in a gorge and that alone is reason enough to visit. It's also an important destination for ethnologists and party-goers alike when the Laufarija, the ancient Shrovetide celebration, takes place. Cerkno's ski centre, around 10km away, is one of Slovenia's best, ensuring a busy winter season.

It's best not to visit Cerkno on a Monday, when both the museum and the TIC are closed.

⊙ Sights

★**Franja Partisan Hospital**   MEMORIAL
(Partizanska Bolnica Franja; ☑05-372 31 80; www.muzej-idrija-cerkno.si; adult/child €5/3; ⊙9am-6pm Apr-Sep, to 4pm Oct) This clandestine hospital, hidden in a canyon near Dolenji Novaki, about 5km northeast of Cerkno, treated wounded Partisan soldiers from Yugoslavia and other countries from late 1943 until the end of WWII. A memorial to humanity and self-sacrifice, it had more than a dozen wooden cabins, including treatment huts, operating theatres, X-ray rooms and huts for convalescence. Some 578 wounded were treated here, and of these only 78 died.

The complex, hidden in a ravine by a stream, had an abundance of fresh water, which was also used to power a hydroelectric generator. Local farmers and Partisan groups provided food, which was lowered down the steep cliffs by rope; medical supplies were diverted from hospitals in occupied areas or later air-dropped by the Allies. The hospital came under attack by the Germans twice but it was never taken.

The hospital was almost entirely destroyed by flood in 2007, and has been completely reconstructed. It's extremely well done, with detailed information panels in both English and Slovene in each building; access is via a lovely 500m stream-side walking path.

🏃 Activities

The brochure *Cerkno Map of Local Walks*, available from the TIC and Hotel Cerkno, lists eight walks in the Cerkno Hills (Cerkljansko Hribovje), most of them pretty easy and lasting 1½ to four hours return. One walk leads to the Franja Partisan Hospital. The *Cerkno Cycling Tracks* brochure outlines five mountain-biking routes in the hills; hire bikes from Hotel Cerkno.

Cerkno Ski Centre   SKIING
(☑05-374 34 00; www.ski-cerkno.com; adult/child day pass €30/17.50; ⊙approx Nov-Mar) This family-friendly ski resort, 10km north of Cerkno, is consistently voted among Slovenia's best ski resorts. It's certainly one of the more modern with eight lifts, 18km of slopes and 5km of cross-country ski trails. There's a

THE 'LAUFARIJA' TRADITION

Ethnologists believe that the Laufarija tradition and its distinctive masks came from Austria's South Tyrol. *Lauferei* means 'running about' in German, and that's just what the crazily masked participants do as they nab their victims.

Special (and mostly male) Laufarji societies organise the annual event. Those aged 15 and over are allowed to enter, after proving themselves as apprentices by sewing costumes. Outfits are made fresh every year, with leaves, pine branches, straw or moss stitched onto a hessian backing. They take quite a beating during the festivities.

The action takes place on the Sunday before Ash Wednesday and again on Shrove Tuesday. The main character is the Pust, with a horned mask and a heavy costume of moss. He's the symbol of winter and the old year – and he *must* die.

The Pust is charged with many grievances – a bad harvest, inclement weather, lousy roads – and always found guilty. Other Laufarji characters represent crafts and trades – Baker, Thatcher, Woodsman – with the rest including the Drunk and his Wife, the Bad Boy, Sneezy and the accordion-playing Sick Man. The Old Man, wearing Slovenian-style lederhosen and a wide-brimmed hat, executes the Pust with a wooden mallet, and the body is rolled away on a caisson.

good mix of beginner, intermediate and expert downhill trails.

Rental of skis, helmet, boots and poles costs €24/20 per day per adult/child.

⭐ Festivals & Events

Laufarija   CULTURAL
(www.60let.laufarija-cerkno.si; ⊙ Feb/Mar) The biggest annual event in these parts unfolds on Glavni trg in the days before Lent begins (the Sunday and Tuesday before Ash Wednesday). This ancient carnival sees masked participants chasing and executing the Pust, a character representing winter and the old year. It's a fabulous time to be in town.

🛏 Sleeping & Eating

There's not a whole lot of choice when it comes to accommodation in Cerkno - the two options are adequate if uninspiring. You'll need to book weeks or even months ahead if you plan to be here during festival time; otherwise, you'll have to stay in Idrija, 20km away.

A handful of simple restaurants around the town centre will ensure you don't go hungry, although neither will you eat anywhere that lives long in the memory. The best place to eat is Gačnk v Logu, 3.5km out of town.

Gačnk v Logu   GUESTHOUSE $
(☑ 05-372 40 05; www.cerkno.com; Dolenji Novaki 1; r per person €22-31; 🐾) This century-old inn is close to the turn-off for the Franja Partisan Hospital. It has nine homely rooms (including family-sized ones), a kids' play area, and a restaurant (mains €7 to €13) serving locally grown ingredients – specialities include mushroom soup, fresh trout, *žlikrofi* and venison. It's a lovely setting, too.

Hotel Cerkno   HOTEL $$
(☑ 05-374 34 00; www.hotel-cerkno.si; Sedejev trg 8; budget s/d €33.50/50, standard €60/90; @ 🐾 ⊠) The decor at this large hotel is tired but facilities are decent and service is excellent. Standard rooms are quite pricey for what you get – better value are the budget 'hostel' rooms (which still have private bathrooms, TV and wi-fi). There's an indoor pool and free bike use for guests, plus a restaurant and a cafe.

ℹ Information

Tourist Information Centre (TIC; ☑ 05-373 46 45; www.turizem-cerkno.si; Močnikova ulica 2; ⊙ 9am-4pm Tue-Fri, 8am-3pm Sat & Sun) Just off Glavni trg.

ℹ Getting There & Away

On weekdays, there are hourly bus departures to Idrija (€3.25, 28 minutes, 21km), and up to eight buses daily to Ljubljana (€7.80, 1¾ hours, 77km). Services drop by about half on weekends.

Southwestern Slovenia

Best Places to Eat

➡ Gostilna Pri Lojzetu (p145)

➡ Hiša Torkla (p162)

➡ Capra (p150)

➡ Pri Mari (p158)

➡ Restaurant Proteus (p134)

➡ Cantina Klet (p158)

Best Places to Stay

➡ Art Hotel Tartini (p157)

➡ Stara Šola Korte Guesthouse (p162)

➡ Majerija (p144)

➡ Lipizzaner Lodge (p133)

➡ Kempinski Palace Portorož (p161)

Why Go?

Slovenia's astonishing diversity comes to the fore in this region. By travelling short distances, you can traipse through remarkable Unesco-recognised caves that yawn open to reveal karstic treasures, go bear-watching in dense green forests, or admire the Venetian history and architectural legacy of photogenic seaside towns.

Continue the winning mix of history-meets-scenery: view dancing white Lipizzaner horses at the estate that first bred them in the late 16th century, then inspect the marvellous detail of the 15th-century *Dance of Death* fresco at remote Hrastovlje. Visit the historic salt pans of Sečovlje, then enjoy a salt scrub at the stylish open-air day spa in their midst.

Flavours are equally diverse and delectable. Lunch on *pršut* (dry-cured ham) accompanied by ruby-red teran wine for the definitive taste of the Karst, or dine on seafood washed down with local *malvazija* wine on the coast – best savoured with a sunset view of the Adriatic.

When to Go
Piran

°C/°F **Temp**   **Rainfall** inches/mm

Jul & Aug The summer peak: prime weather, with crowds, beaches and activities (including | bear-watching) in full swing.
May & Jun Fewer crowds, good for Adriatic swimming. | **Sep & Oct** The grape harvest; ideal for wine and food touring in Goriška Brda and the Vipava Valley.

Southwestern Slovenia Highlights

1 Piran (p153) Enjoying seafood amid Venetian architecture.

2 Postojna Cave (p131) Marvelling at this cathedral-like cave.

3 Lož Valley (p138) Tracking bears in one of Europe's best wildlife experiences.

4 Church of the Holy

Trinity (p143) Being dazzled by frescoes in Hrastovlje.

5 Goriška Brda (p145) Touring idyllic, villages in Slovenia's winemaking region.

6 Predjama Castle (p134) Admiring the castle perched in a cliffside cave.

7 Korte (p162) Escaping the crowds in this village.

8 Vipava Valley (p142) Dining superbly and tasting indigenous wine varieties.

9 Škocjan Caves (p139) Descending into the netherworld with a subterranean boat tour.

10 Lepa Vida Thalasso Spa (p162) Unwinding in the salty Sečovlje Salina Nature Park.

SLOVENIAN KARST

The Karst region (Kras in Slovenian; www.visitkras.info) is a limestone plateau stretching from the Gulf of Trieste to the Vipava Valley. Rivers, ponds and lakes can disappear and then resurface in the Karst's porous limestone through sinkholes and funnels, often resulting in underground caverns like the fabulous caves at Škocjan and Postojna.

Along with caves, the Karst is rich in olives, fruits, vineyards producing ruby-red teran wine, *pršut,* old stone churches and red-tiled roofs.

Postojna

05 / POP 9423 / ELEV 546M

The karst cave at Postojna is one of the largest in the world, and its stalagmite and stalactite formations are unequalled anywhere. Among Slovenia's most popular attractions, it's a busy spot – the amazing thing is how the large crowds at the entrance seem to get swallowed whole by the size of the cave, and the tourist activity doesn't detract from the wonder. It's a big, slick complex, and it doesn't come cheap. But it's still worth every minute you can spend in this magical underground world. The adjacent town of Postojna serves as a gateway to the caves and is otherwise a fairly attractive provincial Slovenian town.

History

The cave has been known – and visited – by residents of the area for centuries (you need only look at the Passage of New Signatures inside the Vivarium Proteus). But people in the Middle Ages knew only the entrances; the inner parts were not explored until April 1818, just days before Habsburg Emperor Franz I (r 1792–1835) came to visit. The following year the Cave Commission accepted its first organised tour group, including Archduke Ferdinand, and Postojna's future as a tourist destination was sealed.

Since then more than 36 million people have visited the cave (with some 6000 a day in August; rainy summer days bring the biggest crowds).

◉ Sights

★ Postojna Cave   CAVE

(Postojnska Jama; 05-7000100; www.postojnska-jama.eu; Jamska cesta 30; adult/child €25.80/15.50, with Predjama Castle €35.70/21.40; ⊙ tours hourly 9am-6pm Jul & Aug, to 5pm May-Jun & Sep, 10am, noon & 3pm Nov-Mar, 10am-noon & 2-4pm

Apr & Oct) The jaw-dropping Postojna Cave system, a series of caverns, halls and passages some 24km long and two million years old, was hollowed out by the Pivka River, which enters a subterranean tunnel near the cave's entrance.

Visitors get to see 5km of the cave on 1½-hour tours; 3.2km of this is covered by a cool electric train. Postojna Cave has a constant temperature of 8°C to 10°C, with 95% humidity, so a warm jacket and decent shoes are advised.

The train takes you to the **Great Mountain** cavern, on a trip that's like entering the secret lair of a James Bond villain. From here a guide escorts you on foot through tunnels, halls, galleries and caverns in one of four to six languages (audioguides are available in many more tongues).

These are dry galleries, decorated with a vast array of stalactites shaped like needles, enormous icicles and even fragile spaghetti. The stalagmites take familiar shapes but there are also bizarre columns, pillars and translucent curtains that look like rashers of bacon.

From the Velika Gora cavern you continue across the **Russian Bridge**, built by prisoners of war in 1916, through the 500m-long **Beautiful Caves** that are filled with wonderful ribbon-shaped stalactites and stalagmites that are two million years old (it takes 30 years to produce 1mm of stalactite). The halls of the Beautiful Caves are the farthest point you'll reach; from here a tunnel stretches to the **Black Cave** (Črna Jama) and **Pivka Cave** (these can also be visited on additional tours).

The tour continues south through the **Winter Hall**, past the 5m, snow-white **Brilliant** stalagmite (also sometimes called the Diamond) and the neighbouring **baroque pillar**, which have become symbols of the cave. You then enter the **Concert Hall**, which is the largest in the cave system and can accommodate 10,000 people for musical performances. In the week between Christmas and New Year, the Live Christmas Crib (Jaslice) – the Nativity performed by miming actors – also takes place in the cave. Visitors reboard the train by the Concert Hall and return to the entrance. The river continues its deep passage underground, carving out several series of caves, and emerges again as the Unica River.

Green felt capes can be hired at the entrance for €3.50. There are few steps to climb. Check the website for package deals,

THE HUMAN FISH

Postojna is home to the blind eel-like *Proteus anguinus,* or olm. A kind of salamander with a colour not unlike pink human flesh, it lives hidden in the pitch black for up to a century and can go a decade without food.

The chronicler Janez Vajkard Valvasor wrote about the fear and astonishment of local people when an immature 'dragon' was found in a karst spring in the late 17th century. Several other reports about this four-legged 'human fish' (*človeška ribica,* as it's called in Slovene) were made before a Viennese doctor described it for science in 1786, naming it for the protector of Poseidon's sea creatures in Greek mythology and the Latin word for 'snake'.

Proteus reaches 30cm long, with a swimming tail and stubby legs. Although blind, with atrophied eyes, *Proteus* has an excellent sense of smell and is sensitive to weak electric fields in the water, which it uses to move around in the dark, locate prey and communicate. It breathes through frilly, bright-red gills. Its skin entirely lacks pigmentation but looks pink in the light due to blood circulation.

Cool pitch-black caves slow down life cycles – the gills are a strange evolutionary throwback to the animals' tadpole stage, which it never fully outgrows, instead reaching sexual maturity at 14 years, with an estimated lifespan of 58 to 100 years! No wonder it's always been a creature of local fascination.

You can see *Proteus* inside the Postojna Cave, or at the Vivarium Proteus.

including various combination tickets that include Vivarium Proteus, the new Expo and the don't-miss Predjama Castle (p134). Postojna is a less-strenuous option than Škocjan Caves (p139).

Vivarium Proteus
MUSEUM

(☑ 05-700 01 00; www.postojnska-jama.eu; adult/child €9.90/5.90, with Postojna Cave €31.80/19.10; ☉ 8.30am-6.30pm Jul & Aug, to 5.30pm May, Jun & Sep, 9.30am-5.30pm Apr, to 4.30pm Oct, to 3.30pm Nov-Mar) Just near the entrance to the Postojna Cave is the Vivarium, the cradle of a special branch of biology: speleobiology. Postojna provides shelter to dozens of cave-dwelling animal species – visitors can get to know some of the most interesting ones in more detail here, including the 'human fish', as well as the slenderneck beetle, cave squid and cave centipede.

Expo Postojna Cave Karst
MUSEUM

(☑ 05-700 01 00; www.postojnska-jama.eu; adult/child €9.90/5.90, with Postojna Cave €31.80/19.10; ☉ 9am-6pm Jun-Aug, to 5pm May & Sep, 10am-4pm Apr & Oct, to 3pm Nov-Mar) This well-designed, kid-friendly space displays details of karst phenomena in an engaging manner, and tracks cave exploration. Most interesting is all the memorabilia and vintage posters detailing the 200-year history of tourism to Postojna Cave (like the fact that the cave got electric lighting in 1883, a decade before Ljubljana).

Planina Cave
CAVE

(Planinska Jama; ☑ 041 338 696; www.planina. si; Planina; adult/child €10/7; ☉ 3pm Sat, 3pm & 5pm Sun Apr-Sep) Planina Cave, 12km to the northeast of Postojna Cave, is the largest water cave in Slovenia and a treasure-trove of fauna (including *Proteus anguinus*). The cave's entrance is at the foot of a 100m rock wall. It's 6.5km long, and you are able to visit about 900m of it in an hour. There are no lights, so take a torch.

With prior warning, tours can be arranged most days in July and August – including a longer, five-hour tour with a boat (€30).

🏃 Activities

As you'd imagine, proper caving is an option here, although experienced spelunkers will find what's on offer to be pretty tame – it's a safe adventure for your average punter.

The forested hills to the east and southeast of Postojna are rich in brown bears and a couple of operators offer tours in search of these soulful creatures.

Underground Adventures
ADVENTURE

(☑ 05-700 01 00; www.postojnska-jama.eu; tours from adult/child €40/25) Want to escape the crowds and get a taste of spelunking? Guided tours have been designed to visit Pivka Cave and Black Cave, parts of the Postojna cave system that are not open on regular tours. These tours can be relatively tame, or involve hardhats, overalls, water obstacles and a little abseiling, depending on your wishes.

Tours last from 1½ to six hours, with expert guiding and equipment provided. They are available year-round; bookings must be made at least three days in advance.

Slovenia4Seasons WILDLIFE WATCHING

(☑ 040 387 887; www.slovenia4seasons.com; per person from €195; ☺ May-Oct) This upmarket operator runs bear-watching excursions – they claim a 90% success rate and offer a 50% discount on a second tour if the first one is unsuccessful. They can pick you up from your hotel or the tourist office in Postojna.

Forest Adventures WILDLIFE WATCHING

(☑ 040 187 309; www.forest-adventures.eu; Ulica Vilka Kledeta 6; per person from €60; ☺ May-Oct) This Postojna-based outfit offers a handful of bear-watching excursions, which range from three to seven hours and involve a mix of hiking and time spent in a hide. They also offer hiking.

🛏 Sleeping

Postojna has good accommodation, both in the town itself, out at the cave complex and in the surrounding region. Kompas Postojna (p135) organises private rooms (per person from €18) in town and farmhouse stays (per person from €20) further afield in Narin (15km southwest) and Razdrto (11km west).

★ Youth Hostel Proteus Postojna HOSTEL $

(☑ 05-850 10 20; www.proteus.sgls.si; Tržaška cesta 36; dm/s/d €15/23/34; ⓟ@🛜) Don't be fooled by the institutional exterior – inside, this place is a riot of colour. It's surrounded by parkland and is a fun, chilled-out space, with three-bed rooms (shared bathrooms), kitchen and laundry access, and bike rental. The year-round hostel shares the building with student accommodation, so facilities are good. It's about 500m southwest of Titov trg.

Camping Pivka Jama CAMPGROUND $

(☑ 05-720 39 93; www.camping-postojna.com; Veliki Otok 50; campsite adult/child €11.90/8.90, 4-bed bungalow €74-99; ☺ Apr-Oct; ⓟ🛜🏊) This large, attractive forested site is about 4km past the Postojna Cave complex, near the entrance to Pivka Cave. Some of the cosy, family-sized, stone-and-wood bungalows have kitchens. There's a swimming pool, restaurant and activity options. Note: campervanners might wish to simply overnight at the parking stop by the cave complex (per 24 hours €18).

★ Lipizzaner Lodge GUESTHOUSE $$

(☑ 040 378 037; www.lipizzanerlodge.com; Landol 17; s/d/q from €55/80/100; ⓟ🛜) In a relaxing rural setting 9km northwest of Postojna Cave, a Welsh-Finnish couple have established this very hospitable, affordable guesthouse. They offer seven well-equipped rooms (including family-sized, and a self-catering apartment); great-value, three-course evening meals on request (€20); brilliant local knowledge (check out their comprehensive website for an idea); forest walks (including to Predjama in 40 minutes); and bike rental.

Rooms & Apartments Proteus GUESTHOUSE $$

(☑ 081 610 300; www.postojnska-jama.eu; Titov trg 1a; d €82-114, q €140-176; ⓟ❄🛜) Above and behind the excellent Proteus Restaurant on Postojna's main square, this complex of 15 sparkling rooms and apartments offers fresh decor and good facilities (including air-con and free parking). Apartments have a kitchen and can sleep up to six. Breakfast is additional (€8).

★ Hotel Jama HOTEL $$$

(☑ 05-700 01 00; www.postojnska-jama.eu; Jamska cesta 30; r from €129) This huge, concrete, socialist-era hotel is part of the Postojna Cave complex and has undergone a stunning renovation, reopening in 2016 with slick,

SOUTHWESTERN SLOVENIA POSTOJNA

HIKING THE VIA DINARICA

The Via Dinarica, which begins at Nanos west of Postojna, could become one of Europe's most rewarding long-distance hiking trails. Although it's playing catch-up with other long-distance trails thanks to the Balkan conflict of the 1990s, that also means numbers remain low compared with other epic pan-European hikes.

The trail hooks up past Predjama Castle, down through Cerknica and the Green Karst, twisting and turning all the way to the Croatian border at Babno Polje, 137km after it began. But the Slovenian leg is just the beginning of an odyssey that follows the high peaks and ridgelines of the Dinaric Alps. The entire trail currently runs for 1261km, although there are ongoing plans for an extension of the route into Macedonia. Until it does, the trail passes through Slovenia, Croatia, Bosnia-Herzegovina, Montenegro, Albania and Kosovo.

For more information visit https://trail.viadinarica.com.

PREDJAMA CASTLE

Nine kilometres from Postojna, is one of Europe's most dramatic **castles** (Predjamski Grad; ☑ 05-700 01 00; www.postojnska-jama.eu; Predjama 1; adult/child €13.80/8.30, with Postojna Cave €35.70/21.40; ☺ 9am-7pm Jul & Aug, to 6pm May, Jun & Sep, 10am-5pm Apr & Oct, to 4pm Nov-Mar). It teaches a clear lesson: if you want to build an impregnable fortification, put it in the gaping mouth of a cavern halfway up a 123m cliff. Its four storeys were built piecemeal over the years from 1202, but most of what you see today is from the 16th century. It looks simply unconquerable.

An audioguide (available in 15 languages) details the site's highlights and history. The castle has great features for kids of any age – holes in the ceiling of the entrance tower for pouring boiling oil on intruders, a very dank dungeon, a 16th-century chest full of treasure (unearthed in the cellar in 1991), and an eyrie-like hiding place at the top called **Erazem's Nook**, named for Erazem (Erasmus) Lueger.

Lueger was a 15th-century robber-baron who, like Robin Hood, stole from the rich to give to the poor. During the wars between the Hungarians and the Austrians, Lueger supported the former. He holed up in Predjama Castle and continued his daring deeds with the help of a secret passage that led out from behind the rock wall. In 1484 the Austrian army besieged the castle, but it proved impregnable. Lueger mocked his attackers, even showering them with fresh cherries to prove his comfortable situation. But the Austrians had the last laugh – finally hitting him with a cannonball as he sat on the toilet. An ignoble fate for a dashing character.

The cave below the castle is part of the 14km Predjama cave system. It's open to visitors from May to September (but closed in winter so as not to disturb its colony of bats during their hibernation). Another adventure option is to visit the narrow Erazem's Passage, through which the besieged knight was connected with the outside world (some climbing skills are required for this). Tours need to be booked at least three days in advance; caving tours range in price from €24 to €80.

Joint tickets can be bought for the castle and Postojna Cave. In July and August, a handy shuttle-bus service runs between the cave and the castle; it's free for guests who buy a combined ticket for both attractions.

contemporary rooms with striking colour schemes and lovely glass-walled bathrooms. It's worth paying extra (anywhere between €10 and €30) for a room with a view. There's also a restaurant and a bar, and the excellent buffet breakfast costs €12.

✗ Eating

★ **Restaurant Proteus**   SLOVENIAN **$$**
(☑ 081 610 300; Titov trg 1; mains €12-22; ☺ 8am-10pm) The fanciest place in town: inside is modern and white, with booths fringed by curtains, while the terrace overlooking the main square is a fine vantage point. Accomplished cooking showcases fine regional produce – house specialities include venison goulash and steak with teran (red wine) sauce. It's hard to go past the four-course Chef's Slovenian Menu (€38) for value and local flavour.

Magdalena Food & Fun   INTERNATIONAL **$$**
(www.postojnska-jama.eu; Postojna Cave complex; mains €7-16; ☺ 11am-5pm) One of the better options inside the cave complex, this place

next to the entrance to Hotel Jama is slick yet casual and does terrific burgers – its cave burger is our pick for Postojna's best burger.

Modrijan Homestead   SLOVENIAN **$$**
(☑ 05-700 01 00; www.postojnska-jama.eu; Postojna Cave complex; mains €12-22; ☺ 10am-6pm Apr-Sep) As you'd imagine, eating at the touristy complex surrounding Postojna Cave is not cheap, but here you'll get some very tasty grilled meats to fuel exploration. The menu lists an impressive seven languages and includes grilled trout, salmon and veggies. The meats – roast suckling pig, *klobasa* (sausage) and *čevapčiči* (spicy meatballs) – are excellent.

❶ Information

TOURIST INFORMATION
Tourist Information Centre Galerija (☑ 040 122 318; www.visit-postojna.si; Trg Padlih Borchev 5; ☺ 9am-5pm Mon-Sat, to 3pm Sun) Well-stocked tourist office in the town centre.

Tourist Information Centre Postojna (TIC; ☑ 064 179 972; www.visit-postojna.si; Tržaška cesta 59; ⊗8am-4pm Mon-Fri, 10am-3pm Sat) A smart new pavilion has been built in the town's west, on the road into town. It's handy for those driving into town and there's adequate parking.

TRAVEL AGENCIES

Kompas Postojna (☑05-721 14 80; www.kompas-postojna.si; Titov trg 2a) In town, this travel agency arranges private rooms. Note, however, that it's privately run, and not a tourist office.

ⓘ Getting There & Away

BUS

Postojna's **bus station** (Titova cesta 2) is about 200m southwest of Titov trg. Note that some intercity buses will stop at the cave complex too (on timetables this is Postojnska jama).

Bus destinations from Postojna include:

Cerknica (€2.90, 27 minutes, seven daily)

Divača (for Škocjan; €3.90, 30 minutes, seven daily)

Koper (€7.50, 1¼ hours, up to eight daily)

Ljubljana (€6.80, one hour, hourly)

Piran (€9.60, 1¾ hours, four daily)

Trieste (€7.30, 1¼ hours, two to three daily)

Vipava (€3.90, 34 minutes, 12 daily)

TRAIN

The train station is on Kolodvorska cesta about 800m east of the square.

Postojna is on the main train line linking Ljubljana (€5.80, one hour) with Sežana and Trieste via Divača, and is an easy day trip from the capital. As many as 20 trains a day make the run from Ljubljana to Postojna and back.

You can also reach Koper (€6.99, 1½ hours) on the coast. There are up to six trains a day; some may require a change at Divača.

ⓘ Getting Around

In July and August there's a free shuttle bus from the train station to Postojna Cave.

Enquire at your accommodation for the closest bike rental, or head to Youth Hostel Proteus Postojna (p133).

For a taxi, call ☑031 777 974 or ☑031 413 254.

The Green Karst

The undulating, heavily forested Notranjska (Inner Carniola) region – which encompasses Postojna and Predjama – is full of woodlands, castles, caves, and sinkholes created by 'disappearing' rivers and lakes. Its isolated setting has spawned some of Slovenia's most cherished myths and legends, notably that of the Turk-slayer Martin Krpan, made famous in Fran Levstik's book of the same name.

The region has recently been repackaged and promoted as the 'Green Karst' (Zeleni Kras; www.zelenikras.si) – it's an apt name, as this is a peaceful rural pocket that flies under the radar of most travellers' attention. This may change when word spreads about its natural beauty, friendly tourist farms, and world-class bear-spotting potential.

Cerknica & Around

☑01 / POP 4018 / ELEV 572M

Cerknica is the largest town on a lake that isn't always a lake – one of Slovenia's most unusual natural phenomena. It's a good springboard for the gorge at Rakov Škocjan and Notranjska Regional Park as a whole, not least because it's a quiet little place that gets none of the tourist buses that can plague nearby Postojna. If you'll be in the area in the week before Ash Wednesday, don't miss Cerknica's fun carnival (p136) celebrations.

⊙ Sights

Lake Cerknica   LAKE
(Cerniško Jezero) Since ancient times, periodic Lake Cerknica (Cerniško Jezero) has baffled and perplexed people, appearing and disappearing with the seasons. Cerknica is a *polje*, a field above a collapsed karst cavern riddled with holes like a Swiss cheese. During rainy periods, usually in the autumn and spring, water comes rushing into the *polje*. As the water percolates between the rocks, the sinkholes and siphons can't handle the outflow underground, and the *polje* becomes Lake Cerknica – sometimes in less than a day.

Notranjska Regional Park   NATURE RESERVE
(Notranjski Regijski Park; www.notranjski-park.si) This 222-sq-km park is a real biodiversity hot spot and holds within its borders a good deal of the region's karst phenomena, including the intermittent Lake Cerknica, forests, meadows, wetlands, caves (including Križna Cave) and Rakov Škocjan gorge. There is also a wealth of cultural heritage in the form of orchards, preserved buildings and old hayracks. Great hiking, cycling and birdwatching lie within its borders. The area's tourist office (p136) can provide info.

Rakov Škocjan   GORGE
Rakov Škocjan is a beautiful, 2.5km-long gorge lying some 6km west of Cerknica. The Rak River, en route to join the Pivka River at Planina Cave, has sculpted 2.5km of hollows, caves, springs and rocky arches – including the **Veliki** and **Mali Naravni Most**, the Big

THE DISAPPEARING LAKE

When it's present, which can be for nine months of the year, Lake Cerknica (p135) begins in the north at the village of Dolenje Jezero, 2.5km south of Cerknica. At its most expansive, the surface area of the lake can reach 38 sq km (under ordinary conditions it usually reaches around 28 sq km), but it is never more than a few metres deep. When full it is an important wetland, attracting up to 276 species of birds each year, as well as 125 butterfly species (a remarkable one-third of Europe's entire stock of butterfly species), and 15 amphibian species (three-quarters of Slovenia's total). During dry periods (usually July to September or later), farmers drive cattle down to the *polje* to graze among the sinkholes.

When the waters disappear underground, they filter down through the caves of the karst system, with some appearing as the Rak River in Rakov Škocjan, and even reaching as far afield as the Ljubljana Marshes.

In the village of Dolenje Jezero you will find the **Museum of Lake Cerknica** (Muzej Jezerski Hram; ☑ 01-709 40 53, 051 338 057; www.jezerski-hram.si; Dolenje Jezero 1e; adult/child €7/5; ☺ guided tour 3pm daily Jul & Aug, Sat Apr-Jun & Sep-Oct, by appointment Nov-Mar), with a 5m-by-3m, 1:2500-scale working model of the lake. It shows how the underground hydrological system actually works in a 1¼-hour demonstration and video about the lake during the four seasons. There are also ethnological exhibits about local fishing and boat building.

Fishing and explorations in flat-bottomed boats are possible – contact the tourist information centre in Cerknica for information.

and Little Natural Bridges. There are lots of hiking and biking trails through and around the gorge, and it is surrounded by Notranjski Regional Park.

Heritage House CULTURAL CENTRE
(Hiša Izročila; ☑ 01-709 63 10; www.hisaizrocila.si; Dolenja Vas 70c) This project, which opened in 2015, aims to preserve the cultural and natural heritage of the Notranjska Regional Park, and to that end it stages public events and organises unique activities and workshops. This could be a guided walk, birdwatching, boat-building demonstration, or an evening of folk music and storytelling. Advance booking required; check the website for info.

✯ Festivals & Events

★ **Pust v Cerknici** RELIGIOUS
(www.pust.si; ☺ Feb-Mar) Cerknica is famous for its pre-Lenten carnival, Pust, which takes place for four days over the weekend before Ash Wednesday. Mask-wearing merrymakers and witches parade up and down while being provoked by *butalci* (hillbillies) with pitchforks.

🛏 Sleeping & Eating

Places to eat are fairly thin on the ground out here, but most accommodation options also offer meals and there are occasional restaurants as well. Postojna, not far away, has plenty of choice.

Hotel Rakov Škocjan HOTEL $
(☑ 031 391 195; Rakov Škocjan 1; d from €48; ❋ 🖰) Set in lovely woodland surrounds, Hotel Rakov Škocjan gets good reviews from travellers for its location (5km west of Cerknica). The carpeted rooms are a little old-fashioned, but they're otherwise fine. The restaurant serves a buffet breakfast, and steaks for lunch or dinner.

Prenočišča Miškar GUESTHOUSE $
(☑ 081 602 284; www.miskar.si; Žerovnica 66; s/d/tr €35/50/66; 🅿🖰) This four-room guesthouse is a very good choice, on forested grounds about 7km southeast of town (and only about 5km from Križna Cave). The owners are friendly, the balcony views superb. Bears wander the surrounding woods.

Valvasorjev Hram SLOVENIAN $
(☑ 01-709 37 88; Partizanska cesta 1; mains €8-17; ☺ 8am-11pm Mon-Sat, 3-10pm Sun) This simple eatery serves hearty dishes like *jota* (bean soup) and *klobasa* as well as pizza. It has its own wine cellar, and outside seating in summer.

ⓘ Information

Tourist Information Centre (TIC; ☑ 01-709 36 36; ticerknica@cerknica.si; Tabor 42; ☺ 8am-4pm Mon-Sat, to noon Sun) For local information, including for Notranjska Regional Park. Bike rental available.

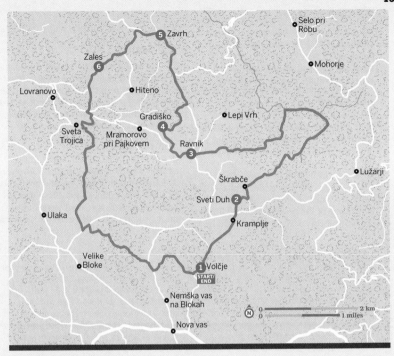

🏃 Walking Tour
Bloke Plateau

START VOLČJE
END VOLČJE
LENGTH 22.5KM; FOUR TO SEVEN HOURS

This appealing walk is the ultimate Slovenian escape from the tour buses, allowing you to stretch your legs among some of the loveliest scenery the Green Karst region has to offer. Fit hikers can accomplish the entire loop in four hours, while six hours is the norm for inexperienced walkers of average fitness. Although there are plenty of rises and falls along the way, the walk is considered an easy walk. The trail is generally open from May to September.

Along the way, watch for traditional sawmills, quiet villages that rarely see tourists and local *pajštaba* (areas traditionally used for drying fruit), old bridges that cross Bloščica Creek and a handful of quietly pretty churches.

Begin in ❶ **Volčje** and, skirting Lake Bloke, continue northeast to ❷ **Sveti Duh** (1.4km); after a further 1km, the trail really starts to climb. After cresting at 785m above sea level, the trail dips down to 713m, before swinging northwest near Laze and climbing

pretty relentlessly to 852m at the trail's northernmost point, around 12km after you began. Along the way, you'll pass through ❸ **Ravnik** and ❹ **Gradiško**, with splendid views of the Notranjska Regional Park and surroundings as you climb. Close to the trail's summit, you'll pass through the tiny settlement of ❺ **Zavrh**; watch in particular for the church of St Ulrich and the remnants of Fajgl Homestead where Martin Krpan lived.

From just beyond Zavrh, the trail descends quite sharply in places, down through the forests all the way to ❻ **Zales**, with occasional openings in the canopy offering fine views. Beyond Bočkovo, you'll reach the lowest point of the trip at 674m, around 15km after you began. As the trail continues south and then southeast, it climbs again, more gradually this time, to 807m above sea level. With a couple of short descents and climbs, you'll be back in Volčje in no time.

Part of the trail follows the pan-Balkan Via Dinarica (p133).

ⓘ Getting There & Away

Bus connections from Cerknica:

Ljubljana (€6.50, 1¼ hours, up to 17 daily)
Postojna (€2.90, 27 minutes, six daily)
Ratek (€1.40, nine minutes, nine daily) The closest train station.

Lož Valley

📍 01 / ELEV 586M

The secluded Lož Valley (Loška Dolina), southeast of Cerknica, is a green and tranquil taste of rural Slovenia. In summer look out for its trademark *ostrnice* (tall slender haystacks) in mowed meadows. There's also a world-class cave experience and a stirring castle to visit. But the main reason to come here is one of the best chances in Europe to see brown bears – we saw them right by the roadside between Grahovo and Žerovnica, as well as on a bear-watching safari from Lož.

⊙ Sights

The beautiful scenery of the Lož Valley is best appreciated on the pretty drive between Grahovo and Lož – take the southern route via Žerovnica and Podcerkev. Most bear-watching excursions will take you deep into the forests of the region.

★ **Križna Cave**   CAVE
(Križna Jama; ☑ 041 632 153; www.krizna-jama.si; adult/child €9/6; ⊙ tours 11am, 1pm, 3pm & 5pm Jul & Aug, 11am, 1pm & 3pm Sep, 3pm Sat & Sun Apr-Jun) You can explore most Slovenian caves on foot, but Križna (Cross) Cave, one of the most magnificent water caves in the world,

---

WHERE TO SEE BROWN BEARS

There is a good-sized bear population in the forests of Notranjska Regional Park and around, and experienced guides can help you observe them in their natural habitat from April to September. Sometimes the season lasts into October, or doesn't begin until May – it all depends on weather conditions; a long winter will mean that bears stay in hiding for longer, while a longer summer may keep them active until later in the year. When looking for bears, keep an eye out for lynx and/or wolves, which also reside in local forests, although both species are extremely elusive.

Most tours involve a drive into the forest, followed by a short walk to an observation hide overlooking a clearing which bears are known to frequent. Then you'll end up sitting in absolute silence for two hours or more, waiting for the bears to appear.

Gostišče Mlakar (☑ 041 582 081; www.slovenianbears.com; Markovec 15a; per day €80-€120) From his family's guesthouse in the hamlet of Markovec, Miha runs customised nature programs, from multiday wildlife photography workshops to seasonal bear-watching tours. He offers a network of 20 observation hides and professional photography hides in pristine forest.

Tourist Information Centre Tours (TIC; ☑ 081 602 853; www.loskadolina.info; Cesta 19 Oktobra 49, Lož; 1/2/3 people €100/130/165) The TIC in Lož can arrange an evening with a local guide at an elevated wildlife observation lookout. The tour begins at the TIC, takes around three to four hours (including a short forest walk to the lookout), and there is a maximum of three on the tour. Advance bookings required. It also offers the excellent 'A Day Out with the Bear', an entire day's expedition spent learning about brown bears, tracking techniques, local food and farming and, of course, an evening spent waiting for bears from the hide. This tour begins at 1pm and can last as late as 9pm.

Forest Adventures (p133) This Postojna-based outfit offers a handful of bear-watching excursions, which range from three to seven hours and involve a mix of hiking and time spent in a hide.

Slovenia4Seasons (p133) This upmarket operator runs bear-watching excursions – they claim a 90% success rate and offer a 50% discount on a second tour if the first one is unsuccessful. They can pick you up from your hotel or the tourist office in Postojna.

Bears & Wildlife (KTC; ☑ 041 201 232; www.bearsandwildlife.si; Hrib 14, Loški Potok; per person €90; ⊙ 4-10pm) Over the mountains east of the Lož Valley in the village of Loški Potok, this outfit runs bear-watching and other nature tours with a wildlife focus; you can even sleep overnight in the forest. Tours begin at 4pm and last until around 10pm, depending on the time of sunset and the success of the tour in finding bears.

THE EURASIAN LYNX

One of the most widespread of all cat species, the Eurasian lynx ranges from the Balkans and northern Europe all the way across Siberia and Central Asia to Russia's Far East. It's also the largest of the four lynx species – the others are the Iberian lynx, Canada lynx and bobcat – with which it shares a spotted coat, hind legs that are longer than those at the front, and affecting ear tufts. The Eurasian lynx hunts at night and is capable of bringing down red deer that, at 225kg, can be more than 10 times the weight of an adult lynx. They're also opportunists and can hunt birds, hares, wild boar and other smaller prey. Lynx can live up to 20 years in the wild.

The Eurasian lynx has been wiped out in Western Europe, and the entire European population is estimated at no more than 8000, thinly spread across the Balkans, Eastern Europe and Scandinavia. At last count, the Eurasian lynx was considered critically endangered in the Balkans, with just 80 to 200 individuals. Threats to the lynx come from over-hunting of their prey and loss of habitat associated with an increasing human population.

In Slovenia, the lynx was considered regionally extinct until 1973 when three males and three females from Slovakia were reintroduced. No-one knows how many survive in Slovenia, although the population is estimated at no more than 40. Although elusive and difficult to spot, the Eurasian lynx is believed to inhabit the forests of southwestern Slovenia, close to the border with Croatia, so always keep an eye out if you're looking for bears.

is one of few where you can take a **subterranean boat ride**. This is also Slovenia's only tourist cave without electric lighting – visitors are given lamps (and boots) for their visit, which lasts one to 1½ hours and tours the dry part of the cave, including a short boat ride at the first lake. Book ahead.

Snežnik Castle CASTLE
(Grad Snežnik; ☑ 01-705 78 14; www.nms.si; Kozarišče 67; adult/child €5/3; ⊘ tours hourly 10am-6pm Apr-Sep, to 4pm Tue-Sun Oct-Mar) Surrounded by parkland, the restored 16th-century Renaissance Snežnik Castle is one of the loveliest and best-situated fortresses in Slovenia. Entrance is via a 45-minute guided tour. The four floors are richly decorated with period furniture and portraits – the household inventory of the Schönburg-Waldenburg family, who bought the castle in 1853 and used it as a summer residence and hunting lodge until WWII.

🍽 Sleeping & Eating

Meals are possible at Gostišče Mlakar. Otherwise, you'll need to bring your own supplies or eat in Cerknica or Postojna.

★**Gostišče Mlakar** GUESTHOUSE **$$**
(☑ 01-705 86 86, 041 582 081; mlakar.markovec@gmail.com; Markovec 15a; per person from €35; ℗ 🛜) In the hamlet of Markovec, Miha and his family run a comfy five-room guesthouse and a restaurant beloved of locals, serving homemade regional specialities. The cherry on top: Miha runs customised nature programs.

ℹ Information

Tourist Information Centre (TIC; ☑ 081 602 853; www.loskadolina.info; Cesta 19 Oktobra 49, Lož; ⊘ 10am-6pm May-Sep, to 4pm Mon-Fri Oct-Apr) Friendly, helpful office in the wee hamlet of Lož. This is the starting point for excellent bear-watching tours, but it also has general information about the region.

ℹ Getting There & Away

There is very little public transport through the Lož Valley, and certainly none at the after-sunset time when you're likely to be returning from watching bears – you'll need your own wheels to explore the area.

Škocjan Caves
☑ 05 / ELEV 402M

The immense system of karst caves at Škocjan, a Unesco World Heritage site, easily rival those at Postojna, and for many travellers a visit here will be a highlight of their Slovenia trip – a page right out of Jules Verne's *A Journey to the Centre of the Earth*.

⊙ Sights & Activities

★**Škocjan Caves** CAVE
(Škocjanske Jame; ☑ 05-708 21 00; www.park-skoc janske-jame.si; Škocjan 2; cave tour Jul & Aug adult/child €20/10, Mar-Jun, Sep & Oct €18/9, Nov-Feb

€16/7.50; ⊙tours hourly 10am-5pm Jun-Sep, 10am, noon, 1pm & 3.30pm Apr, May & Oct, 10am & 1pm Mon-Sat, 10am, 1pm & 3pm Sun Nov-Mar) Touring the huge, spectacular subterranean chambers of the 6km-long Škocjan Caves is a must. This remarkable cave system was carved out by the Reka River, which enters a gorge below the village of Škocjan and eventually flows into the Dead Lake, a sump at the end of the cave where it disappears. It surfaces again as the Timavo River at Duino in Italy, 34km northwest, before emptying into the Gulf of Trieste. Dress warmly and wear good walking shoes.

There are two options for touring the caves. The first is a two-hour guided tour through the caves (the most popular option for visitors, called Through the Underground Canyon). Visitors walk in groups from the ticket office for about 600m down a gravel path to the main entrance in the Globočak Valley. Through a 116m-long tunnel built in 1933, you soon reach the head of the so-called Silent Cave, a dry branch of the underground canyon that stretches for 500m. The first section, called Paradise, is filled with beautiful stalactites, stalagmites and flowstones that look like snowdrifts; the second part (called Calvary) was once the riverbed. The Silent Cave ends at the Great Hall, 120m wide and 30m high. It is a jungle of exotic dripstones and deposits; keep an eye out for the mighty stalagmites called the Giants and the Pipe Organ.

The sound of the Reka River heralds your entry into the Murmuring Cave, with walls 100m high. To get over the Reka and into Müller Hall, you must cross Cerkevnik Bridge, suspended nearly 50m above the riverbed and surely the highlight of the trip.

Schmidl Hall, the final section, emerges into the Velika Dolina (Big Valley). From here you walk past Tominč Cave, where finds from a prehistoric settlement have been unearthed, and over a walkway near the Natural Bridge. The tour ends at a funicular lift that takes you back to the entrance (or you can opt to walk, which takes about 30 minutes).

The caves are home to a surprising amount of flora and fauna; your guide will point out mounds of bat guano. The temperature is constant at 12°C so bring along a jacket or sweater. Also note the paths are sometimes slippery. In total, visitors walk 3km on this tour. There's a 'no photos' rule.

From April to October, visitors can choose a second tour option, called Following the Reka River Underground. This is a guided (or self-guided) 2km walk following the path of the Reka River, entering the first part of the cave through the natural entrance carved by the river below the village of Škocjan. A combined ticket with Through the Underground Canyon costs €24/12.50.

Škocjan Education Trail   WALKING

If you have time before or after your cave tour, follow the circular, 2km Škocjan Education Trail around the collapsed dolines of the cave system and into nearby hamlets. If time is short, take the path leading north and down some steps from the caves' ticket office – after 250m you'll reach a viewpoint that enjoys a superb vista of the Velika Dolina and the gorge where the Reka starts its subterranean journey.

🛏 Sleeping & Eating

Pr' Vncki Tamara   GUESTHOUSE $$

(☑ 05-763 30 73, 040 697 827; pr.vncki.tamara@gmail.com; Matavun 10; d €70; Ⓟ) This welcoming, relaxed spot in Matavun is just steps south of the entrance to the caves. It has four traditionally styled rooms with a total of 10 beds in a charming old farmhouse; we love the rustic old kitchen with the open fire. Bikes can be rented; meals can be arranged (and are highly praised).

Etna   ITALIAN $$

(☑ 031 727 568; www.etna.si; Kolodvorska ulica 3a, Divača; mains €8-19; ⊙ 11am-11pm Tue-Sun) Etna takes the classic pizza-pasta-meat menu and gives it a creative twist, with surprisingly tasty (and beautifully presented) results. All the essentials are homemade (pasta, pizza dough from wholemeal flour); pizza choices are divided between classic or seasonal. The desserts are pretty as a picture.

ⓘ Getting There & Away

The Škocjan Caves are about 4.5km by road southeast of Divača. A bus connection runs from Divača's neighbouring train and bus stations to the caves a couple of times a day – the caves office recommends you call for times, as these change seasonally. Alternatively, there's a one-hour signed walking trail to the caves.

Buses between Ljubljana and the coast stop at Divača. Destinations include:

Koper (€5, 45 minutes, up to 11 daily)

Ljubljana (€8.50, 1½ hours, seven daily)

Postojna (€3.90, 30 minutes, seven daily)

Train destinations from Divača:

Koper (€4.28, 50 minutes, five daily)

SAMPLING WINES FROM THE KARST

If you have your own wheels and a taste for wine and scenery, you might like to explore the picturesque Karst Wine Region. Here, the *terra rossa* (iron-rich red soil) of the Karst region produces full-bodied, ruby-red teran, a genuine Slovenian wine with designated origin, made from refošk grapes and perfect to pair with another local speciality: *pršut* (dry-cured ham). Also grown here are *vitovska grganja* (an old local grape variety that produces a dry white) and malvasia (a Mediterranean grape that grows well in the Karst and produces a moderately dry white).

The **Karst Wine Road** (www.vinskacestakras.si) connects dozens of small family-owned producers; pick up maps and brochures from local tourist information centres. There are charming villages and back roads to explore – a favourite destination is the ancient fortified village of **Štanjel** (population 370; www.stanjel.eu), which has its own castle and some lovely gardens just outside its walls.

Highlights include:

Lisjak (☑041 652 039; www.lisjak.si; Dutovlje 31; ☺Fri-Sun by appointment) This winery is one of the most beautiful in the Karst region, and the award-winning wines live up to the surroundings – mostly teran reds, but they also produce 'Sara', an intriguing teran, merlot and cabernet sauvignon blend.

Tavcar Marjan (☑05-764 22 55; www.vinarstvo-tavcar.com; Dutovlje 50; ☺by appointment) In the heart of the Karst winemaking area centred on Dutovlje, Tavcar Marjan makes the usual teran reds, malvasia whites and a handful of liqueurs, and serves them up at their bar in the village centre. It also arranges proper tastings and cellar tours if you get enough people together.

Širka Kodrič (☑041 740 560; www.sirca-kodric.si; Godnje 19, Dutovlje; ☺by appointment) One of a number of wineries that produce the ruby-red teran grape, as well as cabernet sauvignon, malvasia and liqueurs – ring ahead to arrange a visit and tastings.

Ljubljana (€7.70, 1½ hours, up to 14 daily)
Postojna (€3.44, 35 minutes, up to 14 daily)

Lipica

☑05 / POP 105 / ELEV 396M

The impact of Lipica, some 9km southwest of Divača and 2km from the Italian border, has been far greater than its size would suggest. This tiny village lives for and on its white Lipizzaner horses, which were first bred here for the Spanish Riding School in Vienna in the late 16th century. Horses remain the main appeal of a visit here.

History

In 1580 Austrian Archduke Charles II founded a stud farm here for the imperial court in Vienna. Andalusian horses from Spain were coupled with the local Karst breed that the Romans had once used to pull chariots – and the Lipizzaner was born. But they weren't quite the white horses we know today. Those didn't come about for another 200 years, when white Arabian horses got into the act.

The breed has subsequently become scattered – moved to Hungary and Austria after WWI, to the Sudetenland in Bohemia by the Germans during WWII, and then shipped off to Italy by the American army in 1945. Only 11 horses returned when operations resumed at Lipica in 1947.

Today more than 300 Lipizzaners remain at the original stud farm while others are bred in various locations around the world, including Piber in Austria, which breeds the horses for the Spanish Riding School. Everyone claims theirs is the genuine article – Slovenia even has a pair of Lipizzaners on the reverse side of its €0.20 coin.

◉ Sights

★**Lipica Stud Farm** FARM
(☑05-739 15 80; www.lipica.org; Lipica 5; tour adult/child €16/8, incl performance €23/12; ☺tours 10am-5pm Apr-Oct, 10am-3pm Nov-Mar, live performances 3pm Tue, Fri & Sun, 11am Sat Jun-Aug, 3pm Tue, Fri & Sun May & Sep, 3pm Sun Apr & Oct) The stud farm can be visited on very popular, 50-minute guided tours. The interesting, informative tours are available in a number of languages; a tour covers the farm's unique heritage and the breeding

of the horses, and visits the pastures and stables. It ends at the very good, hands-on museum called Lipikum (entrance included in tour). A highlight is the performance of these elegant horses as they go through their complicated paces, pirouetting and dancing to Viennese waltzes with riders en costume.

On Wednesday, Thursday and Saturday, you can watch training sessions at 10am and 11am (adult/child €14/7 including guided tour). It pays to check the website or call to confirm times, rather than arrive and be disappointed. In April and October there are a reduced number of performances and training sessions; from November to March there are none.

Horse-drawn carriage jaunts around the estate might appeal (15/30/60 minutes €20/30/50). They run 10am to 2pm and 4pm to 6pm Tuesday to Sunday from April to October, and from 11am to 3pm Saturday and Sunday from November to March.

You can still take a tour in winter, but there are fewer horses around. Avoid visiting on Mondays, when there are no performances, training sessions or carriage rides.

🏃 Activities

Lipica Stud Farm HORSE RIDING
(☑ 05-739 1696; www.lipica.org; Lipica 5; 1½hr trail ride €61) Experienced riders only can sign up for a 1½-hour trail ride – these must be arranged at least three days in advance, and proper riding gear must be worn. There is also a five-day riding program involving lessons and grooming (€382, including meals and accommodation). Again, experience (and pre-booking) is a must.

🛏️ Sleeping & Eating

Hotel Maestoso HOTEL $$
(☑ 05-739 15 80; www.lipica.org; Lipica 5; d €60–105; P @ 🕸) You get to enjoy the stud farm's bucolic setting without the crowds if you stay at this 59-room hotel on the estate. Rooms are clean and comfy but decor is looking a little timeworn in parts. Facilities are decent – including restaurant, golf course and bike hire.

Casa Krasna Guest House GUESTHOUSE $$
(☑ 040 214 226; www.krasna-hisa.si; Lokev 78; s/d €108/125; P 🕸 🕸) This small but charming five-room guesthouse lies 3.5km southwest of Lipica and is a good base for both a visit to the stud farm and surrounding countryside, provided you have your own wheels.

Rooms are large and light-filled, with wood floors and fresh white linens.

ℹ️ Getting There & Away

Most people visit Lipica as a day trip from Sežana, 6km to the north, or Divača, 10km to the northeast, both of which are on a rail line and accessible from Ljubljana or Koper. An infrequent bus runs from Sežana to Lipica (€2), otherwise a taxi will cost around €10.

ℹ️ Getting Around

At Lipica, bikes can be hired at the golf course reception (per two hours/day €5/10).

WESTERN WINE REGIONS

Welcome to one of our favourite corners of Slovenia. This collection of wine regions out west, close to the Italian border, is a wonderful place to spend a few days. The wineries and excellent dining options are reason enough to visit the Vipava Valley, while the neighbouring Karst Wine Region is a well-kept secret that's worth discovering. But the crowning glory is Goriška Brda, a Tuscany-like land of fortified villages atop rolling hills with boutique family wineries in between.

Vipava Valley

☑ 05 / ELEV 180M
The fertile, wine-rich Vipava Valley (Vipavska Dolina in Slovenian) stretches southeast from Nova Gorica. It's an excellent place to tour by car or bike, with outstanding gourmet treats and idyllic rural scenery. The valley's mild climate encourages the cultivation of stone fruits – the trees are pretty with blossoms in spring, while autumn foliage is deeply colourful and photogenic.

Under the Roman Empire, this was the first important station on the road from Aquileia to Emona (Ljubljana). The landmark Mt Nanos looms above the valley – a mountain plateau from which the Vipava River springs, and a popular recreation area for hiking, mountain biking, climbing and paragliding. There are two main towns in the valley: Ajdovščina (population 6600) and Vipava (population 1950), only about 7km apart. The numerous villages and hamlets are home to family-owned wine producers.

South of Branik is the unofficial border between the Vipava Valley and the Karst Wine Region (p141).

HRASTOVLJE'S DANCE OF DEATH

The tiny Karst village of Hrastovlje is one of southwestern Slovenia's most rewarding excursions. The small Romanesque church here is a dramatic sight, surrounded by medieval stone walls with corner towers, and covered inside with extraordinary 15th-century frescoes, including the famous *Dance of Death*. Getting here involves a few twists and turns – you'll really need your own vehicle – but it's worth it many times over.

The **Church of the Holy Trinity** (Cerkev Sv Trojice; ☑ 031 432 231; adult/child €3/1.50; ☺ 9am-noon & 1-5pm Wed-Mon) is the biggest drawcard of the village; what attracts most people to this little church is the famous *Dance of Death* or *Danse Macabre*, a fresco that shows 11 skeletons leading the same number of people forward to a freshly dug grave. A 12th holds open a coffin. The doomed line-up includes peasants, kings, cardinals, and even a moneylender (who attempts to bribe his skeletal escort with a purse): all are equal in the eyes of God.

The church was built between the 12th and 14th centuries in the southern Romanesque style, with fortifications added in 1581 in advance of the Ottomans. Its sombre exterior is disarming in the extreme.

The *Dance of Death* is not the only fresco; the interior is completely festooned with paintings by John of Kastav, painted around the 1490s. The frescoes helped the illiterate to understand the Old Testament stories, the Passion of Christ and the lives of the saints. Make time for the 12-minute taped commentary (in four languages, including English) that guides you around the little church.

Facing you as you enter the church is the 17th-century altar, the central apse with scenes from the Crucifixion on the ceiling and portraits of the Trinity and the Apostles. On the arch, Mary is crowned queen of heaven. To the right are episodes from the seven days of Creation, with Adam and Eve and Cain and Abel on the right.

On the ceilings of the north and south aisles are scenes from daily life as well as the liturgical year and its seasonal duties. Christ's Passion is depicted at the top of the southernmost wall, including his Descent into Hell, where devils attack him with blazing cannons. Below the scenes of the Passion is the Dance of Death.

Elsewhere in the village, the quiet **Galerija J Pohlen** (☑ 041 398 368; doris.pohlen@ guest.arnes.si; €2; ☺ 10am-noon & 1-5pm Wed-Mon) exhibits works by sculptor Jožeta Pohlen (1926–2005), who hailed from the village. It's one of a number of small galleries to have opened in Hrastovlje in recent years. Opening hours often vary from the official schedule, but someone with a key is never far away; ask at the church if all else fails.

Gostilna Svab (☑ 05-659 05 10; Hrastovlje 53; mains €9-19; ☺ noon-10pm) is a welcoming little country inn with a surprisingly diverse menu of seasonal local specialities and a good selection of Slovenian wines. Dishes include local cheeses, Istrian soups, grilled meats, pasta dishes with truffles and mountain trout. In winter, the fireplace is the place to be.

Hrastovlje is 30km southwest of Divača off the main highway to the coast; Koper is 18km to the northwest. It is hard to reach without a car or bicycle. There is a weekday afternoon train from Koper (€1.95, 16 minutes), but there is no return train. The church is about 1.5km northwest of Hrastovlje's train station.

SOUTHWESTERN SLOVENIA VIPAVA VALLEY

🏃 Activities

★ **Faladur** WINE
(☑ 040 232 987; www.faladur.si; Lokarjev Drevored 8b, Ajdovščina; ☺ 10am-6pm Mon-Fri, to 2pm Sat) Faladur is a wine shop and tasting room where you're in very capable hands: host Matej can recommend wines to try, put together a platter of valley-produced cheeses, hams and olives to accompany them, and tell you about home-grown varietals and la-

bels. Faladur also offers tastings of the craft beer produced in Ajdovščina, Pelicon.

Vinoteka Vipava WINE
(☑ 05-368 70 41; Glavni trg 1, Vipava; ☺ 9am-7pm Jul-Sep, to 6pm Mon-Fri, to 1pm Sat Oct-Jun) Attached to Vipava's tourist information centre, this friendly, well-informed *vinoteka* stocks some 180 bottles from 45 local wine makers. For €5 you can sample 10 wines (refunded if you buy a bottle).

WINE TASTING IN THE VIPAVA VALLEY

The constant winds, plus the proximity of the sea, and the sun on steep slopes, contribute to ideal conditions for wine production. Both reds and whites are produced, including fresh whites from the indigenous zelen and pinela grapes, and a total of 25 different grape varieties are grown across the Vipava's 2500 hectares of vines. The focus is generally on small-scale family producers, boutique wineries and chemical-free production.

It may help to get a big-picture view of wines, producers and flavours before you take to the back roads. For in-town tastings, try Faladur (p143) in Ajdovščina or Vinoteka Vipava in Vipava.

One way to take the hassle out of tracking down each winery (and let someone else do the driving) is by taking a tour. **Winestronaut** (☎040 166 042; www.winestronaut.com; Skrilje 26, Vipava; per person from €49) offers excellent vineyard and tasting tours and can arrange pick-ups around the valley.

Recommended labels to try (and estates to track down) include:

Batič (☎05-308 86 76; www.batic-wines.com; Šempas 130; ⏰by appointment) A versatile biodynamic wine producer, Batič has a winning suite of whites, reds, rosés and dessert wines. Visitors are welcome for tastings and cellar door sales, but ring ahead to let them know you're coming.

Burja (☎070 900 075, 041 363 272; www.burjaestate.com; Podgrič 12, Podnanos; ⏰by appointment) Whites and reds, local zelen grapes and a Vipava version of the Istrian malvasia variety – Burja is a dynamic winery with plenty of local and international awards across its portfolio. Ring ahead to arrange a tasting.

Guerila (☎05-166 02 65, 041 616 091; www.guerila.si; Planina 111, Ajdovščina; ⏰by appointment) This excellent biodynamic, boutique winemaker is the work of Zmago Petrič and his family. They work primarily with the local zelen and pinela vines, in a chemical-free environment. They offer tastings and estate tours if you contact them in advance.

Tilia Estate (☎031 399 748, 05-364 66 84; www.tiliaestate.si; Potoče 41, Dobravlje; ⏰10am-5pm Mon-Sat) This respected winery produces a lot of different varieties on its 10 hectares, and is sometimes called the 'house of pinots', including pinot noir and pinot gris. It also produces merlot, cabernet sauvignon, sauvignon blanc, chardonnay and yellow muscat. Guided tours and tastings are usually possible whenever they're open, although ring ahead just to be sure.

Sleeping

Hotels are fairly thin on the ground, but that gap is filled by plenty of apartments, private rooms and guesthouses that lie scattered throughout the valley. Advance bookings are strongly recommended in summer.

★Youth Hostel Ajdovščina HOSTEL $
(Hiša Mladih; ☎05-368 93 83; www.hostel-ajdovscina.si; Cesta IV Prekomorske 61a; dm €18-21; P@🛜) This is a high-quality hostel, with bright, fresh features and cool design. Rooms sleep four to eight (with a 24-bed room for groups). All bathrooms are shared; there's also a kitchen (breakfast €3) and laundry. It's on the northern edge of Ajdovščina in a great park-like setting, alongside a youth centre, bar and summertime concert venue. There's a craft-beer brewery across the road.

Camp Lijak CAMPGROUND $
(☎05-308 85 57; www.parklijak.com; Ozeljan 6a, Šempas; campsite per adult/child/van €10.70/8.20/5.10; P🛜🏊) About 6km east of Nova Gorica, this year-round campground has a focus on families and activities: summertime hiking, cycling and mountain-biking tours can be arranged, and year-round paragliding. Family-sized bungalows are available (sleeping two/four €66/88); 'hobbit holes' are timber cubicles that sleep one or two (per person €16.30).

★Majerija GUESTHOUSE $$
(☎05-368 50 10; www.majerija.si; Slap 18; s/d €73/98; P🛜) Four kilometres from Vipava in the hamlet of Slap, Majerija has a fun, unique offering: 10 rooms built underground – under the herb garden, in fact. These simple, stylish rooms feature custom-made timber furniture, skylights above the

bed, and a herb theme (they're named for the lavender, basil and assorted plants growing above).

🍴 Eating

The Vipava Valley is well-known for its wines, but local cheeses and air-dried *pršut* make the perfect accompaniment. A handful of rural restaurants, and even the occasional winery restaurant, are also present.

★ Majerija
SLOVENIAN $$

(☑ 05-368 50 10; www.majerija.si; Slap 18; mains €16, 3-/5-course menus €28/37; ☺ noon-3pm & 6-10pm Thu-Sat, noon-5pm Sun, closed 2nd half of Feb & 2nd half of Jul) Local produce shines in skilled, contemporary dishes at this farmhouse idyll – how about Vipava ham with lavender honey and salted peaches as a starter? The multicourse menus are great value. Service is exemplary, the setting is rustic and charming. It closes for two weeks at the end of February and July.

Gostilnica Mandrija
SLOVENIAN $$

(☑ 041 752 584; www.mandrija.si; Ajshevica 81; mains €8-15; ☺ noon-midnight Thu-Mon) Consistently good reviews from travellers mark this out as a worthy pit stop out in the countryside southeast of town. From the wood-beamed ceilings to the local chops, it's a warm and inviting place where the food is good and traditional without too many elaborations.

★ Gostilna Pri Lojzetu
SLOVENIAN $$$

(☑ 05-368 70 07; www.zemono.si; Dvorec Zemono; mains €18-40, 3-/4-/5-course tasting menu €55/65/75; ☺ 5-11pm Wed & Thu, from noon Fri-Sun) For gourmands, this is a must. Make an advance booking, and make the trip 2km north of Vipava to Dvorec Zemono, a frescoed mansion built in 1680. Here, you'll find innovative, Gostilna Pri Lojzetu, ranked among Slovenia's finest restaurants: 'Michelin-star-worthy' is common praise. Try the pork shoulder marinated in honey, or boned wild duck. Better still, opt for a tasting menu.

ℹ Information

Tourist offices in the region have information about visiting local wineries.

Tourist Information Centre Ajdovščina (TIC; ☑ 05-365 91 40; www.tic-ajdovscina.si; Cesta IV Prekomorske 61c, Ajdovščina; ☺ 10am-6pm Mon-Fri, 8am-noon Sat May-Sep, 8am-4pm Mon-Fri, to noon Sat Oct-Apr) At the youth hostel complex.

Tourist Information Centre Vipava (TIC; ☑ 05-368 70 41; www.izvirna-vipavska.si; Glavni

WORTH A TRIP

WORTH A TRIP: SMARTNO & KANAL

The Goriška Brda area has been under the influence of northern and central Italy since time immemorial, and you'll think you've crossed the border as you go through little towns with narrow streets and the remains of feudal castles. One perfect example is Šmartno (San Martino), a photogenic fortified village with stone walls and a 16th-century tower. It's 4km east of Dobrovo.

At the northeastern edge of Goriška Brda, on the road to Tolmin and Most na Soči, lovely Kanal has a beautiful, double-arched bridge over the Soča River; it's worth pulling over and getting out to explore the old town centre and take in the view from and of the bridge.

trg 3, Vipava; ☺ 9am-7pm Jul-Sep, to 6pm Mon-Fri, to 2pm Sat Sep-Jun) In the centre of town.

ℹ Getting There & Away

About a dozen buses daily connect Ljubljana and Nova Gorica, travelling via Postojna, Vipava and Ajdovščina (Ljubljana to Vipava €8.60, 1¾ hours).

In the Vipava Valley, the tourist offices and numerous accommodation providers have bikes for rent.

Goriška Brda

☑ 05 / ELEV UP TO 800M

Picture-perfect Goriška Brda (Gorica Hills) is a tiny wine-producing region that stretches from Solkan west to the Italian border. It's a charmer, reminiscent of Tuscany, full of rolling hills topped with small settlements and churches, its hillsides lined with grapevines and orchards. In short, it's one of Europe's best-kept secrets. A good place to start is **Dobrovo**, 18km northwest of central Nova Gorica, where there's a castle, *vinoteka* and information centre.

In addition to its grapes and wine, Goriška Brda is celebrated for its fruit, cheeses and olive oil, and especially its cherries (usually available from early June).

⦿ Sights & Activities

Wine tasting is the main activity in these parts, although you could also go for a hike or two-wheeled ride in the hills, stopping in pretty villages at regular intervals as you go.

Dobrovo Castle CASTLE

(Grad Dobrovo; ☑ 05-395 95 86; Grajska cesta 10; adult/child €3/1.50; ☺ 8am-4pm Tue-Fri, 1-6pm Sat & Sun) The Renaissance-style Dobrovo Castle, dating from 1606, has a handful of rooms filled with artworks and period furnishings (limited labelling). There's a decent restaurant here, and Vinoteka Brda for wine tasting.

🛏 Sleeping

There are apartments and private rooms for rent across the region – bookings can be made through tourist information centres and booking websites. Šmartno in particular has a few standout options. A number of wineries engage in *agriturismo,* with rooms and meals available – Bjana is one of the best.

⭐ **Hotel San Martin** HOTEL $$

(☑ 05-330 56 60; www.sanmartin.si; Šmartno 11; r/ste/apt €90/110/140; P ⚙ ☎) To stay in the area, atmospheric Šmartno is a top choice. This hotel is close to the entrance to the fortified village and has polished service, bright, good-value rooms (including family-sized)

and a highly regarded restaurant (Tuesday to Sunday) showcasing regional produce and enjoying a view-enriched terrace.

⭐ **Hiša Marica** GUESTHOUSE $$

(☑ 05-304 10 39; www.marica.si; Šmartno 33; s/d €70/100; ⚙ ☎) This charming old inn lies within the fortified walls of Šmartno and offers four excellent, spacious rooms. Also here is a wine bar (Wednesday to Monday) serving up local flavours, including home-cured hams and salamis, and Soča Valley cheeses.

🍴 Eating

Most places to stay have restaurants, and there are a few country inns scattered around. Otherwise, there's a little more choice in Nova Gorica.

Hotel San Martin SLOVENIAN $$

(☑ 05-330 56 60; www.sanmartin.si/en/gastron omy; Šmartno 11; mains €11-20; ☺ noon-3pm & 6-10pm Tue-Thu, noon-10pm Fri & Sat, to 4pm Sun) With fine views from the terrace, a thoughtfully prepared seasonal menu and a com-

---

WINE TASTING IN GORIŠKA BRDA

The hills and valleys of Goriška Brda, hard up against the Italian border, are known for their more than 50 small, boutique, family-run wineries.

As small operations, most have outsourced their tastings and sales to cooperatives set up to market the region's wines.

Vinoteka Brda (☑ 05-395 92 10; www.vinotekabrda.si; Grajska cesta 10; tastings from €7; ☺ noon-8pm Wed-Sat) In the cellar of Dobrovo Castle is Vinoteka Brda, where you can sample the local vintages (white rebula and chardonnay, or pinot and merlot reds), which go nicely with the cheese and nibbles on offer. There are 300 wines from 49 different producers to try.

Vinska Klet Goriška Brda (☑ 05-331 01 44; www.klet-brda.si; Zadružna cesta 9, Dobrovo; ☺ 10am-4pm Mon-Sat) This wine cooperative, just downhill from Dobrovo Castle, has the largest wine cellar in Slovenia. It offers an excellent 90-minute 'Sommelier Tasting' (€20), which includes a tasting of six wines, a quick sommelier primer, a visit to the wine cellar, and cheese and nibbles. Advance bookings are essential; other tours and tastings are also on offer.

If you prefer to go straight to the source, there are also a handful of options. Check out www.brda.si, although most links direct you to one of the cooperatives. Otherwise, try:

Bjana (☑ 05-395 92 30, tastings 031 339 931; www.bjana.si; Biljana 38; ☺ by appointment) One of the longest-standing wineries in the area, Bjana has won numerous awards for its sparkling wines. There are two gorgeous rooms if you're keen to stay overnight, and they arrange tastings if you contact them in advance.

Scurek (☑ 05-304 50 21; www.scurek.com; Pleshivo 44; ☺ by appointment) Almost within sight of the Italian border (some of the vineyards even lie across the border), this family-run producer is known for its full-bodied white and red Stara Brajda blends. If you contact them in advance, they're usually happy to show you around (check out the colourful barrels decorated by artists) and give you a tasting.

THE 'MINI-BERLIN WALL' OF NOVA GORICA

When the town of Gorica was awarded to the Italians under the Treaty of Paris in 1947 and became Gorizia, the Yugoslav government set about building a model town on the eastern side of the border 'following the principles of Le Corbusier'. Appropriately enough, they called it 'New Gorica' and erected a chain-link barrier between the two towns.

This 'mini-Berlin Wall' was finally pulled down to great fanfare in 2004 after Slovenia joined the EU, leaving Trg Evrope (or Piazza della Transalpina, as the Italians call it) straddling the now open border right behind Nova Gorica train station.

A couple of other worthwhile sights here include the **Kostanjevica Monastery** (Samostan Kostanjevica; ☑ 05-330 77 50; www.samostan-kostanjevica.si; Škrabčeva ulica 1; tombs €2, library €1; ⊗ 9am-noon & 3-5pm Mon-Sat, 3-5pm Sun), founded by the Capuchin Franciscans in the early 17th century. It has a library with 10,000 volumes and 30 incunabula. In the crypt of the Church of the Annunciation is the Tomb of the Bourbons, which contains the mortal remains of the last members of the French house of Bourbon. This includes Charles X (1757–1836), who died of cholera while on holiday in Gorizia.

Three kilometres east of the town, the **Goriško Museum** (Goriški Muzej; ☑ 05-333 59 811; www.goriskimuzej.si; Grajska cesta 1, Kromberk; adult/child €2.50/1.25; ⊗ 9am-7pm Mon-Fri, 1-7pm Sun May-Oct, to 5pm Nov-Apr) resides in the impressive, 17th-century Kromberk Castle. The collection spans rich period furnishings to modern artworks, incorporating religious carvings and details of the Vipava Valley in the Roman era. There's a lovely restaurant in the castle too, and summertime music events held here.

The tour company **Slocally** (☑ 041 432 488; www.slocally.com; Ulica Ivana Gradnika 5a, Deskle; guide per hr €25-35), based about 10km north of Nova Gorica in Plave, encourages slow travel and gives curious visitors a range of unique and affordable local experiences (herb-picking, wine or cheese tours, woodcraft, culinary workshops etc).

There are a handful of good places to stay, although most visitors prefer the quieter villages of the Soča or Vipava valleys. There's also the usual Slovenian portfolio of apartments and homestays on offer.

mitment to local ingredients, the restaurant of the hotel of the same name in Šmartno comes highly recommended. Watch for classic mountain dishes like venison ragout or mountain trout, while the desserts are heavenly or sinful, depending on your perspective. Fab wines, too.

Restavracija Grad Dobrovo SLOVENIAN $$ (☑ 05-395 95 06; Grajska cesta 10; mains €9-17; ⊗ noon-3pm & 7-10pm Fri-Wed) This atmospheric place inside Dobrovo's castle gets mixed reviews from travellers – word on the street is that the service sometimes goes missing and the quality is not what it was. But it's worth it for the atmosphere alone, with a standard range of seafood, grilled meats and pasta on the menu.

❶ Information

Tourist Information Centre (☑ 05-395 95 94; www.brda.si; Grajska cesta; ⊗ 9am-5pm Mon-Fri, 10am-6pm Sat & Sun Mar-Oct, 9am-4pm Mon-Fri Nov-Feb) Information on the Goriška Brda region.

❶ Getting There & Away

Public transport out here is nearly nonexistent – your own wheels (two or four) are recommended for explorations.

SLOVENIAN COAST

Slovenia has just 47km of coastline on the Adriatic Sea, but it certainly makes the most of it. Three seaside towns – Koper, with its medieval core, Izola, known for its good restaurants, and glorious Piran – are full of important Venetian Gothic architecture, and have clean beaches, boats for rent and rollicking bars. That said, the coast is overbuilt, and jammed with tourists from May to September. If you're looking for solitude, head for the hinterland to the south or east where 'Slovenian Istria' still goes about its daily life.

Koper

☑ 05 / POP 25,500

Coastal Slovenia's largest town, Koper (Capodistria in Italian) is something of a well-concealed secret. At first glance, it appears

Koper

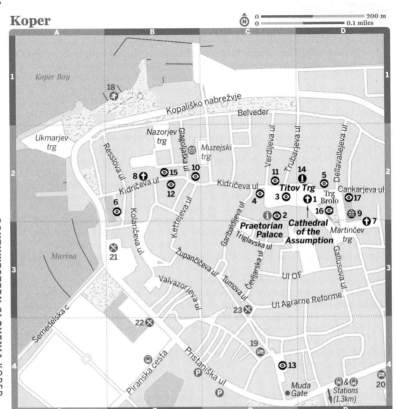

to be a workaday port city that scarcely gives tourism a second thought. Your first impression may be even more underwhelming as you see all the industrial areas and shopping malls on the outskirts. But Koper's central core is delightfully medieval and far less overrun than its ritzy cousin Piran and well worth a day visit at the very least.

Koper's recreational area, the seaside resort of Ankaran, is to the north across Koper Bay.

History

Koper has been known by many names during its long history – as Aegida to ancient Greeks, Capris to the Romans and Justinopolis to the Byzantines. In the 13th century it became Caput Histriae – Capital of Istria – from which its Italian name Capodistria is derived. Its golden age was during the 15th and 16th centuries under the Venetian Republic, when the town monopolised the salt trade. But when Trieste, 20km to the northeast,

was proclaimed a free port in the early 18th century, Koper lost much of its importance.

Between the world wars Koper was controlled by the Italians. After WWII the disputed Adriatic coast area – the so-called Free Territory of Trieste – was divided into two zones, with Koper going to Yugoslavia and Trieste to Italy. Today Koper is the centre of the Italian ethnic community of Slovenia.

⊙ Sights & Activities

Although the city has no standout attractions, it's a great place to wander and enjoy its architectural riches. The easiest way to see Koper's Old Town is to walk from the marina on Ukmarjev trg east along Kidričeva ulica to Titov trg and then south down Čevljarska ulica, taking various detours along the way.

★ Titov Trg   SQUARE

In the centre of old Koper, Titov trg is a Venetian-influenced stunner; mercifully,

Koper

like much of the Old Town's core, it is closed to traffic. On the north side is the arcaded Venetian Gothic Loggia built in 1463 (a perfectly placed cafe lives here); attached is the Loggia Gallery, with changing art exhibits.

To the south is the Praetorian Palace, once the symbol of Venetian power in the region. On the square's western side, the Armoury was a munitions dump four centuries ago and is now university offices. Opposite is the Cathedral of the Assumption and its belfry.

★**Praetorian Palace** NOTABLE BUILDING
(Pretorska Palača; ☏05-664 64 03; Titov trg 3; adult/child €4/2.50; ⊙tours 10am, noon, 2pm, 4pm & 6pm Jul-Sep, 11am, 1pm & 3pm Oct-Jun) On the southern side of Titov trg is the white Praetorian Palace, a mixture of Venetian Gothic and Renaissance styles dating from the 15th century and the very symbol of Koper. Now serving as the town hall, it contains a reconstructed old pharmacy and the tourist information office on the ground floor, plus exhibits on the history of Koper and a ceremonial hall for weddings on the 1st floor. Access is via guided tour.

The facade of the palace, once the residence of Koper's mayor who was appointed by the doge in Venice, is festooned with medallions, reliefs and coats of arms.

★**Cathedral of the Assumption** CATHEDRAL
(Stolnica Marijinega Vnebovzetja) Plumb on Titov trg is the Cathedral of the Assumption and its 36m-tall belfry, now called the City Tower (adult/child €3/2; ⊙9am-1pm & 4-8pm Jul-Sep, 9am-5pm Oct-Jun), with 204 climbable stairs to superb views. The cathedral, partly Romanesque and Gothic but mostly dating from the mid-18th century, has a white classical interior with a feeling of space and light that belies the sombre exterior.

Behind the cathedral to the north is a circular Romanesque **Rotunda of John the Baptist** (Rotunda Janeza Krstnika), a baptistery *(krstilnica)* dating from the second half of the 12th century, with a ceiling fresco.

Trg Brolo SQUARE
Linked to Titov trg to the east, Trg Brolo is a wide and leafy square of fine old buildings, including the late-18th-century baroque Brutti Palace, now the central library, to the north. On the eastern side is the 17th-century Vissich-Nardi Palace, containing government offices and the Fontico, a granary where the town's wheat was once stored, with wonderful medallions and reliefs. Close by is the disused **Church of St James** (Martinčev trg) dating from the 14th century.

Kidričeva Ulica STREET
On the north side of Kidričeva ulica are several churches from the 16th century, including the **Church of St Nicholas** (Cerkev Sv Nikolaja; ⊙hours vary), plus some restored Venetian houses and the 18th-century baroque **Totto Palace** (Palača Totto), with winged lion relief. Opposite the palace are wonderful medieval town houses, with protruding upper storeys painted in a checked red, yellow and green pattern.

Carpacciov Trg SQUARE
One of the most colourful streets in Koper, Kidričeva ulica, starts at Carpacciov trg, where the **Column of St Justina** (Steber Sv

THE PARENZANA TRAIL

You can sample a portion (or all) of the Parenzana Trail, a 130km walking and cycling trail (numbered D8) that runs along the old narrow-gauge Parenzana railway, which once connected Trieste in Italy with Poreč in Croatia. About 30km of the trail runs through Slovenian Istria. See www.parenzana.info for more details, including two-, three- and five-day itinerary suggestions.

Justine) commemorates Koper's contribution – a galley – to the Battle of Lepanto in which Turkey was defeated by the European powers in 1571. Just north is a large Roman covered basin that now serves as a fountain. The western edge of the square is marked by the large arched Taverna, a one-time salt warehouse dating from the 15th century.

Prešernov Trg SQUARE

The 17th-century Italian family who erected the fountain in Prešernov trg was named Da Ponte; thus it is shaped like a bridge (*ponte* in Italian). At the square's southern end is the **Muda Gate** (Vrata Muda). Erected in 1516, it's the last of a dozen such entrances to remain standing. On the south side of the archway you'll see the city symbol: the face of a youth in a sunburst.

Beach BEACH

(Mestno Kopališče; Kopališko nabrežje; ☺ 8am-7pm May-Sep) Buzzing in summer, Koper's tiny beach lies on the northwest edge of the Old Town. It has a small bathhouse with toilets and showers, grassy areas for lying in the sun, and a bar and cafe. On hot summer nights, people pay little heed to the 'closing' hour and swim until late.

🛏 Sleeping

Hostel Histria HOSTEL $

(☎ 070 133 552; www.hostel-histria.si; Ulica pri Velikih Vratih 17; dm €15-23; ❄ @ 🛜) Supremely placed in the core of the Old Town, this cosy place is in a 200-year-old house, with decent facilities (including air-con and laundry). Dorms have six or eight beds; bathrooms are shared.

Camping Adria Ankaran CAMPGROUND $

(☎ 05-663 73 50; www.adria-ankaran.si; Jadranska cesta 25; campsite adult €11.50-13, child €5-8; ☺ mid-Apr–mid-Oct; 🅿 @ 🛜 🏊) This enormous, well-run campground is on the seashore in Ankaran, 10km to the north, and is the closest site to Koper (with regular bus connections). Choose from 430 pitches, plus cabins, apartments and hotel rooms and loads of facilities (bowling, mini-golf, wellness centre, water sports). The camping charge includes use of the seawater swimming pools (nonguests on weekdays/weekends €5/7).

★ Hostel Villa Domus HOSTEL $$

(☎ 030 468 777; www.villa-domus.si; Vojkovo Nabrežje 12; dm from €17, r €54-77; ❄ 🛜) On the southern fringe of the old city, this well-regarded hostel has simple but modern dorms and doubles or twins that put most hotels in the area to shame. Some rooms from the upper floors have fine views and the rooms themselves, though on the small side, are terrific value.

🍴 Eating

Fritolin FISH & CHIPS $

(Pristaniška ulica 2; dishes €2.50-8) There's an outdoor fresh-food market not far from the shore, and it's surrounded by cheap eating spots and cafe-bars popular with locals. We love tiny Fritolin for its fish and chips: calamari fried or grilled, sardines, portions of seabass or bream, or *fritto misto* (mixed fried seafood). There are benches out front, or a park nearby.

Istrska Klet Slavček SLOVENIAN $

(☎ 05-627 67 29; Župančičeva ulica 39; mains €7-12; ☺ 8am-10pm Mon-Fri) The Istrian Cellar, situated below the 18th-century Carli Palace, is one of the most colourful places for a meal in Koper's Old Town. Come for authentic home cooking (hearty soups and stews, roast pork), wine from the barrel, and truly vintage decor that hasn't changed in 30-odd years.

★ Capra MEDITERRANEAN $$

(☎ 041 602 030; www.capra.si; Pristaniška ulica 3; mains €9-23; ☺ noon-11pm) Capra is a sexy new indoor–outdoor venue with a touch of Scandi style. Its appeal extends all day, from coffee to lounge-y cocktails, and the creative, ambitious menu covers many bases with great seafood, salad and pasta options (how's homemade pasta with scampi and truffle?). Presentation is first-class, as are the desserts.

ℹ️ Information

MONEY
Banka Koper (Kidričeva ulica 14; ⊙8.30am-12.30pm & 2-5pm Mon-Fri)

POST
Post Office (📋05-666 66 90; Muzejski trg 3; ⊙8am-6pm Mon-Fri, to noon Sat)

TOURIST INFORMATION
Tourist Information Centre (TIC; 📋05-664 64 03; www.koper.si; Titov trg 3; ⊙9am-8pm Jul-Sep, to 5pm Oct-Jun) Friendly office on the ground floor of the Praetorian Palace.

TRAVEL AGENCIES
Kompas (📋05-663 05 84; www.kompas.si; Pristaniška ulica 17; ⊙8am-7pm Mon-Fri, to 1pm Sat) Travel agency which can arrange local tours as well as apartment accommodation.

ℹ️ Getting There & Away

The joint bus and train station is 1.5km southeast of the Old Town on Kolodvorska cesta.

There's a handy central bus stop for local services (including to other coastal cities) on Piranška ulica (just south of the market).

BUS
Arriva (📋090 74 11; www.arriva.si) is the bus operator on the coast; see its website for schedules. Buses go to Izola (€2, 15 minutes), Portorož (€3, 40 minutes) and Piran (€3, 45 minutes) up to three times an hour on weekdays (hourly on weekends). Five daily buses make the run to Ljubljana (€11.50, 1¾ hours).

Arriva and Croatian-based Črnja Tours (www.crnja-tours.hr) run regular buses to Italian and Croatian destinations. Buses to Trieste (€3.60, 45 minutes) run up to nine times daily Monday to Saturday. Črnja Tours has a daily service to Venice (€19.50, three hours). Destinations in Croatia include Rovinj (€12, three hours) via Umag, Novi Grad and Poreč.

TRAIN
Five trains a day link Koper to Ljubljana (€11.36, 2½ hours) via Postojna (€8.79, 1½ hours) and Divača (€6.08, 45 minutes).

To get to Buzet and Pula in Croatia from Koper, you must change at Hrpelje-Kozina for any of two to three trains a day.

ℹ️ Getting Around

Parking in much of the Old Town is severely restricted – or banned altogether – between 6am and 3pm. Ask your accommodation provider for advice, or leave your vehicle in the pay car parks along Pristaniška ulica.

BUS
Red local buses link the bus and train stations to the rest of the town; line L2 ans 2A will get you to the Tržnica stop (Piranška ulica), by the market. Line 7 does a circle around the Old Town. Local buses are €1.50 if you pay the driver, €0.80 if you pre-purchase your ticket (from vending machines or kiosks).

Izola
📋05 / POP 11,162

Izola, a fishing port 7km southwest of Koper, has traditionally been considered the poor relation among the historical towns of Slovenia's short but crowded coastline. Perhaps this is why it is often bypassed by foreign visitors. And yet Izola does have a certain Venetian charm, together with a large marina, some narrow old winding streets and excellent restaurants and bars where you might linger. If Piran is solidly booked (or its prices too high), Izola makes a good, atmospheric fallback.

History
The Romans built a port called Haliaetum at Simon's Bay (Simonov Zaliv) southwest of the Old Town, and you can still see parts of the original landing when the tide is very low. While under the control of Venice in the Middle Ages, Izola – at that time an island (*isola* is Italian for 'island') – flourished, particularly in the trading of such commodities as olives, fish and wine. But a devastating plague in the 16th century and the ascendancy of Trieste as the premier port in the northern Adriatic destroyed the town's economic base. During the period of the Illyrian Provinces in the early 19th century, the French pulled down the town walls and used them to fill the channel separating the island from the mainland. Today, Izola is the country's foremost fishing port.

⊙ Sights & Activities
There are popular pebble beaches to the north and southeast of the Old Town, but the best one is at **Simon's Bay** about 1.5km to the southwest. It has a grassy area for sunbathing.

Besenghi degli Ughi Palace NOTABLE BUILDING
(Besenghijeva Palača; Gregorčičeva ulica 76) Izola's most beautiful building – albeit looking a little worse for wear – is this late-baroque palazzo below the Parish Church of St Maurus. Built between 1775 and 1781, the mansion has windows and balconies adorned with

Izola

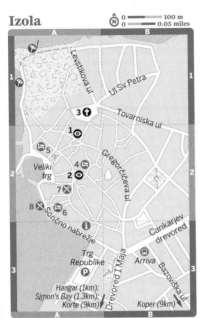

N
0 ——— 100 m
0 ——— 0.05 miles

stuccos and wonderful wrought-iron grilles painted light blue. It is now a music school.

Parish Church of St Maurus CHURCH
(Župnijska Cerkev Sv Mavra; Garibaldijeva ulica; ⊙ hours vary) This renovated, salmon-coloured, 16th-century church and its detached bell tower are on the hill above the town. The views are the main reason to climb up here, but take a peek inside if it's open.

Strunjan Landscape Park NATURE RESERVE
(Krajinski Park Strunjan; www.parkstrunjan.si; Strunjan 152) For centuries the people who lived at Strunjan, a peninsula halfway between Izola and Piran, were engaged in salt-making. Today the old salt-pan area is protected, along with other natural and cultural heritage sites, inside Strunjan Landscape Park. Although there has been much development (resorts and public beach areas) around Strunjan Bay to the southwest, much of the peninsula's northern coast is remarkably unspoiled.

🛏 Sleeping

★ Hostel Alieti HOSTEL $
(☑ 051 670 680; www.hostel-alieti.si; Dvoriščna ulica 24; dm €18-23; ✱ 🛜) This might just be the coast's best hostel. Tucked away off a winding alley, it's small and modern with fresh

decor – beds are in dorms sleeping four to six (shared bathrooms; kitchen facilities). Plus there's air-con, and a simple breakfast included in the price. Owner Uroš is friendly and welcoming.

Laguna Izola ACCOMMODATION SERVICES $$
(☑ 05-640 02 78; www.lagunaizola.com; Istrska Vrata 7; apt for 2 €48-129) This central agency can help with accommodation in and around Izola – rooms, apartments, hotels. Details including locations, photos and prices are on its website.

Hotel Marina HOTEL $$$
(☑ 05-660 41 00; www.hotelmarina.si; Veliki trg 11; s €65-140, d €80-210; 🅿 ✱ @ 🛜) Behind its somewhat incongruous chocolate-brown exterior, this super-central, 52-room hotel offers friendly service, a popular seafood restaurant and appealing extras (bike hire, boat trips, wellness centre). Rates vary with the season and room type: superior rooms have sea views and terraces, standard rooms have neither, but all are comfy and well-equipped.

✖ Eating & Drinking

Izola is the best place on the coast to enjoy a seafood meal, with a range of restaurants serving the freshest catch. Always ask the exact price of the fish: seafood is sold by decagram (usually abbreviated as *dag* on menus) or kilogram, so you might end up eating (and paying) a lot more than you expected.

★ Marina Restaurant SEAFOOD $$
(☑ 05-660 41 00; www.hotelmarina.si; Veliki trg 11; mains €9-21; ⊙ noon-10pm) At the Marina Hotel, this much-loved restaurant serves a stellar

range of seafood (with accessible prices): fish soup, salt-crusted seabass, and lobster with pasta. Meat dishes are no slouch (pork fillet with olive polenta and fresh truffle). There are a range of good-value set menus available, including the daily three-course menu (€18).

Gostilna Sidro SEAFOOD $$
(☑05-641 47 11; Soncno Nabrezje 24; mains €9-22; ☺11am-10pm Fri-Wed) Fresh fish and all manner of seafood overlooking Izola's harbour. Friendly service. A price–quality ratio other seaside restaurants along this coast would do well to mimic. Bliss.

Gostilna Bujol SEAFOOD $$
(☑041 799 490; Verdijeva ulica 10; mains €9-19; ☺11am-10pm Wed-Sun) A place recommended by locals (especially for its cod-fish pate, or *bakalar na belo*), rustic Bujol has a selection of fresh fish offered fried or grilled (the menu is only in Slovenian but staff are helpful). Mussels, calamari and pasta with seafood are all good choices.

Hangar BAR
(☑05-640 05 05; www.facebook.com/izolahangar bar; Tomažičeva ulica 10a; ☺noon-midnight Sun-Thu, to 2am Fri & Sat) With a cafe ambience by day, and cool background music and cocktails by night, Hangar is a terrific place for a drink. They pride themselves on their bottled beers from around the world.

Manzioli Wine Bar WINE BAR
(☑041 738 947; Manziolijev trg 5; ☺noon-midnight Sun-Thu, to 1am Fri & Sat) This rather lovely stone-walled wine bar, inside a Venetian Gothic mansion, serves fabulous regional wines, accompanied by enticing boards of cheeses and cured meats. Tables spill out onto the street in summer.

ℹ Information

Tourist Information Centre (☑05-640 10 50; www.izola.eu; Ljubljanska ulica 17; ☺9am-8pm Jun-Aug, shorter hours rest of year) Signposted from the waterfront promenade, it has plenty of useful information on Izola and the rest of the Slovenian coast.

ℹ Getting There & Away

Arriva (☑090 74 11; www.arriva.si) buses serve the coast. Buses run east to Koper (€2, 15 minutes) and west to Portorož (€2, 25 minutes) and Piran (€2.50, 30 minutes) up to three times an hour on weekdays (hourly on weekends).

Up to seven daily buses make the run to Ljubljana (€11.80, 2½ hours), via Koper.

International routes include two buses a day to Trieste (€4.80, one hour) in Italy; and two in summer to Umag (€5.60, 40 minutes), Pula (€7.80, 1½ hours) and Rovinj (€11, 2½ hours) in Croatia.

ℹ Getting Around

You can rent bicycles from **Koloset** (☑05-997 78 86; www.koloset.si; Gorkijeva ulica 8; per day from €12; ☺9am-1pm & 4-7pm Mon-Fri, 9am-1pm Sat) or the Hotel Marina (three hours/all day €5/12).

Buses **stop at Cankarjev drevored** (Cankarjev drevored); to reach the Old Town and its main square, Veliki trg, walk north along the waterfront promenade. From June to August a tourist train does an hourly loop around town from Trg Republike, stopping at beaches and the Belvedere resort (adult/child €4/2.50).

Order a taxi on ☑040 602 602 or ☑041 706 777.

Piran

☑05 / POP 3804

One of the loveliest towns anywhere along the Adriatic coast, picturesque Piran (Pirano in Italian) sits prettily at the tip of a narrow peninsula. Its Old Town – one of the best-preserved historical towns anywhere in the Mediterranean – is a gem of Venetian Gothic architecture, but it can be a mob scene at the height of summer. In quieter times, it's hard not to fall instantly in love with the atmospheric winding alleyways, the sunsets and the seafood restaurants.

◉ Sights

★ Tartinijev Trg   SQUARE

The pastel-toned Tartinijev Trg is a marble-paved square (oval, really) that was the inner harbour until it was filled in 1894. The statue of a nattily dressed gentleman in the centre is of native son, composer and violinist Giuseppe Tartini (1692–1770). East is the 1818 **Church of St Peter** (Cerkev Sv Petra). Across from the church is **Tartini House** (Tartinijeva Hiša; ☑ 05-671 00 40; www.pomorskimuzej.si; Kajuhova ulica 12; adult/child €2/1; ⊙ 9am-noon & 6-9pm Jul & Aug, shorter hours Sep-Jun), the composer's birthplace. The **Court House** (Sodniška Palača) and the porticoed 19th-century **Municipal Hall** (Občinska Palača), home to the tourist information centre, dominate the western edge of the square.

Venetian House   HISTORIC BUILDING

(Benečanka; Tartinijev trg 4) One of Piran's most eye-catching structures is the red mid-15th-century Gothic Venetian House, with its tracery windows and balcony, in the northeast of Tartinijev trg.

There is a story attached to the stone relief between the two windows – a lion with a banner in its mouth and the Latin inscription *Lasa pur dir* above it. A wealthy merchant from Venice fell in love with a beautiful local girl, but she soon became the subject of local gossips. To shut them up (and keep his lover happy), the merchant built her this little palace complete with a reminder for his loose-lipped neighbours: 'Let them talk'.

★ Cathedral of St George   CATHEDRAL

(Župnijska Cerkev Sv Jurija; www.zupnija-piran.si; Adamičeva ulica 2) A cobbled street leads from behind the Venetian House to Piran's hilltop cathedral, baptistery and bell tower. The cathedral was built in baroque style in the early 17th century on the site of an earlier church from 1344.

The cathedral's doors are usually open and a metal grille allows you to see some of the richly ornate and newly restored interior, but full access is via the **Parish Museum of St George** (☑ 05-673 34 40; Adamičeva ulica 2; adult/child €2/1; ⊙ 9am-1pm & 5-7.30pm

Mon-Fri, 9am-2pm & 5-8pm Sat, from 11am Sun), which includes the church's treasury and catacombs.

Items of interest include a silver-plated figure of St George slaying a dragon, and a wooden model of the church dating from 1595.

The highlight of the cathedral interior (not visible from the grille) is the remarkable, early-14th-century wooden sculpture, The Crucified from Piran, depicting Christ on the cross.

★ Bell Tower   TOWER

(Zvonik; Adamičeva ulica; €1; ⊙ 10am-8pm summer, shorter hours rest of year) The Cathedral of St George's free-standing, 46.5m bell tower, built in 1609, was clearly modelled on the campanile of San Marco in Venice and provides a fabulous backdrop to many a town photo. Its 147 stairs can be climbed for fabulous views of the town and harbour. Next to it, the octagonal 17th-century baptistery contains altars and paintings. It is now sometimes used as an exhibition space. To the east is a 200m-long stretch of the 15th-century town wall.

★ Mediadom Pyrhani   MUSEUM

(☑ 08-205 52 72; www.mediadom-piran.si; Kumarjeva 3; adult/child €5/2; ⊙ 9am-noon & 6-10pm Jul & Aug, 9am-noon & 4-7pm May & Jun, 10am-5pm Apr & Sep, to 4pm Oct-Mar) This exciting new multimedia, interactive museum takes you on an innovative journey through Piran's historical story, with a 'time machine' and numerous exhibits that take a fresh look at the town's fascinating history. Archaeological finds and restored interiors add to the atmosphere.

Minorite Monastery   MONASTERY

(Minoritski Samostan Sveti Frančiška v Piranu; Bolniška ulica 20) The Minorite Monastery has a lovely cloister, and the attached Church of St Francis Assisi was built originally in the early 14th century but enlarged and renovated over the centuries. Inside are ceiling frescoes and the Tartini family's burial plot. The doors are generally left open.

Sergej Mašera Maritime Museum   MUSEUM

(Pomorski Muzej Sergej Mašera; ☑ 05-671 00 40; www.pomorskimuzej.si; Cankarjevo nabrežje 3; adult/child €3.50/2.10; ⊙ 9am-noon & 5-9pm Tue-Sun Jul & Aug, 9am-5pm Tue-Sun Sep-Jun) Located in the 19th-century **Gabrielli Palace** on the waterfront, this museum's focus is the sea, with plenty of salty-dog stories relating to Slovenian seafaring. In the archaeological section, the 2000-year-old Roman amphorae beneath the glass floor are impressive. The antique model ships upstairs are very fine; other rooms are filled with old figureheads and weapons, including some lethal-looking blunderbusses. The folk paintings are offerings placed by sailors on the altar of the pilgrimage church at Strunjan for protection against shipwreck.

Trg 1 Maja SQUARE
(1st May Square) Trg 1 Maja may sound like a socialist parade ground, but it was the centre of Piran until the Middle Ages, when it was called Stari trg (Old Square). The surrounding streets are a maze of pastel-coloured overhanging houses, vaulted passages and arcaded courtyards.

The square is surrounded by interesting baroque buildings, including the former town pharmacy on the north side (now the Fontana restaurant). In the centre of the square is a large baroque cistern *(vodnjak)* that was built in the late 18th century to store fresh water; rainwater from the surrounding roofs flowed into it through the fish borne by the stone putti cherubs in two corners.

Punta Lighthouse LIGHTHOUSE
(Punta Rt Madona) Punta, the historical 'point' of Piran, still has a lighthouse, but today's is small and relatively modern. Attached to it, however, is the round, serrated tower of the Church of St Clement (Cerkev Sveti Klementa; Prešernovo nabrežje), which evokes the ancient beacon from which Piran got its name. The church was originally built in the 13th century but altered 500 years later; it has a lovely (though decrepit) stuccoed ceiling.

🏃 Activities

Boating & Cruises
Several agencies in Piran and Portorož can book you on boat cruises and bus excursions – from a loop that takes in the towns along the coast to day-long excursions to Slovenian highlights (Bled or Postojna, for example), or to Venice and Trieste in Italy.

Subaquatic BOATING
(☑ 041 602 783; www.subaquatic.si; Piran Marina; adult/child €15/10; ☉ cruises 10am, 2pm, 4.15pm & 6.30pm Apr-Sep) Subaquatic offers 1½-hour coastline cruises from Piran to Fiesa and Strunjan (and back). Panoramas are enjoyed above and under the water, with windows under the deck. Check tour schedules online – in cooler months, there may be only two a day.

Sailing Piran BOATING
(☑ 040 669 961; sailingpiran@gmail.com; 4/8hr excursions per person €55/75, boat rental per 4/8hr €240/320; ☉ 9am-1pm & 2-6pm) Take to the Adriatic aboard a yacht for a lovely day or half-day out. The views back towards Piran are worth every euro.

Swimming & Diving
Piran has several 'beaches' – rocky areas along Prešernovo nabrežje – where you might get your feet wet, although they're not the main reason you'd come to Piran. They are a little better on the north side near Punta (and you can hire umbrellas and sun-lounges), but keep walking eastward on the paved path for just under 1km to Fiesa, which has a small beach.

Sub-Net DIVING
(☑ 05-673 22 18, 041 746 153; www.sub-net.si; Prešernovo nabrežje 24; shore/boat dive €35/50) Organises shore and boat-guided dives, runs PADI open-water courses and hires equipment.

⭐ Festivals & Events

Piran Summer Festival CULTURAL
(www.piranfestival.si; ☉ Jul or Aug) For a little over two weeks in late July or early August, performers (dance and music of varying genres) take to a stage in Tartinijev trg at 9pm for free performances.

Tartini Festival MUSIC
(www.tartinifestival.org; ☉ Aug-Sep) The month-long Tartini Festival of classical music takes place in venues throughout Piran, including the vaulted cloister of the Minorite Monastery. A handful of events are staged in Koper.

🛏 Sleeping

Piran has a number of atmospheric choices and an unusually stable accommodation offering. Prices are higher here than elsewhere along the coast, and you'd be crazy to arrive without a booking in summer. If you're looking for a private room, start at Maona Tourist Agency (p159) or Turist Biro (p159).

Kamp Fiesa CAMPGROUND $
(☑ 05-674 62 30; www.facebook.com/kamp.fiesa; Fiesa 57b; adult/child €12/free; ☉ May-Sep; Ⓟ) The closest campground to Piran is at Fiesa, 4km by road but about 1km if you follow the coastal path east. It's tiny and becomes crowded in summer, but it's in a valley by two small, protected ponds and right by the beach.

Piran

Bathing Area

Prešernovo nabrežje

Punta

Pebble
Beach

Pusterla

10
5

Vegova ul

Bonifacijeva ul

Prešernovo nabrežje

Gregorčičeva ul

18

Židovski
trg

Trubarjeva ul

24
14

Verdijeva ul

Trg 1
Maja

Levstikova ul

Kosovelova ul

Obzidna ul

Zelenjavni
trg

Vidalijeva ul

*Piran
Bay*

29

Tomažičev
trg

Tomažičeva ul

Bathing
Area

20 Stjenkova ul

Marina

28

Kidričeva nabrežje

*ADRIATIC
SEA*

*Piran
Harbour*

Venezia
Lines

Customs
Wharf

Trieste
Lines

25

Dantejeva ul

*Pri Mari (65m);
Rizibizi (1.2km);
Dive Strong (1.8km);
Portorož (5km)*

Arriva

⭐ **Max Piran** B&B $$

(☎ 041 692 928; www.maxpiran.com; Ulica IX Korpusa 26; d €70-88; ❄ 🛜) Piran's most romantic accommodation has just six handsome, compact rooms, each bearing a woman's name rather than a number, in a delightful, coral-coloured, 18th-century townhouse. It's just down from the Cathedral of St George, and is excellent value.

Miracolo di Mare B&B $$

(☎ 051 445 511, 05-921 76 60; www.miracolodi mare.si; Tomšičeva ulica 23; r €60-80; 🛜) A lovely and decent-value B&B, the Wonder of the Sea has a dozen charming (though smallish) rooms, some of which (like No 3 and the breakfast room) give on to a pretty garden. Floors and stairs are wooden and original.

⭐ **PachaMama** GUESTHOUSE $$$

(PachaMama Pleasant Stay; ☎ 05-918 34 95; www. pachamama.si; Trubarjeva 8; r €80-175; ❄ 🛜) Built by travellers for travellers, this excellent guesthouse sits just off Tartinijev trg and offers 12 fresh rooms, decorated with timber and lots of travel photography. Cool private bathrooms and a 'secret garden' add appeal. There are also a handful of studios and family-sized apartments dotted around town, of an equally high standard.

⭐ **Art Hotel Tartini** HOTEL $$$

(☎ 05-671 10 00; www.hotel-tartini-piran.com; Tartinijev trg 15; s €130, d €150-220; ❄ 🛜) This attractive, 45-room property faces Tartinijev trg and manages to catch a few sea or square views from the upper floors. A 2018 overhaul has turned the rooms into some of Piran's best – stylish, whitewashed and ever so comfortable. The staff are especially friendly and helpful. The summertime rooftop terrace is a winner.

If you've got the dosh, splash out on the presidential suite (€300); we're suckers for eyrie-like round rooms with million-euro views.

⭐ **Hotel Piran** HOTEL $$$

(☎ 05-666 71 00; www.hotel-piran.si; Stjenkova ulica 1; d €120-180; ❄ 🛜) The town's flagship hotel has a commanding waterside position, great service and a century of history. There are 74 modern rooms and 15 suites – sea view is the way to go, if you can. Downstairs is a wellness centre, cafe and restaurant with large terrace; on the rooftop is a fab summertime champagne bar for hotel guests only.

Piran

✕ Eating

One of Piran's attractions is its plethora of fish restaurants, especially along Prešernovo nabrežje. Most cater to the tourist trade and are rather overpriced, but there are some gems worth tracking down. The seafood pairs well with the local *malvazija* white wine.

★**Cantina Klet**　　　　　　　　SEAFOOD **$**
(Trg 1 Maja 10; mains €5-10; ⊙10am-11pm) This small wine bar sits pretty under a grapevine canopy on Trg 1 Maja. You order drinks from the bar (cheap local wine from the barrel or well-priced beers), but we especially love the self-service window (labelled 'Fritolin pri Cantini') where you order from a small blackboard menu of fishy dishes, like fish fillet with polenta, fried calamari or fish tortilla.

★**Pirat**　　　　　　　　　　　SEAFOOD **$$**
(☑041 327 654; www.facebook.com/PiratPiran; Župančičeva ulica 26; mains €9-21; ⊙11am-10pm) It's not the fanciest place in town, but the atmosphere is top-notch and Rok and his crew do their best to ensure you have a good time. Seafood is king, from the fresh fish carpaccio to pasta with lobster and grilled seabass filleted at the table. It's all nicely accompanied by local *malvazija*.

★**Pri Mari**　　　　　　　MEDITERRANEAN **$$**
(☑041 616 488, 05-673 47 35; www.primari-piran.com; Dantejeva ulica 17; mains €8-24; ⊙noon-4pm & 6-10pm Tue-Sun Apr-Oct, noon-4pm & 6-10pm Tue-Sat, noon-6pm Sun Nov-Mar) This stylishly rustic and welcoming restaurant run by an Italian-Slovenian couple serves the most inventive Mediterranean and Slovenian dishes in town – lots of fish – and a good selection of local wines. Space is limited, so it pays to book ahead.

Gostilna Park　　　　　　　SLOVENIAN **$$**
(☑05-992 17 51; Župančičeva 21; mains €9-19; ⊙noon-11pm) Tucked a little away from the main tourist drag, this fine little place doesn't mess with the basics: fresh seafood, grilled or lightly fried; *čevapčiči* and excellent meat platters; and light salads to keep things fresh. It's all nicely cooked and served with a smile.

Casa Nostromo　　　　　　SEAFOOD **$$**
(☑030 200 000; www.piranisin.com; Tomšičeva ulica 24; mains €9-24; ⊙6pm-1am) Making a big splash on the Piran culinary scene these days is decorated chef Gradimir Dimitrič's new eatery serving seafood and Istrian specialities. Highlights include the octopus salad, the whole seabass (filleted at your table) and the excellent wine list.

🍺 Drinking & Nightlife

★**Café Teater**　　　　　　　　　　　BAR
(☑041 638 933; Stjenkova ulica 1; ⊙9am-midnight) With a grand waterfront terrace and faux antique furnishings, this is where anyone who's anyone in Piran can be found.

Perfect for sundowners. During the day, it's as much coffee as cocktails, but the latter take over late afternoon.

Cafinho BAR
(☑040 554 410; www.facebook.com/Cafinho; Prvomajski trg 3; ☺8am-3am) The name, including the Portuguese spelling, should give a hint at what's on offer here – good coffee in the morning, fine cocktails (including caipirinhas, of course) and a good range of beers the rest of the day. It's right by the water, too.

🛍 Shopping

⭐**Nika's Tiny House** ARTS & CRAFTS
(☑040 156 945; www.facebook.com/nikastiny house; Ulica IX Korpusa 9; ☺10am-1pm & 4-8pm) Nika Domnik creates gorgeous little Piran homes, boats and other locally themed items from driftwood found on local beaches. She's often to be found here at work in her small studio, just where the street starts to climb the hill up to the Cathedral of St George. She also runs occasional workshops for kids.

⭐**Čokoladnica Olimje** FOOD
(☑03-777 41 03; www.cokoladnica-olimje.si; Tartinijev trg 5; ☺9am-7pm Mon-Fri, to 8pm Sat & Sun) Slovenia's best-known chocolate is produced by this chocolaterie, based in the hamlet of Olimje in the east of the country. This boutique outlet is a Willy Wonka world of deliciousness.

Piranske Soline GIFTS & SOUVENIRS
(☑05-673 31 10; www.soline.si; Tartinijev trg 4; ☺9am-9pm) In the Venetian House, this place sells nicely packaged cooking salts and bath sea salts, along with other products all made from the salt of Sečovlje.

ⓘ Information

MONEY
Banka Koper (Tartinijev trg 12; ☺8.30am-12.30pm & 2-5pm Mon-Fri)

POST
Post Office (Cankarjevo nabrežje 5; ☺8am-6pm Mon-Fri, to noon Sat)

TOURIST INFORMATION
Tourist Information Centre (TIC; ☑05-673 44 40; www.portoroz.si; Tartinijev trg 2; ☺9am-10pm Jul & Aug, to 7pm May, to 5pm Sep-Apr & Jun) Your first stop for information on Piran and Portorož. It's in the impressive Municipal Hall.

TRAVEL AGENCIES
Maona Tourist Agency (☑05-674 03 63; www.maona.si; Cankarjevo nabrežje 7; ☺9am-8pm Mon-Sat, 10am-1pm & 5-7pm Sun) Travel agency organising everything from private rooms to activities and cruises.

Turist Biro (☑05-673 25 09; www.turist-biro-ag.si; Tomažičeva ulica 3; ☺9am-1pm & 4-7pm Mon-Sat, 10am-1pm Sun) Travel agency opposite Hotel Piran. Can book rooms and apartments all over the coast.

ⓘ Getting There & Away

BUS
Arriva (☑090 74 11; www.arriva.si) buses serve the coast; see the website for schedules and prices.

From the **bus station** (Dantejeva ulica) south of the centre, buses run frequently to Portorož (€1.40, eight minutes), and up to four times an hour to Izola (€2.50, 30 minutes) and Koper (€3, 45 minutes).

Three buses daily make the journey to Ljubljana (€13, three hours), via Divača and Postojna.

For international destinations, one bus daily goes to Trieste (€6.40, 1½ hours) in Italy, and one bus daily in summer heads south for Croatian Istria, stopping at Umag, Poreč and Rovinj (€9.75, 2¾ hours). There are more frequent services from Izola and Koper.

FERRY
From late June through August, **Trieste Lines** (☑040 200 620; www.triestelines.it) operates a daily (except Wednesday) catamaran from Piran's harbour to Trieste in Italy (€9.60, 30 minutes), and in the other direction to Rovinj in Croatia (€23, 70 minutes). Buy tickets through the tourist office.

Venezia Lines (☑05-242 28 96; www.venezia lines.com) runs a summer-only (usually mid-June to mid-September) catamaran service on Saturdays between Piran and Venice (adult/child €67/42, 3¾ hours).

ⓘ Getting Around
From the southwest corner of Tartinijev trg, free, frequent minibuses shuttle to Piran's bus station and the Fornače car park near the entrance of town. Timetables are posted – in high summer, the shuttles operate roughly every 15 minutes from 5.25am to 1.46am.

Portorož
☑05 / POP 2928

Every country with a coast needs a swish beach resort and Portorož (Portorose in Italian) is Slovenia's. There is a sense that this could be anywhere in the northern Mediterranean, which is fine if that generic experience is what you're looking for. But Slovenia's other coastal towns have significantly more charm and character.

Portorož's beaches are relatively clean (if wall-to-wall with people in summer), and there are spas and wellness centres where you can take the waters or cover yourself in curative mud. The vast array of accommodation options makes Portorož a useful (if less atmospheric) fallback if everything's full in Piran, which is only 4km up the road.

⦿ Sights

Forma Viva PARK

`FREE` Perched atop the Seča Peninsula south of town (beyond the marina), Forma Viva is an outdoor sculpture garden with some 130 works carved in stone. The real reason for coming is the peace and quiet, and the fantastic view of Portorož and Piran Bays. The saltpans at Sečovlje are a short walk to the south.

🏃 Activities

Spas, boat excursions and other waterborne activities are Portorož specialities. Diving is possible, while guided snorkelling trips are also an excellent, easy way to explore the underwater marine environment.

Boating & Cruises

In summer, a couple of boats make runs from the main pier in Portorož to explore the immediate coastline, visiting various combinations of Piran, Izola and Koper, possibly including Strunjan or the saltpans at Sečovlje.

Full-day trips are offered in high season to Venice (by boat or bus) for around €70, and there are bus excursions to Slovenia's big-ticket attractions (Ljubljana, Bled, Postojna).

Stroll along the pier to see the offerings, or visit travel agencies like **Go Portorož** (✆ 040 461 000; www.goportoroz.si; Obala 14).

Spas

All the major hotels have wellness centres. If this is your cup of tea, don't miss the Lepa Vida Thalasso Spa (p162) at Sečovlje Salina Nature Park.

Terme & Wellness LifeClass SPA

(✆ 05-692 90 01, 05-692 80 60; www.lifeclass.net; Obala 43) The 'LifeClass' hotel group includes six hotels in town (chief among them the four-star Grand Hotel Portorož). Part of the offering is this comprehensive spa, offering 'medical wellness', relaxation, spa and recreation facilities – everything from palatial indoor swimming pools to a 'sauna park', gym,

Thai massage, thalassotherapy centre and ayurveda clinic. Activities, opening hours and prices vary greatly – check online.

Swimming & Diving

Portorož Central Beach BEACH

(Centralna Plaza Portorož) Portorož Central Beach accommodates 3300 fried and bronzed bodies. There are loads of water slides and kiddie playgrounds; beach chairs (€5) and umbrellas (€5) are available for rent. Beaches are patrolled by lifeguards during the day, and are off limits between 11pm and 6am. Sleeping overnight on the beach is strictly forbidden.

Dive Strong DIVING

(✆ 040 792 651; www.divestrong.si; Obala 2, Hotel Resort Bernardin; guided dive incl equipment from €30) This dive shop and dive centre offers an excellent introduction to scuba diving – its three-hour 'Discover Scuba Diving' course is aimed at beginners and costs €60 – although it also caters to experienced divers, and offers excellent guided snorkelling trips (from €25 per person).

Cycling

All Year Biking CYCLING

(✆ 041 395 396; www.allyearbiking.com; Šentjane 25; tours per person €21-79) This well-run outfit in the hills high above Piran and Portorož offers tours by electric bike, ranging from a two-hour Piran exploration or a three-hour trip to the saltpans, to a six-hour trip around local villages.

★☆ Festivals & Events

Slovenian Film Festival FILM

(www.fsf.si; ☺ Sep) The biggest night of the year in the Slovenian cinema world, this three-day festival in Portorož in late September sees screenings and awards.

🛏 Sleeping

Portorož counts dozens of hotels; few of them fit into the budget category. Rates peak during summer; many places close in October or November and reopen in April.

Travel agencies can help with private rooms and apartments. Some of the cheapest rooms are on the hillside, quite a walk from the beach. Finding a room for fewer than three nights, or a single at any time, can be difficult.

★ **Kaki Plac** CAMPGROUND $

(✆ 041 359 801; www.adrenaline-check.com/sea; Liminjan 8, Lucija; tent site per person €13, with hired tent €15, lean-to €22-35; ⊙May-Nov; P 🛜) A small, chilled-out and eco-friendly retreat tucked into the woods outside Lucija, on the outskirts of Portorož. Tents with air mattresses can be hired – some sit snugly under thatched Istrian lean-tos, and include linen. There's a sociable communal eating area, free bike hire, and welcoming owners can arrange activities and give great local recommendations.

Europa Hostel   HOSTEL $
(📞05-903 25 74; www.ehp.si; Senčna pot 2; per person €23-29; P ❄ 🛜) This is a good, central budget choice, close to the bus station and with the Auditorium as its neighbour. It's geared to travellers, with bunk-filled rooms named after European destinations. Private rooms are possible, with and without bathrooms. Bonuses: parking, air-con, garden terrace. Note: no kitchen.

★Kempinski Palace Portorož   HOTEL $$$
(📞05-692 70 00; www.kempinski.com/portoroz; Obala 45; s/d from €140/175; P ❄ @ 🛜 🏊) This 19th-century grande dame is a 181-room, five-star masterpiece in the Kempinski stable, with a new and an old wing masterfully combining traditional and contemporary design, with all the required bells and whistles.

🍴 Eating & Drinking

Oštarija   SLOVENIAN $$
(📞05-674 40 04; www.ostarija.eu; Obala 16; mains €7-25; ⊙10am-midnight) Big, bustling and beachfront, but maintaining quality and reasonable prices – there's a lot to like here. The menu rolls through classic Istrian specialities; good choices include *pršut* with truffles, fish soup, calamari in various guises, and fresh fish sold by the gram.

★Montagu   INTERNATIONAL $$$
(📞05-990 04 77; www.montagu.si; Obala 14b; mains €7-49; ⊙noon-midnight) Super-chic, this new restaurant and cocktail bar shines like a beacon on the main strip. The short menu hones in on some serious steak (eg Argentinian Black Angus) with price tags to match, but rice dishes, salads and burgers come in at considerably cheaper rates. You can opt to simply sup wine or cocktails on the handsome, sprawling beachfront terrace.

★Rizibizi   SLOVENIAN $$$
(📞05-993 53 20; www.rizibizi.si; Vilfanova 10; mains €18-30; ⊙noon-11pm) In a tucked-away, elevated position (signed off the road between Portorož and Piran), Rizibizi earns accolades as one of the coast's finest dining options. Savour sea views and a locavore ethos – best value are the various tasting menus (€40 to €60). Truffle-lovers, your dreams have come true: six courses, every one with a truffle flavour, for €60. Bookings advised.

★Kavarna Cacao   BAR
(📞05-674 10 35; www.cacao.si; Obala 14; ⊙8am-1am Sun-Thu, to 3am Fri & Sat) This place wins the award as the most stylish cafe-bar on the coast and boasts a fabulous waterfront terrace thronged by beachgoers. The menu is rich with coffee, juices and smoothies, cocktails, ice creams and cakes, served into the wee hours.

Kanela Bar   BAR
(📞068 139 765; Obala 14a; ⊙10am-3am) Secreted between the beach and the Cacao, the 'Cinnamon' is a workhorse of a rock-and-roll bar up late (and early) with frequent live concerts and a crowd ready for a good time.

ℹ Information

Tourist Information Centre (📞05-674 22 20; www.portoroz.si; Obala 16; ⊙9am-10pm Jul & Aug, to 5pm Sep-Jun) Helpful office opposite the Kempinski; bike rental available.

ℹ Getting There & Away

Arriva (📞090 74 11; www.arriva.si) buses serve the coast; see the website for schedules and prices. Buses stop opposite the main beach on Postajališka pot.

Buses run frequently to Piran (€1.40, eight minutes), and up to four times an hour to Izola (€2, 30 minutes) and Koper (€3, 40 minutes). These buses all stop at Lucija, Bernardin and Strunjan.

Three buses daily make the journey to Ljubljana (€12.80, 2¾ hours), via Divača and Postojna.

For international destinations, one bus daily goes to Trieste (€6.40, 1½ hours) in Italy, and one bus daily in summer heads south for Croatian Istria, stopping at Umag, Poreč and Rovinj (€9.75, 2¾ hours). There are more frequent services from Izola and Koper.

Sečovlje

📞05 / POP 625 / ELEV 2.5M

Salt-making is a centuries-old business along the Slovenian coast. The best place to get a briny taste is at the old saltpans of the Sečovlje Salina Nature Park, right on the Croatian border.

ESCAPE THE CROWDS IN KORTE

If the coast is too crowded for your liking, retreat is possible: head inland. Korte is a sweet hilltop village about 9km from Izola. The contrast between the narrow streets lined with stone-walled or pastel-hued houses and the sweeping views from its perch is a huge part of Korte's appeal. It's not that there are many things to see or do here. Instead, the essence of Korte's appeal is simple: it is just a lovely little place to visit.

Buses connect Korte with Izola only a handful of times a day (€2.50, 15 minutes).

Stara Šola Korte Guesthouse (📞 05-642 11 14, 031 375 889; www.stara-sola.com; Korte 74; r €45-105, apt €69-119; 🅿 ❄ 🛜) This renovated old school is home to 17 bright, modern rooms with two to four beds (with shared or private bathrooms), plus a couple of two-bedroom apartments. It's beautifully done, with idyllic views and pretty common areas. Apartments have a kitchen but there are no cooking facilities for room guests. Breakfast is available (€5) and Korte has two excellent restaurants.

Hiša Torkla (📞 05-620 96 57; www.hisa-torkla.si; Korte 44b; mains €16-29; ⊙ noon-10pm Wed-Sun) One of our most memorable meals was enjoyed here, where Andreja and Sebastijan provide warm service in a stylish setting, with fine local flavours accentuated by accomplished, not-too-fussy cooking (like Black Angus steak cooked to perfection on an indoor flame-grill). The chef's menu is outstanding value (three/four/five plates for €30/43/55). Be guided by staff on local wine choices. Bookings advised.

◉ Sights & Activities

Sečovlje Salina Nature Park   NATURE RESERVE
(Krajinski Park Sečoveljske Soline; 📞 05-672 13 30; www.kpss.si; adult/child €7/5; ⊙ 7am-9pm Jun-Sep, to 5pm Oct-May) This 750-hectare saltpan-studded area, criss-crossed with dikes and channels, has a wealth of birdlife – 290 species have been recorded here.

It's important to note that there are two sections of the park: the main (north) part is at Lera, just south of Seča and off the main road from Portorož. The south part is at Fontanigge, right on the border with Croatia; to reach it you must pass through Slovenian immigration and customs, so don't forget your passport.

The Lera and Fontanigge sections are not connected – they are separated by the Drnica Channel, and different entrances must be used for each. You can get around each section on bike or foot. The area was once a hive of salt-making activity and was one of the biggest money-spinners on the coast in the Middle Ages.

Lera, where salt is still harvested using traditional methods, is home to a **multimedia visitor centre** and cafe. It also has a shop selling Piranske Soline salt products (cooking salt and beauty products; www.soline.si). Lera is also home to the Lepa Vida spa, away to the north in an oasis of calm.

★ Lepa Vida Thalasso Spa   SPA
(📞 05-672 13 60; www.thalasso-lepavida.si; Lepa; 2/4hr incl park entry €18/30; ⊙ 9am-9pm mid-May–Sep) This gorgeous open-air spa sits at the breezy northern end of the saltpans. There's a great set-up: saltwater swimming pool, brine pools for soaking, and a massage pavilion and cafe (drinks only). It's peaceful and quiet, with a maximum 50 guests (no kids under 12). Bookings are essential; a golf cart will shuttle you from the park entrance to the spa.

ℹ Getting There & Away

If driving, follow the signs to reach the park at Lera. The nicest way to arrive is by bike, along the coastal bike trail from Lucija. A few tour companies offer cruises that stop at Lera.

Southeastern Slovenia & the Krka Valley

Why Go?

Slovenia's southeast doesn't announce itself as loudly as other parts of the country, preferring subtle charms over big-ticket attractions. This is a region where life slows down considerably – all the better to enjoy meandering rivers and rolling hills covered with forest, orchards and grapevines. Here, villages cluster around church spires, and distinctive *toplarji* (double-linked hayracks) shelter neat woodpiles.

Low-key tourist attractions come in the shape of grand monasteries, restored castles and easygoing days out exploring local wine roads while enjoying countryside views. For more active ways to discover the region, head out on the back roads by bike, or explore the green-blue waters of the Kolpa or Krka Rivers by canoe, kayak or raft. With some time up your sleeve and a desire to see beyond Slovenia's headline acts, you can craft an itinerary where slow travel brings its own rewards.

Best Places to Eat

➡ Ošterija Debeluh (p188)

➡ Oštarija (p170)

➡ Grad (p176)

➡ Don Bobi (p173)

Best Places to Stay

➡ Hotel Balnea (p170)

➡ Šeruga Farmhouse (p175)

➡ Madronič (p182)

➡ Domačija Novak (p168)

➡ Vila Castanea (p185)

When to Go

Novo Mesto

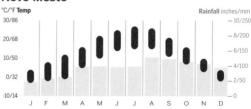

Mar–May Put on your hiking boots as spring blooms and temperatures warm up.

Jun–Sep Mix summer sun with kayaking on the Kolpa or Krka Rivers.

Sep–Oct Take to the cycling trails during cooler autumn days, and enjoy the grape harvest.

Southeastern Slovenia & the Krka Valley Highlights

1 Bizeljsko-Sremič wine country (p189) Embracing local wine culture by touring the flint-stone cave cellars around the village of Bizeljsko.

2 Posavje Museum (p186) Goggling at fresco overload within the Knights' Hall of Brežice's castle-museum.

3 Kostanjevica na Krki (p183) Admiring this teensy island village while canoeing on the Krka River before exploring the art that fills the ancient monastery outside town.

4 Kolpa River (p182) Rafting the rapid-water run on the river from Stari Trg to Vinica.

5 Novo Mesto (p171) Strolling the lanes of the compact Old Town and soaking up its pretty riverfront position.

6 Balnea Wellness Centre (p169) Taking a time-out for a spot of relaxation and pampering in Dolenjske Toplice.

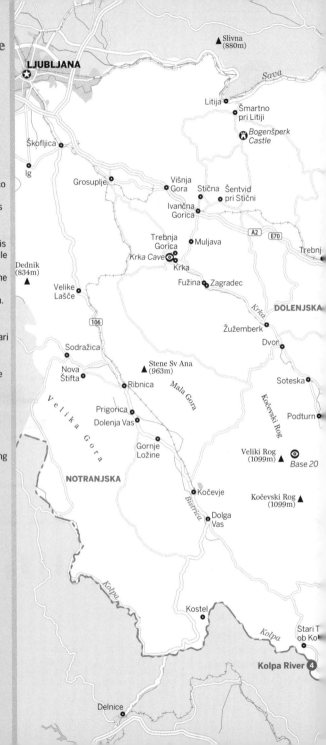

DOLENJSKA

The Dolenjska area follows the dark-cyan waters of the Krka River as it gently winds from its cave source in Krka village, cutting through a deep valley and passing through blink-and-you-miss-them settlements down to Novo Mesto, the region's main town. Along the way, a handful of castles and historical churches provide stop-offs for travellers who prefer to go slow; those after a spa break make a beeline straight for Dolenjske Toplice for relaxing treats.

Ribnica & Around

🖉 01 / POP 3550 / ELEV 493M

Ribnica is the oldest and most important settlement of western Dolenjska. It sits in the area known locally as Kočevsko – all woods, underground rivers and brown bears. It is a good springboard for the unspoiled forests of the Kočevski Rog (p170), and worth a stop for anyone interested in local handicraft traditions.

Ribnica's main street, Škrabčev trg, lies on the east bank of the tiny Bistrica River and runs parallel to it.

Note, too, that if you're searching online for Ribnica, there are a few Slovenian towns by the same name; Ribnica na Pohorju in northeast Slovenia has a stronger online presence. This town is Ribnica na Dolenjskem in online bus schedules etc.

OFF THE BEATEN TRACK

ŠKRILJ NUCLEAR BUNKER

The Škrilj underground **bunker** (🖉059 959 204; www.kocevsko.com/en/visits-and-excursions/the-mysterious-bunker-skrilj;bunker.skrilj@kocevsko.com; TIC Kočevska Reka, Kočevska Reka 5; adult/child €16/7), 22km south of Ribnica in the village of Kočevska Reka, was built in the 1950s to house Slovenia's top brass in case of nuclear war. In 2017 the dimly lit underground corridors and rooms (furnished with bulky old-fashioned communications equipment) were opened to the public for the first time by guided tour. Unfortunately, it can be difficult for independent travellers to access as tours are normally held for a minimum of 15 people. Contact the Kočevska Reka TIC to organise a visit.

◉ Sights

Ribnica Handicraft Centre CULTURAL CENTRE
(Rokodelski center Ribnica; 🖉 01-836 11 04; www.rokodelskicenter-ribnica.si; Cesta na Ugar 6; ⊙9am-5pm Mon-Fri, to 1pm Sat) FREE This is a great addition to the town – a centre tasked with preserving and promoting the area's long-standing handicraft traditions. The *suha roba* made in the region can be translated as 'dry goods', but that doesn't quite do justice to the finely crafted wooden and wicker implements (pottery is another local product). Stop by to see the shop here, and learn about production methods. There are occasionally workshops where you can see local artisans in action.

Church of the Assumption of Mary CHURCH
(Cerkev Marijinega Vnebovzetja; 🖉 01-836 99 43; Nova Štifta 3; ⊙10am-noon & 2-6pm) The church at Nova Štifta, in the foothills of the Velika Gora 7km west of Ribnica, is one of the most important pilgrimage sites in Slovenia. Completed in 1671, the baroque church is unusual for its octagonal shape. The interior of the church, with its golden altars and pulpit, is blindingly ornate.

In the courtyard opposite the Franciscan monastery (where the church key is kept) stands a wonderful old *toplar* and a linden tree, planted in the mid-17th century, complete with a tree house that has been there for over a century.

Ribnica Castle & Museum CASTLE
(Muzej Ribnica; 🖉 01-835 03 76; www.muzej-ribnica.si; Gallusovo nabrežje; adult/child €2.50/1.70; ⊙10am-1pm & 4-7pm Tue-Sun May-Oct) Ribnica Castle was originally built in the 11th century and expanded over hundreds of years. Only a small section – a Renaissance wall and two towers – survived bombings during WWII. Today the castle is set in lovely parkland and houses a small museum detailing the traditional crafts of the area plus an interesting exhibition on local witch trials from the 15th century.

Parish Church of St Stephen CHURCH
(Župnijska Cerkev Sv Štefana; Škrabčev trg) Built in 1868 on the site of earlier churches, this parish church would not be of much interest were it not for the two striking towers added in 1960 to replace the ones toppled during WWII; the towers use the steeple design created for the church by Slovenian architect Jože Plečnik.

THE STIČNA CISTERCIAN ABBEY: DOLENJSKA'S RELIGIOUS CENTRE

Established in 1136 by the Cistercians (famous for their vows of silence), the **Stična Cistercian Abbey** (Cistercijanska Opatija Stična; ☑ 01-787 78 63; www.mks-sticna.si; Stična 17; adult/child €7/2; ☉ tours 8.30am, 10am, 2pm & 4pm Tue-Sat, 2pm & 4pm Sun) was for centuries the most important religious, economic, educational and cultural centre in Dolenjska. The walled monastery, an incredible combination of Romanesque, Gothic, Renaissance and baroque architecture, currently has 14 monks in residence. Only 35km from Ljubljana, approximately midway between the capital and Novo Mesto, it's an easy day trip from either.

Entry is on the east side of the monastery, across a small stream. On the north side of the central courtyard is the **Old Prelature**, a 17th-century Renaissance building which contains the **Slovene Museum of Christianity** (Muzej Krščanstva na Slovenskem), a hotchpotch mix of antique clocks, furniture, icons and old documents (though note, the medieval ones are facsimiles).

On the west side of the courtyard is the **Abbey Church** (1156), a buttressed, three-nave Romanesque cathedral rebuilt in the baroque style in the 17th and 18th centuries. Look inside for the Renaissance red-marble tombstone of Abbot Jakob Reinprecht in the north transept and the blue organ cupboard with eight angels (1747) in the choir loft. The greatest treasures here are the Stations of the Cross paintings (1766) by Fortunat Bergant.

South of the church is Stična's vaulted **cloister**, mixing Romanesque and early Gothic styles. The arches and vaults are adorned with frescoes of the prophets and Old Testament stories and allegorical subjects. The carved stone faces on the west side were meant to show human emotions and vices.

On the south side of the cloister is a typically baroque monastic **refectory**, with an 18th-century pink ceiling with white stucco decoration. **Neff's Abbey**, built in the mid-16th century by Abbot Volbenk Neff, runs to the west. The arches in the vestibule on the ground floor are painted with a dense network of leaves, blossoms, berries and birds.

The Cistercians sell their own products (honey, wine, herbal teas, liqueurs) in a small shop inside the complex.

Stična is served by up to a dozen buses a day from Ljubljana (€4.10, 50 minutes, 35km) on weekdays, with fewer on weekends. Another option is the train, which stops at Ivančna Gorica, a larger town 2.5km south of the abbey; frequent Ljubljana–Novo Mesto trains stop here (€3.44, 50 minutes in either direction).

🏃 Activities

Ribnica is the base for many excellent walks. Ask at the TIC (p168) for information.

The Walls of St Anne HIKING
(Stene Sv Ana) A well-marked trail leads northeast of Ribnica for about 4.5km to **Stene Sv Ana** (the Walls of St Anne; 963m), with fantastic views over the Ribnica Valley.

This hilltop is one of the points along the **Ribnica Hiking Trail**, with 17 points scattered around the valley and surrounding mountains. The trail's highest peak is Turn (1254m), southwest of town.

🛏 Sleeping & Eating

⭐**Harlekin Gostilna** GUESTHOUSE $$
(☑ 01-836 15 32; www.harlekin.si; Gorenjska cesta 21; s/d €50/80; 🕿) The nicest place in town

to bed down, with a half-dozen large modern timber-floored rooms above an excellent restaurant.

Gostišče-Penzion Makšar GUESTHOUSE $$
(☑ 01-837 31 60; http://penzion-maksar.si; Breže 18a; s/d €50/80) This guesthouse, located in a hamlet 5km northwest of Ribnica, has simple, agreeable rooms. There's also a well-priced traditional restaurant here, and the chance to try the Makšar beer made in the small on-site brewery.

Harlekin Pizzerija SLOVENIAN $
(☑ 01-836 15 32; www.harlekin.si; Gorenjska cesta 21; mains €7-15; ☉10am-10pm; 🕿🌙) Offering much more than the big range of wood-fired pizzas that it's known for, Harlekin's menu rambles from homemade gnocchi and tagliatelle with truffles to local flavours including

forest-mushroom soup and wild boar goulash. There's a good variety of dishes for vegetarians too.

ℹ Information

Tourist Information Centre (TIC; ☑ 01-836 11 04; Cesta na Ugar 6; ⊘ 9am-5pm Mon-Fri, to 1pm Sat)

ℹ Getting There & Away

Buses run every one to two hours north to Ljubljana (€5.60, 65 minutes, 47km). There are 12 services daily heading south to Kočevje (€2.70, 25 minutes, 17km). The bus stop is on Škrabčev trg in front of the church (p166).

Žužemberk

☑ 07 / POP 1000 / ELEV 220M

This old market town is a good spot for a stop-off on a road trip to stretch your legs with a ramble around the castle and to impress the locals with your Slovenian pronunciation (it's *zhoozh*-em-berk).

◎ Sights

Žužemberk Castle CASTLE
(Grajski trg 1; ⊘ 9am-6pm Mon-Fri, 7am-8pm Sat & Sun) FREE The mighty 13th-century Žužemberk Castle perches photogenically on a terrace overlooking the Krka River. It was refortified in the 16th century, only to be all but flattened during air raids in WWII.

Its towers have been partially reconstructed, and the Renaissance walls, the roof, the courtyard and the wine cellar have been restored and are open for a quick ramble through.

⌑ Sleeping & Eating

You're better off heading out of town to the scatter of guesthouses in nearby villages or, for more choice, heading on to Dolenjske Toplice or Novo Mesto.

Koren GUESTHOUSE $
(☑ 07-308 72 60; www.turizem-koren.com; Dolga vas 5; per person €30; P 🛜) At Žužemberk's southern end, a sign points the way down to a riverside village below town where you'll find Koren, with glorious views up to the castle. Small rooms are low on frills but spic and span. The restaurant's riverside tables and wholesome simple dishes (mains €6 to €12; try the *štruklji* – cheese dumplings with mushrooms) are the real drawcards here. You can also rent kayaks here.

★**Domačija Novak** GUESTHOUSE $$
(☑ 041 343 000; www.novakdoma.eu; Sadinja vas pri Dvoru 7; s/d €30/60; P 🛜) Earning raves from smitten guests, this farmhouse offers simple accommodation, top-notch food (much of it home-grown) and local wines, and good activity options – including free bike usage and opportunities for fishing,

---

VALVASOR, SLOVENIA'S RENAISSANCE MAN

Most of our knowledge of Slovenian history, geography, culture and folklore before the 17th century comes from the writings of one man, Janez Vajkard Valvasor – and more specifically his work *The Glory of the Duchy of Carniola*.

Valvasor was born in Ljubljana's Old Town in 1641 to a noble family from Bergamo. After a Jesuit education in Ljubljana and Germany, he joined Miklós Zrínyi, the Hungarian count and poet, in the wars against the Turks and travelled widely, visiting Germany, Italy, North Africa, France and Switzerland. He collected data on natural phenomena and local customs as well as books, drawings, mineral specimens and coins.

In 1672 Valvasor installed himself, his books and his precious collections at **Bogenšperk Castle** (Grad Bogenšperk; ☑ 01-898 76 64; www.bogensperk.si; Bogenšperk 5; adult/child €4.50/3.50; ⊘ 10am-6pm Tue-Sat, to 7pm Sun Jul-Aug, 9am-5pm Tue-Fri, 10am-5pm Sat, to 6pm Sun Apr-Jun, Sep & Oct, 10am-5pm Thu-Sun Nov & Mar), where he conducted scientific experiments (including alchemy) and wrote. In 1689 he completed his most important work, *The Glory of the Duchy of Carniola*. It ran to four volumes, comprising 3500 pages with 535 maps and copper engravings, and remains one of the most comprehensive works published in Europe before the Enlightenment. It's such a wealth of information on the Slovenian patrimony that it's still explored and studied to this day.

Valvasor never enjoyed the success of his labours. Publishing such a large work at his own expense ruined him financially and he was forced to leave Bogenšperk in 1692. He died a year later at Krško, 65km to the east on the Sava River.

kayaking and even cooking classes. It's sign-posted about 3km south of Žužemberk.

If you want to experience rural-style roughing-it you can opt to sleep in the hayloft (€25 per person, with sleeping bag, torch and pillows provided as well as hay).

Nonguests can dine here too (three-course lunch/dinner from €20/25) but bookings are essential.

Gostilna Pri Gradu   SLOVENIAN $
(☑ 07-308 72 90; www.gostilna-prigradu.si; Grajski trg 4; mains €7-18; ☺ 6am-11pm) There ain't much going on foodwise in the heart of town but this old-style restaurant, under a linden tree in front of Žužemberk Castle, serves up classic hearty fare. There's a nice outdoor terrace open in the warmer months.

❶ Getting There & Away

The bus stop is in front of the post office on Grajski trg. Popular destinations:
Dolenjske Toplice (€2.70, 24 minutes, 18km) One to four daily.
Ljubljana (€6, one hour, 53km) Three to eight daily.
Novo Mesto (€2.30, 20 minutes, 19km) One to two daily.

Dolenjske Toplice

☑ 07 / POP 810 / ELEV 176M

Within striking distance of Novo Mesto, this small thermal resort is one of Slovenia's oldest spa towns. The pools are its main attraction, and while a large proportion of Dolenjske Toplice's visitors are here for medical purposes, the very swish Hotel Balnea (p170) and connected wellness centre are geared towards pampering and have brought spa-break tourism to town.

Located in the karst valley of the Sušica (a tributary of the Krka River) and surrounded by the wooded slopes of Kočevski Rog (p170), it's also an excellent place in which to hike and cycle if you can pull yourself away from massages, sweat baths and thermal water soaks.

History

The first spa was built here in 1658. The Kopališki Dom (Bathers' House), complete with three pools, was built in the 18th century. Despite getting its own guidebook, tourism didn't really take off until 1899, with the opening of the Zdravilišči Dom (Health Resort House). Strascha Töplitz, as it was then

called, was a great favourite of Austrians from around the turn of the 20th century up to WWI.

☂ Activities

Thermal Spas

Balnea Wellness Centre   THERMAL BATHS
(☑ 07-391 97 50; www.terme-krka.com; Zdraviliški trg; pools day pass adult/child/family Mon-Thu €10/8/32, Fri-Sun €14/12/42; ☺ lagoon 9am-9pm Sun-Thu, to 11pm Fri & Sat) The main reason people come to Dolenjske Toplice is this attractive, well-run spa centre. The **Lagoon** has outdoor (May to September) and indoor (year-round) pools with thermal water between 27°C and 32°C; the **Oasis** section hosts saunas, a Japanese sweat bath and a chill-out terrace; and the swish **Treatment** section is where you go for pampering facials and rejuvenating massages.

For nonguests as well as those staying at Hotel Balnea (p170) there are day-long relaxation packages available, combining lagoon access, sauna, massage and beauty treatment.

As you drive into town, the centre is in pretty parkland just north of the hotels – it's connected to the Hotel Balnea by a walkway.

Hotel Vital   THERMAL BATHS
(☑ 07-391 97 50; Zdraviliški trg 11; adult/child Mon-Thu €7/5, Fri-Sun €9/7; ☺ 7am-8pm) The 36°C mineral water gushing from 1000m below the three indoor thermal pools at the Hotel Vital is used primarily for therapeutic and medical purposes rather than geared to tourism like at the Balnea.

Hiking & Cycling

A dozen trails are outlined on the free *Dolenjske Toplice Municipal Tourist Trails* handout, but without any explanatory detail. You need to ask at the TIC (p171) for more detailed information – it has some two dozen separate sheets with themed hikes, walks and cycle tours.

One is a 2.5km **archaeological walk** west to Cvinger (263m), where Hallstatt tombs and iron foundries have been unearthed. Nature lovers may be interested in the 8km **herbal trail**, a loop south to Sela and Podturn and back via forest roads, which takes in a herb farm and the 15th-century Church of the Holy Trinity at Cerovec. Further afield is the 2km **Dormouse Trail**, which makes a loop from Kočevske Poljane, about 4.5km southwest of Dolenjske Toplice, and could be combined with a hike to Base 20 (p170).

SOUTHEASTERN SLOVENIA & THE KRKA VALLEY DOLENJSKE TOPLICE

OFF THE BEATEN TRACK

THE VIRGIN FORESTS OF KOČEVSKI ROG

One of Slovenia's most pristine areas, the virgin forests of Kočevski Rog, about 9km southwest of Dolenjske Toplice, have been a protected nature area for more than a century. As many as 250 brown bears are believed to live here, as well as lynx and fox. Ten hiking trails, mostly using old forestry roads, wind their way through dense fir and beech trees, leading to small caves and sinkholes, hill peaks (the highest, Veliki Rog, is 1099m), the ruins of the 13th-century Rožek Castle, and many WWII sites.

During WWII, Partisans under Marshal Tito's command used this forest as headquarters; the nerve centre was **Base 20** (Baza 20; ☎041 315 165; www.dolenjskimuzej.si/en/locations/kocevski-rog; ⏱exhibition huts 9am-4pm) FREE, where 26 barracks homed the Partisan leadership in 1943 and 1944. Two of the huts (Nos 16 and 22) house exhibits about the role of Base 20 and of Kočevski Rog during WWII. A plaque erected near the site in 1995 diplomatically pays homage to everyone involved in the 'national liberation war', presumably including the thousands of Domobranci (Home Guards) executed here by the Partisans in 1945.

Base 20 is also the trailhead for one of Kočevski Rog's shorter hiking trails. The circular Resistance Trail takes you past various memorial cemeteries and the Jelendol Partisan Hospital, which treated the injured from 1943.

For more information on all of the hiking trails, ask the Dolenjske Toplice TIC for the *Kočevski Rog Excursion Map*, which marks all of the trails and historic and natural sites in the forest.

Skiing

Gače Ski Centre SKIING
(Smučarski Center Gače; ☎041 182 513; https://scgace.si; Komarna vas 155; day pass adult/child €24/19; ⏱8am-4pm roughly late Nov-Feb) The Gače Ski Centre is on the edge of the Kočevje forest, 16km south of Dolenjske Toplice en route to Črnomelj. It has 6km of slopes and 7km of cross-country trails on Mt Gače at altitudes between 700m and 965m.

Sleeping

It's all about the spa-resort here but if your budget doesn't stretch to that there are also a couple of good guesthouse options.

Hotel Pri Mostu GUESTHOUSE $
(☎041 755 363; Pionirska cesta 2; r s/d €40/50, studio s/d €43/59; P❄📶) The seven rooms above the Pri Mostu bar are a solid, central choice though some tend to be on the small side. If you're staying a few days, the studios (with kitchenette) are a good option. Breakfast is €5.

Kamp Dolenjske Toplice CAMPGROUND $
(☎040 466 589; www.camping-potocar.si/kamp-dolenjske-toplice; per adult/child €12/6; ⏱year-round; P📶) This small campground sits in a pretty riverside position with plenty of trees for shade. It's just off the northern end of Zdraviliški trg, more or less opposite the Balnea spa complex. It's open as a camper van stop in winter too. Bike rental available.

Hotel Oštarija GUESTHOUSE $$
(☎031 413 588; www.ostarija.si; Sokolski trg 2; s/d €40/60, apt d/q €65/72; P❄📶) Don't fancy staying at one of the big spa-hotels? Then this super-friendly guesthouse is by far the top choice, with the bonus of the town's best restaurant downstairs. Spotless rooms have a bright, contemporary feel and are comfortably kitted out. When we last pulled through town, management was adding a dash of character by giving each room individual herbal themes.

★**Hotel Balnea** SPA HOTEL $$$
(☎07-391 94 00; www.terme-krka.com; Zdraviliški trg 11; r s/d €126/182, ste s/d €141/232; P❄📶🏊) Few newly built hotels in Slovenia can compare with this sleek 63-room four-star in terms of design and facilities. Heavy on timber, natural materials and nature-inspired colours, the spacious contemporary rooms (nearly all with big balconies complete with sun loungers) are just the ticket for a relaxing getaway. Bag a back-facing room for views over the park.

Eating & Drinking

★**Oštarija** SLOVENIAN $$
(☎051 262 990; www.ostarija.si; Sokolski trg 2; mains €9-25; ⏱noon-11pm Tue-Sat, to 4pm Sun; ❄📶) There are few eating options in town, so it's a joy to find this place, a foodie's treat with a menu based around seasonal local

produce. Drop in for its three-course lunches (Monday to Friday €10, Saturday €12, Sunday €14) and marvel at the bargain of a five-course dinner for €27 (eight courses for €38).

Kolesar EUROPEAN $$
(☏ 07-306 50 03; www.gostisce-kolesar.com; Dolenje Sušice 22; mains €8-25; ☺ 10am-11pm Mon-Sat) Local trout, plenty of steaks and a range of wood-fired pizzas are the name of the game at this spot, popular with local families for a lazy lunch or dinner thanks to its garden setting and playground to keep the kids happy. It's 2.5km to the southeast of town.

Pri Mostu BAR
(Pionirska cesta 2; ☺ 7am-11pm) About as central as you'll find, this lively cafe-bar has an outside terrace along the narrow Sušica and offers all-day coffee, booze and snacks.

ℹ️ Information

Terme Krka Dolenjske Toplice (☏ 08-205 03 00; www.terme-krka.si) Central contact for bookings at the three main hotels and their spas' beauty and medical treatment packages.

Tourist Information Centre Dolenjske Toplice (TIC; ☏ 07-384 51 88; www.dolenjske-toplice.si; Sokolski trg 4; ☺ 9am-noon & 2-6pm Mon-Fri, 10am-noon & 2-4pm Sat & Sun) Well-informed and friendly office with plenty of maps and information on sights and activities in the area.

ℹ️ Getting There & Away

The main bus stop is right in the centre of town. Useful bus services include:

Črnomelj (€4.10, 50 minutes, 33km) One bus daily.

Ljubljana (€7.20, 1½ hours, 73km) Two daily.

Novo Mesto (€2.30, 20 minutes, 13km) Hourly until 7pm.

Žužemberk (€2.70, 25 minutes, 18km) Two services daily.

Novo Mesto

☏ 07 / POP 23,300 / ELEV 169M

Situated on a sharp, scenic bend of the Krka River, with its tranquil turquoise waters running through the town, Novo Mesto is a surprising omission from most travellers' Dolenjska itineraries. The gateway to the lower Krka's castles and sights, as well as to Croatia (Zagreb is a mere 75km away), most people breeze through on their way to somewhere else.

Oh well. That leaves the Old Town's clutch of cobblestone alleys, on a rocky promontory above the river's left bank, refreshingly empty for you to wind your way past riverfront cottages, to the museum and then on to the fine main square, Glavni trg, for a relaxed drink.

History

Novo Mesto was settled during the late Bronze Age around 1000 BC, and helmets and decorated burial urns unearthed in surrounding areas suggest that Marof Hill, northwest of the Old Town, was the seat of Hallstatt princes during the early Iron Age (8th to 4th centuries BC). The Illyrians and Celts came later, and the Romans maintained a settlement here until the 4th century AD.

During the early Middle Ages, Novo Mesto flourished as a marketplace at the centre of the estates owned by Stična abbey (p167). But by the 16th century, plague, fires and raids by the Turks on their way to Vienna took their toll on the city.

Prosperity returned in the 18th and 19th centuries: a college was established in 1746, Slovenia's first National Hall (Narodni Dom) opened here in 1875 and a railway line linked the city with Ljubljana in the 1890s. Heavy bombardments during WWII severely damaged the city.

◉ Sights

⭐ **Dolenjska Museum** MUSEUM
(Dolenjski Muzej; ☏ 07-373 11 30; www.dolenjski muzej.si/en; Muzejska ulica 7; adult/child €5/3; ☺ 9am-7pm Tue-Sat Jul-Aug, to 5pm Apr-Jun, Sep & Oct, to 4pm Nov-Mar) The Dolenjska Museum's impressive collection is spread over a campus of buildings. The oldest, which once belonged to the Knights of the Teutonic Order, houses a valuable collection of archaeological finds unearthed in the southern suburb of Kandija in the late 1960s. Don't miss the fine bronze *situlae* (pails) from the 3rd or 4th century BC embossed with battle and hunting scenes, and the Celtic ceramics and jewellery (particularly the bangles of turquoise and blue glass).

Jakac House GALLERY
(Jakčev Dom; ☏ 07-373 11 31; www.dolenjskimuzej. si/en; Sokolska ulica 1; adult/child €3/2 or free with Dolenjska Muzej ticket; ☺ 9am-7pm Tue-Sat Jul-Aug, to 5pm Apr-Jun, Sep & Oct, to 4pm Nov-Mar) The Dolenjska Museum administers

Novo Mesto

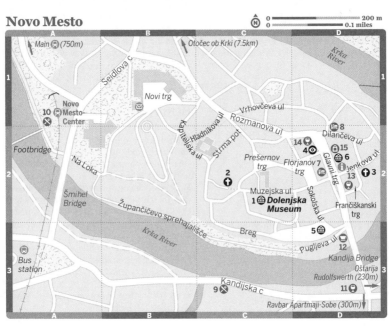

Novo Mesto

Jakac House, which exhibits some of its 830-odd works by prolific painter and local boy Božidar Jakac (1899–1989). The artist visited dozens of countries in the 1920s and 1930s, painting and sketching such diverse subjects as Parisian dance halls, Scandinavian port towns, African villages and American city skylines. But his best works are of Novo Mesto's markets, people, churches and rumble-tumble wooden riverside houses.

Glavni Trg SQUARE
(Main Sq) The Old Town's main square, home to the neo-Renaissance **town hall** (Rotovž; Glavni trg), was busy undergoing a restoration in 2018; expect it to be fully brushed up when you pass through town.

Cathedral of St Nicholas CATHEDRAL
(Stolna Cerkev Sv Nikolaja; http://zupnija-stolna-nm.rkc.si; Kapiteljska ulica; ⏱9am-2pm) Perched above the Old Town, this Gothic cathedral is Novo Mesto's most important historical monument. It has a 15th-century vaulted (and very floral) presbytery and crypt, plus wall frescoes, a belfry that once had been a medieval defence tower, and an altar painting of the church's eponymous saint supposedly painted by the Venetian master Jacopo Tintoretto (1518–94).

Franciscan Church of St Leonard CHURCH
(Frančiškanska Cerkev Sv Lenarta; Frančiškanski trg) Southeast of Glavni trg is the yellow Franciscan Church of St Leonard, originally built by monks fleeing the Turks in Bosnia in 1472, and the attached Franciscan monastery, which has a library containing some 12,000 volumes, including 12th-century incunabula.

⚡ Activities

Equestrian School Sport
Centre Češča Vas HORSE RIDING
(KŠŠC Češča Vas; ☑ 07-337 30 40, 041 554 265; www.konji-cescavas.si; per hr €10-20; ⊙ by appointment) About 5km west of Novo Mesto, just south of Prečna, this equestrian centre has a riding school and offers cross-country rides by arrangement.

🛏 Sleeping

Novo Mesto's accommodation scene is small but the budget and midrange options are all solid, good value and centrally located.

The TIC (p174) has a list of private rooms (from €25 per person). The closest campgrounds are at Otočec ob Krki (p175), 10km northeast, and at Dolenjske Toplice (p170), 13km southwest.

★ Hostel Situla HOSTEL $
(☑ 07-394 20 00; www.situla.si; Dilančeva ulica 1; dm €13.50-19, s/d without bathroom €25/44; P @ 🛜) One of Slovenia's nicest hostels, partially built within the walls of an 18th-century town house with rooms over five floors. Iron Age–style art sets off the cosy rooms; we love the attic dormitory under the mansard roof, but perhaps not in midsummer heat. There's no kitchen for guests, but breakfast is included; the on-site bar-restaurant has a set lunch from €4.

Ravbar Apartmaji-Sobe GUESTHOUSE $
(☑ 041 738 309, 07-373 06 80; www.ravbar.net; Smrečnikova ulica 15-17; s/d/tr from €28/38/60, apt for 2/4 from €48/80; P ✳ 🛜) This family-run guesthouse has a bundle of rooms and apartments – all are homely, well-equipped and spotless. It's in a leafy and quiet suburban area south of the river but only a short walk to the centre. The welcome is warm, the prices more than reasonable and keen cyclist host Jože can help you plan cycling routes.

Center Hotel HOTEL $$
(☑ 07-302 18 00; www.hotel-center.si; Glavni trg 23; s/d €60/90, without bathroom €45/70; P ✳ 🛜) You don't get more central than this aptly named new kid on the block. On the main square, Center's good-sized standard rooms are decked out in a suave, contemporary style with roomy walk-in showers and ridiculously large satellite TVs on the wall. The top floor, under the eaves, is home to budget rooms which all share exceedingly nice bathrooms.

🍴 Eating

Don Bobi ITALIAN $
(☑ 07-338 24 00; www.don-bobi.si; Kandijska cesta 14; mains €7-15; ⊙ 10am-11pm Mon-Fri, noon-11pm Sat; ✳ 🛜) Considerably fancier than the name might suggest, this place does a menu of straight-up Italian with really good gnocchi dishes as well as pasta, steak, fish and pizza that wins plenty of local plaudits.

Gostišče Loka INTERNATIONAL $
(☑ 07-332 11 08; www.gostisce-loka.si; Župančičevo sprehajališče 2; mains €6.50-19; ⊙ 7am-10pm Mon-Thu, to 11pm Fri, 9am-11pm Sat, 9am-9pm Sun; ✳ 🛜 🍴) This riverside spot with a huge outdoor terrace, just beyond the footbridge linking the two banks, is the most happening place in town. The short menu covers all the bases with burgers, pasta and risotto, more expensive steak and fish dishes, and a small – but welcome – vegetarian section. It's equally good for a cuppa-and-cake or an evening glass of wine.

There's playground equipment here to keep the kids entertained.

Oštarija Rudolfswerth SLOVENIAN $$
(☑ 07-332 33 35; www.ostarija-rudolfswerth.si; Kandijska cesta 35; mains €5-20; ⊙ 7am-10pm Mon-Sat; ✳ 🛜) The roadside location is uninspiring but the food is excellent and the decor stylish and detail-oriented – brass buckets used as light fittings, rustic timber and brick, a menu printed on handmade paper. Meals range from beef tenderloin to trout fillet, and there's local game and Krka River fish, plus creative pizza options.

🍸 Drinking

Vovko Arkade Bar BAR
(Rozmanova ulica 1; ⊙ 6am-10pm Mon-Thu, to midnight Fri & Sat, to 8pm Sun; 🛜) This small and rather slick bar-cafe has a great people-watching position right on the entry to

Glavni trg under the arcade. Sit and watch the world go by while sipping a wine or a coffee.

Bar Boter   BAR
(☑040 799 990; Kandijska cesta 9; ⊙7am-midnight) The riverfront deck of this pub, just south of the Old Town, is one of the nicest places to head for a drink as the sun dips behind the lush hills and the Old Town houses on the bank in front take on a golden hue. You can also rent boats and canoes here.

Čajarna Stari Most   CAFE
(☑07-337 01 60; www.starimost.si; Glavni trg 17; ⊙7am-10pm Mon-Thu, to midnight Fri, 9am-midnight Sat, to 10pm Sun) Cute, colourful and family-friendly space right beside the bridge into the Old Town. It serves many varieties of tea, as well as coffee, beer, ice cream and cakes.

Lokal Patriot   BAR
(☑07-337 45 10; www.lokalpatriot.si; Glavni trg 11; ⊙9am-11pm Mon-Wed, to midnight Thu, to 2am Fri, 5pm-2am Sat) The venue of choice among Novo Mesto's students, this bar-club-cafe has programs throughout the week and DJs (and sometimes live music) at the weekend.

🛍 Shopping

Knjigarna-Kavarna Goga   BOOKS
(☑07-393 08 01; www.goga.si; Glavni trg 6; ⊙9am-7pm Mon-Fri, to 1pm Sat) Lovely arcade bookshop stocking the best of Slovene literature, plus a cultural centre staging events, with a small gallery space and a cafe.

ℹ Information

Kompas Novo Mesto (☑07-393 15 20; www.kompas-nm.si; Novi trg 10; ⊙8am-6pm Mon-Thu, to 5pm Fri, 9am-noon Sat) Organises excursions and adventure sports in the Dolenjska and Bela Krajina regions.

Post Office (Novi trg 7; ⊙8am-6pm Mon-Fri, to noon Sat)

Tourist Information Centre (TIC; ☑07-393 92 63; www.visitnovomesto.si; Glavni trg 6; ⊙9am-6pm Mon-Fri, to 2pm Sat) Next door to the town hall (p172). Can arrange guiding, and has bikes for rent (per day €7).

ℹ Getting There & Away

BUS
The **bus station** (Topliška cesta) is southwest of the Old Town across the Krka River on Topliška cesta.

Useful bus services include:

Brežice (€5.60, 1¼ hours, 45km) Two to four daily.

Črnomelj (€5.60, 1¼ hours, 46km) Two daily.

Dolenjske Toplice (€2.30, 20 minutes, 13km) Hourly services until 7pm.

Kostanjevica na Krki (€3.60, 45 minutes, 30km) Four to six daily.

Ljubljana (€7.20, 65 minutes, 72km) Four to eight daily.

Otočec ob Krki (to the castle; €1.80, 17 minutes, 8km) Up to 10 daily.

TRAIN
Novo Mesto has two train stations: the main one on Kolodvorska ulica, and little Novo Mesto-Center on Ljubljanska cesta at the western edge of the Old Town. Only about 1km separates the two stations.

Črnomelj (€3.45, 40 minutes, 31km) eleven trains daily on weekdays, two to five daily on weekends.

Ljubljana (€6.60, 1½ to two hours, 76km) fourteen services daily on weekdays, four to seven daily on weekends.

Metlika (€4.30, one hour, 46km) ten trains daily on weekdays, two to five on weekends. From Metlika there are connections to Karlovac in Croatia.

ℹ Getting Around

Book taxis by calling ☑041 625 108 or ☑040 550 785. The TIC rents bicycles (per day €7).

Otočec & Around
☑07 / POP 790 / ELEV 167M

The castle at Otočec, on a tiny island in the middle of the Krka River, is one of Slovenia's loveliest and most complete fortresses – and the setting is a delight. It now houses a luxurious hotel. For those just passing through, get close-up castle views with a drink in the courtyard (p176).

The first castle here stood on the right bank of the river, but during the Mongol onslaught of the mid-13th century, a canal was dug on the south side, creating an artificial island. The present castle dates from the 16th century.

◉ Sights

Otočec Castle   CASTLE
(Grad Otočec; www.grad-otocec.com; Grajska cesta 2) Perched in the centre of the Krka River and reached via a wooden bridge, Otočec Castle, 1.5km east of Otočec village, showcases both late-Gothic and Renaissance influences. The castle consists of two wings and an

entrance block connected by a pentagonal wall with four squat, rounded towers with conical roofs at each end. Although the castle is now a hotel and restaurant (p176), nonguests can admire it from the courtyard terrace cafe.

Trška Gora
VIEWPOINT

Vineyard-covered Trška Gora (428m) can be reached by road from Mačkovec, about 5km southwest of Otočec. From there, follow the road north for 1km to Sevno then continue along the winding track for 2km until you reach the summit and the Church of St Mary, from where there are wonderful panoramas of the Gorjanci Mountains, Kočevski Rog (p170) and the Krka Valley.

Alternatively, from Otočec another track, popular as a cycling route, leads north for 3.5km via Črešnjice to Trška Gora.

🏃 Activities

With the sports centre and golf course, the area around Otočec – the gateway to the lower Krka and the Posavje region – has become something of a recreational centre.

Kamp Otočec
CANOEING

(☑040 466 589; www.camping-potocar.si/kamp-otocec; ☉Apr-Oct) For exploration, rent canoes (€9/20 for three hours/day) and bikes (€5/10 for three hours/day).

Otočec Sports Centre
SWIMMING

(Športni center Otočec; ☑07-384 86 56; www.terme-krka.com; Hotel Šport, Grajska cesta 2; pool adult/child/family €11/8/30, pool & adventure park adult/child €23/12; ☉8am-9pm) The facilities at **Hotel Šport** (☑07-384 86 00; www.terme-krka.com; s/d €80/120; @ 🛜 🌊) – gym, tennis courts and basketball courts – are all open to the public but for travellers the pool area is probably of most interest. Those with kids that need to work off more energy should beeline to the Otočec Adventure Park on the hotel grounds with its treetop course combining ziplines and rope-bridges.

Šmarješke Toplice Park
THERMAL BATHS

(☑08-205 03 20; www.terme-krka.com; Šmarješke Toplice 100; adult/child €10/8; ☉indoor pools 10am-9pm Sun-Thu, to 11pm Fri & Sat year-round, outdoor pools 10am-6pm Jun & Sep, to 8pm Jul & Aug) For years, the thermal pools of Šmarješke Toplice have been drawing people to this resort in the green hills 5km north of Otočec. There are five pools here: two indoor and three outdoor. Our favourite is the oak-

framed wooden pool dating back to the late 18th-century and built directly atop a thermal spring (hence the steady temperature of 32°C).

Golf Grad Otočec
GOLF

(☑07-307 56 27, 041 304 444; www.golf-otocec.si; Grajska cesta 2; green fee 18/9 holes €60/30; ☉Mar-Nov) Along the Krka, about 800m from Otočec Castle, this is a scenic 18-hole golf course (par 72). Hiring a set of clubs costs €10 and an electric cart is €25. Bookings advised.

🛏 Sleeping

Most travellers choosing to bed down in Otočec are doing so regal-style within the castle. There are more accommodation options out of town and in nearby Novo Mesto.

Kamp Otočec
CAMPGROUND $

(☑040 466 589; www.camping-potocar.si/kamp-otocec; per adult/child €11/5.50; ☉Apr-mid-Oct; 🛜) This idyllic campground has it all: riverside location, castle views, canoes and bikes for rent. It's on a 2-hectare strip of land running along the south bank of the Krka – to reach it from the castle, cross the bridge, turn left (east) and walk for 300m.

★ Šeruga Farmhouse
GUESTHOUSE $$

(☑07-334 69 00; www.seruga.si; Sela pri Ratežu 15; s/d €40/70, granary for 2 people €70; 🛜) This farm, in a small valley with a babbling brook, sits in a hamlet about 4km south of Otočec. Rooms, with rustic wood-detailing and balconies, are the quintessential rural idyll, but the prize booking is the self-contained Granary, built in 1831. You'd be mad not to take half-board (single/double per person extra €12/€7.50) for the organic produce and time-honoured recipes.

Otočec Castle Hotel
HOTEL $$$

(☑07-384 89 00; www.grad-otocec.com; Grajska cesta 2; r/ste from €108/170; P ❄ 🛜) Appropriately regal and refined, the five-star Otočec Castle Hotel is one of the most atmospheric places to stay in Slovenia, and a member of the prestigious Relais & Chateaux group of luxury hotels. The 10 rooms, decorated in soothing neutrals, come with polished parquet floors, marble-topped tables and large baths, while the suites are suitably huge.

There's a range of packages involving weekends, romance, golf and/or cuisine.

VINEYARD COTTAGES

Farmstays have long been popular in Slovenia, but in recent years there's been a growing trend for vineyard stays.

Traditional vineyard cottages are a feature of the Dolenjska, Bela Krajina and Bizeljsko-Sremič wine districts. They stand on the edge of vineyards, on the sunny sides of hills, and offer wonderful views over the surrounding landscape of rolling hills and grapevines, perhaps with church spires and small villages in the panoramic sweep. Vineyard owners have generally built and maintained these cottages (*zidanice* in Slovenian; singular *zidanica*) for themselves, using them while tending their vines. Many of them have now been renovated in a new tourism trend to rent them to travellers; they are often well-priced and family-friendly (sleeping four and starting around €60 per night), with kitchen facilities. If you're lucky, the owners will include a bottle or two of wine as well.

If you're seeking authentic rural charm and tranquillity, check out the vineyard cottages listed on the local site www.zidanice.si.)

Eating

Gostilna Vovko
SLOVENIAN $

(☑ 07-308 56 03; www.gostilna-vovko.si; Ratež 48; mains €8-16; ☺ noon-10pm Tue-Sat, to 4pm Sun; 🛜) Head a couple of kilometres south from Otočec to Ratež village to feast on local flavours at this very fine *gostilna* (inn-like restaurant). The setting is farmhouse-chic, the wine options are varied and the food highlights local seasonal produce with a menu that skips from snails to wild boar. Dessert options include pear stewed in Cviček wine.

★ Grad
SLOVENIAN $$

(☑ 07-384 89 01; www.grad-otocec.com; Grajska cesta 2; mains €13-28; ☺ 7am-10pm; 🅿🛜) Otočec Castle's restaurant is as fancy as you would hope: ancient stone walls, stained glass and locally made artisanal furniture. It's formal, but not at all stuffy and service is excellent. The mains aren't as expensive as the setting would lead you to believe – and the degustation menu may be worth the splurge, at €55 for six courses.

The same menu is served all day, with wide-ranging prices – from a cheaper chicken or trout fillet to fancy beefsteak with truffles. We like that anyone can drop in for a coffee in the courtyard. Dinner bookings advised.

❶ Getting There & Away

Buses link Novo Mesto with Otočec (€1.80, 17 minutes, 8km) up to 10 times daily and stop at the bridge leading to the castle (p174).

BELA KRAJINA

Flying well under the radar of most travellers, Bela Krajina, the 'White March', is separated from Dolenjska by the scenic Gorjanci Mountains. The 600-sq-km region takes its name from the countless stands of birch trees here, and is a treasure trove of Slovenian folklore.

The sinuous Kolpa River is the main draw for rafting and other active pursuits, but the vineyard country north of Metlika offers up a more gentle activity: wine tasting. Tourism is a different beast in this far southeastern corner of the country – the well-oiled tourism machine of the Julian Alps or Soča Valley is nowhere to be found, and that, for some travellers, may be a key part of Bela Krajina's appeal.

Metlika

☑ 07 / POP 3200 / ELEV 156M

Metlika lies in a valley at the foot of the Gorjanci Mountains. While the town itself doesn't have much to do or see of note, it acts as a springboard for hiking and cycling in the area. Metlika is surrounded by Croatia on three sides; the Kolpa River and its 'beaches' lie about 1km to the south.

There was a major Hallstatt settlement here during the early Iron Age, and the Romans established an outpost in Metlika on the road leading to the important river port of Sisak in Croatia. During the Turkish onslaught of the 15th and 16th centuries, Metlika was attacked 17 times and occupied in 1578.

◉ Sights

Mestni Trg SQUARE
(Town Sq) Metlika's town square contains 18th- and 19th-century buildings, including the neo-Gothic **town hall** (Mestni trg 24). At the southern end of the square is the **Commandery** (Komenda; Mestni trg 14), with a Maltese Cross above the entrance. To the northwest is the **Parish Church of St Nicholas** (Farna Cerkev Sv Nikolaja; Mestni Trg).

Bela Krajina Museum MUSEUM
(Belokranjski Muzej; ☑07-306 33 70; www.belo kranjski-muzej.si; Trg Svobode 4; adult/child €4/3; ⊙9am-5pm Mon-Sat, 10am-2pm Sun) Located in **Metlika Castle**, the Bela Krajina Museum's small collection is an eclectic grab bag of minor finds from local archaeological sites (Iron Age and Roman era) and ethnographic displays relating to art, craft and village life as well as a room dedicated to Bela Krajina's role in WWII. It's all pepped up somewhat by audio soundtracks that blast out with startling velocity when you step close to some exhibits.

Slovenian Firefighters' Museum MUSEUM
(Slovenski Gasilski Muzej; ☑07-305 86 97; Trg Svobode 5; €2; ⊙9am-2pm Tue-Sat) Metlika was the first town in Slovenia to have its own fire brigade (1869), commemorated by the Slovenian Firefighters' Museum, which is just outside the castle. There are old fire trucks with enormous wheels, ladders and buckets.

✶ Activities

If you want to go swimming, head to the riverfront at Podzemelj campground (p178). The Kolpa River is clean and very warm (up to 28°C to 30°C in summer).

Hiking & Walking

There are a lot of hikes and walks in Metlika's surrounding areas, outlined on the map *Hiking Trails through Bela Krajina*, available at the TIC (p179). Walk No 19 is an easy 8km trail around Metlika including its old town. No 13 is the circular, 6.3km **Urban Walking Trail** through vineyards to Grabrovec and back via Veselica, a 233m-high small hill less than 1km north of Metlika with great views over the town. No 12 is the 2km **Educational Path Zdenc to Vidovec**, from the village of Božakovo to the Zdenc and Vidovec karst caves.

Wine Tasting

The hills to the north and northeast of Metlika are some of the Bela Krajina wine district's most important areas, producing such distinctive wines as Metliška Črnina (the ruby-red 'Metlika Black') and a late-maturing sweet 'ice wine' called Kolednik Ledeno Vino. These hills are also superb areas for easy walking.

On the way to **Drašiči**, an important wine town 6km from Metlika, you'll see (or walk through) *steljniki*, stands of birch trees growing among ferns in clay soil – the very symbol of Bela Krajina. Drašiči itself is well known for its folk architecture, and you can sample local wines at several places on the route here. Phone beforehand to arrange your tour. Some of our favourites are:

Pečarič (☑07-305 90 16, 041 753 263; www. pecaric.com; Čurile 7; tasting tours €10-25; ⊙by appointment) Tours here take in a trip to the cellar and a range of tasting choices; opt to either concentrate on sampling dessert wines or sparkling options or getting stuck into the heady reds or fruity whites. In Čurile.

Vinska Klet Prus (☑07-305 90 98; www. vinaprus.si; Krmačina 6; tasting tour per person €10; ⊙by appointment) The standout cellar in the Metlika area. The one- to two-hour tours take in the old and new cellars before a five-wine tasting with local snacks. In Krmačina.

Šuklje (☑041 554 120; http://suklje.com; Trn-ovec 22; tasting tours €4-12; ⊙by appointment) After a tour of the brick-lined cellar, sit down to taste the winery's modra frankinja (Blaufränkisch), sauvignon and Laški riesling. Book in for a post-tasting meal at its restaurant, which does excellent local dishes. In Trnovec.

✦ Festivals & Events

Vinska Vigred WINE
(Vineyard Spring; www.metlika-turizem.si/en/port-folio_page/vinska_vigredvinska-en; ⊙May) Metlika's main event is the Vinska Vigred festival held on the first weekend after 15 May. Local wines, foods, folk dancing and music contribute to a merry, much-loved event that's enjoyed by more than 20,000 attendees.

⌷ Sleeping

As a base while you're exploring the Bela Krajina region, Metlika has a couple of options but the out-of-town campgrounds (with cabins if you don't have a tent or motor home) are a nicer choice.

SOUTHEASTERN SLOVENIA & THE KRKA VALLEY METLIKA

Metlika

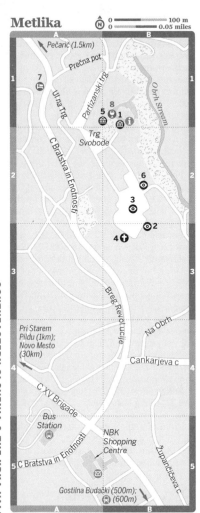

N 0 ————————— 100 m
   0 ————————— 0.05 miles

the 'glamping' option: timber cabins made for two.

Has baby-changing facilities on-site.

Hotel Bela Krajina HOTEL **$$**

(☏07-305 81 23; www.hotel-belakrajina.si; Cesta Bratstva in Enotnosti 28; d/tr from €65/90; P❄🖥) A former socialist holdover pulled into the 21st century with air-con and upgraded furnishings. Look past the orange exterior to find simple but spotless and comfy lodgings, welcoming service and a good onsite restaurant. There's one room with full wheelchair accessibility.

🍴 Eating & Drinking

Pri Starem Pildu INTERNATIONAL **$**

(☏07-305 87 21; Cesta XV Brigade 39; mains €4-13; ⊙8am-11pm Mon-Thu, to midnight Fri & Sat, 1-11pm Sun) The location – on the tip of the city limits – is terrible but this bright pink place is Metlika's best bet for cheap, tasty meals. This is burger, pizza and pasta territory with salads and some (completely unauthentic) Mexican dishes thrown in for good measure. The outdoor terrace is the place to be in Metlika for a drink in the evening.

Hotel Bela Krajina SLOVENIAN **$**

(☏07-305 81 23; Cesta Bratstva in Enotnosti 28; mains €6-14; ⊙7am-10pm; ❄🖥) This convivial place, which starts you off with *belokranjska pogača* (local flatbread, not unlike Italian focaccia), is the best place for a meal in Metlika, with house specialities including herb-crusted lamb or venison medallion. Try the *žlikrofi* (dumplings stuffed with potato, bacon and herbs) in mushroom sauce, or the excellent trout in Belokranjec

Camping Bela Krajina – Podzemelj CAMPGROUND **$**

(Kamp Podzemelj; ☏040 753 188; www.kamp-podzemelj.si; Škrilje 11; campsite pitch/adult/child €5/10.50/7.50, mobile homes d/tr/q from €65/90/100, cabin €79; ⊙mid-Apr–Sep; P🖥🏊) This large campground sits on the Kolpa River 7km southwest of Metlika in Podzemelj. It's packed with facilities including a restaurant, rental of bikes and canoes, playground and adventure climbing park and a river-swimming area, making it a great choice for families. Noncampers can rent family-sized mobile homes or go for white wine. There are even a few good vegetarian options.

Gostilna Budački   SLOVENIAN $
(⤳07-363 52 00; Ulica Belokranjskega Odreda 14; mains €7-16; ⊙8am-10pm Mon-Sat, noon-5pm Sun) This bright-yellow *gostilna* serves up standard Slovenian fare plus pizzas. Nothing's going to rock your world flavour-wise but it's a solid bet for decent food. It's 1km south of the town centre, not far from the train station.

Grajska Klet   WINE BAR
(⤳031 632 470; Trg Svobode 4; ⊙7am-11pm Mon-Thu, to 1am Fri & Sat, 8am-noon Sun) To try some Bela Krajina wine, head for this *vinoteka* (wine bar) in the castle courtyard. This is the cellar for Šturm label wines, and you can sample Pinot Blanc, Chardonnay, Rieslings and sweet *rumeni muškat* (yellow muscatel). Do try the Metliška Črnina, unique to Bela Krajina.

ⓘ Information

Post Office (NBK 2, off Cesta XV Brigade; ⊙8am-6pm Mon-Fri, to noon Sat)
Tourist Information Centre (TIC; ⤳07-363 54 70; www.metlika-turizem.si; Trg Svobode 4; ⊙8am-5pm Mon-Fri, 9am-1pm Sat Jun-Aug, 8am-4pm Mon-Fri, 9am-noon Sat Sep-May) In the castle courtyard. Hands out a decent map of the surrounding area.

ⓘ Getting There & Away

BUS
The **bus station** (Cesta XV Brigade) is 650m south of the Old Town on Cesta XV Brigade, opposite a shopping centre. You'll need to be an early riser to catch most bus services starting from Metlika. In general, it's better to take the train.

Destinations served include:
Črnomelj (€2.30, 30 minutes, 15km) Six on weekdays, one daily on weekends.
Novo Mesto (€3.60, one hour, 30km) Six on weekdays, two daily on weekends.
Vinica (€3.10, one hour, 34km) One daily.

TRAIN
The train station is on Kolodvorska ulica, about 1km southeast of the town centre.
Ljubljana (€8.49, 2½ to three hours, 122km) Nine services daily on weekdays, two to five daily on weekends. These all run via Novo Mesto (€4.28, one hour, 47km) and Črnomelj (€1.85, 18 minutes, 15km).

There are also two services daily to Karlovac in Croatia.

Črnomelj
⤳07 / POP 5580 / ELEV 145M

The capital of Bela Krajina and its largest town, Črnomelj (pronounced cher-*no*-ml) is on a promontory in a loop where the Lahinja and Dobličica Rivers meet. This is the 'folk heart' of Bela Krajina, and its popular Jurjevanje (p181) festival attracts hundreds of dancers and singers from the region. For the rest of the year, Črnomelj presses the snooze button and goes back to sleep. The town itself has little to make you linger but it's a gateway to scenic surrounds.

Legend has it that Črnomelj (a corruption of the words for 'black miller') got its name when a beggar, dissatisfied with the quality of the flour she'd been given, put a curse on the local miller. The town's symbol today is a smiling baker holding a pretzel.

MITHRA & THE GREAT SACRIFICE

Mithraism, the worship of the god Mithra, originated in Persia. As Roman rule extended west, the religion became extremely popular with traders, imperial slaves and mercenaries of the Roman army, and spread rapidly throughout the empire in the 1st and 2nd centuries AD. In fact, Mithraism was the principal rival of Christianity until Constantine, a Christian convert, came to the throne in the 4th century.

Mithraism's devotees guarded its secrets well. What little is known of Mithra, the god of justice and social contract, has been deduced from reliefs and icons found in temples, such those at Rožanec (p180) near Črnomelj and at Ptuj in eastern Slovenia. Mithra is portrayed in Persian dress sacrificing a white bull in front of Sol, the sun god. From the bull's blood sprout grain and grapes, and from its semen animals grow. Sol's wife Luna, the moon, begins her cycle and time is born.

Črnomelj

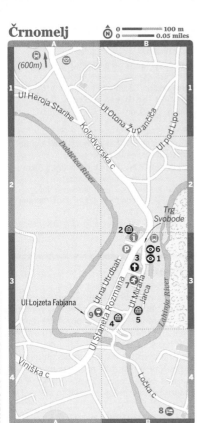

N 0 — 100 m
0 — 0.05 miles

Parish Church of St Peter CHURCH
(Cerkev Sv Petra; Ulica Staneta Rozmana) The church dates to the 13th century but what you'll see today is a standard-issue baroque structure with a single spire. There are Roman tombstones built into the walls, and on the western exterior above the main entrance is a fresco of St Christopher.

Town Museum Collection MUSEUM
(Mestna Muzejska Zbirka; ☎07-620 08 97; www.muzej-crnomelj.si; Ulica Mirana Jarca 3; adult/child €4/1.50; ⊙noon-4pm Tue, Wed & Fri, to 6pm Thu, 11am-3pm Sat) Houses a bright, interesting take on the history of the town and Bela Krajina.

Primožič House GALLERY
(Primožičeva Hiša; Ulica Mirana Jarca 18; ⊙by arrangement) This cute green house is home to displays of local arts and crafts including embroidery, woodwork and Bela Krajina's renowned *pisanice,* intricately painted Easter eggs. TIC staff will open it for you.

Mithraeum HISTORIC SITE
(Mitrej; Rožanec) About 4km northwest of Črnomelj is Rožanec village; to reach it turn west just after Lokve. From the village centre, a sign points along a trail leading about 400m to the Mithraeum, a temple in a cavern dedicated to the god Mithra, dating from the 2nd century AD. One of the exposed limestone faces is a 1.5m-high carved relief of Mithra sacrificing the sacred bull, watched by the sun and moon with a dog, serpent and scorpion at his feet.

History

Črnomelj's Roman presence is evident from the Mithraic shrine at Rožanec, about 4km northwest of the town. During the Turkish invasions in the 15th and 16th centuries, the town was attacked incessantly; due to its strong fortifications and excellent hilltop lookouts it was never taken. After the 1943 surrender of Fascist Italy – which had occupied Ljubljana and the southeastern region of Slovenia since 1941 – the town functioned for a time as Slovenia's capital.

◎ Sights

Trg Svobode SQUARE
(Freedom Sq) The main square is surrounded by some of the town's oldest and most important buildings: the **castle** (Črnomeljski Grad), the mid-17th-century **Commandery** (Komenda) and a grand old bank from the turn of the 20th century.

⚞ Activities

Hiking

Some great hikes and walks in the surrounding areas are outlined on the map *Hiking Trails through Bela Krajina,* available from the TIC. A number of them connect the smaller villages to Črnomelj's south. Walk No 1 is a 13km path from Dragatuš to Vinica dedicated to a local poet. No 2 is a 6km circular path beginning from Obrh (south of Dragatuš) that takes in forest scenery plus vineyards, castle ruins and village churches.

Wine Tasting

Črnomelj Wine Cellar WINE
(Črnomaljska Klet; ☑ 07-305 65 30; Ulica Mirana Jarca 2; ⊙ by arrangement) This wine cellar, in the basement of a beautifully renovated music school, offers tastings from the Bela Krajina wine-growing district with *belokranjska pogača* (local flatbread) and cheese. Generally, it only opens for groups of 10 or more, and tastings need to be arranged through the TIC.

⚟ Festivals & Events

Jurjevanje CULTURAL
(www.jurjevanje.si; ⊙ late Jun) The oldest international folklore festival in Slovenia, Jurjevanje is five days of music, dance and bonfires at the fairground near the train station and other locations around town in late June. It's based on the Zeleni Jurij (Green George), an early Slavic deity of vegetation, fertility and spring.

⏾ Sleeping

There's not a lot of choice for rooms, and the hostel is pretty grim – best to stock up on local maps and groceries and head out of town, where there are some great guesthouses and glamping options (p182).

Nearby riverside campgrounds include those at Podzemelj (p178), 10km northeast of Črnomelj, and Adlešiči (p183), 12km to the southeast.

Gostilna Müller GUESTHOUSE $
(☑ 07-356 72 00; www.gostilna-muller.si; Ločka cesta 6; s/d €30/50; 🅿 ❄ 🛜) Črnomelj's best restaurant is also its best bet for bedding down for the night in town. The four chalet-style rooms are bright and come with office-style furniture. It's an easy walk into central Črnomelj from here.

⚟ Eating & Drinking

Gostilna Müller SLOVENIAN $
(☑ 07-356 72 00; www.gostilna-muller.si; Ločka cesta 6; mains €5-14; ⊙ 8am-11pm Tue-Fri, 11am-midnight Sat, to 10pm Sun; 🛜) Črnomelj's eating options may be slim but at least what they do have is good. This local favourite – with timber interior, plants and a nice outdoor terrace – has a menu which covers all the classic Slovenian staples as well as some more local Bela Krajina dishes such as goat ragout. There's grilled trout and steaks plus a kids' menu too.

Črnomaljska Kavarna BAR
(☑ 040 741 006; Ulica Lojzeta Fabjana 7; ⊙ 9am-2pm daily plus 6-11pm Mon-Thu, 6pm-1am Fri & Sat, 5-10pm Sun; 🛜) Just below the bridge over the Lahinja River, this place with the shaded leafy terrace is a tranquil spot for a cold drink, coffee or beer. There's also a menu of burgers for the hungry.

ⓘ Information

Post Office (Kolodvorska cesta 30; ⊙ 8am-6pm Mon-Fri, to noon Sat)
Tourist Information Centre (TIC; ☑ 07-305 65 30; www.belakrajina.si; Trg Svobode 3; ⊙ 8am-4pm Mon-Fri, 9am-noon Sat) On the ground floor of Črnomelj Castle. Helpful office, with additional Saturday hours (3pm to 7pm) in July and August.

ⓘ Getting There & Away

BUS

Črnomelj's bus stop (Trg Svobode) is on Trg Svobode. Bus connections are lousy and as they're tailored towards students and workers, the services they do have are mostly in the early morning hours. There is a handful of departures to local villages and Kolpa Valley destinations. Services include:

Ljubljana (€9.20, two hours, 100km) Two daily.
Metlika (€2.30, 30 minutes, 15km) Seven on weekdays, two daily on weekends.
Novo Mesto (€5.20, 70 minutes, 44km) Two daily.

TRAIN

The train station is about 1.5km north of the old town, on Železničarska cesta.
Ljubljana (€7.70, two to 2½ hours, 107km) ten trains daily on weekdays, two to five daily on weekends. All these trains go via Novo Mesto (€3.45, 40 to 50 minutes, 32km).
Metlika (€1.85, 18 minutes, 15km) Heading in the other direction, there are nine services

LANDSCAPES & GLAMPING SOUTH OF ČRNOMELJ

The **Lahinja Landscape Park** (Krajinski Park Lahinja), about 9km south of Črnomelj, is a protected karst area of about 200 hectares rich in birdlife and the source of the Lahinja River. Trails criss-cross the fields, forest and wetlands. It's possible to access the park via two 'entrances': at the villages of Pusti Gradec and Veliki Nerajec.

The latter is the best option – there's a simple information point at Veliki Nerajec 18a, where you can get a map and basic information for walks. Vera, the owner of the house at Veliki Nerajec 18a, displays and sells local handicrafts, including distinctive 'kingfisher' ceramic whistles she makes, and the *gudalo*, a remarkable local musical instrument.

Walks 1 and 24 outlined on the *Hiking Trails through Bela Krajina* map cover areas of the park.

Not far away, **Glamping Malerič** (☑ 07-305 71 20; http://glamping.turizemmaleric.si/en; Podlog 3c; apt for 4 from €105; ❄ 🕿 🗷), in the tiny hamlet of Podlog, is a complex of four futuristic pod-style apartments arranged in front of a natural swimming pool, with splendid rural outlooks. The pods are stylishly compact, each with two bedrooms (sleeping four) plus bathroom, kitchenette, living space and sundeck.

daily on weekdays, and two to five daily on weekends.

❶ Getting Around

You can hire bikes from **L Šport** (☑ 07-305 24 81; Kolodvorska cesta 13; per day from €10; ☺ 8am-7pm Mon-Fri, to noon Sat).

Kolpa Valley

☑ 07 / ELEV UP TO 370M

For watery pursuits, make a beeline to the banks of the Kolpa. The meandering 118km-long river marks the border with Croatia and is the warmest and one of the cleanest rivers in the country. The villages of Adlešiči and, to the west, Stari Trg ob Kolpi make good bases for those keen on rafting, boating, fishing and swimming. Kolpa Landscape Park is a popular recreation area.

Facility-wise, Vinica is the largest village, with amenities including a grocery store.

◉ Sights & Activities

Kolpa Landscape Park PARK
(Kolpa Krajinski Park; www.kp-kolpa.si) This protected area follows the meandering path of the Kolpa River from the brilliantly named village of Fučkovci (*fuch*-kow-tse), just north of Adlešiči, as far southwest as Stari Trg ob Kolpi. It's a popular recreation area for swimming, fishing and boating, especially around Vinica, Adlešiči and Stari Trg ob Kolpi.

Grand Kolpa RAFTING
(☑ 041 740 798; www.grandkolpa.si; Stari Trg ob Kolpi 15; rafting per person 1/2 days from €20/36;

☺ Apr-Sep) From its base in the village of Stari Trg ob Kolpi, this company offers river rafting trips ranging from a family-friendly 8km to a longer 25km.

Cycling

There are excellent cycling trails along the river valley. Get a copy of the *Cycling Trails through Bela Krajina* map – routes 1 and 5 are especially good for exploring this area.

Hiking

On the *Hiking Trails through Bela Krajina* map, walks 3, 4, 5 and 18 are good. Walk 18 describes the 'Castle Footpath along the Kolpa River', a flat 26km path through the most attractive part of the park, from the sweet hamlet of Žuniči (full of traditional architecture) to Dragoši.

🛏 Sleeping & Eating

If your main aim is getting on the water, the Kolpa riverbank is home to a couple of the best sleeping choices in Bela Krajina.

★ **Madronič** GUESTHOUSE $
(☑ 031 627 952; www.gostinstvo-madronic.si; Prelesje 10; campsite/hay barn dm/r per person €9/9/29; 🕿) About 4km downhill from Stari Trg ob Kolpi in the hamlet of Prelesje, this is a handsome riverside complex in a beautiful setting. There's a restaurant to feed you, a choice of sleeping arrangements (from a campsite to smart, renovated rooms – and also the chance to sleep in a hayloft) and lots of activities, from fishing to rafting to swimming.

Kamp Jankovič   CAMPGROUND **$**
(☑ 041 622 877; www.kolpas.si; Adlešiči 24a; campsite adult/child €10/7, hut €42; ☺ mid-Apr–Sep; Ⓟ) At the southern end of Adlešiči, take the signposted turning and follow the road for about 1km to reach this fabulous, friendly spot. It's a simple riverside camp area with extras including swimming platform, canoe and SUP rental, three small timber glamping huts and a great barn-like restaurant-bar known as Stari Pod.

❶ Getting There & Away

There are infrequent buses to the Kolpa Valley – these link Vinica with Črnomelj via Dragatuš, or Adlešiči to Črnomelj – but they are geared to the needs of local workers and students. Bus timetables are at www.mpov.si.

❶ Getting Around

This is an area best explored with your own wheels (car or bike).

POSAVJE

The Posavje region (www.posavje.com) covers the lower Sava River valley as it extends towards the border with Croatia. Although often overlooked by travellers zooming between Ljubljana and Zagreb, dilly-dallying for a day or two in its rolling hills of vineyards and forests is a great way to see a slice of rural Slovenia. The Bizeljsko-Sremič wine district was made for puttering between boutique wineries on an afternoon's drive or cycle. Brežice has a castle-museum with a whopper of a frescoed hall, and island-bound Kostanjevica na Krki is charmingly teensy as well as being home to an engrossing art museum. Throw in a couple of excellent restaurants, and you're set for the day.

Kostanjevica na Krki

☑ 07 / POP 720 / ELEV 149M

Situated on an islet just 500m long and 200m wide in a loop of the Krka River, sleepy Kostanjevica is Slovenia's smallest town and, with a charter that dates back to 1252, one of its oldest. Apart from the excellent Božidar Jakac Art Museum, the main highlight of a visit here is taking a simple stroll on the island with its handful of historical buildings, admiring the serene atmosphere.

If you're road-touring, Kostanjevica makes for a good stop-off to stretch your legs; if you enjoy a quiet village atmosphere, it's a very tranquil base for the night. Kostanjevica's historical sights are on the island; further amenities are on the mainland to the northwest or southeast, reached by two small bridges.

◉ Sights

★**Božidar Jakac Art Museum**   MUSEUM
(Galerija Božidar Jakac; ☑ 07-498 81 40; www.galerija-bj.si; Grajska cesta 45; adult/child €6/free; ☺ 10am-6pm Tue-Sun) This is an unexpected treat: superbly varied art in a magnificent setting, surrounded by a garden full of sculptures. The museum's galleries showcase the works of Slovenian artists.

About 1.5km southwest of town, this former Cistercian monastery was a very wealthy institution in the Middle Ages, but abandoned in 1786 when monastic orders were dissolved. The beautifully painted main entrance through two squat, candy-striped towers leads to an enormous courtyard enclosed by a cloister with 230 arcades across three floors.

To the west stands the disused Church of the Virgin Mary containing elements from the 13th to 18th centuries; it is now used to great effect as an exhibition space. Upstairs is an exhibition on the monastery's history and its masterful restoration.

The galleries of the museum itself exhibit the works of eight Slovenian artists, encompassing paintings, drawings, graphic art and sculpture. Chief among the artists is the expressionist Božidar Jakac (1899–1989) and brothers France (1895–1960) and Tone Kralj (1900–75), who painted expressionist and surrealist-cum-socialist-realism canvases respectively. France Kralj was particularly prolific and his sculptures are captivating. There's also a permanent collection of old masters from the Carthusian monastery at Pleterje.

The grounds of the Božidar Jakac Art Museum are home to more than 100 large wooden sculptures from Forma Viva, sculptural symposia that were held in several places in Slovenia from 1961 to 1988 and have been revived in recent years. At these symposia, sculptors work with materials associated with the area. Here it was oak, in Portorož stone, iron at Ravne in Koroška and concrete in Maribor.

PLETERJE MONASTERY

Located 10km southwest of Kostanjevica na Krki, the enormous **Pleterje Monastery** (Samostan Pleterje; www.kartuzija-pleterje.si; Drča 1; ☺church 7.30am-6pm) belongs to the Carthusians, the strictest of all monastic orders. The **Gothic Holy Trinity Church** (also called the Old Gothic Church or Stara Gotska Cerkev), 250m up a linden-lined path from the car park, is the only part of the complex open to the public but the location, in a narrow valley between slopes of the Gorjanci Mountains, is so attractive that it's worth a visit in any case.

Pleterje was built in 1407 by the Counts of Celje. It was fortified with ramparts, towers and a moat during the Turkish invasions, and all but abandoned during the Protestant Reformation in the 16th century. The Carthusian order, like all monastic communities in the Habsburg Empire, was abolished in 1784. When French Carthusian monks returned in 1899, they rebuilt to the plans of the order's charterhouse at Nancy in France.

You may catch a glimpse of some of the white-hooded monks quietly going about their chores – they take a strict vow of silence – or hear them singing their offices in the Gothic church at various times of the day. But the ubiquitous signs reading Klavzura – Ni Vstopa (Enclosure – No Admittance) and Območje Tišine (Area of Silence) remind visitors that everything apart from the church is off limits.

Above the ribbed main portal of the austere church (1420) is a fresco depicting Mary being crowned and the Trinity. Inside, the rib-vaulted ceiling with its heraldic bosses and the carved stone niches by the simple stone altar are worth a look, as is the medieval rood screen, the low wall across the aisle that separated members of the order from lay people.

There's a **monastery shop** (☺7.30am-5.30pm Mon-Sat) where the monks sell some of their own products. The **Open-Air Museum Pleterje** (Muzej na Prostem Pleterje; ☏041 639 191, 07-308 10 50; www.skansen.si; Drča 1; adult/child/family €4/3/8; ☺10am-5pm Apr-Oct by appointment) is to the west of the monastery car park.

Old Town
AREA

No one's going to get lost or tired touring the itsy-bitsy Old Town island of Kostanjevica – walk 400m up Oražnova ulica and 400m down Ulica Talcev and you've seen the lot.

Cross the southern bridge onto Kambičev trg to the tiny, late-Gothic **Church of St Nicholas** (Cerkev Sv Miklavža; ☏for interior viewings 07-498 70 26; Kambičev trg; ☺interior viewed by prior arrangement). About 200m northwest along Oražnova ulica is a 15th-century manor house containing the **Lamut Art Salon** (☺10am-6pm Tue-Sun Apr-Oct, to 4pm Nov-Mar) **FREE**.

Continue along Oražnova ulica, passing a somewhat crumbling fin-de-siècle house (No 24), to the 13th-century Romanesque Parish Church of St James.

Loop from there onto Ulica Talcev, lined with attractive 'folk baroque' houses, to stroll back to the Church of St Nicholas.

Parish Church of St James
CHURCH

(Župnijska Cerkev Sv Jakoba; ☏for viewing appointments 07-498 70 26; Oražnova ulica; ☺interior viewed by prior arrangement) This 13th-century Romanesque building has a mostly baroque interior. Above the carved stone portal on the western side are geometric designs and decorative plants and trees. On the south side is a 15th-century depiction of Jesus rising from the tomb, as well as 1800s grave markers embedded in the wall.

Kostanjevica Cave
CAVE

(Kostanjeviška Jama; ☏07-498 70 88, 041 297 001; www.kostanjeviska-jama.com; Dolšce 24; adult/child €8/4; ☺tours 10am, noon, 2pm, 4pm & 6pm weekends mid-Apr–Oct, daily Jul & Aug) This small cave, about 1.5km southeast of town, has 40-minute tours in spring, summer and autumn. The guide will lead you 250m in, past a small lake and several galleries full of stalactites and stalagmites. The temperature is a constant 12°C.

🏃 Activities

Čolnarna
WATER SPORTS

(☏040 883 007; www.facebook.com/mestnacolnarna; Oražnova 14) From a house in the village, a local guy rents out canoes, rowboats and SUP boards. If you can't find him, ask at Bar Štraus on the riverfront.

Cviček Wine Cellar WINE

(Vinska Klet Cviček; ☎07-498 81 40; info@galerija-bj.si; Grajska cesta 45; €8 per person, groups of 10 or more only; ⊙by arrangement Tue-Sun) Inside the ancient monastery that's home to the Božidar Jakac Art Museum (p183) is the Cviček Wine Cellar. This is a true cellar if there ever was one, with ancient casks and mould a-blooming in the vaulted ceiling. Cviček's 40-minute tasting sessions usually consist of three different wines.

Hosta Stud Farm HORSE RIDING

(Kobilarna Hosta; ☎031 220 059, 041 690 066; www.hosta-lipizzans.eu; Sela pri Šentjerneju 6; per hr €15-22; ⊙11am-7pm Sat & Sun) Some 9km southwest of Kostanjevica, this horse stud is one of the largest private Lipizzaner breeders in Slovenia (and Europe), with 50 horses. It offers rides from two hours to two days in beautiful rolling countryside; it can arrange riding lessons too. Bookings are required.

Sleeping

Although sleeping options are otherwise thin, the two main places to stay are solid choices.

Gostilna Žolnir GUESTHOUSE $

(☎07-498 71 33; www.zolnir.eu; Krška cesta 4; s/d €30/50; P 🛜) This friendly *gostilna*, about 500m northeast of the island, has 12 double rooms; decor is basic but comfy. The best reason to stay here is the on-site restaurant.

★**Vila Castanea** GUESTHOUSE $$

(☎031 662 011; www.vila-castanea.si; Ulica Talcev 9; d €69-83, f €110; P ❄ 🛜) A swish renovation has breathed new life into this gracious Old Town villa, and the result is an appealing nine-room guesthouse with elegant decor and muted tones. Superior rooms are lovely and spacious (two have a balcony), while larger rooms can accommodate families.

Eating & Drinking

Gostilna Žolnir SLOVENIAN $

(☎07-498 71 33; www.zolnir.eu; Krška cesta 4; mains €8-18; ⊙7am-10pm; 🛜) It's a short walk northeast of the island to this local favourite, which wins praise for its traditional food: lots of *štruklji* options, grilled calamari, gnocchi with game ragu and venison fillet, a speciality of the house. Its decor is a blend of old and new, with an appealing courtyard space.

Kitcher Brewery MICROBREWERY

(Pivovarna Kitcher; ☎041 639 193; www.pivovarnakitcher.si; Oražnova ulica 19; ⊙10am-7pm) This small local brewery produces four craft beers including its IPA Kitcher Ribič and a stout, Kitcher Jamar. You can tour the brewery here and have a beer tasting.

Bar Štraus BAR

(☎07-498 75 30; Ulica Talcev 31; ⊙5.15am-midnight) Fronting the Krka by the northern bridge, this little cafe-bar is the best place for a drink in town, though to be fair it has little competition. The narrow riverfront terrace is where you come to while away a warm and lazy afternoon in Kostanjevica. Don't bother with the coffee; opt for a beer or cold drink instead.

Information

Tourist Information Centre (TIC; ☎07-498 81 50; tic-gbj@galerija-bj.si; Grajska cesta 45; ⊙9am-6pm Tue-Sun Apr-Oct, to 4pm Tue-Sun Nov-Mar) In an old mill at the entrance to the Božidar Jakac Art Museum (p183); like the museum, it's closed Mondays.

Getting There & Away

Buses (Ljubljanska cesta) drop off and pick up from the car park on Ljubljanska cesta that connects the footbridge to the island.

Useful bus services include:

Brežice (€2.70, 30 minutes, 20km) Three to six daily.

Ljubljana (€9.20, 1¾ hours, 97km) Four to five daily.

Novo Mesto (€3.60, 40 minutes, 30km) Four to five daily.

Brežice

☎07 / POP 6800 / ELEV 163M

This sleepy provincial town is a great place for a layover while you're exploring the southeast. View the flashy frescoes of the Knights Hall inside the sturdy walls of Brežice Castle then stroll the main street, rimmed by well-cared-for Renaissance and late-baroque facades, and watch the world go by from one of the pavement cafes. The town's laid-back appeal is further enhanced by having the vast Terme Čatež resort right on its doorstep. If you're travelling with children, this hugely family-focused thermal baths complex makes Brežice the perfect pit stop for a day of downtime off the road.

History

Situated near where the Krka flows into the Sava, Brežice was an important trading centre in the Middle Ages. Its most dominant feature has always been its castle, mentioned in documents as early as 1249. In the 16th century the original castle was replaced with a Renaissance fortress to strengthen the town's defences against the Turks and later marauding peasants who, during one uprising, beheaded nobles at the castle and impaled their heads on poles. Today the castle houses the Posavje Museum.

◉ Sights

★ Posavje Museum   MUSEUM

(Posavski Muzej; ☑ 07-466 05 17; www.pmb.si; Cesta Prvih Borcev 1; adult/child/family €4/2.50/7; ☺ 10am-8pm Mon-Sat, 2-8pm Sun Jun-Aug, 10am-6pm Tue-Sat, 2-6pm Sun Apr-May & Sep-Oct, 8am-4pm Tue-Sat, 1-4pm Sun Nov-Mar) Housed in **Brežice Castle**, the Posavje Museum is one of provincial Slovenia's richest museums, particularly for its archaeological and ethnographic collections – and for its stunning fresco-filled Knights' Hall.

From the courtyard, ascend the staircase; its walls and ceiling are illustrated with Greek gods, the four Evangelists and the coat of arms of the Attems family, who owned the castle for 250 years. Rooms on the 2nd floor feature archaeological exhibits; look out for the 7th-century-BC bronze horse bridle and the Celtic and Roman jewellery. In the ethnographic rooms, along with the details of local winemaking, flax weaving and master pottery, there is a strange beehive in the shape of a soldier from the early 1800s.

Rooms on the 1st floor cover life in the Posavje region in the 19th century and during the two world wars, with special emphasis on the deportation of Slovenes by the Germans during WWII. There are also galleries of religious artworks and more contemporary pieces.

The museum's real crowd-pleaser is the **Knights' Hall** (Viteška Dvorana), an Italian baroque masterpiece where everything except the floor is painted with landscapes, classical gods, heroes, allegories and muses. Concerts and events are sometimes held here.

☂ Activities

You can rent bikes (per hour/day €3/15) from the TIC (p188). Ask for a free copy of the *Cycling Booklet*, outlining four themed regional rides.

Terme Čatež   THERMAL BATHS

(☑ 07-493 67 00; www.terme-catez.si; Topliška cesta 35) The thermal spring just east of Čatež ob Savi (3km southeast of Brežice) has attracted rheumatics since the late 18th century. Today, the huge Terme Čatež spa and holiday complex is every bit as much a recreational area, popular all year. There's an outdoor pool playground, year-round indoor complex, saunas, three hotels, enormous campground, wellness centre and various family-friendly activities.

Its huge **Summer Thermal Riviera** (Poletna Termalna Riviera; ☑ 07-493 67 00; www.terme-catez.si; Topliška cesta 35; day pass adult/child €13/10.50 Mon-Fri, €17/13 Sat & Sun; ☺ late-Apr–early Oct) area is packed with family-friendly fun and is tremendously popular on summer weekends.

Open year-round, the indoor, dome-topped **Winter Thermal Riviera** (Zimska Termalna Riviera; ☑ 07-493 67 00; www.terme-catez.si; Topliška cesta 35; day pass adult/child €13/10.50 Mon-Fri, €17/13 Sat & Sun; ☺ year-round) is a massive complex spanning 2300 sq metres; it has a pirate ship ensconced in one pool, plus a wave pool. Water temperatures tip 33°C.

There are at least half-hourly bus services (€1.30, five minutes, 3km) between Brežice and Terme Čatež.

SUP Čatež   WATER SPORTS

(☑ 040 649 265; www.supcatez.com; Velike Malence, Terme Čatež; per person per hr €10; ☺ May-Oct) These guided stand-up paddle tours along the Krka River begin from near the Tochka beach bar (p188). Book beforehand.

✸ Festivals & Events

Seviqc Brežice   MUSIC

(www.seviqc-brezice.si; ☺ late-Jun–mid-Aug) Culture vultures, this is for you. This is an acclaimed summer-long series of concerts, featuring international early music performances (classical music with authentic instruments), set exclusively at venues of Slovenian cultural heritage – for example, the stunning Knights' Hall at Brežice Castle, and **Mokrice Castle** (Grad Mokrice; Rajec 4; ☺ 8am-10pm) FREE. Full program online.

⌂ Sleeping

A great hostel and a solid midrange choice make Brežice one of the best bases for ex-

Brežice

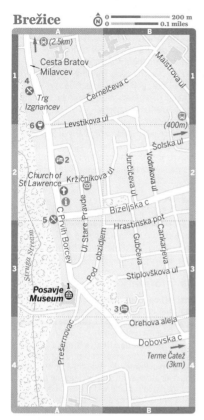

N · 0 — 200 m
0 — 0.1 miles

Brežice

⊙ **Top Sights**
1 Posavje Museum.................................A3

🛏 **Sleeping**
2 Hotel Splavar.....................................A2
3 MC Hostel Brežice.............................B3

🍴 **Eating**
Gostilna Splavar..........................(see 2)
4 Ošterija Debeluh..................................A1
5 Santa Lucija.......................................A2

🍷 **Drinking & Nightlife**
6 Jazz Pub...A2

campground at the Terme Čatež resort is chockers with families thanks to masses of kid-friendly facilities including playgrounds, sports courts and an animation program. Not got a tent? There are family-sized tepees plus a 'Pirates Bay' complex: bungalows built over the water in the middle of the campground's lake.

Rates include day-long passes to the thermal baths. Outside of holidays, expect more breathing space.

Hotel Splavar
HOTEL **$$**
(☎07-499 06 30; www.splavar.si; Cesta Prvih Borcev 40a; s/d/tr €55/80/100; P🖥) The hotel's central position, on Brežice's main street above the Gostilna Splavar, makes the 16 rooms here a convenient choice. The plain, good-sized rooms are comfortable, though they can get stuffy in the heat. Along with the top-notch location, the best reasons to stay here are the chirpy staff and the easy accessibility to the ice cream downstairs.

Hotel Terme
HOTEL **$$$**
(☎07-493 67 00; www.terme-catez.si; Topliška cesta 35; s/d €132/220; P❄🖥🏊) Out of the three large run-of-the-mill hotels at the Terme Čatež complex, this is the nicest. Rooms are rather retro beige-on-beige but all come with balconies; the hotel benefits from being tucked away a little from the crowds. Prices are indeed high while style points are low, but rates do include thermal bath entry.

🍴 Eating & Drinking

Gostilna Splavar
EUROPEAN **$**
(☎07-499 06 30; www.splavar.si; Cesta Prvih Borcev 40a; mains €6-16; ⊙7am-10pm; 🖥) This friendly *gostilna* has a cosy pub-like interior plus street-side terrace. Steaks and other

ploring the Posavje region. There's also plenty of top-end accommodation (and a campsite) at Terme Čatež just down the road if you're looking for a resort break.

★ MC Hostel Brežice
HOSTEL **$**
(☎05-908 37 97; www.mc-hostel.si; Gubčeva ulica 10a; dm €15, d with/without bathroom €48/36; P🖥) Just a short walk through parkland from the town's castle and museum, this hostel is a breath of fresh air: bright and colourful with spic-and-span six-bed dorms and light-filled private rooms. It's got all the facilities you need – an outdoor terrace, kitchen and laundry plus a bar serving beers from around the globe.

Camping Terme Čatež
CAMPGROUND **$**
(☎07-493 67 00; www.terme-catez.si; Topliška cesta 35; campsite or motorhome adult/child from €20/10, tepee/bungalow from €73/102; ⊙year-round; P🖥🏊) Don't come here looking for peace and quiet in summer – this mega-

SOUTHEASTERN SLOVENIA & THE KRKA VALLEY BREŽICE

MOKRICE CASTLE

Ten kilometres southeast of Brežice, is the loveliest **fortress** (Grad Mokrice; Rajec 4; ◷8am-10pm) in the Posavje region. The castle dates from the 16th century, but there are bits and pieces going back to Roman times built into the structure. The castle is home to a **hotel** (www.terme-catez.si; d from €90) with an 18-hole golf course but its lovely grounds – including a 20-hectare 'English park' full of rare plants, a large orchard of pear trees and a small disused Gothic chapel – are open to all at no charge.

It's supposedly haunted by the ghost of the 17th-century countess Barbara, who committed suicide here after her lover failed to return from sea. She's particularly active on her name day (4 December) when she spends the night rolling cannonballs around the joint. A trip to the castle makes a lovely excursion from Brežice, especially by bike; take the secondary road from Čatež ob Savi that runs parallel to the highway.

meaty mains hold sway on the menu, all presented with modern panache. Seasonal offerings including nettle soup are a strong point. The best is kept for last: Splavar is celebrated for its homemade ice cream. Try the balsamic and orange flavour and you'll see why.

Santa Lucija
PIZZA $

(☏07-499 25 00; http://santa-lucija.si; Cesta Prvih Borcev 15; mains €6.50-12; ◷11am-11pm) Head for the terrace out the back during summer or dine inside, where the walls are daubed with some rather eccentric frescoes. The large pizza menu won't exactly set your taste buds buzzing but it's a decent, well-priced standby in the centre.

★Ošterija Debeluh
EUROPEAN $$

(☏07-496 10 70; www.debeluh.si; Trg Izgnancev 7; mains €12-25; ◷noon-10pm Mon-Sat; ❊ 🖥) This fine-dining restaurant, with a French-countryside interior, serves inventive European cuisine with local twists, from the chef's signature beef tartare with foie gras, to trout served on a bed of roast pear and horseradish sauce. The wine list is large, the strudel desserts excellent and the advice sage. A four-/six-course tasting menu is €38/50. Bookings advised.

Tochka Beach Bar
BAR

(www.facebook.com/beachbartochka; Velike Malence, Terme Čatež; ◷2pm-midnight Mon-Fri, 10am-midnight Sat & Sun May-Sep) This bright-yellow shack on the bank of the Krka River (on the Terme Čatež side of town) is the place to be during summer. There's a shaded terrace as well as wooden seating on the grassy riverbank, so pull up a pew, have a beer or cocktail and chill out for the afternoon.

Jazz Pub
PUB

(☏031 412 797; www.jazzpub.si; Trg Izgnancev 2; ◷7am-midnight) Come for the pub's popular outdoor terrace, good coffee and the beautiful timber-lined old-world interior. No live jazz, alas.

❶ Information

Post Office (Ulica Stare Pravde 34; ◷8am-6pm Mon-Fri, to noon Sat) In a new building behind the **Church of St Lawrence** (Župnijska Cerkev Sv Lovrenca; Cesta Prvih Borcev).

Tourist Information Centre Brežice (TIC; ☏064 130 082; www.discoverbrezice.com; Cesta Prvih Borcev 22; ◷10am-6pm Mon-Sat) Souvenir store, wine shop and tasting room and tourist information all in one caboodle. Has some brochures but actual information is thinner on the ground here than in other TICs.

Tourist Information Centre Terme Čatež (☏07-620 70 35; www.discoverbrezice.com; Topliška cesta 35; ◷10am-noon & 6-10pm Jun-Aug, 10am-6pm Sep-Nov & Mar-May, to 2pm Dec-Feb) Helpful branch at the Terme Čatež resort (p186).

❶ Getting There & Away

BUS

The **bus station** (Cesta Svobode 11) is about 1km northeast of the castle (p186).

Useful services include:

Kostanjevica na Krki (€2.70, 30 minutes, 20km) Three to five daily.

Ljubljana (€10.70, 2¼ hours, 117km) Three to five daily.

Novo Mesto (€5.20, 70 minutes, 45km) Three to five daily.

Terme Čatež (€1.30, five minutes, 3km) At least half-hourly services.

TRAIN

There are excellent connections to Ljubljana with 17 trains a day on weekdays and 10 daily on weekends (€7.70, 1½ to two hours, 107km). Unfortunately, the station is quite inconvenient, about 3km north of the castle (p186) at Trg Vstaje 3.

ⓘ Getting Around

You can rent bikes (per hour/day €3/15) from the tourist information centres.

Bizeljsko-Sremič Wine District

🖉 07 / ELEV 175M

Cycling the 17km from Brežice to Bizeljsko is a great way to experience the picturesque Bizeljsko-Sremič wine country, stopping off whenever you see a *vinska klet* (wine cellar) that takes your fancy.

This area is interesting for its use of flint-stone caves (*repnice* in Slovene; singular *repnica*), which once stored *repa* (turnips) but are now used to store and mature wine. On the main road to Bizeljsko, follow the signs for 'Repnice/Bresovica' to reach a pocket of small wineries, each with their own *repnica,* which you can visit before getting down to some wine tasting.

🏃 Activities

Repnica Vino Graben   WINE

(🖉 07-495 10 59; www.vino-graben.com; Kumrovška 6, Bizeljsko; tour & tasting per person €6; ☺ 9am-7pm Fri-Sun, by appointment rest of week) There are plenty of different drops to try at this local winery which produces herb and fruit wines as well as a selection of whites and reds. Tours take in the caves used to store and mature the wines before tasting.

Penine Istenič   WINE

(🖉 07-495 15 59; www.istenic.si; Stara Vas 7; per wine sample €1.50) One of Slovenia's biggest and best sparkling wine producers, Istenič has a *vinska klet* (wine cellar) in the hamlet of Stara Vas, surrounded by an emerald-green lawn. Stop in to sample a few bubbly varieties (the Prestige extra brut is the pick, but Desiree is the big seller) alongside some charcuterie (€4 to €7).

Tastings with an included cellar tour can be arranged for groups of 10 or more with an advance booking; they cost according to the number of wine samples (between €3 and €14 per person).

There is also stylish accommodation here with rooms in the Istenič Villa starting from €75.

Repnice Najger   WINE

(🖉 07-495 11 15; repnicanajger@siol.net; Brezovica 32; tour & tastings €4; ☺ 9am-9pm) Family-run Najger offers a fun tour of its large cave, first carved out in the 19th century, with tastings of homemade wines including its Laški Riesling.

🍴 Eating & Drinking

Many of the wine cellars serve charcuterie platters and other snacks. There are also simple *gostilne* scattered along the wine district route. For hearty pub grub, pull into Pivoteka Bizeljsko.

Gostilna Kocjan   SLOVENIAN **$$**

(🖉 07-495 10 90; www.gostilnakocjan.si; Stara Vas 63; mains €9-27; ☺ 7am-10pm) One of the best places in the area for typical, hearty Slovenian and continental European dishes, plus excellent charcuterie platters if you're looking for nibbles rather than a full-on meal.

Pivoteka Bizeljsko   PUB

(🖉 041 662 848; Stara Vas 58; ☺ 10am-midnight Mon-Thu & Sun, to 3am Fri & Sat) A surprise among the vineyards – but a fun one. This is a big barn of a pub, with a wide beer selection and hearty beer snacks to enjoy on the chilled-out terrace. Hungry? Order a metre of chicken wings or a metre of *čevapčiči* (spicy meatballs) – enough to feed four.

ⓘ Getting There & Away

You'll need your own transport to explore this area. Bicycles can be hired from Brežice's TIC.

Eastern Slovenia

Best Places to Eat

➜ Hiša Denk (p226)

➜ Gostilna Grabar (p215)

➜ Restavracija Mak (p223)

➜ Gostilna Ribič (p215)

➜ Gostilna Rajh (p232)

➜ Gostilna Kmetec (p203)

Best Places to Stay

➜ DomKulture MuziKafe (p215)

➜ Lenar Farmhouse (p198)

➜ Hotel Mitra (p215)

➜ Hotel Maribor (p222)

➜ Herbal Glamping Resort Ljubno (p198)

➜ MCC Hostel (p202)

Why Go?

The heartland of the country, Eastern Slovenia is often ignored by visitors heading west to the country's big highlights. If you want to explore further than the main tourist routes, this region offers outdoor activities aplenty and three grand historical centres where you can wander freely without squeezing between tour-group crowds.

For stupendous mountain views with a spot of hiking and mountain biking, make a beeline to the highland pastures of Velika Planina, the glacial valley of Logarska Dolina or the forest-clad peaks of the Pohorje Massif. Afterwards, add in a slice of culture amid the cobblestone quaintness of Ptuj, Maribor's buzzing cafes or the Roman heritage of Celje. Ramble through the undulating hills of the Jeruzalem-Ljutomer Wine Road, or take time out for a soak at a thermal spa. This chunk of the country is tailor-made for those who prefer a scenic dawdle rather than zipping between sights.

When to Go
Maribor

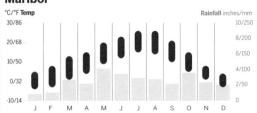

Feb Ptuj's masked Kurentovanje carnival is one of Slovenia's best cultural festivals.

Jun–Sep Pull on your hiking boots; the season to soak up the alpine views of Logarska Dolina and Velika Planina.

Dec–Feb Ski-bunnies head to Maribor Pohorje, Slovenia's biggest alpine skiing centre.

KAMNIK-SAVINJA ALPS

Within easy reach of the capital, this area is a prime day-tripping destination for Ljubljana locals itching for some nature. Krvavec is where city-slickers head for skiing in the winter and mountain biking in summer, while the high green pastures of Velika Planina, trimmed by snowcapped peaks, are made for mountain rambling.

Kamnik

📞 01 / POP 13,700 / ELEV 375M

The historical town of Kamnik, just 23km northeast of Ljubljana, is often missed by travellers drawn directly to Bled or Bohinj. But Kamnik's attractive medieval core is worth a visit, and the town is surrounded by great side trips, not least of which is the beautiful mountain pastures of Velika Planina.

◎ Sights & Activities

Šutna STREET

Kamnik's main street is trimmed with fine pastel-washed buildings, some dating back to the medieval era. Many sport guild and craft signs from when this street was a centre for craftspeople. Also look out for the many plaques (with English explanations) on the facades, commemorating important ex-residents. In the centre of Šutna stands the **Church of the Immaculate Conception** (built in the mid-18th century), with a detached Gothic spire.

Mali Grad VIEWPOINT

(entry off Šutna) From near central Glavni trg (main square), climb the steps up history-filled Mali Grad hill to enjoy great panoramas from the 'balcony of Kamnik', taking in red rooftops against the backdrop of the Kamnik-Savinja Alps.

In summer you can visit the unique, three-level **Romanesque Chapel** (adult/child €2.50/1.50; ⊙ 9am-7pm mid-Jun–mid-Sep) here (two storeys plus a crypt), with its 15th-century frescoes and Gothic stone reliefs.

Arboretum Volčji Potok GARDENS

(📞 01-831 23 45; www.arboretum-vp.si; Volčji Potok 3; adult/child/family €8.50/6/21; ⊙ 8am-8pm Apr-Aug, shorter hours Sep-Mar) About 6km south of Kamnik is Volčji Potok, Slovenia's largest and most beautiful garden. The 80-hectare arboretum has more than 2500 varieties of trees, shrubs and flowers from all over the world; spring is, needless to say, abloom with colour (April's tulips are especially magnificent).

Franciscan Monastery MONASTERY

(Frančiškanski Samostan; 📞 01-831 80 37; www.franciskani-kamnik.rkc.si; Frančiškanski trg 2; ⊙ by appointment) West of Glavni trg, the Franciscan monastery has a rich 10,000-volume library of manuscripts and incunabula (including an original copy of the Bible translated into Slovene by Jurij Dalmatin in 1584). Next door is the 1695 **Church of St James**, and just off the main altar is the tent-like **Chapel of the Holy Sepulchre**, which was designed by Jože Plečnik in 1952. The church and chapel are usually open daily.

Terme Snovik THERMAL BATHS

(📞 01-834 41 00; www.terme-snovik.si/en; Snovik 7, Laze v Tuhinju; day pass adult/child Mon-Fri €14/11, Sat & Sun €16/13; ⊙ indoor pools 9am-8pm year-round, outside pools Jun-Sep) Terme Snovik is a year-round thermal water park with indoor and open-air pools in the emerald-green Tuhinj Valley, 10km east of Kamnik. Water temperatures range from 26°C outdoors up to 36°C inside and there are water slides to keep the little ones happy. For those after more than a dip, there are a swag of wellness services on offer.

🍴 Sleeping & Eating

Although there's not a wide range of accommodation, Kamnik has two good options: the hostel and Gostilna Repnik (p191).

Hostel Pod Skalo HOSTEL $

(📞 01-839 12 33; www.hostel-kamnik.si; Maistrova ulica 32; dm/s/d/tr €19/36/60/84; 🅿🛜) The cosy dorm here, with 10 beds under a wooden ceiling, is a first-rate budget option, while the 10 private rooms (all with en suite) are modern and bright. The hostel is attached to a pub with a great terrace and occasional live music – try the local Mali Grad beer. It's about 500m east of the centre, opposite a public swimming pool.

Picerija Napoli PIZZA $

(📞 01-839 27 44; www.picerijanapoli.com; Sadnikarjeva ulica 5; pizzas €7-9; ⊙ 11am-10pm) South of Mali Grad, this homey pizzeria is one of the few places for a meal in central Kamnik. It has a shady terrace and does takeaway as well.

★ Gostilna Repnik SLOVENIAN $$

(📞 01-839 12 93; www.gostilna-repnik.si; Vrhpolje 186; mains €12-18; ⊙ 10am-10pm Tue-Fri, noon-

Eastern Slovenia Highlights

1 **Ptuj** (p214) Exploring the skinny cobbled streets of this preserved medieval town, the jewel of Eastern Slovenia.

2 **Logarska Dolina** (p195) Soaking up the pristine alpine views amid this glacial valley.

3 **Maribor** (p216) Stand-up paddleboarding down the Drava River, for the best

views of the Old Town's grand architecture.

4 **Velika Planina** (p194) Hiking this high pasture pinned between lofty snowcapped peaks.

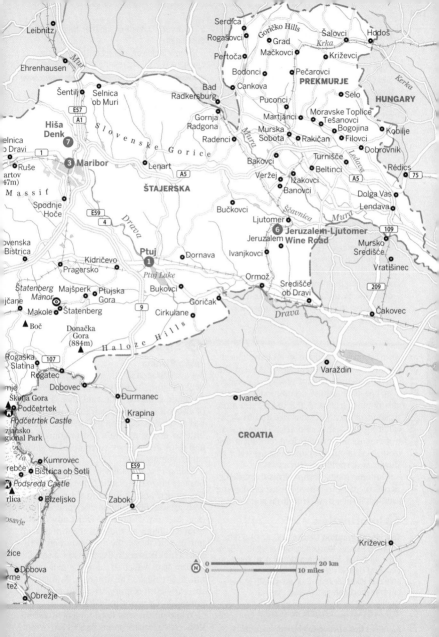

5 Celje (p199) Putting your history hat on to delve into this old Roman centre's museums.

6 Jeruzalem-Ljutomer Wine Road (p217) Discovering the lush, gentle hills of this vineyard-strewn corner and getting stuck into some of its wine.

7 Hiša Denk (p226) Relishing the genius flavour combinations at this top foodie haunt.

8 Rogla (p226) Enjoying the winter wonderland and uncrowded skiing amid the Pohorje Massif.

KRVAVEC – SKIING & HIGH-ALTITUDE DINING

25km north of Ljubljana, is the **Krvavec Ski Centre** (☑ 04-25 25 911; www.rtc-krvavec.si; Cerklje; day pass adult/child €33/18; ☉ 9am-7pm), one of the most popular skiing areas in Slovenia. Thirty kilometres of ski runs are maintained at 1450m to 1971m, and there are all the required ski rental, ski school and après-ski activities. Access is via a cable car near the village of Cerklje na Gorenjskem.

In summer, the cable car grants access to lots of hiking and biking trails – as well as the cable car dining event, whereby each cabin is converted into a dining car. If you feel like dining at altitude, once or twice a month a dinner (per person €50) is held, and diners are served three courses over three hours, while riding their private cabin up and down the mountain (each cabin holds two to four guests). Find details at www.jezersek.si/en/events.

10pm Sat, noon-3pm Sun; P ✳ 🛜) Long a locals' favourite for top-notch Slovenian cuisine, Gostilna Repnik (1.5km east of the centre) also boasts boutique accommodation (singles/doubles from €55/90) to give you more reason to linger. Great service and fresh, local produce are the hallmarks. There's usually no menu, but a well-priced offering of, say, trout, veal shank and delicious dessert – all showcasing tradition with a twist.

The nine rooms feature stylishly rustic design elements; guests have free use of bikes and excellent insider travel trips from host Peter.

ℹ Information

Tourist Information Centre (TIC; ☑ 01-831 82 50; www.kamnik-tourism.si; Glavni trg 2; ☉ 9am-9pm Jul & Aug, 10am-6pm Mon-Sat, to 2pm Sun Sep-Jun) Helpful office with hiking maps available and bikes for rent. Can assist with working out transport details to Velika Planina.

ℹ Getting There & Away

Kamnik's **bus station** (off Maistrova ulica) is smack in the centre of town.

Buses to/from Ljubljana (€3.10, 50 minutes) run two to four times an hour (less frequently on weekends).

In July and August there are four services from Kamnik's bus station north to Kamniška Bistrica via the cable-car stop for Velika Planina (€2.30,

20 minutes). Outside of summer, there are three buses daily.

Kamnik is also on a direct rail line to/from Ljubljana (€2.58, 40 minutes, up to 15 a day).

Kamniška Bistrica & Velika Planina

☑ 01 / ELEV 1666M

Loosely translated as 'Great Highlands', Velika Planina combines stunning mountain scenery with traditional heritage; the herding and dairy economy on these high pastures has changed little for hundreds of years. It's a popular day trip for everyone from dog walkers and amblers to more serious hikers.

Take the looping road north from Kamnik for 9.5km, beside the Kamniška Bistrica River, to arrive at the lower station, from where you access Velika Planina by cable car.

For a much less busy trekking scene, follow the road for a further 3km and you'll arrive at the hamlet of Kamniška Bistrica, launching pad for hikes in the Kamnik-Savinja Alps.

◉ Sights

Velika Planina   MOUNTAIN
(www.velikaplanina.si) The journey to the top of Velika Planina unfolds in two stages: first a dramatic cable-car ride, and then a choice of either a 15-minute chairlift or hiking the rest of the way. Once on the pastures, there's little to do except walk the pristine fields and drink in the views, surrounded by snow-capped mountains.

Velika Planina is where traditional dairy farmers graze their cattle between June and September, and the pastures are scattered with around 60 traditional shepherds' huts (and the tiny **Church of Our Lady of the Snows**) unique to the area. Regrettably, all but one of these, the tiny two-room **Preskar Hut** (Preskarjeva Bajta; Velika Planina; €2; ☉ 10am-4pm) which is now a small museum, are replicas. The originals, dating from the early-20th-century, were burned to the ground by Germans in WWII.

While on the top, have a meal at **Zeleni Rob** (Velika Planina; mains €5.50-8.50; ☉ 8am-4pm Mon-Thu, to 5pm Fri-Sun), a small restaurant a short walk from the middle stop on the chairlift. It's said by some to serve Slovenia's best *štruklji* (cheese dumplings). In summer, the area's friendly shepherds in their big black hats will sell you curd and white cheese.

Kamniška Bistrica NATURE RESERVE

This pretty little settlement in a valley near the source of the Kamniška Bistrica River is 12km north of Kamnik, and well worth a drive for its delightful setting: crystal-clear springs, alpine backdrop, a chapel, and a lodge with beds and food. Kamniška Bistrica is the springboard for popular hikes in the Kamnik-Savinja Alps.

More ambitious treks include one to **Grintovec** (2558m; nine hours return), the highest peak in the range and a popular destination. Shorter hikes head northwest to the mountain pass at **Kokra Saddle** (Kokrsko Sedlo; 1793m), and north to **Kamnik Saddle** (Kamniško Sedlo; 1876m). Both passes have mountain huts open in summer. Ask at the TIC, or see more at www.hiking-trail.net.

🛏 Sleeping

Kamp Alpe CAMPGROUND $

(📞 041 816 477; www.kamp-alpe.com; Kamniška Bistrica 2; campsite per person/tent/motorhome €9/6/8, alpine hut €40; ⊙ May-Sep; P 🅿 🛜) This shady campground sits in the area surrounding the cable car to Velika Planina (9.5km from Kamnik) and has a small cafe on-site. For those who want a tad more comfort than a tent, it also has cute wooden huts made for two.

ℹ Getting There & Away

Three daily buses (four in summer) travel from Kamnik to Kamniška Bistrica, all via the cable-car stop for Velika Planina (€2.30, 20 minutes). Check the latest bus schedule at www.kam-bus.si or at Kamnik's TIC.

A taxi between the cable-car stop and Kamnik costs €10.

The **cable car** (📞 031 680 862; www.velika planina.si; adult/child return incl chairlift €15/11, cable car only €13/9; ⊙ twice hourly 8.30am-6pm Jun-Sep, 9am, 10am, noon, 2pm & 4pm Mon-Thu, hourly 9am-5pm Fri-Sun Oct-May) to Velika Planina runs year-round but has less services outside of the June to September high season. From October to May, the chair lift only runs from Friday to Sunday.

Upper Savinja Valley

The beautiful Upper Savinja Valley (Zgornja Savinjska Dolina) is bound by forests, ancient churches, traditional farmhouses and high alpine peaks. There are activities here to suit every taste and inclination – from hiking, mountain biking and rock climbing to fishing, kayaking and swimming in the Savinja.

The valley has been exploited for its timber since the Middle Ages. Rafters transported the timber from Ljubno to Mozirje and Celje and some of the logs travelled as far as Romania. The trade brought wealth to the valley, evident from the many fine buildings still standing.

Logarska Dolina

📄 03 / POP 110 / ELEV UP TO 1250M

Squeezed between craggy snowcapped peaks, this narrow glacial valley (7.5km long and no more than 500m wide) is the archetype vision of Slovenia's alpine countryside. Hikers, bikers and fresh-air fiends flock here through the warmer months to soak up the lush green meadows, thick forest-clad hills and majestic mountain panoramas.

This 'pearl of the alpine region' was declared a country park in 1987 and its mere 24 sq km are scattered with caves, springs, peaks, rock towers and waterfalls to explore as well as endemic flora (golden slipper orchids) and rare fauna (mountain eagles, peregrine falcons) to spot. It's one of the most magically pretty corners of the country. Bedding down here – to wake up to those jaw-dropping mountain views out your window – is one of the great joys of any Slovenia journey.

⊙ Sights & Activities

The tourist office (p198) can organise any number of activities – from guided mountaineering and rock climbing (per hour €25) to paragliding (€75) and canyoning (€110). It also rents mountain bikes (per hour/day €3/12), as does Hotel Plesnik (p198). The valley has the very basic **Logarska Dolina ski grounds** (📞 03-838 90 04; www.logarska-dolina. si; day pass adult/child €10/7), a 1km-long slope and 13km of cross-country ski trails served by two tows.

Logarska Dolina Country Park NATIONAL PARK (Krajinski Park Logarska Dolina; www.logarska-dolina.si; per car/motorcycle €7/5 Apr-Oct, pedestrians & cyclists free; ⊙ year-round) This glacial valley, hidden between the grandiose peaks of the Kamnik-Savinja Alps, is a paradise for nature fans and those seeking out hiking and biking. It's one of the most beautiful spots in Slovenia. A road goes past a chapel and through the woods to the 90m-high **Rinka Waterfall** (Slap Rinka) at 1100m, the park's most popular highlight, but there are plenty of trails to explore and up to 20 other waterfalls in the area.

Spas & Thermal Resorts

Slovenia has around 20 thermal-spa resorts: two on the coast and the rest in the east. Some specialise in old-world atmosphere, others in modern luxury, and still others in water slides and family fun.

Traditional Treatments

The older, more atmospheric spas are big on 19th-century architecture and traditional, medicinal treatments. For that fin-de-siècle feel, it's hard to beat Rogaška Slatina (p207), Slovenia's oldest spa, dating to the 16th century. You'll sense the history through the impressive neoclassical, Secessionist and Plečnik-style buildings.

Luxury Pampering

The southwestern part of the country has the most modern and luxurious spas. In Portorož, the Terme & Wellness LifeClass spa (p160) offers palatial swimming pools, sauna 'parks', massage, a thalassotherapy centre and an Ayurveda clinic. Another luxury choice, Lepa Vida Thalasso Spa (p162), along the coast at Sečovlje, tosses health-inducing salt treatments into the mix.

1. Vis Vita Spa, Grand Hotel Rogaška (p207) **2.** Terme & Wellness LifeClass, Portorož (p160) **3.** Facade of the Grand Hotel Rogaška (p207)

Family Fun

There's no shortage of places for fun in the sun. The most popular include Terme Čatež (p186), Terme Olimia (p204) and Terme Ptuj (p211). Forget facials, these are about wave pools and water slides.

For more information, check the websites of the Slovenian Tourist Board (www.slovenia.info) and the Association of Slovenian Spas (http://en.slovenia-terme.si).

The bottom of the Rinka Waterfall is a 10-minute walk from the end of the valley road. The climb to the top takes about 20 minutes; it's not very difficult, but it can get slippery. From the top to the west you can see three peaks reaching higher than 2250m: Kranjska Rinka, Koroška Rinka and Štajerska Rinka. Until 1918 they formed the triple border of Carniola (Kranjska), Carinthia (Koroška) and Styria (Štajerska). Ask the tourist office for the *Trail through the Logar Valley* brochure, a 14km hike which will take you through the valley in about five hours.

Opposite Dom Planincev is a trail leading to Sušica Waterfall and Klemenča Cave, both at about 1200m.

Fairytale Forest   AMUSEMENT PARK
(Pravljični Gozd; ☑ 031 249 441; Logarska Dolina 14; adult/child €3.50/2.50, free for guests of Pension Na Razpotju; ☺ 9am-6pm) A series of trails through 2 hectares of forest next to the Pension Na Razpotju takes children of all ages past three-dozen recreated staged fairy stories – both Slovenian and international. A great way to get kids to do some walking.

Matkov Kot   AREA
Much less explored than neighbouring Logarska Dolina, this magnificent 6km-long valley runs parallel to Logarska Dolina and the border with Austria. Reach here by road, turn west as you leave Logarska Dolina.

🛏 Sleeping & Eating

Planšarija Logarski Kot   CABIN $
(☑ 041 210 017; www.logarski-kot.si; Logarska Dolina 15; dm/d without bathroom €20/44; ☺ May-Oct; ℗) Close to the Rinka falls, this locally run hut is a peaceful base with simple rooms and good local food. Breakfast is extra (adult/child €7/4).

★ Lenar Farmhouse   FARMSTAY $$
(☑ 03-838 90 06, 041 851 829; www.lenar.si; Logarska Dolina 11; d/tr/q €80/114/127, apt €80-120, hayloft per person €12; ℗ 🛜) For the great outdoors on your doorstep, you can't beat this farmhouse with helpful owners and rooms, with balconies, in cosy-countryside style. Breakfast, full of local produce, sets you up for the day while their garden is a relaxing idyll after hiking or biking, with a kid's play area and plenty of seating for admiring the grand mountain views.

Pension Na Razpotju   GUESTHOUSE $$
(☑ 03-839 16 50, 031 249 441; www.logarska-narazpotju.si; Logarska Dolina 14; s/d €59/88; ℗ 🛜)

This cheerful guesthouse has colourful, spacious rooms all with balconies, and a good bar-restaurant set up. It's a family-friendly place with an indoor playroom packed full of games, an outdoor area with a caboodle of playground equipment and the guesthouse's adorable Fairytale Forest (open to nonguests) just next door.

Hotel Plesnik   HOTEL $$
(☑ 03-839 23 00; www.plesnik.si; Logarska Dolina 10; r €81-91; ℗ @ 🛜 🏊) This 29-room hotel in the centre of the valley pretty much is Logarska Dolina. There's a pool, sauna, ayurveda spa treatments, a fine restaurant (8am to 10pm) and a relaxed, friendly vibe. Its annexe, the **Vila Palenk** (www.plesnik.si/en/vila-palenk; s/d/f €50/90/150; 🛜), with 11 comfortable rooms done up in generic 'alpine style', takes the overflow.

**★ Herbal Glamping
Resort Ljubno**   RESORT $$$
(☑ 051 611 777; www.charmingslovenia.com; Ter 42, Ljubno ob Savinji; 4-person tent €320; ℗ 🏶 🛜 🏊) Camping doesn't get more swish than this intimate resort, 23km southeast of Logarska Dolina. Scattered around a wood-decked swimming pool, the 10 tents (if they can really even be called that) come with two double beds, en suites and private outdoor jacuzzis. The herbal garden here is put to good use in the resort's range of beauty and wellness treatments.

Orlovo Gnezdo   CAFE $
(Eyrie; ☑ 070 847 639; Logarska Dolina; dishes €4-6; ☺ 10am-6pm) In the valley itself, the 'Eagle's Nest' is a simple cafe-pub with snacks, housed in a tall wooden tower overlooking the falls and reached by a steep set of steps.

ℹ Information

Center Rinka (☑ 03-839 07 10; www.solcavsko.info; Solčava 29; ☺ 8am-5pm Jul & Aug, to 3pm Sep-Jun) In Solčava, 4km before the entrance to the valley, this multipurpose centre has a cafe, exhibition space and a shop with local products for sale as well as a tourist information counter.

Tourist Information Centre (TIC; ☑ 051 626 380, 03-838 90 04; www.logarska-dolina.si; Logarska Dolina 9; ☺ 9am-5pm Jul & Aug, to 2pm Jun) In a small wooden kiosk opposite the Hotel Plesnik car park.

ℹ Getting There & Away

Logarska Dolina isn't well-served by public transport.

From the first weekend of June to the first weekend of September there's a bus service from Celje (€7.20, two hours) every Saturday and Sunday. The bus leaves Celje at 7.10am and 1.10pm and returns from Logarska Dolina at 10am and 6pm.

Otherwise, some accommodation in the valley, such as Lenar Farmhouse, can organise transfers for guests from Gornji Grad, which has five daily bus services from Ljubljana on weekdays, and one daily on weekends (€6, 1¾ hours).

ⓘ Getting Around

You can rent bicycles (per hr/day €4/12) from the tourist office and the Hotel Plesnik. The latter also has electric bikes (per hr/day €4/16).

Celje

☑ 03 / POP 38,000 / ELEV 238M

With its time-warp historical centre, fabulous architecture, excellent museums and enormous castle looming over the picturesque Savinja River, Celje might appear to have won the tourism sweepstakes. But as the town often gets overlooked in favour of Maribor and Ptuj, visiting can feel like something of a discovery.

Celje's compact Old Town sits north of the Savinja River, bordered by the Lower Castle area to the west and the train tracks to the east. The town has two main squares: Glavni trg, at the southern end of pedestrian Stanetova ulica, and Krekov trg, opposite the train station.

History

Celeia was the administrative centre of the Roman province of Noricum between the 1st and 5th centuries. In fact, it flourished to such a degree that it gained the nickname 'Troia secunda', the 'second Troy'.

Celje's second Camelot came in the mid-14th century when the Counts of Celje took control of the area. The counts (later dukes), one of the richest and most powerful feudal dynasties in medieval Central Europe, were the last on Slovenian soil to challenge the absolute rule of the Habsburgs, and they united much of Slovenia for a time. Part of the counts' emblem – three gold stars forming an inverted triangle – has been incorporated into the Slovenian national flag and seal.

Celje was more German than Slovene until the end of WWI, when the town government passed into local hands for the first time.

◉ Sights

Old Castle Celje CASTLE
(Stari Grad Celje; ☑ 03-428 79 36, 03-544 36 90; www.grad-celje.com; Cesta na Grad 78; adult/child €4/1; ⊙ 9am-9pm Jun-Aug, to 8pm May & Sep, to 7pm Apr, to 6pm Mar & Oct, to 5pm Feb & Nov, 10am-4pm Dec & Jan) The largest fortress in Slovenia, this castle is perched on a 407m-high escarpment about 2km southeast of the Old Town; the walk up via a footpath from Cesta na Grad takes about half an hour. The castle was originally built in the early 13th century and went through several transformations, especially under the Counts of Celje in the 14th and 15th centuries. A large portion of the walls remain intact and have been restored, including 23m-high Frederick's Tower (Friderikov Stolp).

When the castle lost its strategic importance in the 15th century it was left to deteriorate, and subsequent owners used the stone blocks to build other structures, including parts of the Princes' Palace and the Old Counts' Mansion. Due to this, there's not much inside, though concerts are staged and medieval-themed events take place in the warmer months.

Celje Regional Museum MUSEUM
(Pokrajinski Muzej Celje; ☑ 03-428 09 50; www.pokmuz-ce.si/en; Muzejski trg 1; adult/child/family incl Princes' Palace €5/3/10; ⊙ 10am-6pm Tue-Sun Mar-Oct, to 4pm Tue-Fri, 9am-1pm Sat Nov-Feb) This branch of the Celje Regional Museum's collection is housed in a grand Renaissance building called the Old Count's Mansion. The 1st floor is home to a dozen rooms featuring interiors from the baroque to Secessionist periods with the museum's show-stopper Celje Ceiling looming down on the central main hall. This enormous trompe l'oeil painting of columns, towers, frolicking angels, noblemen and ladies was completed in about 1600 by an unknown Italian artist.

On the ground floor you'll find glassware displays as well as a small but interesting exhibit on Celje's own Alma M Karlin (1889–1950), the most daring and voracious early-20th-century traveller you've probably never heard of. From 1919 to 1927 Karlin globe-trotted solo, taking in places as diverse as Japan, New Caledonia, New Zealand and Peru and picking up nine languages along the way. Various ethnographic objects she collected on her travels are displayed here as well as photos and information (in Slovene;

Celje

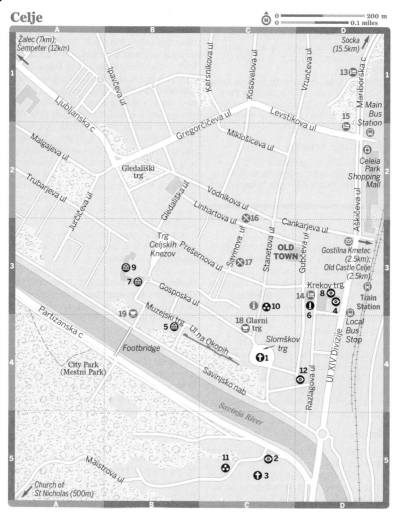

Celje

◎ Sights

◎ Sleeping

◎ Eating

◎ Drinking & Nightlife

staff will hand you an English-language pamphlet) on her extraordinary life.

The museum's biggest highlight, however, is a very recent discovery. Excavations inside the cellar (which usually houses the lapidarium) have unearthed the remains of a 1st-century Roman villa replete with vividly coloured, intact frescoes (the only intact Roman frescoes discovered in Slovenia). Preservation work was still ongoing during our last visit, scheduled to be completed in early 2019. Once opened to the public, the in situ frescoes will be the star attraction.

Princes' Palace   MUSEUM
(Spodnij grad; www.pokmuz-ce.si/en; Trg Celjskih Knezov 8; adult/child/family incl Celje Regional Museum €5/3/10; ⊙10am-6pm Tue-Sun Mar-Oct, to 4pm Tue-Fri, 9am-1pm Sat Nov-Feb) This 4th-century structure houses an important branch of the Celje Regional Museum (p199). In the cellar is the City under the City exhibition: partial remains of Roman Celeia's 3rd-century *decumanus maximus* (main west-east road) brilliantly displayed with excavated statuary, Roman villa ruins, parts of the old city walls and traces of the medieval buildings built on top, all aided by thorough explanation panels. On the 1st floor you'll find beautifully curated displays of neolithic, Bronze Age and Iron Age finds.

Half of the 1st floor and the entire 2nd floor are devoted to (rather sparse) exhibits tracing the history of the Counts of Celje. One room houses a display of 18 of the noble skulls spookily set out in back-lit cases.

The southern wing of the building is home to the **Gallery of Contemporary Art** (Galarija Sodobnih Umetnosti; ☑03-426 51 60; ⊙11am-6pm Tue-Sat, 2-6pm Sun) FREE, with thematic exhibitions of work by both local and foreign artists.

Krekov Trg   SQUARE
The mammoth **Celje Hall** (Celjski Dom), with its turreted neo-Gothic facade, dominates Krekov trg. It was built in 1907 as the social centre for German-speaking Celjani. In the middle of the square a bronze statue celebrating Alma M Karlin, Celje's renowned traveller, writer and polyglot, takes pride of place. To the south, connected to the Hotel Evropa, is the 16th-century **Defence Tower** (Obrambni Stolp; Razlagova ulica), and about 150m further on, the **Water Tower** (Vodni Stolp; Razlagova ulica 19), part of the city wall and ramparts, built between 1451 and 1473.

Roman Celeia   RUINS
(Rimska Celeja; Glavni trg 17; ⊙10am-7pm Mon-Fri, to 5pm Sat & Sun) In 2013 archaeologists unearthed the remnants of two late-3rd-century Roman villas, complete with surviving mosaic flooring, along Celje's main square. The ruins are now beautifully presented within a glassed-in building complete with plenty of explanation panels (and with Celje's TIC office (p203) sitting behind).

Abbey Church of St Daniel   CHURCH
(Opatijska Cerkev Sv Danijela; Slomškov trg; ⊙9am-7pm) Dating from the early 14th century, this church has some magnificent frescoes and tombstones, but its greatest treasure is a 15th-century carved wooden pietà in the **Chapel of the Sorrowful Mother** to the left of the sanctuary. The chapel has carved stone walls and vaults with remnants of frescoes from the early 15th century and carved effigies of the Apostles.

Breg   AREA
On the Savinja River's south bank, a stairway at Breg 2 leads to the **Capuchin Church of St Cecilia** (Kapucinska Cerkev Sv Cecilije). The Germans used the nearby monastery (now apartments) as a prison during WWII. Between the church and City Park are the scant remains of the Roman **Temple of Hercules** (Heraklejev Tempelj; Maistrova ulica) dating from the 2nd century AD. Further south, walk up 396m-high **Nicholas Hill** (Miklavški Hrib), topped by the **Church of St Nicholas** (Cerkev Sv Miklavža), for views across to the Old Town and the castle.

🏃 Activities
Celje's tourist information centre (p203) has brochures listing a number of **walks** and **hikes** into the surrounding countryside lasting from one to several days. An easy walk leads southeast to **Mt Tovst** (834m) and the picturesque village of Svetina via the **Celjska Koča** (☑059 070 400, 041 718 274; www.celjska-koca.si; Pečovnik 31; d/q/f €80/110/120; 🏠🎿), a mountain hut at 650m that has metamorphosed into a delightfully modern three-star hotel with adjacent skiing piste. Ask for the *Dežela Celjska: Vodnik za Pohodnike* (Land of Celje: Guide for Hikers). The tourist office also distributes the *Dežela Celjska: Turistična Karta za Kolesarje in Pohodnike* (Land of Celje: Tourist Map for Cyclist and Hikers), with more than 40 routes outlined for Celje and surroundings.

ŽALEK & ŠEMPETER

Heading west from Celje, the endless fields marked out by pole and wire trellises announce your arrival deep in the heart of hop-growing country. The tidy little town of Žalec, 10km west, is a worthy side trip for beer fans, with two sights celebrating its hops heritage. After Žalec's beer-themed sights you could also carry on another 2km west to the bland town of Šempeter, which has a small but archaeologically significant Roman site and a cave nearby.

Eco Museum of Hop Growing (Eko Muzej Hmeljarstva; ☑ 03-710 04 34; www.ekomuzej-hmelj.si; Cesta Žalskega tabora 2, Žalec; adult/child €4/3; ⊙ 9am-6pm Tue-Sun) This museum, based in Žalec's old hop-drying house, is dedicated to the history of hop growing in the area. Before technology lightened the farming load somewhat, around 30,000 hop-pickers used to flood into town during the picking season, and the exhibits here concentrate on their back-breaking work. The friendly staff will guide you around, explaining the history and processes involved in hop growing. Don't miss the brilliant black-and-white documentary showing Žalec during the mid-20th century.

Green Gold Beer Fountain (Fontana Piv Zeleno Zlato; www.beerfountain.eu; Savinjska cesta 11, Žalec; tastings €8; ⊙ 10am-11pm Mon-Sat, to 10pm Sun Jun-Aug, 10am-9pm Mon-Sat, to 8pm Sun Apr-May & Sep-Oct) Most towns just have a water fountain. Žalec went one better than that. Yep, it's the world's first beer fountain. Don't expect free-flowing amber nectar, though. Buy your micro-chipped glass from either the Green Gold kiosk next to the fountain or Žalec's **TIC** (☑ 03-710 04 34; www.turizem-zalec.si; Šlandrov trg 25, Žalec; ⊙ 9am-6pm Mon-Fri, to noon Sat & Sun) and then pour yourself six tastings. The beers on offer include the malty ale Svarun from the Lobik microbrewery, Mali Grad's Šlagerica lager and the mildly bitter Loko Loko beer.

Šempeter Roman Necropolis (Roman Necropolis; ☑ 031 645 937, 03-700 20 56; www.td-sempeter.si; Ob Rimski Nekropoli 2, Šempeter; adult/child €5/4; ⊙ 10am-5pm May-Sep, to 3pm Apr, to 4pm Sat & Sun Oct) This is the site of a reconstructed Roman necropolis of wealthy families living in the area. Scattered around the grassy plot are four complete tombs plus a variety of columns, stelae and fragments carved with portraits, mythological creatures and scenes from daily life. Although undoubtedly archaeologically important, the site is probably only of interest to serious history buffs.

Pekel Cave (Pekel Jama; ☑ 03-570 21 38, 035 702 138; adult/child €8/5; ⊙ tours hourly 10am-6pm Jun-Sep, 10am, noon, 2pm & 4pm Apr & May) Four kilometres north of the necropolis you'll find the 'Hell Cave'. One hour tours take you 1200m from the lower wet area to the upper dry section. Among the highlights, you'll pass a 4m-high waterfall, the Silent Hall with perfect acoustics and the Hall of Fantasy, where stalactites and stalagmites become snakes, pigeons, cauliflowers and frogs. It's 10°C in there and very slippery; take a wrap and wear sturdy shoes.

🛏 Sleeping

★ MCC Hostel
HOSTEL $

(☑ 03-490 87 42, 040 756 009; www.hostel-celje.com; Mariborska cesta 2; dm/s/d €16/22/44; 🛜) This hostel with on-the-ball staff, a great cafe-bar with craft beer and good coffee, and regular social events is a real find. Both dorms and the small private rooms with shower (toilets are shared) are immaculately presented, and each is decorated by local artists to tell a story from Celje's crazy past.

Hotel Celeia
HOTEL $$

(☑ 03-426 97 00; www.hotel-celeia.si; Mariborska cesta 3; s €46-67, d €68-90, ste €98-120; P ✳ 🛜)

Popular with business travellers, the Celeia has a 'pop-art' theme with Warhol-style portraits of Elvis, Marilyn and even Obama strewn around common areas. The theme doesn't really carry through into the rooms, which are briskly bland. The single rooms in particular could do with refurbishment. Light sleepers should eschew front-facing rooms due to traffic noise.

Hotel Evropa
HISTORIC HOTEL $$$

(☑ 03-426 90 00; www.hotel-evropa.si; Krekov trg 4; s €87-129, d €99-149; P ✳ 🛜) One of Slovenia's oldest hotels, the Evropa has been in business since 1873. Don't expect that historic ambience to follow you into the rooms though; they're modern and comfortable, but stripped of all character. Enter from Razlagova ulica.

✖ Eating

Stari Pisker
BURGERS $

(✆ 03-544 24 80; Savinova ulica 9; ⊙ 10am-10pm Mon-Thu, to midnight Fri & Sat; 🛜) This pub-restaurant is all about gourmet burgers, served with onion rings and some of the best chips you'll get in Slovenia. We like the umami burger with sundried tomatoes and parmesan crisp. There are also steak dishes, craft beer and a large wine list.

★ Gostilna Kmetec
SLOVENIAN $$

(✆ 03-544 25 55, 041 333 831; www.tlacan.si; Zagrad 140a; mains €8.50-25; ⊙ noon-10pm Wed-Fri, 10am-10pm Sat, to 6pm Sun) One of our favourite *gostilna* (inn-like restaurant) anywhere, the Kmetec sits high in the hills, looking Celje's old castle square in the face. Offerings are on the meaty side – venison, boar, steak cooked in hay – but don't fail to try the creamy pumpkin souffle (€4.60). It's heavenly.

Gostilna Oštirka
BISTRO $$

(Linhartiova ulica 6; mains €7.50-19.50; ⊙ 6am-10pm Mon-Thu, to 11pm Fri & Sat; 🛜) Casual-chic dining comes complete with charming service at this glass-walled restaurant across the road from the market. The menu here is stronger on smaller dishes than meat and seafood mains, with soups to die for (we had a wild garlic soup with micro-vegetables, milk foam and shrimp ravioli). Risotto and homemade gnocchi starters are vibrant with herbs.

▼ Drinking & Nightlife

Kavarna Oaza
CAFE

(Glavni trg 13; ⊙ 7am-10pm Mon-Thu & Sun, to midnight Fri & Sat; 🛜) Great location, on-the-ball staff and something for everyone on the vast drinks menu. Grab a coffee or one of the multitude of teas in the morning, and a beer or smoothie later on. The interior is slick and contemporary, but in the summer the prime spots are the tables spilling out onto Glavni trg.

Miško Knjižko
CAFE

(✆ 031 377 480, 03-426 17 52; www.ce.sik.si; Muzejski trg 1a; ⊙ 7am-10.30pm Mon-Sat, 8am-9pm Sun) This modern cafe at the Celje Central Library, just at the footbridge over the Savinja, is a lovely place to put your feet up and enjoy the riverfront with a coffee and a slice of something sweet (cakes €2 to €3.50).

Kavarna Evropa
CAFE

(✆ 03-426 96 07; Krekov trg 4; ⊙ 7am-11pm Mon-Thu, 11am-midnight Fri & Sat, 8am-10pm Sun) This 'old-world' cafe in the Hotel Evropa – all dark-wood panelling, gilt mouldings and chandeliers – is prime meet-up territory for Celje locals and serves decent cakes as well as drinks. The outdoor seating spreads out onto the square during warmer months.

ℹ Information

MONEY
Abanka (Aškičeva ulica 10; ⊙ 8am-5pm Mon-Fri, 8-11am Sat)
Banka Celje (Vodnikova ulica 2; ⊙ 8.30-11.30am & 2-5pm Mon-Fri) In a building designed by Jože Plečnik in 1930.

POST
Post Office (Krekov trg 9; ⊙ 8am-6pm Mon-Fri, to noon Sat)

TOURIST INFORMATION
Tourist Information Centre Celje (TIC; ✆ 03-428 79 36; www.celje.si; Glavni trg 17; ⊙ 10am-7pm Mon-Fri, to 5pm Sat & Sun) Winner of the most creatively located tourist office in Slovenia, in our opinion. Celje's TIC is based in a glass-fronted office behind and on top of the ruins of the excavated Roman villa on Glavni trg. Staff have plenty of information and give out free maps of the town.

There's also a TIC branch at the entrance to the Old Castle Celje (p199), open when the castle is, which rents bicycles (per three hours/six hours/one day €3/5/10).

ℹ Getting There & Away

BUS
The **main bus station** (Aškičeva ulica) is 300m north of the train station, opposite the huge Celeia shopping mall. **Local buses** (Ulica XIV Divizije) to Šempeter and Žalec also stop south of the train station.

You can check up-to-date bus schedules on www.izletnik.si.

Buses from Celje
Ljubljana (€7.50, 1¾, 8 Mon-Fri, 2-5 Sat & Sun)
Maribor (€6.30, 1¾, 6 Mon-Fri)
Mozirje (4€.10, ¾, At least hourly Mon-Fri, 3 Sat & Sun)
Podčetrtek (€4.70, 1, 4-6 Mon-Sat, 1 Sun)
Rogaška Slatina (€4.10, 1, 13 Mon-Fri, 3-4 Sat & Sun)
Rogatec (€5.20, 1¼, 13 Mon-Fri, 3-4 Sat & Sun)

Šempeter (€2.60, ¼, Frequent Mon-Fri, 3-6 Sat & Sun)

Žalec (€1.80, ¼, Frequent Mon-Sat, 8 Sun)

TRAIN

As well as having good rail connections to Ljubljana, Celje is on the line linking Zidani Most (connections to and from Ljubljana and Zagreb) with Maribor and the Austrian cities of Graz and Vienna. A third line connects Celje with Zabok in Croatia via Rogaška Slatina and Rogatec.

Trains from Celje

Ljubljana (€7-12.30, 1½hrs, 12 direct trains daily)

Maribor (€5.80-10.50, 1hr, At least hourly Mon-Fri, reduced services Sat & Sun)

Podčetrtek (€3.45, ¾hr, 3 direct trains Mon-Sat, 1 on Sun)

Ptuj (€7.60-10.50, 1hr, 3 direct trains Mon-Fri, 2 on Sat & Sun)

Rogaška Slatina (€3.45, ¾hr, 7 direct trains Mon-Fri, 2 on Sat & Sun)

Rogatec (€4.30, 1hr, 7 direct trains Mon-Fri, 2 on Sat & Sun)

Šempeter (€1.85, 15 mins, 12 trains Mon-Fri, 4 on Sat)

Žalec (€1.30, 15 mins, 12 trains Mon-Fri, 4 on Sat)

KOZJANSKO REGION

Kozjansko is a remote region along the eastern side of the Posavje Mountains and the 90km-long Sotla River, which forms part of the eastern border with Croatia. It is an area of forests, rolling hills, vineyards and scattered farms. It's also the site of one of Slovenia's three regional parks, with much to offer visitors in the way of spas, castles, hiking, cycling and excellent wine.

Podčetrtek

🖉 03 / POP 530 / ELEV 212M

Most people make their way to this village, on a little bump of land extending into Croatia, to relax at the Terme Olimia thermal spa. Looming overhead are the remains of a castle originally built in the 11th century and an important fortification during the wars with the Hungarians 300 years later.

The town's seemingly unpronounceable name (pronounced pod-*che*-ter-tek) comes from the Slovenian word for 'Thursday' – the day the market took place and the district court sat.

◉ Sights

Podčetrtek Castle   CASTLE

(Grad Podčetrtek; Cesta na Grad) The enormous Renaissance-style Podčetrtek Castle, atop a 355m-high hill to the northwest of town, went up some time in the mid-16th century but was badly damaged by an earthquake in 1974. It's not open to the public but offers stunning views. To get here, walk north along Trška cesta and then west on Cesta na Grad for about 1.5km.

Olimje Minorite Monastery   MONASTERY

(Minoritski Samostan Olimje; 🖉 03-582 91 61; www.olimje.net; Olimje 82; pharmacy adult/child €1/0.50; ⊗ 8am-7pm) The Minorite Olimje Monastery, 3km southwest of Podčetrtek, was built as a Renaissance-style castle in about 1550. Its **Church of the Assumption** contains 17th-century ceiling paintings in the presbytery, one of the largest baroque altars in the country and the ornate **Chapel of St Francis Xavier**. On the ground floor of the corner tower to the left of the main entrance is the monastery's greatest treasure: a 17th-century **pharmacy** painted with religious and medical scenes.

Land of Fairytales & Fantasy   PARK

(Koča Pri Čarovnici; 🖉 031 309 103; www.carovnica. si; Olimje 104; adult/child €3/2; ⊗ 10am-6pm; 🖈) This little trail in the forest, 1.5km above the Olimje Minorite Monastery, was laid out by the former local school principal and leads you past dozens of fairy-tale characters made of recycled materials. There's also a small museum of local life a century ago and a room filled with souvenirs from around the world. A charming short diversion if you have little ones with you.

🏃 Activities

Some of the most rewarding hikes and bike trips in Slovenia can be found in this region. The free *Občina Podčetrtek Sprehajalne Poti* (Podčetrtek Municipality Walking Trails) map outlines several excursions for hikers on marked trails. The 1:50,000-scale *Obsotelje in Kozjansko* cycling map from the TIC (p206) outlines 10 paths of varying difficulty for cyclists and mountain bikers.

Terme Olimia   SPA

(🖉 03-829 70 00; www.terme-olimia.com; Zdraviliška cesta 24; 🖈) Some 1.2km northeast of Podčetrtek centre, this vast spa-resort has thermal water (28°C to 35°C) full of magnesium and calcium for health. The

Podčetrtek Area

emphasis here though is very much on recreation.

The resort's 2000-sq-metre **Termalija thermal bathing complex** (☏ 03-829 78 05; day pass adult/child Mon-Fri €13/8.50, Sat & Sun €15/10; ⊙ 8am-10pm Sun-Thu, to midnight Fri & Sat; ♿) has a range of saunas and both indoor and outdoor pools, featuring geysers,

water jets and a water slide. It was undergoing a thorough and very swish upgrade when we last passed through, due to be completed by mid-2018.

In summer the outdoor **Thermal Park Aqualuna** (Zdraviliška cesta 9; day pass adult/child Mon-Fri €12/9.50, Sat & Sun €15/11.50; ⊙ 10am-7pm Mon-Fri, from 9am Sat & Sun Jun-Sep; ♿), near Kamp Natura, throws open its doors for 3000 sq metres of thermal water pools dedicated solely to family-friendly days out. There are oodles of water slides, a wave pool and an aqua-jungle adventure course –tots are looked after with their own shallow pool and gentle water slide.

The complex offers accommodation in two hotels, an apartment complex and a tourist village. In addition, the resort has two wellness centres: the **Spa Armonia** at the Hotel Sotelia and the luxurious **Orchidelia**.

🛏 Sleeping

Apart from the campground, this area veers mostly into the high-end category. The biggest choice of hotels is within the Terme Olimia spa complex. For budget and midrange options, the TIC (p206) has a list of families offering private rooms (per person from €20) in Podčetrtek and the surrounding area.

Kamp Natura CAMPGROUND $
(☏ 03-829 78 33; www.terme-olimia.com; Zdraviliška cesta; campsite with pool entrance per person €16.50-21; ⊙ mid-Apr–mid-Oct; P🐾) Owned and operated by Terme Olimia, this 1-hectare campground with 200 sites is about 1km north of the spa complex, on the edge of the Sotla River. It's fairly standard, but the location by the Croatian border is stunning. There are also holiday cottages available.

★ Jelenov Greben FARMSTAY $$$
(☏ 03-582 90 46; www.jelenov-greben.si; Olimje 90; s/d €59/108, 4-person apt €100; P🐾♿) Set on a ridge some 500m south of Olimje at Ježovnik this working farm, with 100 head of deer roaming freely on 6 hectares of land, has 15 cosy rooms and apartments (some with balconies). Along with a popular restaurant, there is a superb wine cellar, a spa and sauna, and a shop selling farm products.

Ortenia Apartments in Nature DESIGN HOTEL $$$
(Ortenia Apartmajo v Naravi; ☏ 040 373 331; www.ortenia.com; Škofja Gora 36; apt €198; P✳🐾♿) This award-winning property with a mouthful of a name counts six luxurious

KOZJANSKO REGIONAL PARK

Established in 1999, the 206.5-sq-km **Kozjansko Park** (Kozjanski Park; ☑03-800 71 00; www.kozjanski-park.si; Podsreda 45; ☺visitor centre 8am-4pm Mon-Fri) stretches along the Sotla River, from Bizeljsko in the south to Podčetrtek in the north. Named a Unesco biosphere reserve in 2010, the park's forests and meadows harbour a wealth of flora and fauna, notably butterflies, reptiles and birds, including corncrakes and storks.

There are a number of trails, including the circular 32km-long Podsreda Trail (Pešpot Podsreda), which ends at the wonderfully preserved **Podsreda Castle** (Grad Podsreda; ☑03-580 61 18; www.kozjanski-park.si; Podsreda; adult/child/family €4/2.50/10; ☺10am-6pm Tue-Sun Mar-Nov). Set amid the hills of the Kozjansko region, the castle is one of the best-preserved Romanesque fortresses in Slovenia. It looks pretty much the way it did when it was built in the mid-12th century, thanks to renovations completed in 2015.

The rooms in the castle wings, some with beamed ceilings and ancient chandeliers, now contain a glassworks exhibit (crystal from Rogaška Slatina, vials from the Olimje pharmacy, green and blue Pohorje glass). The fabulous wood-panelled Renaissance Hall hosts classical concerts and, of course, weddings. In the room next to it is a wonderful collection of prints of Štajerska's castles and monasteries taken from Topographii Ducatus Stiria (1681) by Georg Mattäus Vischer (1628–96).

apartments with kitchens in three ultra-modern 'pods' – each with enormous glass windows looking up to the castle. The 'nature' part of the name is well-deserved; all materials are natural, with wood and stone in profusion. There's a sauna and small pool, and breakfast comes in a basket.

✕ Eating

Gotišče Jelenov Greben SLOVENIAN $
(☑03-582 90 46; Olimje 90; mains €8-16; ☺7am-10pm Mon-Fri, to 11pm Sat & Sun; ☎) This rustic-by-design restaurant at the 'Deer Ridge' farm is celebrated, not surprisingly, for its venison, as well as its wild mushroom dishes. Desserts emerge from its own in-house bakery. The set lunch is a wallet-friendly €12 (or €20 if you want venison).

🛍 Shopping

Olimje Chocolatier CHOCOLATE
(Čokoladnica Olimje; ☑03-810 90 36; www.cokoladnica-olimje.si; Olimje 61; ☺9am-7pm Mon-Fri, from 10am Sat & Sun) This boutique factory makes Slovenia's most famous chocolates and the shop stocks the full range of chocaholic delights. It's next door to the Olimje Minorite Monastery.

ℹ Information

Banka Celje (Zdraviliška cesta 27c; ☺8.30-11.30am & 2-5pm Mon-Fri) In the shopping mall between the village centre and spa complex.

Post Office (Zdraviliška cesta 27c; ☺8am-9.30am & 10am-5pm Mon-Fri, 8am-noon Sat) Some 200m north of the village centre and next door to Banka Celje.

Tourist Information Centre Podčetrtek (TIC; ☑03-810 90 13; www.turizem-podcetrtek.si; Cesta Škofja Gora 1; ☺8am-3pm Mon-Fri, 8am-noon Sat, 9am-noon Apr-Sep, closed Sun Oct-Mar) At the central roundabout.

ℹ Getting There & Away

BUS
The centre of Podčetrtek is at the junction of four roads. All buses stop at the crossroads as well as at the spa and the camping ground. Monday to Saturday, four to six buses daily pass by Podčetrtek and Terme Olimia on their way from Celje (€4.70, one hour) to Bistrica ob Sotli (€2.30, 20 minutes) and vice versa. On Sunday there's usually only one service.

TRAIN
Podčetrtek is on the rail line linking Celje (via Stranje) with Imeno. There are three train stations. For the village centre and the castle, get off at Podčetrtek. Atomske Toplice is good for Terme Olimia and the spa hotels. Podčetrtek Toplice is the correct stop for the camping ground. Four to six trains leave the main Podčetrtek station daily Monday to Saturday for Celje (€3.45, 50 minutes).

On Saturdays in May, June and September a heritage train runs between Celje and Podčetrtek (€10, one hour, two services each way).

Rogaška Slatina

📌 03 / POP 4950 / ELEV 227M

Rogaška Slatina is Slovenia's oldest and largest spa town, a veritable 'cure factory' with most visitors here to undergo the various medical treatments and therapies offered by the renowned Rogaška Medical Center. Its location, set among scattered forests in the foothills of the Macelj range, does attract some, mostly older, recreational visitors, who come for the area's hiking and cycling opportunities.

The hot spring here was known in Roman times but first made it onto the map in 1572, when the governor of Styria took the waters on the advice of his physician. A century later visitors started arriving in droves and by the early 19th century, Rogaška Slatina was an established spa town.

The heart of Rogaška Slatina is the spa complex, an architecturally important group of neoclassical, Secessionist and Plečnik-style buildings surrounding a long landscaped garden called Zdraviliški trg, or Health Resort Sq.

⊙ Sights

Ana's Mansion   MUSEUM
(Anin Dvor; 📌 03-620 26 51; www.turizem-rogaska.si; Cvetlična hrib 1a; adult/child/family €5/3.50/10; ⊙9am-5pm Tue-Sun) This ambitious, though rather odd, museum is divided into several distinct sections including a water-based art installation, a collection of tree bark, a small exhibit on Rogaška's important glass-making industry (with little in the way of explanation), a collection of lovely engravings of Rogaška Slatina, donated to the town by Swiss collector Kurt Müller, and a rather eccentric exhibit of letters and memorabilia from the Yugoslav kingdom plus autographs of the great, good and infamous, all amassed by one man.

Rogaška Glassworks   FACTORY
(Steklarska Rogaška; 📌 03-818 20 27; www.rogaska-crystal.com; Ulica Talcev 1; ⊙9am-1pm Mon-Fri) Rogaška Slatina is as celebrated for its crystal glass as it is for its mineral water. Individuals are welcome to take a guided tour of the town's glass-making factory to see the production from glass-blowing to decorating. The shop here has a wide range of leaded crystal items for sale. It's 2km southeast of the centre.

🏃 Activities

Hot Springs & Spas

Vis Vita Spa   SPA
(📌 03-811 24 70; www.rogaska-resort.com; Zdraviliški trg 11; 1-day pool & sauna pass €20; ⊙8am-9pm) The Grand Rogaška Hotel's in-house spa specialises in mineral baths (€25), therapeutic and relaxation massages, and body wraps (from €39) to aid weight loss. There is also a range of top-to-tail beauty treatments from facials to pedicures. On-site is a 15m-long indoor pool at 31°C and four saunas.

Pivnica   HEALTH & FITNESS
(Zdraviliški trg; single drink €3, 3-/5-day pass €20/30; ⊙7am-1pm & 3-7pm Mon-Sat, 7am-1pm & 4-7pm Sun) It's all about the mineral water (called Donat Mg) at Rogaška Slatina and this round, glassed-in drinking hall is where it's dispensed direct from the springs. Donat Mg contains the highest magnesium content found in water anywhere in the world. A 'drinking treatment' based around this salty and slightly metallic-tasting water is said to aid digestion, alleviate constipation and lower both blood pressure and blood sugars. Enter via the Rogaška Medical Center.

Rogaška Medical Center   HEALTH & FITNESS
(📌 03-811 70 15; www.rogaska-medical.com; Zdraviliški trg 9; ⊙7am-8pm Mon-Fri, 8am-noon & 4-8pm Sat & Sun) Most visitors to Rogaška Slatina are here specifically to undergo treatments and therapies at this medical centre with specialist units for physiotherapy, gastroenterology and cardiology as well as spa services. Rejuvenating and pampering treatments include facials (from €35), algae body wraps (€48), mineral baths (€25) and a full range of massages from medical therapeutic (€41) to ayurvedic (€67).

Rogaška Riviera   THERMAL BATHS
(📌 03-818 19 50; Celjska cesta 5; day pass adult/child Mon-Fri €11/7, Sat & Sun €13/9; ⊙9am-8pm Apr-Oct, outdoor pools mid-Jun–mid-Sep) Rogaška Slatina's main baths complex has a 34m-long indoor pool and a connected 26m-long outdoor pool with water temperatures peaking at 31°C. If that's not hot enough, dip into the two whirlpools at 35°C. Two extra outdoor pools open during midsummer. The pools are good for a soak, but note there's no kid-friendly water-park equipment and no cafe here.

Rogaška Slatina

Rogaška Slatina

Hiking

Walking trails fanning out into the surrounding hills and meadows are listed in the free *Rogaška Slatina & the Surrounding Area* brochure available from the TIC. One trail leads 15km to the hilltop Church of St Florian, and to Ložno, from where you can continue on another 4km to Donačka Gora, a 1374m-high hill east of Rogatec. To return, walk two hours down to Rogatec to catch a bus or train back.

The walk to Boč (979m), northwest of Rogaška Slatina and in the centre of the 886-hectare Boč Country Park (Krajinski Park Boč; www.boc.si), will take you about five hours, though you can drive as far as Dom na Boču, a category III mountain hut a couple of kilometres south of the peak at 658m, with 47 beds in 15 rooms.

🛏 Sleeping

Big-hitter spa hotels dominate the accommodation scene. For something less pricey, holiday apartments are catching on in popularity. The TIC has a list of private rooms (per person €16 to €20) and apartments (from €80).

Apartman Ina   APARTMENT $

(☏ 041 604 522; www.apartman-ina.com; Ulica XIV Divizije 6; apt s/d/tr/q from €28/37/46/55; 🅿✳🛜) These seriously good-value apartments run by a local family (good German spoken but little English) are a real find and just a hop-skip-jump from all the spa action. They all have well-equipped kitchens, comfortable living areas with huge satellite TVs, and a separate bedroom. The biggest apartment can sleep up to six, with an extra mezzanine bedroom.

Eco Vila Mila   GUESTHOUSE $$

(☏ 03-166 18 00; www.ecovila-mila.si; Kamence 19; s/d/tr €37/52/72; 🛜) This modern villa, 5km south of Rogaška Slatina, has six bright, minimalist bedrooms upstairs, all with pine furniture and balconies. All can be converted to fit a family of four and there's also one room fully fitted out for wheelchair users. The restaurant here wins local plaudits for its homestyle cooking and reasonable prices.

Grand Hotel Sava   SPA HOTEL $$$

(☏ 03-811 40 00; www.rogaska.si; Zdraviliški trg 6; incl half board Sana s €120-185, d €180-250, Zagreb s/d €110/180; 🅿✳🛜⊠) There are two separate wings here: the Sava, with 'superior' rooms, and the older rooms of the Zagreb. The Sava's rooms are some of the nicest and most comfortable in town, all peachy-beige tones and leafy views from the balcony. Don't bother with the Zagreb wing; rooms could do with a refurbishment.

🍴 Eating

Gostilna Bohor   SLOVENIAN $

(☏ 03-581 41 00; Kidričeva ulica 23; mains €6-20; ⊗ 8am-10pm Mon-Thu, to 11pm Fri & Sat, 10am-10pm Sun) This popular local restaurant-bar is where you come for good-value Slovenian staples with hearty soups, stews, and grilled

ROGATEC

This small town, about 7km east of Rogaška Slatina, accessible by bus and train, has two important sights well worth a short visit.

Strmol Manor (Dvorec Strmol; ☑ 03-810 72 22; www.rogatec.si; Pot k Ribniku 6, Rogatec; adult/child/family €3/2.60/6; ☺10am-6pm Tue-Sun Apr-Oct, Sat only Nov-Mar) This restored 15th-century castle has exhibits in 15 rooms on five floors. There's a 17th-century chapel with baroque and Renaissance murals, a baroque salon with pink stucco work, and an original open-hearth 'black kitchen' *(črna kuhinja)*. In the loft, an exhibit recreates a mid-19th-century country kitchen, complete with original fittings and furnishings. On the 2nd floor, work from the local artists' colony is displayed.

Rogatec Open-Air Museum (Muzej na Prostem Rogatec; ☑ 03-818 62 00; www.rogatec.si; Ptujska cesta, Rogatec 23; adult/child/family €3/2.30/6; ☺10am-6pm Tue-Sun Apr-Nov) This is Slovenia's largest *skanzen* (open-air village museum) with regular displays of traditional activities such as weaving, bread-making and stone-cutting. Within the complex there are more than a dozen (mostly original) structures, moved here in the early 1980s. The central farmhouse, built by the Šmit family in the early 19th century, barn, a *toplar* (double hayrack), forge, grocery shop and vintner's cottage replicate a typical Styrian hamlet of the 19th and early 20th centuries.

meat and fish dishes. There's also a separate menu listing a multitude of pizzas and burgers. The daily three-course lunch menu (€10) will fill you up for the rest of the day.

Restavracija Kaiser EUROPEAN $$$
(☑ 03-811 47 10; Zdraviliški trg 6; mains €12-55; ☺noon-11pm; ☏) Rogaška Slatina's fancy-pants restaurant (part of Grand Hotel Sava) dishes up classic European cooking. Both smaller dishes, such as mushroom risotto with parmesan foam, and mains, such as duck with polenta and truffles, are served with suitable pomp and panache. Prime seating is on the outdoor terrace so you can gaze out over leafy Zdraviliški trg while you dine.

ℹ Information

Post Office (Kidričeva ulica 3; ☺8am-6pm Mon-Fri, to noon Sat) Just south of the bus station.

SKB Banka (Kidričeva ulica 11; ☺8am-5pm Mon-Fri) Next to the post office.

Tourist Information Centre Rogaška Slatina (TIC; ☑ 03-581 44 14; www.rogaska-slatina.si; Zdraviliški trg 1; ☺8am-7pm Mon-Fri, to noon Sat & Sun Jul & Aug, 8am-4pm Mon-Fri, to noon Sat Sep-Jun) Helpful, friendly and clued-up staff dish out bundles of brochures and maps.

ℹ Getting There & Away

BUS

Rogaška Slatina's **bus station** (Celjska cesta) is just south of Zdraviliški trg. Buses to Celje (€4.10, one hour) and Rogatec (€1.80, 10

minutes) leave Rogaška Slatina every one to two hours on weekdays with less services on weekends.

Check up-to-date bus schedules at www.izletnik.si.

TRAIN

The **train station** (Kidričeva ulica) is 300m south of the bus station. Rogaška Slatina is on the train line linking Celje (€3.45, 50 minutes) with Rogatec (€1.30, 10 minutes). There are seven services on weekdays and one to two on weekends. A few of these services carry on to Zabok in Croatia (change here for Zagreb).

Ptuj

☑02 / POP 17,800 / ELEV 225M

Rising gently above a wide valley, Ptuj (p-too-ee) forms a symphony of red-tile roofs best viewed from across the Drava River. One of the oldest towns in Slovenia, Ptuj equals Ljubljana in terms of historical importance. The compact medieval core, with its cobblestone alleys rimmed by interesting facades, scattered with ornate monasteries and topped by a grand whitewashed castle, may be easily seen in a day, but the laid-back ambience, cafe culture and great hotels may convince you to base yourself here for a while longer. There are plenty of interesting side trips and activities in the area if you do decide to linger.

History

Ptuj began life as a Roman military outpost on the south bank of the Drava River and later grew into a civilian settlement called Poetovio on the opposite side. By the 1st century AD, Poetovio was the largest Roman township in what is now Slovenia, and the centre of the Mithraic cult; several complete temples have been unearthed in the area.

Ptuj received its town rights in 977 and grew rich through river trade. By the 13th century it was competing with the 'upstart' Marburg (Maribor) upriver, in both crafts and commerce. Two monastic orders – the Dominicans and the Franciscan Minorites – settled here and built important monasteries. The Magyars attacked and occupied Ptuj for most of the 15th century.

When the railroad reached Eastern Slovenia from Vienna on its way to the coast in the mid-19th century, the age-old rivalry between Maribor and Ptuj turned one-sided: the former was on the line and the latter missed out altogether. The town remained essentially a provincial centre with a German majority until WWI.

◉ Sights

Ptuj's Gothic centre, with its Renaissance and baroque additions, is a joy to wander around. If you want to dig a bit deeper into the history behind the facades, the TIC (p216) can organise private walking tours (€50).

On our last visit it was also planning a daily group walking tour focused on Ptuj's Roman heritage to run during July and August – enquire at the office for updates.

★ Ptuj Castle   CASTLE
(Grad Ptuj; ☑ castle 02-748 03 60, museum 02-787 92 30; www.pmpo.si; Na Gradu 1; adult/child €5/3; ⊙ 9am-6pm Mon-Fri, to 8pm Sat & Sun Jul & Aug, 9am-6pm May-Jun & Sep–mid-Oct, to 5pm mid-Oct–Jun) Ptuj Castle is an agglomeration of styles from the 14th to the 18th centuries, but it is nonetheless a majestic sight, sitting high on the hill overlooking the red-roofed burger houses of Ptuj and the Drava River. It houses the Ptuj-Ormož Regional Museum but is equally worth the trip for the views of Ptuj and the river. The shortest way to the castle is to follow narrow Grajska ulica, east of the Hotel Mitra, which leads to a covered wooden stairway and the castle's Renaissance Peruzzi Portal (1570).

As you enter the castle courtyard, look to the west at the red marble tombstone of Frederick IX, the last lord of Ptuj (he died in 1438). In the former stables just past the ticket office is a large collection of Kurent masks and costumes.

The ground floor of one wing is devoted to an arms collection of some 500 weapons. The suits of armour are particularly fine. Also here is a fascinating musical instruments collection mostly from the 17th to 19th centuries (though there is a Roman double flute from the 2nd or 3rd century AD).

The 1st floor is given over to period rooms – treasure-troves of original tapestries, painted wall canvases, portraits, weapons and furniture mostly left behind by the castle's last owners, the Herbersteins (1873–1945). Notice the coat of arms containing three buckles upon entering the chapel – it belonged to the Leslies, a Scottish-Austrian family who owned the castle from 1656 to 1802. The Chinoiserie Countess's Salon and her rococo bedroom are exquisite.

In Festival Hall you'll find Europe's largest collection of aristocratic Turkerie portraits, some 45 in total – possibly of more historical than artistic interest.

The Castle Gallery on the 2nd floor contains paintings from the 16th to 18th centuries.

Enquire at the museum office if you're interested in visiting Ptuj's unearthed Roman-era Mithraic shrines, dedicated to the sun god Mithras; for a time in the 1st and 2nd centuries AD Mithraism was more widely practised than Christianity. The shrines are located south of the river, a couple of kilometres west of town in suburban Spodnja Hajdina and Zgornji Breg.

Dominican Monastery   MONASTERY
(Dominikanski Samostan; Muzejski trg 1; adult/child/family €4/2/9; ⊙ 10am-6pm Tue-Sun Apr-Sep) Carefully restored and newly reopened to the public, Ptuj's Dominican Monastery was first established in 1230, though much of its original medieval character was replaced by baroque features during the 18th century. Inside, the walls of the Gothic cloister still hold on to scraps of faded frescoes, while the baroque powder-pink refectory is home to swirling plasterwork and colourful murals. The entrance fee includes an audio guide with some good basic historical information on the building.

Slovenski Trg   SQUARE
Funnel-shaped Slovenski trg is the centre of old Ptuj. The 16th-century **City Tower** (Mestni Stolp) dominates the square's eastern side. Roman tombstones and sacrificial altars from Poetovio were incorporated into the walls in

the 1830s – check the reliefs of Medusa's head, dolphins, a lion and a man on horseback.

In front of the tower stands the 5m-tall **Orpheus Monument** (Orfejev Spomenik; Slovenski trg), a 2nd-century Roman tombstone with scenes from the Orpheus myth. It was used as a pillory in the Middle Ages.

On the northern side of the square are several interesting buildings, including the 16th-century **Provost's House** (Slovenski trg 10), the baroque **Old Town Hall** (Mestna Hiša; Slovenski trg 6) and the **Ljutomer House** (Slovenski trg 5), built in 1565 and now housing the TIC (p216).

Prešernova Ulica STREET
Pedestrian Prešernova ulica was the town's market in the Middle Ages. The arched spans above some of the narrow side streets support older buildings. The **Late Gothic House** (Prešernova ulica 1), dating from about 1400, has an unusual projection held up by a Moor's head. Opposite is the sombre **Romanesque House** (Prešernova ulica 4), the oldest building in Ptuj. The renovated yellow pile called the **Little Castle** (Mali Grad; Prešernova ulica 33-35) was the home of the Salzburg bishops and various aristocratic families over the centuries.

Minorite Monastery MONASTERY
(Minoritski Samostan; ☑ 059 073 000; Minoritski trg 1; ⊙ by appointment) This massive Minorite monastery, with its 17th-century **plague pillar**, was established in the 13th century. Because the Franciscan Minorites dedicated themselves to teaching, the order was not dissolved under the edict issued by Habsburg Emperor Joseph II in the 18th century, and has continued to function here for more than seven centuries. Although the main courtyard entrance is often open, to access the rest of the monastery you need to organise a tour. The TIC (p216) can arrange this for you.

The arcaded baroque structure, which dates from the second half of the 17th century, contains a summer refectory on the 1st floor, with beautiful stucco work and a dozen ceiling paintings of St Peter (north side) and St Paul (south side). It also has a 5000-volume library of important manuscripts.

On the northern side of the inner courtyard, the **Church of Sts Peter and Paul** (Cerkev Sv Petra in Pavla; Minoritski trg 1; ⊙ 8am-6pm) is one of the most beautiful examples of early Gothic architecture in Slovenia. Reduced to rubble by Allied bombing in Jan-

uary 1945, it was painstakingly rebuilt over the decades. View fragments of the original church in the side chapel.

Ptuj City Gallery GALLERY
(Mestna Galerija Ptuj; Prešernova ulica 29; ⊙ 10am-6pm Tue-Fri, to 1pm Sat & Sun) **FREE** Ptuj's newly opened city gallery concentrates on contemporary art with a particular emphasis on local artists.

🏃 Activities

Thermal Spa
Terme Ptuj THERMAL BATHS
(www.sava-hotels-resorts.com; Pot v Toplice 9; adult/child Mon-Fri €15/9.90, Sat & Sun €16/10.50; ⊙ indoor complex 8am-10pm Mon-Fri, from 7am Sat & Sun, outdoor complex 9am-8pm May-Sep) Kids need to cool off after trudging the cobblestones? Bring them here. The outdoor complex is a family-fun set-up with a range of water slides, a wave pool and a slow-current 'river' for those who just want to relax on an inner tube. Outside of summer, the indoor complex has seven pools with one water slide.

Wine Tasting
Kobal Wine Shop WINE
(Vinoteka Kobal; ☑ 041 348 596; www.kobalwines.si; Prešernova ulica 4; wine tasting €9; ⊙ by appointment 10am-6pm Mon-Sat) Kobal is one of the Haloze area's most notable boutique wineries, producing a completely luscious sauvignon as well as a richly bodied *šipon*. Its wine shop, inside the Romanesque House (the oldest building in Ptuj) is a suitably atmospheric place to get stuck into some tasting. Phone beforehand to make sure the shop is open.

Ptuj Wine Cellar WINE
(Ptujska Klet; ☑ 02-787 98 27, 041 486 258; www.pullus.si; Vinarski trg 1; tours €7-12; ⊙ by appointment 9am-noon & 1-5pm Mon-Fri, to noon Sat) One of the oldest cellars in Slovenia, this is the place to go if you want to learn about local wine, especially Haloze sauvignon, *šipon* or *laški rizling* (Laški riesling). Book tours in advance. It also holds Slovenia's oldest vintage: Zlata Trta, the 'Golden Vine' sweet wine dating from 1917. You can sample local wines at the attached Pullus Vinoteka (p215).

🎭 Festivals & Events
Kurentovanje CARNIVAL
(www.kurentovanje.net; ⊙ Feb) Ptuj marks Shrovetide with Kurentovanje, a rite of spring

Ptuj

1 Ptuj Castle

2
3
4
5
6
7
8
9
10
11
12
13
14
15

16
17
18
19
20
21
22
23
24
25
26
27
28
29

Bus Station

Drava River

Footbridge

Camping Terme Ptuj (1.3km);
Mithraic shrines (2km)

Town Hall

Ul Viktorina Ptujskega

Trstenjakova ul

Raičeva ul

Osojnikova c

Ormoška c

Vinarski trg

Novi trg

Miklošičeva ulica trg

Heroja Lacka ul

Vodnikova ul

Minoritski trg

Mestni trg

Krempljeva ul

Murkova ul

Slovenski trg

ul Tomaža Šalamuna

Vrazov trg

Jadranska ul

Slomškova ul

Grajska ul

Prešernova ul

Cankarjeva ul

Cvetkov trg

Vošnjakova ul

Dravska ul

Dravska ul

Cafova ul

Na Hribu

Muzejski trg

Cobbled Path

Pot v Toplice

(200m)

200 m
0.1 miles

Ptuj

and fertility that dates to the time of the early Slavs and is now an organised carnival and centrepiece of Ptuj's calendar. Festivities are spread over 11 days in February, culminating in the Kurent parades on the Saturday and Sunday before Shrove Tuesday.

The main character of the rite is Kurent, a Dionysian god of unrestrained pleasure and hedonism. Hundreds of masked and costumed Kurents march through town during the parades, dressed in sheepskins with cowbells dangling from their belts. On their heads they wear huge furry caps decorated with feathers, sticks or horns and coloured streamers. Their leather masks have red eyes, trunk-like noses and enormous tongues hanging down to the chest.

The Kurents process from house to house, scaring off evil spirits with their bells and *ježevke* (wooden clubs) entwined with hedgehog quills. A *hudič* (devil), covered in a net to catch souls, leads each group. Young girls present the Kurents with handkerchiefs, which they then fasten to their belts, and people smash little clay pots at their feet for luck and good health.

Tens of thousands of spectators visit Ptuj for the parades, so book accommodation well in advance.

Days of Poetry & Wine   CULTURAL
(Dnevi Poezije in Vina; www.versoteque.com; ☺Aug) This annual festival held in August gathers Slovenian and international poets, writers, storytellers and musicians for read-

ings, concerts and good wine through the summer evenings.

🛏 Sleeping

Ptuj has some of the most interesting places to stay in Eastern Slovenia, much of them slap bang in the historic central city area. The TIC (p216) can arrange private rooms (per person €20 to €25) both in the centre and on the south side of the Drava near Terme Ptuj.

Panorama Guesthouse   GUESTHOUSE $
(✆02-787 75 70; www.panorama-krapsa.si; Maistrova ulica 19; s €30-35, d €45-50, studio €60; ☎) With a countryside setting, yet still only a 10-minute walk into the centre, this rambling guesthouse has bright, homey rooms, all with fridges, satellite TVs and kettles. The mammoth garden, with chickens and an area set up with playground equipment, makes this a good choice for those travelling with little ones. Bonus points for the beautiful, friendly dog.

Camping Terme Ptuj   CAMPGROUND $
(✆02-749 45 80; www.terme-ptuj.si; Pot v Toplice 9; campsite per person with/without pools entry €18.50/14.50, wine barrels s/d €43/64; P@☎) This 1.8-hectare campground next to Ptuj's thermal baths complex has 120 sites with a decent amount of shade. Those without a tent or motorhome can bed down in one of eight oversized (but still snug) wine barrels.

EASTERN SLOVENIA PTUJ

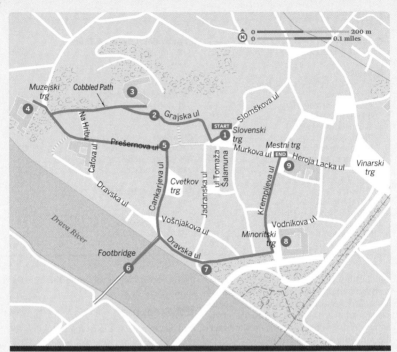

🏃 Walking Tour
Ptuj's Old Town Heritage

START SLOVENSKI TRG
END MESTNI TRG
LENGTH 1.8KM, 1½ HOURS

Begin in front of the **1 Orpheus Monument** (p211), one of the few remnants of Ptuj's Roman heritage. Note the holes on the lower half of the tombstone. During the medieval era, Ptuj's criminals were shackled to iron rings attached to them. Admire the mix-and-match of different facades before taking arched and cobblestoned **2 Grajska ulica** up the hillside as it rims the castle fortifications.

Enter the grounds of **3 Ptuj Castle** (p210) and peer over the walls for the panorama, dominated by the clock tower's dome. From here you can see that the castle-facing side of the tower is missing its clock face. This is because the castle lords didn't chip in for the building costs, so Ptuj's citizens decided to deny them easy viewing of the time.

Once you've visited the exhibits inside the castle, make your way down the cobbled path to the powder-pink stuccoed facade of the

4 Dominican Monastery (p210); its Gothic-baroque interior is open in summer. From the monastery walk down **5 Prešernova ulica** (p211), which had its heyday between the 11th to 14th centuries, when it thrummed with market activity thanks to Ptuj's strategic location upon the trade routes.

Take Cankarjeva ulica, down to the riverfront and cross the **6 bridge** over the Drava River to take in the views back towards the red-roofed Old Town. The entire town was once encased within defensive walls, which during the 16th century helped to repel the Ottoman army. Backtrack over the bridge, to note the riverfront **7 Drava Tower**, the only restored remnant of these fortifications.

From here head up to Minoritski trg dominated by the stucco-facade of its **8 Minorite Monastery** (p211), still home to Minorite order monks today. Walk from here up to Mestni trg, loomed over by the **9 Town Hall** (p213) built by Viennese architect Max Ferstl. Finish up by taking a seat in one of the square's pavement cafes to admire this mustard-yellow pile of a building at leisure.

★**DomKulture MuziKafe** BOUTIQUE HOTEL **$$**
(⌨ 02-787 88 60; www.muzikafe.si; Vrazov trg 1;
s €42-67, d €57-81, f €115, studio €90; ☎) This
quirky cracker of a place is tucked away off
Jadranska ulica. Each room is idiosyncrat-
ically decorated with lashings of retro chic
by the hotel's designer owners; we especially
love rooms 1 and 7. There's a small kitchen
for guest use, plus Ptuj's best cafe down-
stairs with a terrace and vaulted brick cellar
that hosts musical and artistic events.

Šilak B&B GUESTHOUSE **$$**
(⌨ 031 597 361, 02-787 74 47; www.rooms-silak.
com; Dravska ulica 13; s/d/tr/q €48/63/85/98, apt
€74-110; P✳☎) This old tannery building
underwent a painstaking, years-long restoration to be transferred into a good-value
guesthouse. The spacious, simply furnished
rooms, have high, super-comfortable beds,
and there are a range of apartments to accommodate large groups. Breakfast is served
in the old skin-dying warehouse and there's
a peaceful inner courtyard where guests can
put their feet up after sightseeing.

★**Hotel Mitra** BOUTIQUE HOTEL **$$$**
(⌨ 051 603 069, 02-787 74 55; www.hotel-mitra.
si; Prešernova ulica 6; s €62-69, d €106; P✳☎)
With Turkish carpets on the wooden floors
and walls hung with specially commissioned
paintings plus a wellness centre off a tran-
quil internal courtyard, the Mitra is one of
provincial Slovenia's more interesting small
hotels. The 25 good-sized rooms each come
with their own name and theme; rooms on
the top floor have mansard ceilings.

✖ Eating

Teta Frida CAFE **$**
(⌨ 02-771 02 35; Mestni trg 2; cakes €3.10-4.40;
⊙7am-10pm Mon-Thu, to midnight Fri, 8am-mid-
night Sat, 10am-10pm Sun; ☎) Resign yourself
to a trip to the dentist when you get home.
Based in the 18th-century Corner House,
Teta Frida's chocolate torte and *kremšnita*
(mille-feuille-style custard pastry) with
fruity twists are worth it. There's a good
amount of dairy and gluten-free cake op-
tions as well.

★**Gostilna Grabar** EUROPEAN **$$**
(⌨ 02-778 21 40; Rabelčja vas 15; mains €14-24;
⊙10am-10pm Mon-Sat, to 7pm Sun) This unas-
suming restaurant in the suburbs whips up
the most creative modern European cooking
in the area. The menu changes daily, based
on what's in season and what they've pulled

fresh from the garden. Expect seriously good
eating dressed up with a dash of foams-
crumbs-purées frippery, but never just for
the sake of style; it's all about flavour here.

It's 2km north of the centre, signposted
from the corner of Volkmerjeva cesta and
Peršonova ulica.

★**Gostilna Ribič** SLOVENIAN **$$**
(⌨ 02-749 06 35; Dravska ulica 9; mains €12-30;
⊙10am-11pm Sun-Thu, to midnight Fri & Sat; ☎▱)
Ptuj's fanciest restaurant is in a prime po-
sition, with a shady terrace facing the riv-
er. The speciality here is fish – particularly
trout and pike-perch – and local chicken
dishes, but it deserves serious kudos for the
small but way more inventive than most
vegetarian menus (the black risotto with
tofu is divine) and the kids' menu. Service
is exceptional.

Gostilna Amadeus SLOVENIAN **$$**
(⌨ 02-771 70 51; Prešernova ulica 36; mains €7-19;
⊙noon-10pm Mon & Wed-Sat, to 4pm Sun; ☎)
This very pleasant *gostilna* above a pub and
near the foot of the road to the castle serves
a lot of stick-to-the-ribs Slovenian specialities, such as *štruklji* and *ajdova kaša z jurčki* (buckwheat groats with mushrooms),
as well as plenty of grill and seafood dishes.

♙ Drinking & Nightlife

Bo Kava CAFE
(Slovenski trg 7; ⊙9am-11pm) This cafe's outdoor terrace, right behind the Orpheus Monument, is a real winner. We can't think of a
better place to chill out with a wine or beer
on a sunny summer Ptuj afternoon.

Legend Pub PUB
(⌨ 02-749 32 50; Murkova ulica 6; ⊙7am-11pm
Mon-Thu, to 1.30am Fri & Sat, 8am-11.30pm Sun)
Great for a sundowner, this pub attracts a
youngish crowd and is one of Ptuj's most
popular hang-outs after dark. As well as all
the usual offerings, there's a small menu of
global craft beers.

Kavabar Orfej BAR
(⌨ 02-772 97 61; Prešernova ulica 5; ⊙6.30am-
11pm Mon-Thu, to 1am Fri & Sat, 10am-11pm Sun)
The Orfej is the anchor tenant of Prešernova
ulica and is usually where everyone starts
(or ends) the evening. It closes an hour or so
later in summer.

Pullus Vinoteka WINE BAR
(⌨ 02-787 98 10; Vinarski trg 1; ⊙9am-5pm Mon-
Fri, to 1pm Sat) This *vinoteka* is a convenient

way to sample wines if you don't have time for a prearranged tour at the attached Ptujska Klet cellar.

ℹ Information

Nova Ljubljanska Banka (Prešernova ulica 6; ⊙ 8am-5pm Mon-Fri) With an ATM, next door to the Hotel Mitra.

Post Office (Vodnikova ulica 2; ⊙ 8am-6pm Mon-Fri, to noon Sat)

Tourist Information Centre Ptuj (☑ 02-779 60 11; www.ptuj.info; Slovenski trg 5; ⊙ 9am-8pm May–mid-Oct, to 6pm mid-Oct–Apr) Ptuj's very proactive TIC is housed in the 16th-century Ljutomer House (p211) and has plenty of maps and brochures. Check out the side room with a video of the Kurentovanje festival (p211).

ℹ Getting There & Away

BUS

Ptuj's **bus station** (Osojnikova cesta) has decent connections to nearby towns on weekdays.

Maribor (€3.60, one hour) One or two per hour weekdays, five to six services daily on weekends.

Ormož (€3.60, 40 minutes) At least hourly weekdays, none on weekends.

Stuttgart (Germany; €40, 11½ hours) One to two direct services daily, via Munich.

TRAIN

Ptuj train station is on Osojnikova cesta, 1km east of the centre.

Ljubljana (€10 to €14.80, 1¾ to 2½ hours) Two to four direct services daily. Several other trains require a transfer at Zidani Most or Pragersko.

Maribor (€3.45 to €5.25, 50 minutes) Nine direct trains daily on weekdays and five daily on weekends. More services with a change in Pragersko.

Murska Sobota (€5.80 to €7.60, 1¼ hours) Ten services daily on weekdays and eight daily on weekends.

ℹ Getting Around

A free city bus runs a circular route from Ptuj bus station into the city centre (via a trundle into the suburbs) and then out to Terme Ptuj every 30 minutes from 6am to 9pm on weekdays and to 3pm on weekends.

Around Ptuj

◉ Sights

Basilica of the Patroness Mary   BASILICA
(Bazilika Marije Zavetnice; ☑ 02-794 42 31; www.ptujska-gora.si; Ptujska Gora 40; ⊙ 6am-7pm) The pilgrimage Basilica of the Patroness Mary, in Ptujska Gora village 14km southwest of Ptuj, contains one of the most treasured objects in Slovenia: a 15th-century carved caped Misericordia of the Virgin Mary and the Child Jesus. The church itself, built at the start of the 15th century, is the finest example of a three-nave Gothic church in Slovenia. It was named a basilica for its 600th anniversary in 2010.

Among some of the other treasures inside is a small wooden statue of St James on one of the pillars on the south aisle and, under the porch and to the right as you enter, 15th-century frescoes of the life of Christ and of several saints, including St Nicholas and St Dorothy with the Child Jesus. Look behind the modern tabernacle in the chapel to the right of the main altar for faded frescoes of St Peter and St Michael the Archangel. The modern stained glass is exquisite.

The church, perched atop Black Hill (Črna Gora), is an easy 10-minute walk from where the bus headed for Majšperk from Ptuj (up to six a day) will let you off. Dragica is a small bar opposite the church with snacks and views.

🏃 Activities

Haloze Mountain Path   HIKING
(Haloška Planinska Pot) The Haloze Hills extend from Makole, 18km southwest of Ptuj, to Goričak on the border with Croatia. The 12km-long Haloze Mountain Path takes in this land of gentle hills, vines, corn and sunflowers, accessible from near **Štatenberg Manor** (Dvorec Štatenberg; ☑ 040 870 835; www.dvorecstatenberg.si; Štatenberg 89; adult/child €2/1; ⊙ visits by appointment, restaurant noon-7pm Sat & Sun Jun-Aug, to 6pm May, Sep & Oct), an 18th-century pile with grand rooms. The manor is 5km outside Makole; the TIC in Ptuj can help with maps.

Maribor

☑ 02 / POP 94,650 / ELEV 266M

Despite being the nation's second-largest city, Maribor has only about a third of the population of Ljubljana and often feels more like an overgrown provincial town. It has no unmissable sights but oozes charm thanks to its delightfully patchy Old Town along the Drava River. Pedestrianised central streets buzz with cafes and student life, and the riverside Lent district hosts a major summer arts festival. Maribor is the gateway to the Maribor Pohorje, a hilly recreational area to the southwest,

WORTH A TRIP

THE JERUZALEM-LJUTOMER WINE ROAD

The Jeruzalem-Ljutomer Wine Road begins at Ormož, 23km east of Ptuj, and continues for 18km north to Ljutomer, the main seat in the area, via the delightful hilltop village of Jeruzalem. The rural vistas of rolling, vineyard striped hills, speckled with wineries predominantly producing white wines, makes for a scenic cycle tour or easygoing countryside drive.

There are many cellars and small restaurants along the way where you can sample the wines.

Jeruzalem Ormož Winery (☎02-741 57 25; www.visitjeruzalem.com; Kolodvorska 11, Ormož; tasting tour per person €15; ⏰by appointment 8am-4pm Mon-Fri, to noon Sat) The wine shop and cellar of the Puklavec family vineyards, which have been producing wine in the region since the 1930s. Wines include a peppery pinot grigio and the interestingly spicy sweet traminec. Tasting tours visit the cellar and include four wine samples, with bread and cheese. Pre-book tours two days in advance.

Malek Vineyard Cottage (Zidanica Malek; www.visitjeruzalem.com; Svetinje 22; tasting tour per person 3/4/5 wines €6/7/8; ⏰11am-6pm May-early Nov) This tasting room and wine shop is run by the family behind the Jeruzalem Ormož Winery. Tastings don't require pre-booking, so just pull in along the road between Svetinje and Jeruzalem to sample some fine local produce.

Vino Kupljen (☎02-719 41 28; www.vino-kupljen.com; Svetinje 21; tastings 5/10 wines €10/25, min 4 people; ⏰10am-4pm) This boutique winery produces the excellent Stars of Stiria label, including an intense pinot noir and a full-bodied sauvignon blanc. The 10-wine tasting includes a cellar tour. Stick around for lunch or dinner at the restaurant (10am to midnight), which has views of the rolling hills of vineyards.

Enoteka Ljutomer (☎031 229 778; www.enoteka.si; Prešernova ulica 1, Ljutomer; ⏰10am-6pm Mon-Fri, to 1pm Sat) A good place to gather information on the local wine scene, this shop stocks wine from around 25 local producers and offers tastings.

and the Mariborske and Slovenske Gorice wine-growing regions to the north and east.

History

Maribor rose to prominence in the Middle Ages and grew wealthy through the timber and wine trades, financed largely by the town's influential Jewish community. The waterfront landing (Pristan) in the Lent district was one of the busiest river ports in the country. The town was fortified in the 14th century.

Though its fortunes declined in later centuries, the tide turned in 1846 when it became the first town in Slovenia to have train connections with Vienna. Maribor thrived again and began to industrialise.

Air raids during WWII devastated Maribor, and by 1945 two-thirds of it lay in ruin.

👁 Sights

Glavni Trg SQUARE

Maribor's marketplace in the Middle Ages, Glavni trg is just north of the river and the main bridge crossing it. In the centre of the square is Slovenia's most extravagant **plague pillar**, erected in 1743. Behind it is the **town hall** built in 1565 by Venetian craftsmen.

National Liberation Museum MUSEUM

(Muzej Narodne Osvoboditve; ☎02-235 26 00; www.muzejno-mb.si; Ulica Heroja Tomšiča 5; adult/child €3/2; ⏰8am-5pm Mon-Fri, 9am-noon Sat) Housed in a stunning 19th-century mansion, the collections here document Slovenia's struggle for freedom throughout the 20th century, with particular emphasis on the work of the Pohorje Partisans during the Nazi occupation. Riveting.

Maribor Regional Museum MUSEUM

(☎02-228 35 51; www.pmuzej-mb.si; Grajska ulica 2; adult/child €5/3.50; ⏰10am-6pm Tue-Sat) Housed inside 15th-century Maribor Castle, this museum has one of the richest collections in Slovenia, though much of it is not on show. The most interesting section is the ground floor with archaeological and ethnographic exhibits, including 19th-century beehive panels with biblical scenes from the Mislinja and Drava Valleys, models of Štajerska-style hayracks and wax ex voto offerings from the Ptuj area.

Maribor

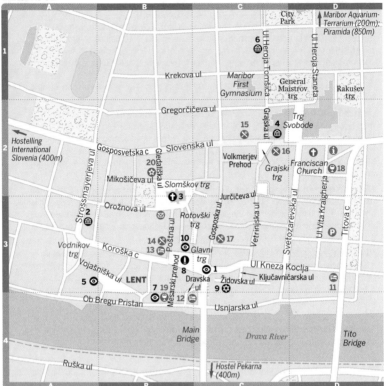

Maribor

◉ Sights

Upstairs are rooms devoted to Maribor's history and its guilds and crafts, an 18th-century pharmacy, and altar paintings and sculptures from the 15th to the 18th centuries. Taking pride of place are the exquisite statues by Jožef Straub (1712–56) taken from the Church of St Joseph in Studenci. The magnificent rococo staircase near

the exit, with its pink walls, stucco work and figures arrayed on the bannisters, is visible from the street when the museum is closed.

Maribor Cathedral
CATHEDRAL

(Stolna Cerkev Maribor; www.stolnicamaribor.si; Slomškov trg; ⊙8am-6pm) Maribor's cathedral faces the square named after Anton Martin Slomšek (1800–62), the Slovenian bishop and politician beatified in 1999 and the first Slovene to earn such distinction. Parts of the imposing structure date from the 13th century, and it shows elements of virtually every architectural style from Romanesque to modern. Of special interest are the flamboyant Gothic sanctuary and the gilded choir stalls, as well as the lovely modern stained glass and the enormous organ.

City Park
PARK

(Mestni Park) City Park is a lovely arboretum with 150 species of trees and three ponds.

Here you'll find the small but diverting **Maribor Aquarium-Terrarium** (Akvarij-Terarij Maribor; ☑02-234 26 80; www.maribor-pohorje.si/aquarium-terrarium; Ulica Heroja Staneta 19; adult/child €4/3.20; ⊙8am-7pm Mon-Fri, 9am-noon & 2-7pm Sat & Sun), with its diverse collection of fresh- and salt-water critters, reptiles and other exotic creepy crawlies. To the northeast is **Piramida** (386m), where the titans of Marchburg once held sway. Here you'll find an archaeological site and a chapel.

Maribor Art Gallery
GALLERY

(Umetnostna Galerija Maribor; ☑02-229 58 60; www.ugm.si; Strossmayerjeva ulica 6; adult/child €3/2; ⊙10am-6pm Tue-Sun) The Maribor Art Gallery, southwest of Slomškov trg, has a permanent collection of modern works by Slovenian artists and excellent changing exhibits.

⊙ Lent

The waterfront Lent district contains some of the most important and interesting historical sights in Maribor, including an ancient vine.

Old Vine
LANDMARK

(Stara Trta; Vojašniška ulica 8) About 150m east along the Pristan embankment is Maribor's most celebrated attraction, the so-called Old Vine, which still produces between 35kg and 55kg of grapes and about 25L of red wine per year, despite being planted more than four centuries ago. It is tended by a city-appointed viticulturist, and the dark-red Žametna Črnina (Black Velvet) is distributed to visiting dignitaries as 'keys' to Maribor in the form of 0.25L bottles.

Learn more about the vine and Slovenian viticulture at the adjacent **Old Vine House** (Hiša Stare Trta; ☑02-251 51 00; www.maribor-pohorje.si; Vojašniška ulica 8; wine tasting €4; ⊙9am-8pm May-Sep, to 6pm Oct-Apr) FREE, where you can taste local wine from its enormous collection. And don't miss the lovely new floor mosaic tracing Maribor's history.

Synagogue
SYNAGOGUE

(☑02-252 78 36; Židovska ulica 4; €1; ⊙8am-4pm Mon-Fri) Just north of the pentagonal 16th-century Water Tower on the waterfront, a set of steps leads up to Židovska ulica (Jewish St), the centre of the Jewish district in the Middle Ages, and home to this 15th-century synagogue. It contains Gothic key stones and tomb fragments; the special exhibitions and 15-minute video are enlightening.

EASTERN SLOVENIA MARIBOR

Jeruzalem-Ljutomer Wine Road (p217) winery **2.** Vintner, Vipava
lley (p144) **3.** Grapes in Črnomelj vineyard (p179)

Exploring Slovenia's Wineries

Slovenia's three major wine-producing regions – Podravje and Posavje in the east and Primorska in the west – are all relatively compact. With some advance planning, it's easy to pair a visit to a region with a tour of the local wineries.

Jeruzalem-Ljutomer Wine Road

Arguably, the country's best-known wine route, the eastern Jeruzalem-Ljutomer Wine Road (p217), begins at Ormož and stretches a scenic 18km to Ljutomer. It's drivable, but better on bike. Wineries here specialise in luscious whites, like as pinot gris and sauvignon, as well as sparkling wines.

Bela Krajina

The Metlika wine area (p177) is rapidly gaining prominence due to the quality of up-and-coming varietals like sauvignon blanc and Blaufränkisch, and the enduring quality of its ice wines. This is home to Metliška Črnina (Metlika Black), a ruby-red unique to the region. Elsewhere, cyclists will want to make the 17km journey from Brežice to Bizeljsko to experience the charming Bizeljsko-Sremič wine district (p189).

The Karst & Vipava Valley

The Karst Wine Region (p141) in the southwest is a good place to sample some of the best reds. The rich, red soil of the Karst is responsible for the dark hue of arguably the country's best-known wine: Teran. A wine road links 170 winemakers, and is best explored by car.

North of the Karst, the wineries of the Vipava Valley (p144) and around Goriška Brda (p146) have earned a reputation as Slovenia's most daring in recent years. Wineries are small-scale and open to visitors. Tour outfits like Winestronaut (p144) can put together a tasting.

Minorite Monastery MONASTERY
(Vojašniški ulica 2a) At the western end of the riverfront Pristan is the renovated 13th-century Minorite Monastery, closed by Joseph II in 1784, later used as a military barracks until 1927, and now reborn as the Maribor Puppet Theatre.

🏃 Activities

Bananaway SUP Tours ADVENTURE SPORTS
(☑ 040 238 756; www.bananaway.si; per person €39; ⊙10am & 5pm Apr-Jun & Sep, 9am & 6pm Jul & Aug) These two-hour SUP tours on the Drava River are a great way to experience Maribor from a different angle. Tours are suitable for complete beginners; pre-booking is mandatory.

Big Guys Wine Tours WINE
(☑ 041 949 635; www.bigguyswinetours.com; half-day tour per person €57-67) These wine tours explore the Podravje wine scene with local sommelier Jernej Lubej. The half-day tour visits two small wineries and includes around 15 wine tastings.

🎆 Festivals & Events

Lent Festival CULTURAL
(www.festival-lent.si; ⊙Jun-Jul) The biggest event on the city's calendar, the Lent Festival is a two-week celebration of folklore, culture and music from late June into July, when stages are set up throughout the Old Town.

Festival Maribor MUSIC
(www.festivalmaribor.si; ⊙Sep) A 10-day extravaganza of music concerts held in venues across town in September.

Old Vine Festival WINE
(⊙Oct) Among the most colourful ceremonies in Maribor is the harvesting of the Old Vine for wine in early October.

🛏 Sleeping

Much of Maribor's accommodation veers towards the business traveller. For a city, mid-range and budget options are thin on the ground; it pays to book ahead. The TIC can organise private rooms (single/double from €25/40) and apartments.

★Hostel Pekarna HOSTEL **$$**
(☑ 059 180 880; www.mkc-hostelpekarna.si; Ob Železnici 16; dm/s/d €21/30/54; P @ 🛜) Part of Maribor's Pekarna alternative cultural centre, this bright and welcoming hostel south of the river is housed in a converted army

bakery (*pekarna* is 'bakery' in Slovene). Accommodation is mostly in four-bed dorms but there are also private studios and apartments with kitchenette. Facilities include a communal balcony, kitchen, cosy TV room and laundry, plus free bike rental.

Hotel Lent HOTEL **$$**
(☑ 059 177 700, 02-250 67 69; www.hotel-lent.si; Dravska ulica 9; s/d €49/69; ❄ 🛜) Chaotically run but enviably located on the river in Lent (though most rooms don't have views), this small hotel has 17 pokey but comfortable rooms. There's a lovely cafe out front.

★Hotel Maribor APARTMENT **$$$**
(☑ 02-234 56 00; www.hotelmaribor.si; Glavni trg 8; apt s/d/f from €109/139/149; P ❄ 🛜) This 18th-century brewery building has been sensitively converted into the nicest digs in town. Spacious, white-on-white apartments (the biggest has four bedrooms) have bags of sleek minimalist style. Some have original stone wall features, while all come with full kitchens, big balconies, repurposed factory lamps swinging over tables and sumptuous bathrooms with walk-in showers. There's a small sauna on-site.

🍴 Eating

There's a good range of eating options in town, from cheap and cheerful joints to restaurants serving classy modern European cookery.

★Malca EUROPEAN **$**
(☑ 059 100 397; www.malcamimogrede.si; Slovenska ulica 4; dishes €4.90-6.60; ⊙10am-4pm Mon-Fri; 🖉) This lunchtime bistro serves some of the freshest dishes based on seasonal ingredients in Maribor. The daily changing menu takes inspiration from across Europe (paella and moussaka were both chalked up on the board the last time we were here) as well as including Slovenian favourites like nettle soup and *žlikrofi* (ravioli of potato, bacon and chives).

Isabella Food & Wine CAFE **$**
(☑ 059 959 450; Poštna ulica 3; mains €2.80-6.50; ⊙8am-midnight Mon-Thu, 9am-2am Fri & Sat, to midnight Sun; 🛜) This pint-sized cafe on Maribor's liveliest street is a great place for a panini, salad or breakfast. It also does some of the best coffee in town and there is a decent selection of craft beers, including Bevog and Pelican.

★ **Restavracija Mak**　　　EUROPEAN **$$**
(✆ 02-620 00 53; www.restavracija-mak.si; Oso-jnikova ulica 20; set lunch/dinner from €25/45; ⊙ noon-3pm & 6-9.30pm Tue-Sat) The restaurant itself, in Obrežje across the Drava River, may not look like much, but you're here for the food not some grand dining hall. Owner-chef David Vračko will guide you through a multiple-course food experience (there's no menu) of creative modern European cuisine. Booking is highly recommended and don't expect to eat and run. This is a three- to four-hour affair.

Gostilna Maribor　　　SLOVENIAN **$$**
(Glavni trg 8; mains €6-26; ⊙ 7.30am-11pm Mon-Thu, to 2am Fri & Sat, 9am-4pm Sun) This great new addition to Maribor's dining scene focuses on bringing contemporary tweaks to traditional Styrian dishes with mains like wild boar with carrot *štruklji* and *spëtzle* (small pasta dumplings) with smoked curd. For lunch it's known for its *žemljica* (traditional bun) sandwiches (€6 to €7) stuffed with ingredients such as beef, horseradish and sauerkraut.

Rožmarin　　　EUROPEAN **$$**
(✆ 02-234 31 80; www.rozmarin.si; Gosposka ulica 8; mains €15-25, set menus 2/3 courses €23/30; ⊙ 7am-midnight Mon-Sat; 🐾🍴) Restaurant, cafe, *vinoteka* and shop; Rožmarin has its finger in many a pie, but the restaurant is where it shines. It's all about modern European cuisine, with good steaks and better than usual vegetarian offerings (we love the asparagus soup spiked with Stilton and the ravioli stuffed with morels and baby onions). Check out the set menus.

Pri Florjanu　　　MEDITERRANEAN **$$**
(✆ 059 084 850; www.priflorjanu.si; Grajski trg 6; mains €10-22; ⊙ 11am-10pm Mon-Thu, to 11pm Fri, noon-11pm Sat; 🐾🍴) A great spot in full view of the Column of St Florian, patron of firefighters, this popular restaurant has both an open front and an enclosed back terrace, with a huge minimalist restaurant in between. It serves a Mediterranean-influenced menu with a good supply of vegetarian options, as well as decent coffee and cakes.

🍸 **Drinking & Nightlife**

★ **Luft Bar**　　　BAR
(✆ 040 413 514; www.luftbar.si; Ulica Vita Kraigher-ja 3; ⊙ 8am-midnight Mon-Fri, 9am-4am Fri & Sat, 10am-10pm Sun; 🐾) Always suckers for views and recycling, we love that the old

Slavija Hotel is now an office building with a two-level rooftop cafe-bar. Floor 11 has a slick bar; go one floor up to the open terrace and you'll be bowled over by the sweeping views of the city and mountains. Service is friendly, the cocktails out of this world.

Mačka　　　BAR
(www.macka-bar.com; Vojašniška ulica 6; ⊙ 9am-midnight Mon-Thu & Sun, to 2am Fri & Sat; 🐾) The front terrace here, facing the Drava River, is a pleasant place to kick back with a wine and watch people out for an evening stroll along the riverfront. There's a good menu of both local and global craft beers as well.

Čajek Cafe　　　CAFE
(www.cajek.com; Slovenska ulica 4; ⊙ 7.30am-10pm Mon-Fri, 9am-10pm Sat, 3-9pm Sun; 🐾) Our favourite cafe in Maribor has an old-fashioned, cosy interior with lots of dark wood and eclectic decor. The menu concentrates on tea (in umpteen different flavours), though there's decent coffee, cold drinks and beer too, as well as homemade cake.

☆ **Entertainment**

Slovenian National Theatre Maribor　　　THEATRE
(Slovensko Narodno Gledališče Maribor; ✆ 02-250 61 00, box office 02-250 61 15; www.sng-mb.si; Slovenska ulica 27; tickets €10-30; ⊙ 10am-1pm & 5-7.30pm Mon-Fri, 10am-1pm Sat & 1hr before performance) This branch of the SNG in Ljubljana has one of the best reputations in the country, and its productions have received critical acclaim throughout Europe. The city's ballet and opera companies also perform here. Enter from Slomškov trg.

Jazz Klub Satchmo　　　JAZZ
(✆ 070 878 387; www.jazz-klub.si; Strossmayerjeva ulica 6; ⊙ 7pm-3am Tue-Thu, to 4am Fri, 8pm-4am Sat) Maribor's celebrated jazz club meets in a wonderful cellar in the art gallery building.

ℹ **Information**

Abanka (Glavni trg 18; ⊙ 8am-5pm Mon-Fri, to 11am Sat) In the mall at the eastern end of Glavni trg.

Post Office (Slomškov trg 10; ⊙ 8am-6pm Mon-Fri, to noon Sat)

Tourist Information Centre Maribor (TIC; ✆ 02-234 66 11; www.maribor-pohorje.si; Partizanska cesta 6a; ⊙ 9am-7pm Mon-Fri, to 5pm Sat & Sun) Helpful TIC in a large kiosk opposite the Franciscan church. Staff can organise city tours with local guides; between June and

October they run group city tours (€8, 1½ hours) on Friday at 4pm and Saturday at 11am.

ℹ Getting There & Away

BUS

You can reach virtually any town in Slovenia (and certain international destinations) from Maribor's huge **bus station** (Minska ulica).

Buses from Maribor

Celje €6.70, 1½hrs, 5 daily weekdays, 1 daily weekends

Ljubljana €12.40, 2-3hrs, 7 daily weekdays, 2-3 daily weekends

Munich (Germany) €48, 6hrs, 9.50pm & 11.45pm daily

Murska Sobota €6.30, 1¼hrs, 8 daily weekdays, 3-5 daily weekends

Ptuj €3.60, ¾hr, At least hourly weekdays, 5-7 daily weekends

Sarajevo (Bosnia) €45, 9hrs, 6.40pm daily & 9.15pm Mon-Thu, Sat & Sun

Slovenj Gradec €7.20, 2hrs, 3 daily

Vienna (Austria) €23, 3½hrs, 8.25am & 8pm daily

TRAIN

As well as direct services, there are many more possible connections to Ljubljana and Ptuj by changing in Pragersko.

International connections to Belgrade (€29, 8½ hours) and Zagreb (€12, three hours) are possible by changing in Zidani Most.

Trains from Maribor

Celje €5.80-7.60, ¾, At least hourly weekdays, every one to two hours weekends

Ljubljana €14.85-24.21, 2, 2 ICS express & 7 regular services daily

Murska Sobota € 7.17, 2, 6 daily weekdays, 5 daily weekends

Ptuj € 3.44, ½, 10 daily weekdays, 6 daily weekends

Vienna (Austria) € 29, 3½, 2 daily

ℹ Getting Around

Maribor and its surrounds are well served by local buses. They depart from the stands south of the train station near Meljska cesta. You can check bus timetables at www.marprom.si. Single-fare tickets bought on the bus cost adult/child €2/1.

The TIC (p223) rents bikes (three hours/one day €5/10). Electric bicycles are available from the **Maribor City Hotel** (🎘 02-292 70 00; www. hotelcitymb.si; Ulica Kneza Koclja 22; s/d from €120/180; 🅿 😊 ❋ 🛜).

Taxi company **Cammeo** (🎘 02-707 12 12; www. cammeo.si; per km €0.85) operates in Maribor. Ring or download the app for a pick-up.

POHORJE MASSIF

The wooded slopes, lush pastures and jagged peaks of the Pohorje Massif are pinned roughly between Slovenj Gradec to the west, Maribor to the east, and Celje to the south. This is Eastern Slovenia's hub for biking and hiking in summer and skiing in winter but, unlike the grander peaks of the Julian Alps, the area remains little known outside of Slovenia. For day hikes or an afternoon's mountain biking, there's easy access to the eastern edge of the mountain range from Maribor. With more time, launch into the region's core from Zreče; travelling the countryside lanes to tiny villages sitting snug between alpine meadows and hillside vineyard rows is Pohorje at its best.

Maribor Pohorje

🎘 02 / ELEV 1347M

The eastern edge of the Pohorje Massif, Maribor's green lung and central playground, is known in these parts as the Maribor Pohorje (Mariborsko Pohorje). It's within easy reach of the city and has countless activities on offer – from skiing and hiking to horse riding and mountain biking.

🏃 Activities

Walking

There are heaps of easy walks and more difficult hikes in every direction from the upper ski station atop Žigartov Vrh (1347m). Following a stretch of the marked Slovenian Mountain Trail, which originates in Maribor and goes as far as Ankaran on the coast, first west and then southwest for 5km, will take you to the two **Šumik waterfalls** and **Pragozd**, one of the very few virgin forests left in Europe. Another 6km to the southwest is **Black Lake** (Črno Jezero), the source of the swift-running Lobnica River, and **Osankarica**, where the Pohorje battalion of Partisans was wiped out by the Germans in January 1943.

PZS produces a 1:50,000-scale *Pohorje* map (€8.10). Kartografija also makes a 1:40,000-scale version (€12).

Biking

Cycling is an ideal way to explore the back roads and trails of the Maribor Pohorje. The

TIC (p223) offers the 1:100,000 *Pohorje Cycling Map* encompassing the entire Pohorje region, and the simple but useful *Kolesarske Poti na Mariborskem Pohorju* (Cycle Trails in the Maribor Pohorje).

The **sport centre** (8am-7pm) rents GT DHI Pro mountain bikes from the lower cable-car station (four hours/one day €40/50).

Skiing

Maribor Pohorje Ski Grounds   SKIING
(☑02-603 65 53; www.mariborskopohorje.si; Pohorska ulica 60; day pass adult/child €24/13; ☺7am-7pm) Maribor Pohorje ski grounds stretch from the Hotel Habakuk (336m) near the lower cable-car station to Žigartov Vrh. With 42km of slopes, 27km of cross-country runs and 22 ski lifts, tows and gondolas, this is Slovenia's largest ski area. Ski equipment rentals are available from the upper cable-car station, and there's a ski and snowboarding school as well.

★☆ Festivals & Events

**Women's World Cup Slalom
and Giant Slalom Competition**   SPORTS
(www.goldenfox.org; ☺Jan-Feb) The annual Women's World Cup Slalom and Giant Slalom Competition – the coveted Zlata Lisica (Golden Fox) trophy – takes place on the main piste of the Maribor Pohorje ski grounds for four days in late January or early February.

🛏 Sleeping & Eating

There are plenty of places to stay in the Maribor Pohorje, including more than a dozen mountain lodges and a lot of private apartments; ask at the Maribor TIC (p223) for a list and basic map.

Almost everyone takes their meals in their hotels in the Maribor Pohorje; there are no independent restaurants except for snack bars. Be on the lookout for dishes and drinks unique to the region, including *pohorski pisker* (Pohorje pot), a kind of goulash, and *pohorska omleta,* a pancake filled with cranberries and topped with cream.

Ruška Koča   CABIN **$**
(☑041 666 552, 02-603 50 46; www.ruskakoca.si; Frajham 64; per person €10-18; 🛜) This charming old mountain lodge, at 1246m, has had a makeover to suit the needs of today's hikers and skiers. Rooms (doubles and singles) are simple but comfortable and the terrace is a great place to relax after a day of activity. You'll need to book as it's hugely popular.

Camping Centre Kekec   CAMPGROUND **$**
(☑040 225 386; www.cck.si; Pohorska ulica 35; adult/child €9.50/6) This friendly, well-run campground with three-dozen pitches is at the foothills of the Maribor Pohorje near the lower cable-car station.

Hotel Bellevue   HOTEL **$$$**
(☑031 691 554, 02-607 51 00; www.terme-maribor. si; Na Slemenu 35; s/d €90/105; 🅿🛜) A Pohorje landmark, this hotel within tumbling distance of the upper cable-car station is the most comfortable place to bed down in the region. Rooms aren't as stylish as the communal areas, but they're spacious, well-maintained and have balconies. Rates include entry to the hotel's fine wellness centre.

ℹ Getting There & Away

BUS

To reach the lower cable-car station from the train station in Maribor take local bus 6 (€1.10, 20 minutes, twice hourly) and get off at the terminus – the cable-car station is just behind the bus stop.

CABLE CAR

An easy – and exhilarating – way to get to the Hotel Bellevue and the heart of the Maribor Pohorje is to take the **cable car** (Vzpenjača; ☑041 959 795; www.visitpohorje.si; adult/child/family return €6/3/12; ☺7am-10pm) from the station in Zgornje Radvanje, 6km southwest of Maribor's Old Town. There are clamps on the outside of each of the cable car cabins for mountain bikes and skis.

The cable car runs every hour daily from 7am to 10pm. Additionally, on weekends it runs continuously between 10am and 6pm.

CAR & MOTORCYCLE

You can drive or, if ambitious, cycle the 20km from the Old Town in Maribor – head south past the Renaissance-style Betnava Castle, turning west at Spodnje Hoče before reaching a fork in the road at a small waterfall. A right turn and less than 4km brings you to the upper cable-car station. Go left and you'll reach the upper station of the ski lift after about 5km.

Rogla & Zreče Pohorje

☑03 / ELEV 1517M

Zreče, some 40km southwest of Maribor, is the springboard for the Zreče Pohorje (Zreško Pohorje) and the ski and sports centre of Rogla. This central zone of the pear-shaped massif presents the Pohorje peaks at their highest and most beautiful. Although

HIŠA DENK

Gregor Vračko's **restaurant** (☑02-656 35 51; www.hisadenk.si; Zgornja Kungota 11A; tasting menu €40-50; ⊙11am-10pm Thu-Mon; 🐾) is all wood and floor-to-ceiling window minimalism. Its chic simplicity is a worthy contrast to the food. This is boldly creative fine dining with an added dash of eccentricity, elevating local Styrian produce to the highest level. There's no menu; just allow the chef to decide, settle back and expect a three- to five-hour dining extravaganza.

Bookings are essential. The restaurant is in the village of Zgornja Kungota, 15km north of Maribor. Rather than having to drive after dinner (there's an exceptional wine list) many foodies choose to make this an overnight trip. Luckily Hiša Denk also has a few rooms (€65 to €75), kitted out in the same simple modern style as the restaurant, so all you have to do after your dining blow-out is crawl upstairs to bed.

it's true that the mountains here can't exactly compete with those of the Julian and Kamnik-Savinja Alps – most barely clear the 1500m mark here – this means that hiking in the Zreče Pohorje can be a year-round activity.

Zreče itself has a modest spa, though it can't be called an attractive town; it's dominated by the tool-manufacturing company Unior. Head north 16km and you'll reach Rogla's ski slopes (1517m) where athletes, including the Slovenian Olympic team, train. The surrounding alpine meadow scenery, scattered with itsy-bitsy hamlets, is prime territory for trekkers and anyone simply wanting to soak up rural views.

🏃 Activities

Hiking & Mountain Biking

Kartografija's 1:40,000 *Pohorje* (€12) map outlines various circular hiking trails that are as short as 2km (30 minutes) and as long as 32km (eight hours), while the free *Rogla-Zreče Karta Pohodnih Poti* hiking map has 14 hikes and walks of between 3km and 33.5km. A good choice outlined on both maps is the 12km hike (three hours) that leads northwest to the **Lovrenc Lakes** (Lovrenska Jezera), a turf swamp with 20 small lakes that are considered a natural phenomenon.

Mountain bikers should get hold of a copy of the excellent free 1:100,000 *Pohorje Cycling Map,* spanning the entire Pohorje area with a dozen trails outlined heading west towards Slovenj Gradec and Dravograd and out east to Maribor. The spa's map/brochure (1:50,000) called *Rogla Terme Radfahrwege/Cycling Paths* is much more basic, but sticks to the local area with nine trails linking Zreče, Rogla and Areh.

Rogla Outdoor Centre HIKING
(Kolesarsko in Pohodriško Center; ☑03-757 74 68; www.rogla.eu; Rogla; bike rental 1hr/day from €10/20; ⊙9am-7pm Thu-Sun May-Jul, daily Aug–mid-Sep) This is the place to rent a bike and find out about cycling and hiking trails in the area. Staff can also organise guiding and rent other outdoor equipment.

Skiing

Rogla Unitur Ski Resort's website (www.rogla.si) is useful, especially for activities.

Rogla Ski Grounds SKIING
(☑03-757 61 55, 03-757 64 40; www.rogla.eu; Rogla; day pass adult/child €33/18; ⊙9am-4pm Mon-Wed, 9am-4pm & 5-9pm Thu-Sun Dec-Apr) The Rogla ski grounds have 13km of ski slopes (mostly easy and intermediate) and 21km of cross-country trails served by two chairlifts and 11 tows. The season is a relatively long one – from the beginning of December to as late as April.

Snowsports School Intersport Rogla SKIING
(Šola Snežnih Športov Intersport Rogla; ☑03-757 74 68; www.solasmucanja.eu; Rogla; beginners 2-day ski course adult/child €80/55; ⊙8.15am-4.15pm in winter) In a little wooden cabin at the base of the ski lift, Rogla's highly recommended snowsports school runs ski and snowboard lessons for beginners through to advanced skiers, as well as cross-country and freestyle ski courses.

Intersport Rent & Ski Servis SKIING
(☑03-757 74 89; Planja Hotel, Rogla; ski rental per day adult/child €22/18; ⊙8.30am-4.45pm, to 9pm winter) All the winter sports equipment you need can be rented at this office at the Planja Hotel.

Thermal Spa

Terme Zreče THERMAL BATHS
(☑03-757 61 56; www.terme-zrece.eu; Cesta na Roglo 15; day pass adult/child Mon-Fri €13/10, Sat & Sun €15/11.50; ⊙9am-9pm Mon-Thu & Sun, to 10pm Fri & Sat) Terme Zreče is a treatment centre for post-operative therapy and locomotor disorders (especially for sports injuries) but its thermal pool complex, with indoor and outdoor pools and water temperatures up to 35°C, is fully set up for recreation. For families, it's best between June and September when the Forest Water-park section is open, with water slides and a kid's splash-pool.

🛏 Sleeping & Eating

Small guesthouses, apartments and farmhouses accepting guests are scattered throughout the Zreče Pohorje region, particularly around Resnik, 7km southwest of Rogla and Skomarje, further to the southwest. Enquire at the TIC in Zreče for a list. Zreče and Rogla are the only places with bigger hotels.

Farmstay Ramšak GUESTHOUSE $$
(☑04-189 16 29; www.kmetija-ramsak.si; Padeški Vrh 2; s/d €30/60; 🅿) This peaceful family-run place with an organic farm and tasty meals (half board is just a couple of euros extra) has five simple rooms with white-washed walls, wood ceilings and balconies. It's halfway between Zreče and Rogla in the settlement of Padeški Vrh.

Pačnik Farmhouse GUESTHOUSE $$
(☑03-576 22 02; www.kmetija-pacnik.net; Resnik 21; d/tr €70/105; 🅿🅷) Pačnik farmhouse has four comfortable rooms and two apartments with lovely views over the mountains. The food here is delicious, prepared with home-grown produce and locally sourced meat and dairy. It's near Resnik, around 7km southwest of Rogla.

Garni Hotel Zvon GUESTHOUSE $$
(☑03-757 36 00; www.garnihotelzvon.si; Slomško-va ulica 2, Zreče; s/d/apt from €47/74/90; 🅿🅷🅐) The homey 'Bell' is just a hop-skip-jump to Terme Zreče and has 15 spotless rooms with balconies, and apartments that can sleep up to six.

Atrij Hotel HOTEL $$$
(☑03-757 60 00; www.terme-zrece.eu; Cesta na Roglo 15, Zreče; s/d €108/156; 🅿🅷🅐🅷🅧) Of Terme Zreče's three flashy hotels, the four-star Atrij at the entrance is the flagship, with 45 spacious and well-designed rooms

and a comprehensive wellness centre. Several rooms are adapted for guests with disabilities. Make sure you get one of the rooms with a balcony. Check the website for ski and wellness packages.

Koča na Pesku SLOVENIAN $
(☑03-757 71 67; www.en.pzs.si; Rogla; dishes €4.50-12.50; ⊙7am-9pm Apr-Oct, 8am-5pm Nov-Mar) This mountain lodge (half board per person €28), 3km north of Rogla on the un-sealed road to Koroška, is a popular place for hearty local dishes, especially its celebrated mushroom soup with buckwheat groats (*gobova kremna juha z ajdovimi žganci;* €5) and *pohorski lonec* (Pohorje pot; €5.50), a kind of goulash.

ℹ Information

Post Office (Cesta na Roglo 11, Zreče; ⊙8am-6pm Mon-Fri, to noon Sat) Southeast of the bank.

Tourist Information Centre Rogla-Zreče (TIC; ☑03-759 04 70; www.destinacija-rogla.si; Cesta na Roglo 11j, Zreče; ⊙8am-4pm Mon-Fri, 9am-noon Sat, to 11am Sun) In the PTC shopping centre. It has a complete listing of private rooms in the area.

ℹ Getting There & Away

On weekdays there are roughly hourly services between Zreče and Celje (€3.60, 45 minutes) via Slovenske Konjice. There is only one evening service on Saturdays and Sundays.

To Rogla, local buses make the run from Zreče bus station and in winter two buses a day from Celje and a couple from Slovenske Konjice stop at Zreče and then carry on to Rogla.

In winter there are special ski buses from Zreče (€3, 30 minutes, five in each direction), as well as Celje and Slovenske Konjice. Also during ski season, Terme Zreče runs free buses hourly from 6am to 8.30pm or 9pm up to Rogla for its guests. During the rest of the year it runs one bus up at 6am, which returns at 10pm.

KOROŠKA

The truncated province of Koroška is essentially just three valleys bounded by the Pohorje Massif to the east; the last of the Karavanke peaks, Mt Peca, to the west; and the hills of Kobansko to the north. Most visitors whizz through the region en route to Austria, but if you're a hiker or cyclist then the countryside around here – particularly the eastern edge of the Pohorje range – is worth checking out if you have time up your sleeve.

The Drava Valley runs east to west and includes the towns of Dravograd, Muta and Vuzenica. The Mežica and Mislinja Valleys fan out from the Drava; the former is an industrial area with such towns as Ravne na Koroškem, Prevalje and Črna na Koroškem, while the latter's main centre is Slovenj Gradec.

Slovenj Gradec & Around

📞 02 / POP 7240 / ELEV 405M

Slovenj Gradec isn't the 'capital' of Koroška – that distinction goes to the industrial centre of Ravne na Koroškem to the northwest – but it is certainly the province's cultural and recreational heart. A number of museums, galleries and historical churches line its main square, while the sporting opportunities in the Pohorje Massif to the east are many.

Slovenj Gradec's main street is Glavni trg, a colourful long 'square' lined with old town houses and shops.

History

The history of Slovenj Gradec is closely tied to Stari Trg, a suburb southwest of the Old Town where there was a Roman settlement called Colatio that existed from the 1st to the 3rd centuries (though there is no trace of it now). At that time, an important Roman road from Celeia (Celje) to Virunum (near Klagenfurt in Austria) passed through Colatio. Slovenj Gradec was an important trade centre in the Middle Ages and minted its own coins. Later it became a cultural and artistic centre, with many artisans and craft guilds. Among the prominent Habsburg nobles based in Slovenj Gradec over the centuries were members of the Windisch-Grätz family, a variant of the German name for the town (Windisch Graz).

🟢 Sights

Koroška Gallery of Fine Arts   GALLERY
(Koroška Galerija Likovnih Umetnosti; 📞 02-882 21 31; www.glu-sg.si; 1st fl, Glavni trg 24; adult/child/family €2.50/1.50/5; ⊙ 9am-6pm Tue-Fri, 10am-1pm & 2-5pm Sat & Sun) The Koroška Gallery of Fine Arts, on the 1st floor of the former town hall, counts among its permanent collection bronze sculptures by Franc Berneker (1874–1932) and naive paintings by Jože Tisnikar (1928–98). Tisnikar is among the most interesting and original artists in Slovenia, and his obsession with corpses, distorted figures and oversized insects is at once disturbing and funny. Check out *Birth and Death, Crows under the Cross* and the amusing *Bare Feet.*

Koroška Regional Museum   MUSEUM
(Koroški Pokrajinski Muzej; 📞 02-884 20 55; www.kpm.si; ground & 2nd fl, Glavni trg 24; adult/child €2.50/1.70; ⊙ 10am-6pm Tue-Fri, 10am-1pm & 2-5pm Sat & Sun) This museum, on two floors of the former town hall, has several permanent collections. They range from ethnological items relating the history of Slovenj Gradec and the Koroška region, from painted beehive panels to models of wartime hospital rooms and schools run by Partisans; to African folk art brought here by Slovenian doctor Franc Tretjak (1914–2009) in the 1950s and '60s; and various bits and bobs amassed by priest Jakob Soklič (1893–1972).

The Soklič Collection on the 2nd floor is a real hotchpotch, including mediocre watercolours and oils of peasant idylls and umpteen portraits of composer Hugo Wolf (born at Glavni trg 38 in 1860), green goblets and beakers from nearby Glažuta (an important glass-manufacturing town in the 19th century), local embroidery, religious artefacts and some 18th-century furniture. Tretjak's African photographs are exhibited in five of the old town hall's jail cells on the ground floor.

🏃 Activities

Slovenian Alpine Trail   HIKING
The Slovenian Alpine Trail passes through Stari Trg and the centre of Slovenj Gradec before continuing up to Mala Kopa (1524m) where it meets the E6. The E6 heads north through Vuhred and Radlje ob Dravi to Austria, and the Slovenian Alpine Trail carries on eastward to Rogla and Maribor. There is accommodation on Velika Kopa at 1377m, at the 60-bed **Grmovškov Dom pod Veliko Kopo** (📞 02-883 98 60, 031 816 754; www.pdsg.si/grmovskov-dom; per person from €22).

Kope Ski Grounds   SKIING
(📞 02-882 27 40; www.ribnisko-pohorje.si; Razborca; day pass adult/child/student & senior €27/17/24; ⊙ 9am-6pm) Three ski slopes are within striking distance of Slovenj Gradec, but the closest is Kope, with skiing above the Mislinja Valley on the western edge of the Pohorje Massif. The ski grounds have 8km of runs, 15km of cross-country trails and eight

lifts and tows on Mala Kopa and Velika Kopa peaks.

Koroški Splavarij RAFTING
(Koroška Rafters; ☑ 02-872 33 33; www.splavar jenje.com) The TIC (p230) can help organise three-hour rafting trips for about €25 per person on the Drava, though they are usually available to groups only. The trip starts at Vrata, about 8km east of Dravograd. The price includes food and drink.

🛏 Sleeping

Slovenj Gradec is the obvious choice to bed down for the night while exploring Koroška, but if you have your own transport Otiški Vrh and Vič, to the north, both have hotels.

Hotel Korošica HOTEL **$$**
(☑ 02-878 69 12; www.korosica.si; Otiški Vrh 25d; s/d €59/85; [P][❄][🌐]) It's a bit of a schlep, 10km northwest of Slovenj Gradec, but this four-star hotel, in the village of Otiški Vrh on the Mislinja River en route to Dravograd, is about the best in the region. The not particularly attractive facade – essentially a big grey and yellow box in a field – hides 30 comfortable rooms, and there's a popular restaurant too.

Hotel Slovenj Gradec HOTEL **$$**
(☑ 02-883 98 50, 051 310 333; www.vabo.si; Glavni trg 43; s/d €40/65; [P][❄][🌐]) The only central hotel option in town is this 68-room property with friendly staff. The rooms have had a fresh-looking makeover with wood furnishings and shiny, modern bathrooms.

🍴 Eating & Drinking

If you're road-tripping through Koroška, the best place to stop for lunch and a rest from the road is Slovenj Gradec. If you're en route to Austria, you might want to wait until to you get to Vič (just before the border) and have a meal at **Fabrika Guest House's** (☑ 041 619 073; www.fabrika-guest-house.slovenia-hotel.com; 22A Vič; s/d €40/60; [🌐]) modern, friendly restaurant.

Restavracija Paradiso INTERNATIONAL **$**
(☑ 02-883 98 50; www.vabo.si; Hotel Slovenj Gra-dec, Glavni trg 43; mains €6.50-16; [🌐]) The closest Slovenj Gradec gets to fine dining is this restaurant in the Hotel Slovenj Gradec. The *plošče* (platters) for sharing are especially good value (€20 to €24), as are the daily set menus (€8 to €9). The menu is a mini

Slovenj Gradec Ⓝ

Slovenj Gradec

◎ **Sights**
1 Koroška Gallery of Fine Arts...............A2
  Koroška Regional Museum ....(see 1)

❸ **Activities, Courses & Tours**
2 Koroški Splavarij....................................A2

🛏 **Sleeping**
3 Hotel Slovenj Gradec...........................A2

✴ **Eating**
4 Restavracija Paradiso A2
5 Šlaščičarna Šrimpf A2

🍷 **Drinking & Nightlife**
6 Mestna Kavarna....................................A2
7 Pisarna Cafe Lounge Bar....................B2

✦ **Entertainment**
8 Slovenj Gradec Cultural Centre..........B1

history lesson on the great and the good of Slovenj Gradec.

Šlaščičarna Šrimpf CAFE **$**
(☑ 02-884 14 82; Glavni trg 14; cakes €1-3; ⏱8.30am-7pm Mon-Sat, from 10am Sun) This long-established cafe draws the crowds with its fabulous cakes. Try the *zagrebska* (€2), a

rich concoction of custard, cream, chocolate and flaky pastry.

Gostilna Murko SLOVENIAN $$
(☑ 02-883 81 03; Francetova cesta 24; mains €12-18; ☺ 8am-10pm Mon-Fri, 10am-10pm Sat, to 5pm Sun) About 400m north of the centre on the Mislinja River, Gostilna Murko is a four-star roadside inn popular with Austrian tourists. It's been here for decades and is still serving solid and reliable Slovenian dishes.

Pisarna Cafe Lounge Bar BAR
(☑ 041 727 984; Poštna ulica 3; ☺ 6am-11pm Mon-Thu, to 2am Fri, 8am-2am Sat, 9am-8pm Sun) This black-and-white themed bar is a popular student hang-out; there's a decent buzz here on weekend evenings.

Mestna Kavarna CAFE
(☑ 041 324 774; Trg Svobode 7; ☺ 7am-10pm Mon-Thu, to 1am Fri, 8am-11pm Sat, to 10pm Sun; 🛜) This retro-style cafe on the corner of Glavni trg is one of the most comfortable places in town to tip back a coffee or maybe even something stronger.

☆ Entertainment

Slovenj Gradec Cultural Centre CONCERT VENUE
(Kulturni Dom Slovenj Gradec; ☑ 02-884 50 05; www.kulturni-dom-sg.si; Francetova ulica 5) Classical music concerts are sometimes held at both the Church of St Elizabeth and this centre, which also has a small cinema showing films between 8pm and 10pm Friday to Sunday.

❶ Information

Nova Ljubljanska Banka (Glavni trg 30; ☺ 8.30am-12.30pm & 2.30-5pm Mon-Fri)

Post Office (Francetova cesta 1; ☺ 8am-6pm Mon-Fri, to noon Sat) At the northern end of Glavni trg.

Tourist Information Centre Slovenj Gradec (TIC; ☑ 02-881 21 16; www.slovenjgradec.si; Glavni trg 24; ☺ 8am-6pm Mon-Fri, 10am-5pm Sat & Sun) On the ground floor of the former town hall. It has reams of material on local activities and places of interest.

❶ Getting There & Away

Slovenj Gradec is not on a train line. The **bus station** (Pohorska cesta 15) is about 500m north-east of the TIC. Destinations served include:

Celje (€7.20, 1½ hours) Two daily Monday to Friday.

Ljubljana (€9.90, two hours) Five daily Monday to Friday, one on Saturday, seven on Sunday.

Maribor (€7.20, two hours) Three daily.

PREKMURJE

Prekmurje is Slovenia's 'forgotten' corner – for the most part a broad, farmed plain 'beyond the Mura River' (as its name describes it). Relatively isolated until the 1920s, Prekmurje has preserved its traditional music, folklore, architecture and a distinct local dialect.

Until the end of WWI, most of Prekmurje belonged to the Austro-Hungarian Empire, and it still has a small Magyar minority, especially around Lendava. In many ways Prekmurje looks and feels more like Hungary than Slovenia, with its white storks, large thatched farmhouses, substantial Roma population, and the occasional Hungarian-style *golaž* (goulash) cooked with paprika.

A natural launching pad into Hungary, it's also a fine place for those with time up their sleeve, to road trip between itsy-bitsy villages and indulge in *gibanica,* a rich local pastry.

Murska Sobota & Around

☑ 02 / POP 11,130 / ELEV 189M

Slovenia's northernmost city, Murska Sobota sits on a plain flatter than a *palačinka,* the pancake filled with jam or nuts and topped with chocolate that is so popular here. The city itself has little to recommend it except for its odd architectural mix of neoclassical, Secessionist and 'socialist baroque' buildings, but it's a useful base for exploring the surrounding countryside and potters' villages.

History

The town of Murska Sobota was once little more than a Hungarian market town until the opening of the railway in 1907, which linked Murska Sobota with Šalovci in Hungary proper. With the formation of the Kingdom of Serbs, Croats and Slovenes in 1918 and the transfer of territory, Murska Sobota found itself more or less in the centre of Prekmurje and development really began.

◉ Sights

Pomurje Museum Murska Sobota MUSEUM
(Pomurski Muzej Murska Sobota; ☑ 02-527 17 06; www.pomurski-muzej.si; Trubarjev drevored 4; adult/child €3/2; ☺ 9am-5pm Tue-Fri, to 1pm Sat, 2-6pm Sun) Housed in 14 rooms of the Renaissance-style Murska Sobota Castle, a sprawling manor house from the mid-16th century, this museum tells the story of life along the Mura River, from prehistoric times to the end of the 20th century. Highlights

EXPLORING PREKMURJE'S RURAL HEARTLAND

A day spent pottering around Prekmurje's teensy villages is the best way to explore this region's proud local heritage. From the last working floating mills on the Mura River to a state-of-the-art winery, this rural, lesser-travelled district throws up plenty of surprises.

Martjanci

The **Parish Church of St Martin** (Župnijska Cerkev Sv Martina; Martjanci) here contains 14th-century frescoes painted on the sanctuary's vaulted ceiling and walls.

Filovci

This village is famed for its *črna keramika* (black pottery). **Keramika Bojnec** (☑041 330 987; www.bojnec.com; Filovci 20; €4), 200m southwest of the main road, invites visitors to watch artisans at work at the ancient kiln in the *skanzen* (open-air museum displaying village architecture) over the road.

Bogojina

Stop here to visit the **Parish Church of the Ascension**, which was redesigned by Jože Plečnik around 1926. The interior is an odd mixture of black marble, brass, wood and terracotta; the oak-beamed ceiling is fitted with Prekmurje ceramic plates and jugs, as is the altar.

Mačkovci

Marof (Vinska Klet Marof; ☑02-556 18 10; www.marof.eu; Mačkovci 35; ⊙10am-4pm Tue-Fri, 1-6pm Sat), one of Prekmurje's leading wineries, is based here. Travellers can tour the cellar before getting stuck into tasting. The label is known for its deeply fruity *modra frankinja*, but also does a lovely chardonnay.

Floating mills, which date back to Roman times, were very popular on rivers that changed their course abruptly or swelled rapidly after rainfall, as they allowed millers to move to the best possible spots for milling. In Slovenia, floating mills were largely built on the Mura River; up until WWII there were dozens of these wooden mills in operation. Today, there are only two left.

Babič Mill (Babičev Mlin; ☑041 694 087; Prvomajska ulica 24, Veržej; ⊙8am-4.30pm Mon-Fri, to 2pm Sat) In business since 1925, this working mill is still grinding grain for clients. It's not set up for visitors, but it's usually OK to take photos (sometimes there's a €1 charge).

Island of Love Mill (Otok Ljubezni Mlin; ☑02-541 35 80; Mladinska ulica 2, Beltinci; entry & ferry ride €3.50; ⊙9am-6pm Apr-Jun, Sep & Oct, to 8pm Jul & Aug) This mill at Ižakovci, southwest of Beltinci, was purpose-built in the mid-1990s to preserve the region's mill heritage. You can tour the small museum here and take a ride across the Mura River on the *kumpi* (traditional ferry worked by pulley).

include the medieval rubbish pit (room 4), the frescoed Baroque Salon (room 9), the old peasant house interiors in room 11 and the former chapel next to room 14.

Murska Sobota Gallery   GALLERY
(Galerija Murska Sobota; ☑02-522 38 34; www.galerija-ms.si; Kocljeva ulica 7; adult/child €2/1; ⊙8am-5pm Tue-Fri, 9am-noon Mon & Sat Sep-Jun, 9am-noon Sat Jul & Aug) The best gallery in Prekmurje, MSG has a permanent collection of more than 500 works – much of it sculpture – as well as some excellent special exhibitions (admission varies).

Evangelical Church   CHURCH
(Evangeličanska Cerkev; Slovenska ulica; ⊙8am-6pm) The neo-Gothic Evangelical Church (1910) is the main Lutheran seat in Slovenia. (The majority of Slovenian Protestants live in Prekmurje.) The interior, painted with geometric shapes and floral motifs in muted shades of blue, green, brown and gold, is a welcome change from the overwrought baroque gold and marble decor found in most Catholic churches here.

🛏 Sleeping

Hotel Štrk   GUESTHOUSE **$$**
(☑02-525 21 58; www.lovenjakov-dvor.si; Polana 40; s/d €41/82; 🅿 ❋ @ 🛜 ⛲) Views of nesting

Murska Sobota

Murska Sobota

◎ Sights
1 Evangelical Church	B1
2 Murska Sobota Gallery	B2
3 Pomurje Museum Murska Sobota	A1

🛏 Sleeping
4 Hotel Diana	C2

✖ Eating
5 Bunker	C2

🍸 Drinking & Nightlife
6 Zvezda Pivnica	B1

storks, comfortable, classically styled rooms, an enclosed pool with thermal water from Moravske Toplice and bike rental for €10 a day; the 25-room 'Stork' at the Lovenjakov Dvor (Lovenjak Court) tourist house is the nicest place in the area to bed down for the night. It's 4km northwest of Murska Sobota.

Hotel Diana　　　　　　　BUSINESS HOTEL **$$**
(☑ 02-514 12 00; www.hotel-diana.si; Slovenska ulica 52; s/d €55/90; ⓟ ❄ 🛜 🏊) Look, the bland rooms may have no 'wow' factor but they're all perfectly functional and well-cared for, plus the staff are a cheerful bunch. There's a glassed-in swimming pool, sauna and fitness room on the 2nd floor, as well as a decent restaurant.

✕ Eating & Drinking

Bunker　　　　　　　　　　　BURGERS **$**
(☑ 031 670 444; Slovenska ulica 47; burgers €4.50-7; ⊙ 8am-11pm Mon-Thu, to 1am Fri, 9am-1am Sat, to 10pm Sun; 🛜) The last thing we were

expecting when we moseyed into Murska Sobota was a dystopian steampunk styled bar-restaurant serving up good burgers and a vast global beer menu. Bunker is all mammoth machine-gun staring out the window, industrial piping and mannequins dressed for the coming apocalypse. Simply the coolest, most fun place for a meal or drink for miles around.

★**Gostilna Rajh**　　　　　　SLOVENIAN **$$**
(☑ 02-543 90 98; www.rajh.si; Soboška ulica 32, Bakovci; mains €9.50-22; ⊙ 10.30am-10pm Tue-Fri, 11am-10pm Sat, 11.30am-4pm Sun) In Bakovci village, 5km southwest of Murska Sobota, this *gostilna* serves local specialities with a modern twist. We love the trout served with pea-mash and parsley oil and the hearty stick-to-your-ribs *bograč golaž* (Hungarian-style goulash soup). Finish with *gibanica* ice cream – what happens when the local pastry gets taken to new heights.

The five-course tasting menu is €38.

Gostilna Lovenjak　　　　SLOVENIAN **$$**
(☑ 02-525 21 53; Hotel Štrk, Polana 40; mains €7.50-20; ⊙ 11am-10pm Mon-Thu, to midnight Fri & Sat, 11am-8pm Sun) The Hotel Štrk's restaurant serves Prekmurje specialities such as roast suckling pig with noodles and indecently rich *prekmurska gibanica,* the local spiced pastry delight. There's a Sunday buffet and live music at weekends. Set lunches are a snip at €10 to €18.

Zvezda Pivnica　　　　　　　　　　PUB
(Star Pub; ☑ 02-539 15 73; www.hotel-zvezda.si; Trg Zmage 8; ⊙ 9.30am-10pm Sun-Thu, to 1am Fri & Sat; 🛜) This pub, with a large outdoor terrace in

WHITE STORKS

The white stork *(Ciconia cicconia)*, or *beli štrk* in Slovene, is Prekmurje's most beloved symbol. Country people consider it a sign of luck and honour for a pair to nest on their rooftop. The storks arrive in spring and spend the warm summer months here. Come mid-August, they migrate south on a 12,000km trek to sub-Saharan Africa for the winter, returning in the spring.

Storks build their nests on church steeples, rooftops or telephone poles. The nest is repaired every year and can weigh as much as 500kg. The birds live on a diet of worms, grasshoppers, frogs and small rodents. If food is scarce, however, it is not unknown for parents to turf their fledglings out of the nest.

Slovenia's stork population (around 350 breeding pairs) has grown over the past two decades. Nevertheless, the white stork remains a vulnerable species, primarily because its hunting and breeding grounds – the meadows – are being destroyed, dried out and regulated.

the centre of town, is Murska Sobota's main drinking hub. There's decent food here too.

ℹ Information

Nova Ljubljanska Banka (Trg Zmage 7; ⊘8.30am-5pm Mon-Fri)

Post Office (Trg Zmage 6; ⊘8am-6pm Mon-Fri, to noon Sat)

Tourist Information Centre Murska Sobota (TIC; ☑02-534 11 30; Slovenska ulica; ⊘9am-6pm Mon-Sat May-Oct, to 4pm Nov-Apr) Murska Sooata's TIC sits inside the town's restored, 100-year-old bank building and is a brilliant combo of cafe, shop selling local Prekmurje wine and food products and clued-up staff who'll fill you in on all there is to do in the region. While there, do have a glass of the local pear juice. It's delicious.

An ambitious tourist centre was being assembled on the outskirts of town at Soboška Lake on our last visit, and was due to open in late 2018. It will host interactive presentations on the Prekmurje region as well as a shop selling local products and a restaurant-cafe.

ℹ Getting There & Away

BUS

Murska Sobota's **bus station** (Zvezda ulica) has solid bus services to destinations within the Prekmurje and to towns further afield. Check the latest bus timetables on www.apms.si.

Dobrovnik (€2.70, 30 minutes) Eight buses daily on weekdays, none on weekends.

Maribor (€6, 1¼ hours) Eight buses daily on weekdays, three to four on weekends.

Moravske Toplice (€1.80, 15 minutes) Buses every 30 minutes in the morning, hourly in the afternoon on weekdays. None on weekends.

Radenci (€2.30, 15 minutes) At least hourly on weekdays, three to four services on weekends.

Ljubljana (€16, three hours) Two to five buses daily.

TRAIN

Murska Sobota has decent rail connections.

Ljubljana (€13 to €21, 2½ to 3½ hours, two to four direct services daily)

Maribor (€7.20 to €10.75, 1½ to two hours, three to six direct services daily)

For more services, transfer in Pragersko. All trains heading west go via Ptuj. From Murska Sobota, trains head east to Budapest (Hungary).

ℹ Getting Around

You can rent bikes from Hotel Štrk for €10 a day.

The town was setting up a bike-hire scheme (from €10) on our last visit. Enquire at the TIC.

Moravske Toplice

☑02 / POP 790 / ELEV 185M

The thermal spa of Moravske Toplice, 7km northeast of Murska Sobota, boasts the hottest water in Slovenia: 72°C at its source, but cooled to a body temperature of 38°C for use in its many pools and basins. Though it's one of the newest spas in the country – the spring was discovered in 1960 during exploratory oil drilling – many young Slovenes consider the clientele too old for their liking, preferring the small, partly *au naturel* spa at Banovci to the southwest. But Moravske Toplice is every bit a health resort geared for recreation, and the Terme 3000 thermal bath complex, with its water-park style facilities, makes a good pit stop if you're travelling with little ones in tow.

🏃 Activities

Terme 3000   THERMAL BATHS
(☑02-512 22 00; www.sava-hotels-resorts.com; Kranjčeva ulica 12; day pass adult/child €15.90/11.90; ⊘8am-9pm May-Sep, from 9am Oct-Apr) The recently fully renovated indoor

section (open year-round) of this complex has four pools split over two levels plus a sauna area, cafe and a wading pool for little ones. The outdoor section (open June to September) is geared towards family fun with seven pools and eight water slides, including the fourth fastest in Europe.

The thermal water here is recommended for relief of rheumatism and certain minor skin ailments.

🛏 Sleeping

The Terme 3000 complex dominates the accommodation scene. Outside the complex, there are a handful of family-run guesthouses with budget and midrange rooms. The TIC can also organise private rooms (per person from €20) and apartments (double €30 to €50).

Maj Inn GUESTHOUSE $
(☑ 070 137 635; www.majinn.si; Kranjčeva ulica 5; s/d/tr €35/40/55; ⓟ🛜) The well-maintained rooms at this central, family-run place are a great-value find. Rooms are simple but well-sized: bag one with a balcony if you can. There's a cafe-bar with a really nice communal terrace on the ground floor.

Hotel Livada Prestige HOTEL $$$
(☑ 02-512 22 00; www.sava-hotels-resorts.com; Kranjčeva ulica 12; r from €128; ⓟ🌀@🛜🏊) Moravske Toplice resort's flagship property is this 122-room behemoth with its own separate pool and spa complex. Rooms are rather outdated in style for the price, but all are spacious and come with balconies – plus most have the added option of using thermal water in your bath or shower. Check its website for package deals.

Eating

Gostilna Kuhar SLOVENIAN $$
(☑ 02-548 12 15; Kranjčeva ulica 13; mains €8-19.50; ⊗ 9am-11pm Tue-Sun) Set back from the road opposite the Terme 3000's main entrance, Gostilna Kuhar serves decent traditional Prekmurje dishes in a homey, simple interior and on a terrace festooned with geraniums.

Oaza Grill STEAK $$
(☑ 051 383 141; www.oaza-grill.com; Mljatinci 39; mains from €11; ⊗ noon-9pm Tue-Thu, to 10pm Fri & Sat, to 3pm Sun; ⓟ🛜) Worth the short drive out of town, this contemporary, upmarket restaurant overlooking a tiny lake in Mljatinci (just south of the pottery village Tešanovci and about 3km southeast of Moravske Toplice) serves up perfectly cooked steak.

ℹ Information

Nova Ljubljanska Banka (Kranjčeva ulica; ⊗ 8am-5pm Mon-Fri) Near the entrance to the Terme 3000 spa.

Post Office (Kranjčeva ulica 5; ⊗ 8am-6pm Mon-Fri, to noon Sat) On the main road.

Tourist Information Centre Moravske Toplice (TIC; ☑ 02-538 15 20; www.moravske-toplice.com; Kranjčeva ulica 3; ⊗ 8am-8pm Mon-Fri, 7am-3pm Sat, 8am-2pm Sun Jul & Aug, shorter hours Sep-Jun) On the main road northwest of the entrance to the Terme 3000 complex.

ℹ Getting There & Away

Buses leave from Kranjčeva ulica. Nearby destinations:

Dobrovnik (€2.30, 15 minutes) Approximately every hour.

Murska Sobota (€1.80, 15 minutes) Roughly every 30 minutes in the morning and hourly in the afternoon on weekdays.

Understand
Slovenia

Slovenia Today

Visitors often glide blissfully through a destination without knowing much about the inner workings of the country they're travelling through. In trying to grasp the essence of a place, though, it can help to feel like you have your finger on the pulse. Some big-picture topics Slovenes are discussing these days include the uncertain future of the country's politics, environmental sustainability, overtourism, and yes, the fact the food is getting better.

Best in Film

Ekspres, Ekspres (*Gone with the Train;* 1997) Surreal comedy on (and off) the rails.

Petelinji Zajtrk (*Rooster's Breakfast;* 2007) Bittersweet romance with lots of laughs.

Razredni Sovražnik (*Class Enemy;* 2013) Tragedy leads students to revolt against their teacher.

Ničija zemlja (*No Man's Land;* 2001) Bosnian war film, shot in Slovenia, won the Oscar for Best Foreign Picture.

Best in Print

Crumbs (Miha Mazzini; 1987) Slovenian anti-hero with a crazy obsession in the final days of Yugoslavia.

Yugoslavia, My Fatherland (Goran Vojnovič; 2015) Son discovers the secret legacy of his long-disappeared soldier father.

Forbidden Bread (Erica Johnson Debeljak; 2009) Young American follows her poet lover to his homeland just after independence.

Veronika Decides to Die (Paulo Coelho; 1989) More uplifting than the title suggests, Coelho's bestseller is set in Slovenia.

A Culinary Revival

Slovenia made culinary headlines in 2017 when 'The World's 50 Best Restaurants' recognised Ana Roš of Kobarid's Hišo Franko as the 'World's Best Female Chef'. Roš, who taught herself to cook, was hailed for reviving the use of locally grown produce in her recipes. A year later, the group recognised Hišo Franko itself as one of the world's 50 best places to eat.

Roš represents the tip of a nationwide trend towards using farm-fresh and locally sourced ingredients. Though a Slovenian restaurant is yet to win a Michelin star, the feeling is that it's just a matter of time.

Slovenes are also undergoing a revived interest in their own culinary heritage. Over the past decade Slovenia has succeeded in gaining protected status within the EU for several regional and national dishes, including in 2015 for the Carniolan sausage *(Kranjska klobasa)*. The trend has been underpinned by the Slovenian Tourist Board, which has launched a campaign to identify and support uniquely Slovenian dishes as part of the country's bid to win designation as a European Gastronomic Region in 2021.

Booming Tourism

The secret is out that Slovenia is a beautiful country and tourism is growing rapidly. The number of tourist arrivals in 2017 reached 4.7 million, a 13% increase from the previous year. The year 2018 was on track for another record.

The increase in tourist arrivals outpaced Europe as a whole, where tourism grew by around 8% in 2017, and exceeded Croatia, where the number of arrivals in 2017 increased by 12%. Though, admittedly, Slovenia is starting from a smaller base.

Most people head to Lake Bled, the coastal resorts and Ljubljana, and these areas can certainly feel very crowded during August. Comparatively, though, Slovenia is still below levels of overtourism seen in some other parts of Europe. The Slovenian Tourist Board is aware of the potential for overtoursim and officials say it intends to focus on promoting smaller-scale 'boutique tourism'. Visitors can avoid crowds by focusing on less high-profile parts of the country.

Keeping Things Sustainable

Slovenia is widely recognised for its pristine environment. Forests cover approximately 58% of the country's land mass, the air is clean and the drinking water is some of the purest in the world. In fact, in 2016 parliament added to the country's constitution its citizens' right to drinkable water.

In 2016 the European Commission awarded Ljubljana the title of European Green Capital in recognition of the pedestrianisation of much of the city centre, the promotion of environmentally friendly transport, such as cycling, and the provision of free drinking fountains to discourage people from buying bottled water.

Ljubljana also became the first EU capital to adopt a zero-waste strategy, which promotes recycling and aims to reduce the amount of waste sent to landfill sites and incinerators to zero. Under this plan, the capital, by 2025, promises to increase the percentage of waste that is separated from its current 60% to a target of over 75%. Other initiatives include promoting composting and encouraging more ecofriendly packaging.

Uncertain Political Times

To travellers not well versed in the ins and outs of Slovenian politics, such a well-run country must appear to be the epitome of consensus. A closer look, though, reveals a society going through a turbulent political period.

In March 2018 Prime Minister Miro Cerar resigned in protest after the country's high court ruled against a railway project he had supported. The resignation prompted early parliamentary elections, in June 2018, that revealed wide societal divisions. The right-leaning Slovenian Democratic Party (SDS), led by former two-time Prime Minister Janez Janša, won the most votes. He had run on a broadly anti-immigrant platform, promising supporters he would not allow a repeat of 2015 and 2016, when half a million refugees travelled through the country on their way north.

SDS, however, took just 25% of the vote, ending up short of the majority needed to form a government in the 90-seat National Assembly and presaging the possibility of a coalition government or yet another election. Eight other parties won parliamentary seats, though none received more than 13% support.

POPULATION: **2 MILLION**

AREA: **20,273 SQ KM**

GDP: **US$48.9 BILLION**

GDP GROWTH: **+5%**

INFLATION: **-0.1%**

UNEMPLOYMENT: **6.2%**

population per sq km

SLOVENIA ITALY UK

≈ 100 people

ethnic groups
(% of population)

83 — Slovenes

17 — Others

population per sq km

SLOVENIA ITALY UK

≈ 100 people

History

Slovenia is as old as the hills and yet as new as a few decades ago. Slovenia as a 'people' can trace its origins back at least a millennium and a half. But Slovenia as a nation-state is a much more recent entity; not until June 1991 did Slovenia arrive as an independent republic. Slovenia's story begins with the mass migration of Celts, but by the late 13th century the Habsburgs moved in and stayed for more than six centuries.

Early Inhabitants

The area of present-day Slovenia has been settled since the Palaeolithic Age. Stone implements that date back to 250,000 BC have been found in a cave near Orehek southwest of Postojna.

During the Bronze Age (roughly 2600 to 800 BC), marsh dwellers farmed and raised cattle in the Ljubljansko Barje – the marshland south of present-day Ljubljana – and at Lake Cerknica. They lived in round huts set on stilts and traded with other peoples along the so-called Amber Route linking the Balkans with Italy and northern Europe.

Around 700 BC the Ljubljana Marsh people were overwhelmed by Illyrian tribes from the south who brought with them iron tools and weapons. They settled largely in the southeast, built hilltop forts and reached their peak between 650 and 550 BC, during what is called the Hallstatt period.

Iron helmets, gold jewellery and *situlae* (embossed pails) with distinctive Hallstatt geometric motifs have been found in tombs near Stična and at Vače near Litija; you'll see some excellent examples of these findings at both the National Museum of Slovenia in Ljubljana and the Dolenjska Museum in Novo Mesto.

Around 400 BC, Celtic tribes from what are now France, Germany and the Czech Republic began pushing southward towards the Balkans. They mixed with the local population and established the Noric kingdom, the first 'state' on Slovenian soil.

A primitive bone flute discovered in 1995 in a cave at Divje Babe, near the town of Cerknica, dating back some 35,000 years, is thought to be the world's oldest known musical instrument. It takes pride of place at the National Museum of Slovenia in Ljubljana.

TIMELINE	2000–900 BC	400 BC	1st century AD
	Bronze Age settlers build wooden huts on stilts, farm, raise cattle and produce coarse pottery in the Ljubljana Barje, a marshy area south of present-day Ljubljana.	Continental Celtic tribes led by the Norics establish a kingdom called Noricum on Slovenian soil near the present-day city of Celje in Eastern Slovenia.	The Romans move into Slovenia from Italy and annex Noricum, marking the beginning of Roman occupation that would last for almost half a millennium.

THE TALE IN THE PAIL

Hallstatt is the name of a village in the Salzkammergut region of Austria where objects characteristic of the early Iron Age (from about 800 to 500 BC) were found in the 19th century. Today the term is used generically for the late Bronze and early Iron Age cultures that developed in Central and Western Europe from about 1200 to 450 BC.

Many regions of Slovenia were settled during this period, particularly the Krka Valley. Burial mounds – more than two dozen in Novo Mesto alone – have yielded swords, helmets, jewellery and especially *situlae* – pails (or buckets) that are often richly decorated with lifelike battle and hunting scenes. Hallstatt art is very geometric, and typical motifs include birds and figures arranged in pairs. The bronze vessel, Vače situla, in the National Museum of Slovenia in Ljubljana is a particularly fine example.

The Romans

In 181 BC the Romans established the colony of Aquileia (Oglej in Slovene) on the Gulf of Trieste in order to protect the empire from tribal incursions. Two centuries later they annexed the Celtic Noric kingdom and moved into the rest of Slovenia and Istria.

The Romans divided the area into the provinces of Noricum, Upper and Lower Pannonia and Histria, later called Illyrium, and built roads connecting their new military settlements. From these bases developed the important towns of Emona (Ljubljana), Celeia (Celje) and Poetovio (Ptuj), where reminders of the Roman presence can still be seen.

The Early Slavs

In the middle of the 5th century AD, the Huns, led by Attila, invaded Italy via Slovenia, attacking Poetovio, Celeia and Emona along the way. On their heels came the Germanic Ostrogoths and then the Langobards, who occupied much of Slovenian territory. The last major wave was made up of the early Slavs.

The ancestors of today's Slovenes arrived from the Carpathian Basin in the 6th century and settled in the Sava, Drava and Mura River valleys and the eastern Alps. In their original homelands, the early Slavs were a peaceful people, living in forests or along rivers and lakes, breeding cattle and farming by slash-and-burn methods.

From Duchy to Kingdom

In the early 7th century, the Alpine Slavs united under their leader, Duke Valuk, and joined forces with the Frankish kingdom. This tribal union became the Duchy of Carantania (Karantanija) – the first Slavic state,

Reminders of the Roman Presence

Citizen of Emona (Ljubljana)

Roman necropolis (Šempeter near Celje)

Mithraic shrines (outside Ptuj and Črnomelj)

Roman villa and preserved frescoes (Celje)

5th century	6th century	7th century	748
In about AD 450, the Huns, led by Attila, invade Italy via Slovenia, attacking the Roman settlements of Poetovio (Ptuj), Celeia (Celje) and Emona (Ljubljana) along the way.	Early Slavic tribes, divided into two distinct but related groups, the Slaveni and the Antes, settle in the valleys of the Sava, Drava and Mura Rivers and the eastern Alps.	A loose confederation of Slavic tribes establishes the Duchy of Carantania, the world's first Slavic political entity, and establishes its capital somewhere near Celovec (now Klagenfurt in Austria).	The Carolingian empire of the Franks incorporates Carantania as a vassal state called Carinthia; with the establishment of a formal church, the Christianisation of the Slovenes begins.

THE PATRIARCHATE OF AQUILEIA

You'd never guess from its present size (population 3370), but the Friulian town of Aquileia north of Grado, in modern-day Italy, played a pivotal role in Slovenian history, and for many centuries its bishops (or 'patriarchs') ruled much of Carniola, the area that includes today's Julian Alps region.

Founded as a Roman colony in the late 2nd century BC, Aquileia fell to a succession of tribes during the Great Migrations and had lost its political and economic importance by the end of the 6th century. But Aquileia had been made the metropolitan see for Venice, Istria and Carniola, and when the church declared some of Aquileia's teachings heretical, it broke from Rome. The schism lasted only a century, and when it was resolved Aquileia was recognised as a separate patriarchate.

Aquileia's ecclesiastical importance grew during the mission of Paulinus II to the Avars and Slovenes in the late 8th century, and it acquired feudal estates and extensive political privileges (including the right to mint coins) from the Frankish and later the German kings. It remained a feudal principality until 1420, when the Venetian Republic conquered Friuli, and Venetians were appointed patriarchs for the first time. Aquileia retained some of its holdings in Slovenia and elsewhere for the next 300 years. But the final blow came in 1751 when Pope Benedict XIV created the archbishoprics of Udine and Gorizia. The once powerful Patriarchate of Aquileia had outlasted its usefulness and was dissolved. The rich archaeological area and cathedral of Aquileia have been on the World Heritage List since 1998.

with its seat at Krn Castle (now Karnburg), near Klagenfurt in modern-day Austria.

Within a century, a new class of ennobled commoners called *kosezi* had emerged, and it was they who publicly elected and crowned the new *knez* (grand duke) on the *knežni kamen* ('duke's rock') in the courtyard of Krn Castle. Such a process was unique in the feudal Europe of the early Middle Ages.

In 748 the Frankish empire of the Carolingians incorporated Carantania as a vassal state called Carinthia and began converting the people to Christianity. By the early 9th century, religious authority on Slovenian territory was shared between Salzburg and the Patriarchate (or Bishopric) of Aquileia, now in Italy. The weakening Frankish authorities began replacing Slovenian nobles with German counts, reducing the local peasants to serfs. The German nobility was thus at the top of the feudal hierarchy for the first time in Slovenian lands. This would later become one of the chief obstacles to Slovenian national and cultural development.

With the total collapse of the Frankish state in the second half of the 9th century, a Carinthian prince named Kocelj established a short-lived (869–74) independent Slovenian 'kingdom' in Lower Pannonia, the area

Best Preserved Castles

Ljubljana Castle (Ljubljana)

Bled Castle (Bled)

Ptuj Castle (Ptuj)

Old Castle Celje (Celje)

Predjama Castle (near Postojna)

869–74	955	970	13th century
Carinthian Prince Kocelj rules a short-lived Slovenian 'kingdom' in Lower Pannonia, the area that stretches southeast from modern-day Austria to the Mura, Drava and Danube Rivers.	The marauding Magyars, who had invaded and settled in Slovenian Pannonia, are stopped in their tracks at a decisive battle at Augsburg by German King Otto I.	Appearance of the *Freising Manuscripts*, the earliest known text written in Slovene (or any Slavic language for that matter), which contain a sermon on sin and penance and instructions for general confession.	The first feudal holdings on Slovenian territory – the provinces of Carniola, Gorizia, Istria, Carinthia and Styria – fall under Habsburg control and remain in their hands until WWI.

stretching southeast from Styria to the Mura, Drava and Danube Rivers. But German King Otto I would soon bring this to an end after defeating the Magyars in the mid-10th century.

German Ascendancy

The Germans decided to re-establish Carinthia, dividing the area into a half-dozen border regions *(krajina)* or marches. These developed into the Slovenian provinces that would remain basically unchanged until 1918: Carniola (Kranjska), Carinthia (Koroška), Styria (Štajerska), Gorica (Goriška) and the so-called White March (Bela Krajina).

A drive for complete Germanisation of the Slovenian lands began in the 10th century. Land was divided between the nobility and various church dioceses, and the German gentry were settled on it. The population remained essentially Slovenian, however, and it was largely due to intensive educational and pastoral work by the clergy that the Slovenian identity was preserved.

From the 10th to the 13th centuries, most of Slovenia's castles were built and many important Christian monasteries – such as Stična and Kostanjevica – were established. Towns also began to develop as administrative, trade and social centres from the 11th century.

Early Habsburg Rule

In the early Middle Ages, the Habsburgs were just one of many German aristocratic families struggling for hegemony on Slovenian soil. Others, such as the Andechs, Spanheims and Žoneks (later the Counts of Celje), were equally powerful at various times. But as dynasties intermarried or died out, the Habsburgs consolidated their power. Between the late 13th century and the early 16th century, almost all the lands inhabited by Slovenes passed into Habsburg hands.

By this time Slovenian territory totalled about 24,000 sq km, approximately 15% larger than its present size. Not only did more towns and boroughs receive charters and rights, but the country began to develop economically, with the opening of ironworks at Kropa and mines at Idrija. This economic progress reduced the differences among the repressed peasants, and they united against their feudal lords.

Raids, Revolts & Reformation

Attacks by the Ottoman Turks on southeastern Europe in the early 15th century helped to radicalise landless peasants and labourers, who were required to raise their own defences *and* continue to pay tribute and work for their feudal lords. More than a hundred peasant uprisings and revolts occurred on Slovenian territory between the 14th and 19th centuries, but they reached their peak between 1478 and 1573. Together with

The early Magyars were such fierce fighters that a common Christian prayer during the Dark Ages was 'Save us, O Lord, from the arrows of the Hungarians'.

The proto-democratic process that elected the grand duke of Carantania at Krn Castle was noted by the 16th-century French political theorist Jean Bodin, whose work is said to have been a key reference for Thomas Jefferson when he wrote the American Declaration of Independence in 1775–76.

1408	1478–1573	1540–85	16th century
Ottoman Turks start their attacks on southeastern Europe, which will continue for over two centuries and bring them to the gates of Vienna several times.	Peasant-led riots are at their peak; along with the Protestant Reformation in the middle of the 16th century, they are considered a watershed of the Slovenian national awakening.	The first printed books appear in Slovene, including a catechism published by Primož Trubar, a complete translation of the Bible by Jurij Dalmatin, and a grammar of Slovene written in Latin.	The Catholic-led Counter-Reformation is in full swing throughout Slovenia; the systematic Germanisation of Slovenia's culture, education and administration begins under the Habsburgs.

the Protestant Reformation at the end of the 16th century, they are considered a watershed of the Slovenian national awakening.

The Protestant Reformation in Slovenia was closely associated with the nobility from 1540 onward and was generally ignored by the rural population except for those who lived or worked on lands owned by the church. But the effects of this great reform movement cannot be underestimated. It gave Slovenia its first books in the vernacular, thereby lifting the status of the language and thus affirming Slovenian culture.

Ivan Cankar's *Hlapec Jernej in Njegova Pravica* (The Bailiff Yerney and His Rights; 1907), a tale of the unequal relationship between servant and master, is read as a metaphor for Slovenia under Habsburg rule.

Habsburg Reforms & Napoleon

Reforms introduced by Habsburg Empress Maria Theresa (1740–80) included the establishment of a new state administration with a type of provincial government; the building of new roads; and the introduction of obligatory elementary school in German and state-controlled secondary schools. Her son, Joseph II (1780–90), went several steps further. He abolished serfdom in 1782, paving the way for the formation of a Slovenian bourgeoisie, and allowed complete religious freedom for Calvinists, Lutherans and Jews. He also made primary education in Slovene compulsory. As a result of these reforms, agricultural output improved, manufacturing intensified and there was a flowering of the arts and letters in Slovenia.

But the French Revolution of 1789 convinced the Austrians that reforms should be nipped in the bud, and a period of reaction began that continued until the Revolution of 1848. In the meantime, however, there was a brief interlude that would have a profound effect on Slovenia and its future. After defeating the Austrians at Wagram in 1809, Napoleon decided to cut the entire Habsburg Empire off from the Adriatic. To do this he created six 'Illyrian Provinces' from Slovenian and Croatian regions, and made Ljubljana their capital.

Although the Illyrian Provinces lasted only from 1809 to 1813, France instituted a number of reforms, including equality before the law and the use of Slovene in primary and lower secondary schools and in public offices. Most importantly, the progressive influence of the French Revolution brought the issue of national awakening to the Slovenian political arena for the first time.

Romantic Nationalism & the 1848 Revolution

The period of so-called Romantic Nationalism (1814–48), also known as the Vormärz (pre-March) period in reference to the revolution that broke out across much of Central Europe in March 1848, was one of intensive literary and cultural activity and led to the promulgation of the first

1782	1809	1821	1848
Habsburg Emperor Joseph II abolishes serfdom, paving the way for the growth of the Slovenian middle classes, and grants complete religious freedom to Calvinists, Lutherans and Jews.	Ljubljana is named the capital of the French-ruled Illyrian Provinces (1809–13), created by Napoleon from Slovenian and Croatian regions in a bid to cut the Habsburgs off from the Adriatic Sea.	Slovenia's capital makes it on the world-conference map when members of the Holy Alliance meet at the Congress of Laibach (Ljubljana) to discuss ways to suppress national movements in Italy.	Slovenian intellectuals issue a national political program called United Slovenia, which demands the unification of all historic Slovenian regions within an autonomous unit under the Austrian monarchy.

Slovenian political program. Although many influential writers published at this time, no one so dominated the period as the poet France Prešeren (1800–49). His bittersweet verse, progressive ideas, demands for political freedom and longings for the unity of all Slovenes caught the imagination of the nation then and it has never let it go.

In April 1848 Slovenian intellectuals drew up their first national political program under the banner Zedinjena Slovenija (United Slovenia). It called for the unification of all historic Slovenian regions within an autonomous unit under the Austrian monarchy, the use of Slovene in all schools and public offices, and the establishment of a local university. The demands were rejected, as they would have required the reorganisation of the empire along ethnic lines. Slovenes of the time were not contemplating total independence. Indeed, most looked upon the Habsburg Empire as a protective mantle for small nations against larger ones they considered predators like Italy, Germany and Serbia.

The only tangible results for Slovenes in the 1848 Austrian Constitution were that laws would henceforth be published in Slovene and that the Carniolan (and thus Slovenian) flag should be three horizontal stripes of white, blue and red. But the United Slovenia program would remain the basis of all Slovenian political demands up to 1918, and political-cultural clubs and reading circles began to appear all over the territory. Parties first appeared towards the end of the 19th century, and a new idea – a union with other Slavs to the south – was propounded from the 1860s onward.

The Kingdom of Serbs, Croats & Slovenes

With the defeat of Austria-Hungary in WWI and the subsequent dissolution of the Habsburg dynasty in 1918, Slovenes, Croats and Serbs banded together and declared the independent Kingdom of Serbs, Croats and Slovenes under Serbian King Peter I. Postwar peace treaties had given large amounts of Slovenian and Croatian territory to Italy, Austria and Hungary, and almost half a million Slovenes now lived outside the borders.

The kingdom was dominated by Serbian control, imperialistic pressure from Italy and the notion of Yugoslav unity. Slovenia was reduced to little more than a province in this centralist kingdom, although it did enjoy cultural and linguistic autonomy. Economic progress was rapid.

In 1929 Peter I's son Alexander seized power, abolished the constitution and proclaimed the Kingdom of Yugoslavia. But he was assassinated five years later during an official visit to France, and his cousin, Prince Paul, was named regent. The political climate changed in Slovenia when the conservative Clerical Party joined the new centralist government in 1935, proving that party's calls for Slovenian autonomy hollow. Splinter

1867	1918	1929	1937
A number of Slovenes are incorporated into Hungary with the Compromise of 1867, an agreement creating the Dual Monarchy of Austria (the empire) and Hungary (the kingdom).	Austria-Hungary loses WWI and the political system collapses with the armistice of 11 November; the Serbia-dominated Kingdom of Serbs, Croats and Slovenes is established.	King Alexander seizes absolute power, abolishes the constitution and proclaims the Kingdom of Yugoslavia; he is assassinated five years later by a Macedonian terrorist in France.	The Communist Party of Slovenia (KPS) is formed under the leadership of Josip Broz Tito and the Communist Party of Yugoslavia (KPJ).

groups began to seek closer contacts with the workers' movements; in 1937 the Communist Party of Slovenia (KPS) was formed under the leadership of Josip Broz Tito and the Communist Party of Yugoslavia (KPJ).

Josip Broz Tito (1892–1980) was born in Kumrovec, just over the southeastern border in Croatia, to a Slovenian mother and a Croatian father.

WWII & the Partisan Struggle

Yugoslavia's involvement in WWII began in April 1941 when the German army invaded and occupied the country. Slovenia was split up among Germany, Italy and Hungary. To counter this, the Slovenian communists and other left-wing groups formed a Liberation Front (Osvobodilne Fronte; OF), and the people took up arms for the first time since the peasant uprisings. The OF, dedicated to the principles of a united Slovenia in a Yugoslav republic, joined the all-Yugoslav Partisan army of the KPJ, which received assistance from the Allies and was the most organised – and successful – of any resistance movement during WWII.

After Italy capitulated in 1943, the anti-OF Slovenian Domobranci (Home Guards) were active in western Slovenia and, in a bid to prevent the communists from gaining political control in liberated areas, began supporting the Germans. Despite this assistance and the support of the fascist groups in Croatia and Serbia, the Germans were forced to evacuate Belgrade in 1944. Slovenia was not totally liberated until May 1945.

The following month, as many as 12,000 Domobranci and anti-communist civilians were sent back to Slovenia from refugee camps in Austria by the British. Most of them were executed by the communists over the next two months, their bodies thrown into the caves at Kočevski Rog.

Postwar Division & Socialist Yugoslavia

The status of the liberated areas along the Adriatic, especially Trieste, was Slovenia's greatest postwar concern. A peace treaty signed in Paris in 1947 put Trieste and its surrounds under Anglo-American administration (the so-called Zone A) and the areas around Koper and Buje (Istria) under Yugoslav control in Zone B. In 1954 Zone A (with both its Italian and ethnic Slovenian populations) became the Italian province of Trieste. Koper and a 47km-long stretch of coast later went to Slovenia while the bulk of Istria went to Croatia. The Belvedere Treaty (1955) guaranteed Austria its 1938 borders, including most of Koroška.

France Štiglic's 1955 film *Dolina Miru* (Valley of Peace) *is* the bittersweet story of an ethnic German boy and a Slovenian girl trying to find a haven during the tumult of WWII.

Tito had been elected head of the assembly, providing for a federal republic in November 1943. He moved quickly after the war to consolidate his power under the communist banner. Serbian domination from Belgrade continued, though, and in some respects was even more centralist than under the Kingdom of Yugoslavia.

Tito distanced himself from the Soviet Union as early as 1948, but isolation from the markets of the Soviet bloc forced him to court the West. Yugoslavia introduced features of a market economy, including workers'

1945	1948	1956	1980
Slovenia, occupied by the Germans in WWII, is liberated by the Partisans in May and 12,000 Domobranci and anti-communist civilians are executed; Slovenia is included in the Federal People's Republic of Yugoslavia.	Yugoslavia distances itself from – and then breaks with – the Soviet Union; exclusion from the markets of the Soviet bloc forces Tito to look to the West.	Tito, in association with India's first prime minister Jawaharlal Nehru and the president of Egypt Gamal Abdul Nasser, founds the Non-Aligned Movement.	Tito, his direct involvement in domestic policy and governing somewhat diminished, dies at age 87, opening the floodgates that lead to the dissolution of the federal republic in the next decade.

self-management. Economic reforms in the mid-1960s as well as relaxed police control and border controls brought greater prosperity and freedom of movement, but the Communist Party saw such democratisation as a threat to its power. What were to become known as the 'leaden years' in Yugoslavia lasted throughout the 1970s until Tito's death in 1980.

Crisis, Renewal & Change

In 1987 the Ljubljana-based magazine *Nova Revija* published an article outlining a new Slovenian national program, which included political pluralism, democracy, a market economy and independence, possibly within a Yugoslav confederation. The new liberal leader of the Slovenian communists, Milan Kučan, did not oppose the demands, and opposition parties began to emerge. But the de facto head of the central government in Belgrade, Serbian communist leader Slobodan Milošević, resolved to put pressure on Slovenia.

In June 1988 three Slovenian journalists working for the weekly *Mladina* (Youth) – including the former prime minister, Janez Janša – and a junior army officer who had given away 'military secrets' were tried by a military court and sentenced to prison. Mass demonstrations erupted throughout the country.

In the autumn Serbia unilaterally scrapped the autonomy of Kosovo (where 80% of the population is ethnically Albanian) granted by the 1974 constitution. Slovenes were shocked by the move, fearing the same could happen to them. A rally organised jointly by the Slovenian government and the opposition in Ljubljana early in the new year condemned the move.

In the spring of 1989 the new opposition parties published the May Declaration, demanding a sovereign state for Slovenes that was based on democracy and respect for human rights. In September the Slovenian parliament amended the constitution to legalise management of its own resources and peacetime command of the armed forces. Serbia announced plans to hold a 'meeting of truth' in Ljubljana on its intentions. When Slovenia banned it, Serbia and all the other republics except Croatia announced an economic boycott of Slovenia, cutting off 25% of its exports. In January 1990 Slovenian delegates walked out on a congress of the Communist Party.

Independence

In April 1990 Slovenia became the first Yugoslav republic to hold free elections. Demos, a coalition of seven opposition parties, won 55% of the vote, and Kučan, head of what was then called the Party of Democratic Renewal, was elected president. The Slovenian parliament adopted a declaration on the sovereignty of the state of Slovenia. Slovenia's own

Slovenia 1945: Memories of Death and Survival after World War II (2010), by John Corsellis and Marcus Ferrar, is the harrowing story of the forced return to Slovenia and execution of thousands of members of the anti-communist Domobranci after WWII.

1988	1989	1990	June 1991
The arrest of three journalists and a junior army officer for passing on 'military secrets' results in mass demonstrations; independent political parties are established for the first time in more than four decades.	The May Declaration calls for a sovereign state based on democracy and respect for human rights; parliament amends the constitution to manage its own resources and take command of the armed forces.	The Slovenian electorate overwhelmingly votes for an independent republic within six months; Belgrade brands the action secessionist and anti-constitutional and raids the state coffers of US$2 billion.	Slovenia quits the Yugoslav Federation; fighting erupts when the Yugoslav army marches on Slovenia and meets resistance; the war lasts 10 days and leaves 66 people dead.

constitution would direct its political, economic and judicial systems; federal laws would apply only if they were not in contradiction to it.

On 23 December 1990, 88.5% of the Slovenian electorate voted for an independent republic, effective within six months. The presidency of the Yugoslav Federation in Belgrade labelled the move 'secessionist' and 'anticonstitutional'. Serbia took control of the Yugoslav monetary system and misappropriated almost the entire monetary issue planned for Yugoslavia in 1991 – US$2 billion. Seeing the writing on the wall, the Slovenian government began stockpiling weapons, and on 25 June 1991 Slovenia pulled out of the Yugoslav Federation for good. 'This evening dreams are allowed', President Kučan told a jubilant crowd in Ljubljana's Kongresni trg the following evening. 'Tomorrow is a new day.'

Indeed it was. On 27 June the Yugoslav army began marching on Slovenia but met resistance from the Territorial Defence Forces, the police and the general population. Within several days, units of the federal army began disintegrating; Belgrade threatened aerial bombardment and Slovenia faced the prospect of total war.

The military action had not come totally unprovoked. To dramatise their bid for independence and to generate support from the West, which preferred to see Yugoslavia continue to exist in some form or another, Slovenian leaders attempted to take control of the border crossings first.

Neil Barnett's slim biography *Tito* (2006), an entertaining read, offers a frank assessment of the limits of holding a state like Yugoslavia together by sheer force of personality.

WAVING THE FLAG

Slovenia had to come up with a national flag and seal at rather short notice after independence and not everyone was happy with the results. Some citizens said the flag resembled a football banner, while others complained the seal was too close to that of neighbouring countries, such as Croatia.

Though the flag's colours – red, white and blue – were decided in 1848, the national seal, in the upper left corner of the flag, was a new design. In order to clear up any confusion, the government information office offered Slovenes and the world an explanation of what the seal means on two levels: the national and universal.

On a national level, the outline of Triglav above a wavy line was said to represent Slovenia's regional space, between the mountains to the north and west, the Adriatic Sea to the south and the plains of the former Pannonian Sea to the east. The three six-pointed stars of the Counts of Celje symbolise the cultural tradition of the Slovenian lands in relation to their inclusion in European history.

The universal explanation went like this: the symbol of a mountain with a water surface along the foothills represents the basic equilibrium of the world. On a human level it demonstrates the balance between men and women and, on a global level, the balance between civilisation and nature. The three gold stars above symbolise spiritual and ethical principles.

October 1991	1992	2004	2007
Keeping its promise it would withdraw the federal army from Slovenia within three months, Yugoslavia recalls the last of its soldiers from Slovenian territory.	The EC formally recognises independent Slovenia; Slovenia is admitted into the UN as the 176th member state; Serbia's and Montenegro's bid for admission as the Federal Republic of Yugoslavia is rejected.	Slovenia enters the EU as a full member along with nine other countries and becomes the first transition country to graduate from borrower status to donor partner at the World Bank.	Slovenia becomes the first of the 10 new EU states to adopt the euro, its fourth currency (Yugoslav dinar, tolar scrip, tolar) since independence.

SLOVENIA'S NATIONAL ANTHEM

The seventh stanza of France Prešeren's popular poem *Zdravljica* (A Toast) forms the lyrics of Slovenia's national anthem:

God's blessing on all nations,
Who long and work for that bright day,
When o'er earth's habitations
No war, no strife shall hold its sway;
Who long to see
That all men free
No more shall foes, but neighbours be.

Apparently Belgrade had never expected Slovenia to resist, believing that a show of force would be sufficient for it to back down.

As no territorial claims or minority issues were involved, the Yugoslav government agreed on 7 July to a truce brokered by leaders of the European Community (EC). Under the so-called Brioni Declaration, Slovenia would put further moves to assert its independence on hold for three months provided it was granted recognition by the EC after that time. The war had lasted just 10 days and took the lives of 66 people.

The Road to Europe

Belgrade withdrew the federal army from Slovenian soil on 25 October 1991, less than a month after Slovenia introduced its own new currency – the tolar. In late December, Slovenia got a new constitution that provided for a bicameral parliamentary system of government. The head of state, the president, is elected directly for a maximum of two five-year terms. Executive power is vested in the prime minister and his cabinet.

The EC formally recognised Slovenia in January 1992, and the country was admitted to the UN four months later as the 176th member state. In May 2004, Slovenia entered the EU as a full member and less than three years later adopted the euro, replacing the tolar as its national currency.

The 2nd edition of *Slovenia and the Slovenes: A Small State and the New Europe* (2010), by James Gow and Cathie Carmichael, offers excellent and independent analysis not just of history and politics but of culture and the arts as well.

2010	2012	2013	2018
The Slovenian parliament ratifies a border arbitration deal with Croatia that is vital for Zagreb's EU membership bid; Croatia becomes a member three years later.	Janez Janša resumes the premiership after 3½ years in opposition. His opponent, Borut Pahor, unseats President Danilo Türk in a landslide victory. Pahor is re-elected to a second term in 2017.	The coalition collapses over disputes about austerity measures and corruption allegations; Janša is sentenced to two years in prison for corruption but the conviction is overturned two years later.	Centre-left Prime Minister Miro Cerar resigns, prompting snap elections in June. The vote was won by former Prime Minister Janša's Democratic Party but left the party short of a majority to form a government.

Slovenian Way of Life

Slovenes are a sophisticated and well-educated people. They have a reputation for being sober-minded, hard-working, dependable and honest – perhaps a result of all those years under the yoke of the Austrian Habsburgs. But they very much retain their Slavic character, even if their spontaneity is sometimes a little more premeditated and their expressions of passion a little more muted than that of their Balkan neighbours. Think quietly conservative, self-confident, broad-minded and tolerant.

Lifestyle

Slovenia's population is divided exactly in half between those who live in towns and cities and those who live in the country. But in Slovenia, where most urban dwellers still have some connection with the countryside – be it a village house or a *zidanica,* a cottage in one of the wine-growing regions – the division is not all that great. And with the arrival of large malls on the outskirts of the biggest cities and a Mercator supermarket in virtually every village, the city has now come to the country.

Most Slovenes believe that the essence of their national character lies in nature's bounty. For them a life that is not in some way connected to the countryside is inconceivable. At weekends many seek the great outdoors for some walking in the hills or cross-country skiing. Or at least a spot of gardening, which is a favourite pastime.

It's not hard to reach deep countryside here. Forest, some of it virgin, and woodland covers more than 58% of the land area, the third-most forested country in the EU after Finland and Sweden. And the figure jumps to 66% if you include land reverting to natural vegetation and agricultural plots that have not been used for more than two decades. Land under agricultural use is rapidly diminishing and now accounts for less than a quarter of the total.

With farmstays a popular form of accommodation in Slovenia, it's relatively easy to take a peek inside a local home. What you'll find generally won't differ too much from what you'd see elsewhere in Central and Western Europe, though you may be surprised at the dearth of children. Slovenes don't have many kids – the nation has one of Europe's lowest rates of natural population increase and women usually give birth on the late side (the average age is almost 29). Most families tend to have just one child and if they have a second one it's usually almost a decade later. And the names of those kids? Luka and Filip for boys and Eva and Ema for girls.

Cleveland, Ohio, in the USA, is the largest 'Slovenian' city outside Slovenia; other American cities with large concentrations of ethnic Slovenes are Pittsburgh, Pennsylvania and Chicago, Illinois.

Population & Multiculturalism

According to national field-census figures, just over 83% of Slovenia's two million people claims to be ethnic Slovene, descendants of the South Slavs who settled in what is now Slovenia from the 6th century AD.

'Others' and 'undeclared', accounting for almost 17% of the population in national field-census figures, include ethnic Serbs, Croats, Bosnians, those who identify themselves simply as 'Muslims' and many citizens of former Yugoslav republics who 'lost' their nationality after independence for fear that Slovenia would not grant them citizenship.

The Italians (0.1% of the population) and Hungarians (0.3%) are considered indigenous minorities with rights protected under the constitution, and each group has a special deputy looking after their interests in parliament. Census figures put the number of Roma, mostly living in Prekmurje and Dolenjska, at about 3300, although unofficial estimates are double or even triple that number.

Ethnic Slovenes living outside the national borders number as many as 400,000, with the majority in the USA and Canada. In addition, 50,000 Slovenes live in the Italian regions of Gorizia (Gorica), Udine (Videm) and Trieste (Trst), another 15,000 or more in Austrian Carinthia (Kärnten in German, Koroška in Slovene) and about 5000 in southwest Hungary.

Slovenes are gifted polyglots, and almost everyone speaks some English, German and/or Italian. The fact that you will rarely have difficulty making yourself understood and will probably never 'need' Slovene shouldn't stop you from learning a few phrases of this rich and wonderful language, which counts as many as three dozen dialects and boasts not just singular and plural but the 'dual' number in which things are counted in twos (or pairs) in all cases. Any effort on your part to speak the local tongue will be rewarded 100-fold. *Srečno* (Good luck)!

An excellent guide to the culture and customs of Slovenia is *Culture Smart! Slovenia* by Canadian and long-term Ljubljana resident, Jason Blake.

Sport

Smučanje (skiing) remains the king of sports. The national heroes have been Primož Peterka, ski-jumping World Cup winner in the late 1990s, and extreme skier Davo Karničar, who has skied down the highest mountains in each of the seven continents, including the first uninterrupted descent of Mt Everest on skis in 2000.

More recent people to follow have been skier Tina Maze, the most successful female racer in Slovenian history. She won no fewer than two golds at the 2014 Winter Olympics at Sochi, Russia, following two silvers at the 2010 Winter Olympics in Vancouver. Peter Prevc, another household name, won a silver and a bronze at Sochi, which were the most successful Olympic games in Slovenian history.

Female skier Petra Majdič, in 2006, became the first Slovenian skier to win a medal in a World Cup cross-country race and went on to collect two dozen more.

Until not so long ago Slovenia was one of the few countries in Europe where football (soccer) was *not* a national passion. But interest in the sport increased after the national team's plucky performance in the 2000

For the latest on Union Olimpija and Slovenian basketball see the Eurobasket (www.eurobasket.com/Slovenia/basketball.asp) website.

SLOVENIA AT THE OLYMPICS

Slovenia occasionally punches above its weight when it comes to winning Olympic medals at the winter and even the summer games.

The 2014 Winter Olympics at Sochi, Russia, ended up being the most successful Olympic games in the country's history. In addition to Tina Maze's two golds, Slovenia bagged a total of eight medals and placed a remarkable 16th in the national medal standings. By contrast, the 2018 Winter Games at Pyeongchang, South Korea, were a relative disappointment. The country won just two medals, and slipped to 24th overall in the medal tables. The only bright spot was the national hockey team, which qualified for the playoff round, but did not win a medal.

In summer Olympic sports, Slovenia tends to excel at the smaller events. At the 2016 Summer Olympics at Rio de Janeiro, Brazil, Slovenian master Tina Trstenjak won gold in judo, repeating a team judo triumph at the London Olympics in 2012. Slovenia also tends to do well in rowing events.

SLOVENIA'S 'FIRST LADY'

With all the notable Slovenes over the years, it's perhaps ironic that arguably the best-known Slovene in the world right now is US First Lady Melania Trump. Born as Melanija Knavs on 26 April 1970 in the city of Novo Mesto in southeastern Slovenia, she spent some of her teenage years in the town of Sevnica, about 50km to the north, before attending university in Ljubljana and later pursuing a modelling career overseas.

The Slovenian Tourist Board has detected what it calls the 'Melania effect': her public profile has helped raise awareness of Slovenia in the USA, and has even prompted more than a few Americans to visit her homeland. However, travellers will find few overt references to the First Lady in Slovenia, even in places like Novo Mesto and Sevnica.

European Championship and in two of three matches at the 2010 World Cup in South Africa, its second appearance at a FIFA World Cup since independence. Slovenia, however, failed to qualify for both the 2014 and 2018 World Cup games.

There are 10 teams in the First Division (Prva Liga), with Maribor, Olimpija Ljubljana and Domžale consistently at the top of the league.

In general *kosarka* (basketball) is the most popular team sport here, and the Union Olimpija team reigns supreme. Other popular spectator sports are *odbojka* (volleyball) and *hokej na ledu* (ice hockey), especially since Anže Kopitar, perhaps the best-known Slovenian athlete in the world, helped the Los Angeles Kings of the US National Hockey League win two Stanley Cups, in 2012 and 2014.

Every third Slovene regularly takes part in some sort of active leisure pursuit; 3500 sport societies and clubs count a total membership of 400,000 – 20% of the population – across the nation.

Religion

Although Protestantism gained a strong foothold in Slovenia in the 16th century, the majority of Slovenes – just under 58% – identified themselves as Roman Catholic in the most recent demographic survey. The archbishop of Ljubljana and primate of Slovenia is Stane Zore.

Other religious communities in Slovenia include Muslims (2.4%), Orthodox Christians (2.3%) and Protestants (less than 1%). Most Protestants belong to the Evangelical (Lutheran) church based in Murska Sobota in Eastern Slovenia.

Jews have played a minor role in Slovenia since they were first banished from the territory in the 15th century. In 2003 the tiny Jewish community of Slovenia received a Torah at a newly equipped synagogue in Ljubljana – basically a room in an office block – the first since before WWII. The chief rabbi of Slovenia is based in Trieste.

Women in Slovenia

Women have equal status with men under Slovenian law but, despite all the work done to eliminate discrimination, bias remains. The share of women in government has improved in recent years: at present more than a third of all MPs are women but only a handful of government departments have a female at the helm. In business, well under half of directorial posts are filled by women.

The Arts

Slovenia is a highly cultured and educated society with a literacy rate of virtually 100% among those older than 15 years of age. Indeed, being able to read and write is so ingrained in the culture that the question 'What is your surname?' in Slovene is 'Kako se pišete?' or 'How do you write yourself?' Though few will be able to enjoy Slovenian literature in the original, music, fine art and film are all widespread and accessible.

Literature

The oldest example of written Slovene can be found in the so-called *Freising Manuscripts (Brižinski Spomeniki)* from around AD 970. They contain a sermon on sin and penance and instructions for general confession. Oral poetry, such as the seminal *Lepa Vida* (Fair Vida), a tale of longing and nostalgia, flourished throughout the Middle Ages, but it was the Reformation that saw the first book in Slovene, a catechism published by Primož Trubar in 1550. A complete translation of the Bible by Jurij Dalmatin followed in 1584. Almost everything else published until the late 18th century was in Latin or German, including an ambitious account of Slovenia, *The Glory of the Duchy of Carniola* (1689), by Janez Vajkard Valvasor (1641–93), from which comes most of our knowledge of Slovenian history, geography, culture and folklore before the 17th century.

The Enlightenment gave Slovenia its first dramatist (Anton Tomaž Linhart), poet (Valentin Vodnik) and modern grammarian (Jernej Kopitar). But it was during the so-called National Romantic Period that Slovenian literature gained its greatest poet of all time: France Prešeren.

The French novelist Charles Nodier (1780–1844), who lived and worked in Ljubljana from 1811 to 1813 during the so-called period of the Illyrian Provinces, described Slovenia as 'an Academy of Arts and Sciences' because of the people's flair for speaking foreign languages.

FRANCE PREŠEREN: A POET FOR THE NATION

Slovenia's most beloved poet was born in Vrba near Bled in 1800. Most of his working life was spent as an articled clerk in the office of a Ljubljana lawyer. By the time he had opened his own practice in Kranj in 1846, he was already a sick and dispirited man. He died three years later.

Although Prešeren published only one volume of poetry (*Poezije;* 1848) in his lifetime, he left behind a legacy of work printed in literary magazines. His verse set new standards for Slovenian poetry at a time when German was the literary *lingua franca,* and his lyric poems, such as the masterpiece *Sonetni Venec* (A Garland of Sonnets; 1834), are among the most sensitive and original works in Slovenian. In later poems, such as his epic *Krst pri Savici* (Baptism by the Savica Waterfall; 1836), he expressed a national consciousness that he tried to instil in his compatriots.

Prešeren's life was one of sorrow and disappointment. The sudden death of his close friend and mentor, the literary historian Matija Čop, in 1835 and an unrequited love affair with a young heiress called Julija Primic brought him close to suicide. But this was when he produced his best poems.

Prešeren was the first to demonstrate the full literary potential of the Slovenian language, and his body of verse – lyric poems, epics, satire, narrative verse – has inspired Slovenes at home and abroad for generations.

In the latter half of the 19th century, Fran Levstik (1831–87) brought the writing and interpretation of oral folk tales to new heights with his legends about the larger-than-life hero *Martin Krpan*, but it was Josip Jurčič (1844–81) who published the first novel in Slovene, *Deseti Brat* (The 10th Brother) in 1866.

Slovenia is the third-smallest literature market in Europe (a fiction 'best seller' means 500 to 800 copies sold) and in the EU only the Danes borrow more library books than the Slovenes; the annual average is 10 books per person.

Contemporary Literature

The first half of the 20th century was dominated by two men who singlehandedly introduced modernism into Slovenian literature: the poet Oton Župančič (1878–1949) and the novelist and playwright Ivan Cankar (1876–1918). The latter has been called 'the outstanding master of Slovenian prose' and works like his *Hlapec Jernej in Njegova Pravica* (The Bailiff Yerney and His Rights; 1907), influenced a generation of young writers.

Slovenian literature immediately before and after WWII was influenced by socialist realism and the Partisan struggle, as exemplified by the novels of Lovro Kuhar-Prežihov Voranc (1893–1950). Since then, however, Slovenia has tended to follow Western European trends: late expressionism, symbolism (poetry by Edvard Kocbek; 1904–81) and existentialism (novels by Vitomil Zupan; 1914–87, and the drama of Gregor Strniša; 1930–87).

The major figures of Slovenian postmodernism since 1980 have been the novelist Drago Jančar (1948–) and the poet Tomaž Šalamun (1941–2014), who has a street in Ptuj named after him. Important writers born around 1960 include the late poet Aleš Debeljak (1961–2016) and the writer Miha Mazzini (1961–), whose *Crumbs* (1987) was the best-ever selling novel in Yugoslavia; Mazzini now has several books published in English. The work of centenarian Boris Pahor (1913–), a member of the Slovenian minority in Trieste, including *Nekropola* (Pilgrim among the Shadows), focuses on the time he spent in a concentration camp at the end of WWII.

Young talent to watch out for today includes authors dealing with sensitive issues such as racism and relations with the former Yugloslav republics. The first novel by Andrej E Skubic (1967–), *Fužinski Bluz* (Fužine Blues; 2004), takes place on the day of the first football match between independent Slovenia and Yugoslavia. Goran Vojnovič (1980–) wrote a satire called *Čefurji Raus!* (2009), which is translated as *Southern Scum Out!* and refers to those from the other former Yugoslav republics living in Slovenia. Vojnovič followed this up in 2015 with the acclaimed *Yugoslavia, My Fatherland*.

One of the finest poets to emerge on the Slovenian literary scene in recent years is Katja Perat (1988–), whose *Najboljši So Padli* (The Best Have Fallen; 2011) won a best debut award.

Music

As elsewhere in Central and Eastern Europe, music – especially the classical variety – is important in Slovenia.

Romantic composers from the 19th century, such as Benjamin Ipavec, Fran Gerbič and Anton Foerster, incorporated traditional Slovenian elements into their music as a way of expressing their nationalism. But Slovenia's most celebrated composer from that time was Hugo Wolf (1860–1903), born in Slovenj Gradec and best known for his *lieder* (highly expressive art songs). Contemporary classical composers whose reputations go well beyond the borders of Slovenia include Primož Ramovš, Marjan Kozina, Lojze Lebič and the ultra modernist Vinko Globokar, who was born in France. Aldo Kumar has received awards for his theatre and film compositions; Milko Lazar is one of the more interesting composer-musicians to emerge in recent years.

FOLK MUSIC

Ljudska glasba (folk music) has developed independently from other forms of Slovenian music over the centuries. Traditional folk instruments include the *frajtonarica* (button accordion), *cimbalom* (a stringed instrument played with sticks), *bisernica* (lute), *zvegla* (wooden cross flute), *okarina* (clay flute), *šurle* (Istrian double flute), *trstenke* (reed pipes), Jew's harp, *lončeni bajs* (earthenware bass), *berdo* (contrabass) and *brač* (eight-string guitar).

Folk-music performances are usually local affairs and are very popular in Dolenjska and Bela Krajina. There's also been a modern folk-music revival in recent years. Listen for the groups Katice and Katalena, who play traditional Slovenian music with a modern twist. Nejc Pačnik is one of the greatest folk accordionists to emerge in the past decades.

Opera buffs won't want to miss out on the chance to hear Marjana Lipovšek and Argentina-born Bernarda Fink, the country's foremost mezzo-sopranos.

Popular music runs the gamut from Slovenian *chanson* as sung by the likes of Vita Mavrič and folk to jazz and mainstream polka, best exemplified by the Avsenik Brothers Ensemble, whose founder Slavko died in 2015. However, it was punk music in the late 1970s and early 1980s that put Slovenia on the world stage. The most celebrated groups were Pankrti, Borghesia and especially Laibach, and they were imitated throughout Eastern Europe. The most popular alternative rock band in Slovenia today remains Siddharta, still going strong after two decades.

Architecture

You'll encounter all styles of architecture – from Romanesque to post-modern – in Slovenia, but it is fair to say that for the most part you'll find baroque, with occasional bits of Gothic and flourishes of art nouveau thrown in to liven things up.

Examples of Romanesque architecture can be found in many parts of Slovenia and include the churches at Stična Abbey in Dolenjska and at Podsreda Castle in southeastern Slovenia.

Much of the Gothic architecture in Slovenia is of the late period; the earthquake of 1511 took care of many buildings erected before then (although both the Venetian Gothic Loggia and the Praetorian Palace in Koper date back a century earlier). Renaissance architecture is mostly limited to civil buildings (eg townhouses in Škofja Loka and Kranj, Brdo Castle near Kranj).

Italian-influenced baroque of the 17th and 18th centuries abounds in Slovenia, particularly in Ljubljana; very fine examples there include the Ursuline Church of the Holy Trinity and the Cathedral of St Nicholas. Classicism prevailed in architecture here in the first half of the 19th century; the Kazina building in Ljubljana's Kongresni trg and the Tempel pavilion in Rogaška Slatina are good examples.

The turn of the 20th century was when the Secessionist (or art nouveau) architects Maks Fabiani and Ivan Vurnik began changing the face of Ljubljana after the devastating earthquake of 1895. We can thank them for symmetrical Miklošičev Park, the Prešeren monument and the splendid Cooperative Bank on Miklošičeva cesta. The tourist information centre in Ljubljana distributes the excellent map-guide *Fabiania's Ljubljana*. But it's safe to say no architect had a greater impact on his city or nation than Jože Plečnik, a man whose work defies easy definition. You'll find most of his creations in Ljubljana, but be on the lookout for buildings like the Parish Church of the Ascension in far-flung Bogojina.

Architectural Guide to Ljubljana (2007), by Andrej Hrausky and Janez Koželj, is a richly illustrated guide to more than 100 buildings and other features in the capital, with much emphasis on architect extraordinaire Jože Plečnik.

SLAVOJ ŽIŽEK: THE WORLD'S BEST-KNOWN PHILOSOPHER

With Slovenia's cultural emphasis on the spoken word, it's not surprising that one of the world's best-known philosophers would end up being a Slovene.

Slavoj Žižek (1941–) was born in Ljubljana and spent his boyhood on the Adriatic. He's authored dozens of philosophical works, appeared regularly in mainstream literary journals like the *London Review of Books*, and starred in several films, including *The Pervert's Guide to Cinema* (2006) and *The Pervert's Guide to Ideology* (2012).

While Žižek cut his philosophical teeth in the neo-Marxism that was fashionable in the 1960s and '70s, today it's hard to pin him down on any hard-and-fast political or philosophical idea. He relishes more the role of the spoiler, staking out unpopular positions on issues and challenging his followers to rebut him.

One area in which he's been relatively consistent is his rejection of the political centre-left, which he accuses of not being radical enough. He famously praised US President Donald Trump in the run-up to the presidential election in 2016 as being preferable to Trump's challenger, Hillary Clinton.

Žižek is widely published in English and any decent bookshop will have an entire shelf of his works. Experts divide his titles between pop and serious philosophy, though none are considered boring.

Appreciation is growing for the country's postwar and Yugoslav-era architecture, which you'll find in abundance in Ljubljana's Center neighbourhood. Edvard Ravnikar's Trg Republike in Center has recently been improved with the removal of the car park from its forecourt. For a fascinating look at the ideas behind the planning of some of the capital's districts, get a copy of the free map-guide *Modernist Neighbourhoods of Ljubljana*.

Among the most interesting contemporary architects working today are the award-winning team of Rok Oman and Špela Videčnik, whose OFIS Architechts designed the Ljubljana City Museum (2004) and the Maribor football stadium (2009), and participated in building the landmark Cultural Centre of European Space Technologies (KSEVT) in Vitanje in 2012. In Ljubljana, Atelier Arhitekti designed the attractive (and useful) Butchers' Bridge (2010) and Fabiani Bridge (2012) over the Ljubljanica River while Vesna and Matej Vozlič have given new life to the riverfront Breg.

Painting & Sculpture

There are three dozen permanent art museums and galleries in Slovenia and hundreds more temporary exhibition spaces, which will give you a good idea of the role that the visual arts play in the lives of many Slovenes.

Examples of Romanesque fine art are rare in Slovenia, surviving only in illuminated manuscripts. Gothic painting and sculpture is another matter, however, with excellent works at Ptujska Gora (the carved altar in the Church of the Virgin Mary), Bohinj (frescoes in the Church of St John the Baptist) and Hrastovlje (*Dance of Death* wall painting at the Church of the Holy Trinity).

For baroque sculpture, look at Jožef Straub's epic plague pillar in Maribor and the work of Francesco Robba in Ljubljana (eg the Carniolan Rivers fountain now in the National Gallery). Fortunat Bergant, who painted the *Stations of the Cross* in the church at Stična Abbey, was a master of baroque painting.

The most important painters of the 19th century include the impressionists Rihard Jakopič, whose *Sunny Hillside* (1903) recalls Van Gogh, and Ivan Grohar, whose pointillist *The Sower* (1926) is recalled on the

€0.05 coin. In the 20th century, the expressionist school of Božidar Jakac and the brothers France and Tone Kralj put a uniquely Slovenian spin on what had previously been primarily a Germanic school. After the war, sculptors Alojzij Gangl, Franc Berneker, Jakob Savinšek and Lojze Dolinar dominated the art scene when art was being used as a great tool of communication and propaganda. The last two in particular would create 'masterpieces' of socialist realism under Tito without losing their credibility or (sometimes) their artistic sensibilities.

From the 1980s and onward postmodernist painting and sculpture has been dominated by the artists' cooperative Irwin, part of the wider multimedia group Neue Slowenische Kunst (NSK). Among notable names today are the artist Tadej Pogačar, sculptor Marjetica Potrč and video artists Marko Peljhan and Marina Gržinič.

Street Art & Squats

One of the most exciting emerging areas of visual arts is street art, which you'll find down alleyways and on building walls in cities around the country. In Ljubljana, two places to check out some of the best are the squats Metelkova Mesto and Tovarna Rog. The sheer visual anarchy, the colours and the designs represent a stark contrast to Jože Plečnik's restrained minimalism, so present around the rest of the capital.

Cinema

Slovenia was never on the cutting edge of filmmaking like some of the former Yugoslav republics (such as Croatia) and produces just five to seven feature films a year. However, it's still managed to produce award-winning films, such as Jože Gale's *Kekec* (1951), the story of a young heroic do-gooder in an idyllic Slovenian mountain village, and France Štiglic's *Dolina Miru* (Valley of Peace; 1955), the philosophical tale of two orphans on the lam in war-torn Yugoslavia.

What is now touted as the 'Spring of Slovenian Film' in the late 1990s was heralded by two films: *Ekspres, Ekspres* (Gone with the Train; 1997) by Igor Šterk, an award-winning 'railroad' film and farce, and *Autsajder* (Outsider; 1997), by Andrej Košak, about the love between a Slovenian girl and a Bosnian boy who doesn't fit in.

Subsequent successes included *Kruh in Mleko* (Bread and Milk; 2001), the tragic story of a dysfunctional small-town family by Jan Cvitkovič,

---

FAVOURITE FILMS OF NEJC GAZVODA

Sometimes it helps to consult an expert. Nejc Gazvoda (1985–) is a well-known Slovenian scriptwriter (he collaborated on Rok Biček's *Class Enemy*) and director, who these days has been dabbling successfully in Slovenian TV. Some of his top Slovenian films of all time:

➡ *Trenutki Odločitve* (Moments of Decision; 1955) by František Čap. Harrowing drama set in Slovenia during WWII.

➡ *Na Papirnatih Avionih* (On Paper Wings; 1967) by Matjaž Klopčič. Sad, funny, quirky romance about love and marriage.

➡ *Odgrobadogroba* (Grave Hopping; 2006) by Jan Cvitkovič: Story of a funeral reader, a dysfunctional family and some hard lessons learned.

➡ *Kratki Stiki* (Short Circuits; 2006) by Janez Lapajne. Series of poignant vignettes reveal the complexities of city life and human emotion.

Gazvoda also highly recommends any of the short films of Karpo Godina (1943–), a cinematographer and film director.

and Damjan Kozole's *Rezerni Deli* (Spare Parts; 2003) about the trafficking of illegal immigrants through Slovenia from Croatia to Italy by a couple of embittered misfits.

Lighter fare is Cvitkovič's *Odgrobadogroba* (*Grave Hopping;* 2006), an Oscar-nominated tragicomedy about a professional funeral speaker, and *Petelinji Zajtrk* (Rooster's Breakfast; 2007), a romance by Marko Naberšnik set in Gornja Radgona on the Austrian border in northeast Slovenia.

More recent productions are *Izlet* (A Trip; 2011), Nejc Gazvoda's low-budget road movie about lost friendship and youth, and the award-winning *Razredni Sovražnik* (Class Enemy; 2013) by Rok Biček about high-school students rebelling against their teacher. *Drevo* (The Tree; 2014) is a slow-moving but touching drama about a girl who loses her father and then starts to hear his whispers through the rustling of branches on the family tree.

Survival Guide

Directory A–Z

Accessible Travel

Slovenia is reasonably accessible for travellers with disabilities. Facilities include public telephones with amplifiers, pedestrian crossings with beepers, Braille on maps at bus stops, sloped pavements and ramps in government buildings, and reserved spaces in many car parks.

Bigger hotels will normally have at least one room designed for disabled guests (bathrooms big enough for a wheelchair user to turn around in, access door on bath tubs etc). Helpful organisations:

Paraplegics Association of Slovenia (Zveza Paraplegikov Republike Slovenije; ☏01-432 71 38; www.zveza-paraplegikov. si/eng; Štihova ulica 14, Ljubljana; ☺7am-3pm Mon-Fri) Produces a guide for members in Slovene only (although the English-language website is fairly complete).

Slovenian Association of Disabled Students (Društvo Študentov Invalidov Slovenije; ☏01-565 33 51; www.dsis-drustvo.si; Kardeljeva ploščad 5, Ljubljana; ☺9am-4pm Mon-Fri) Active group for those with special needs.

Download Lonely Planet's free Accessible Travel guides from http://lptravel.to/AccessibleTravel.

Accommodation

Slovenia has all manner of places to bed down. You'll need to book well in advance if you're travelling during peak season (July and August on the coast and at Bled or Bohinj; spring and autumn in Ljubljana). At other times, you'll have little trouble finding accommodation to fit your budget.

Many local TICs do double-duty as room-finding services and usually list available properties for rent on their websites. If the TIC is closed or the town doesn't have a tourist office and you have exhausted online options, try walking around and looking for signs like 'Sobe' or 'Apartma' or in German, 'Zimmer frei', which indicate the owners have a room available.

Hotels Runs the gamut between family-run operations to five-star boutiques.

Hostels Both indie hostels and HI-affiliated affairs are plentiful.

Pensions & Guesthouses Often family-owned and good value.

Private Rooms Single rooms or fully furnished flats. Locate via tourist information centres.

Mountain Huts Simple beds, with or without facilities, near hiking trails.

Camping

There's a *kamp* (campground) in virtually every corner of the country; seek out the Slovenian Tourist Board's *Camping in Slovenia* brochure. Some also rent inexpensive bungalows. Almost all sites close between mid-October and mid-April. Camping 'rough' is illegal in Slovenia.

Campgrounds generally charge per person. Prices vary according to the site and the season, but expect to pay anywhere from €10 to €20 per person (children are usually charged 20% to 50% of the adult fee). An overnight at one of Slovenia's luxurious 'glamping' spots will cost you considerably more. Many campgrounds offer discounts of 5% to 10% to holders of the Camping Card International (CCI; www.campingcardinterna tional.com).

Farmstays

Hundreds of working farms in Slovenia offer accommodation to paying guests, either in private rooms in the farmhouse itself or in alpine-style guesthouses. Many farms offer outdoor-sport activities and allow you to help out with the farm chores if you feel so inclined.

Expect to pay upwards from €20 per person in a room with a shared bathroom and breakfast (from €30 for half board) in the low season (September to mid-December and mid-January to June), rising in the high season (July and August) to a minimum of €25 per person (or from €40 for half board). Apartments for groups of up to eight people are also available.

Contact the **Association of Tourist Farms of Slovenia** (Združenje Turističnih Kmetij Slovenije; ☑03-491 64 80; www.farmtourism.si; Trnoveljska cesta 1, Celje) or check out the Slovenian Tourist Board's excellent *Farm Stays in Slovenia* brochure, which lists upwards of 185 farms with accommodation.

Holiday Apartments

Some agencies and tourist offices also have holiday apartments available that can accommodate up to six people. One for two/four people could go for as low as €50/70.

Hostels & Student Dormitories

Slovenia has a growing stable of excellent private hostels, including several in Ljubljana and Bled and other places that are popular with visitors. Expect the usual perks at these hostels, including free wi-fi, laundry facilities, lockers and the possibility of purchasing breakfast. Some have shared kitchens where you can prepare you own meals.

In addition to private hostels, throughout the country there are more-modest but usually cheaper *dijaški dom* (college dormitories) or *študentski dom* (student residences), moonlighting as hostels for visitors in July and August. Unless stated otherwise, hostel rooms share bathrooms.

Hostels usually cost €16 to €25 for a bed; prices are at their highest in July and August and during the Christmas break.

Hotels

Most visitors to Slovenia usually stay in standard hotels. Hotels cover the spectrum from midrange to top end, though at a minimum all are clean and well maintained whatever the room price.

Rates vary depending on the location and amenities. Cheaper rooms may have shared facilities. Breakfast is usually, though not always, included in the room rate. Check the booking details to make sure. Air-conditioning may not be available at cheaper places.

Slovenia's hotel rates vary seasonally, with July and August the peak season and September/October and May/June the shoulders. Ski resorts such as Kranjska Gora and Maribor Pohorje also have a peak season from December to March. In Ljubljana, prices are generally constant throughout the year, though weekends are often cheaper at top-end hotels.

Mountain Huts

The **Alpine Association of Slovenia** (PZS; ☑01-434 56 80; www.pzs.si; Ob železnici 30a, Ljubljana; ⊙9am-3pm Mon & Thu, to 5pm Wed, to 1pm Fri) maintains around 180 mountain huts throughout the country and these are ranked according to category. A hut is Category I if it is at a height of over 1000m and is more than one hour from motorised transport. A Category II hut is within one hour's walking distance from motorised transport. A Category III hut can be reached by car or cable car directly. It's important to book in advance, particularly from June to September.

A bed for the night runs from €21 to €27 in a Category I hut, depending on the number of beds in the room, and from €16 to €22 in a Category II hut. Category III huts are allowed to set their own prices but often cost less than Category I huts.

Pensions & Guesthouses

Pensions and guesthouses go by several names in Slovenia. A *penzion* is, of course, a pension, but more commonly it's called a

gostišče – a rustic restaurant with *prenočišče* (accommodation) attached. Generally speaking, a *gostilna* serves food and drink only, but some might have rooms as well. The distinction between a *gostilna* and a *gostišče* isn't very clear – even to most Slovenes.

Pensions represent good value. They are usually more expensive than hostels but cheaper than hotels, and might be your only option in small towns and villages.

Private Rooms & Apartments

You'll find private rooms and apartments through tourist offices and travel agencies in most towns. The Slovenian Tourist Board (www.slovenia.info) website provides photos and the location of the house along with rates.

You don't have to go through agencies or tourist offices; any house with a sign reading 'Sobe' or, in German, 'Zimmer frei' means that rooms are available. Depending on the season, you might save yourself a little money by going direct.

In Slovenia, *registered* private rooms and apartments are rated from one to four stars.

Prices vary greatly according to the town and season, but typical rates cost around €20 to €40 for a single and €40 to €60 for a double. The price quoted is often for a minimum stay of three nights. If you're staying a shorter time, you'll have to pay 30% and sometimes as much as 50% more the first night and 20% to 30% extra the second. The price usually does not include breakfast (from €5 to €8 when available) or tourist tax.

Bargaining

Gentle haggling is common at flea markets; in all other instances you're expected to pay the stated price.

Customs Regulations

Goods brought in and out of countries within the EU incur no additional taxes, provided duty has been paid somewhere within the EU and the goods are for personal use. Duty-free shopping is only available if you're leaving the EU.

Duty-free allowances (for anyone aged over 17) arriving from non-EU countries:

➡ 200 cigarettes or 100 cigarillos or 50 cigars or 250g of loose tobacco or a proportional combination of these goods.

➡ 1L of strong liquor or 2L of less than 22% alcohol by volume, plus 4L of wine, plus 16L of beer.

➡ Other goods up to the value of €300 if arriving by land, or €430 if arriving by sea or air (€175 if aged under 15).

Discount Cards

The **Ljubljana Card** (www. visitljubljana.com/en/ljubljana-card; per 24/48/72hr adult €27/34/39, child aged 6-14 €16/20/23), available from the Tourist Information Centre (TIC) for 24/48/72 hours, offers free admission to 19 attractions, walking and boat tours, unlimited travel on city buses and internet access.

Camping Card International

➡ The Camping Card International (www. campingcardinternational. com) is available free from local automobile clubs, local camping federations such as the UK's Caravan Club (www. caravanclub.co.uk), and sometimes on the spot at selected campgrounds.

➡ It incorporates third-party insurance for damage you may cause, and many campgrounds in Slovenia offer discounts of 5% or 10% if you sign in with one.

Hostel Card

No hostel in Slovenia requires you to be a HI cardholder or a member of a related association, but they sometimes offer a discount if you are.

Hostelling International Slovenia (Popotniško Združenje Slovenije; ☎02-234 21 37; www.youth-hostel.si; Gosposvetska cesta 84, Maribor) Maribor-based organisation representing Slovenia in Hostelling International. Maintains an online database of member hostels in Slovenia.

Student, Youth & Teacher Cards

➡ The International Student Identity Card (€12.20; www. isic.org) provides bona fide students with many discounts on certain forms of transport and cheap admission to museums and other sights.

➡ If you're aged under 31 but not a student, you can apply for ISIC's International Youth Travel Card (IYTC; €12.50) or the Euro<26 card (€19) issued by the European Youth Card Association (EYCA; www.eyca.org), both of which offer the same discounts as the student card.

Electricity

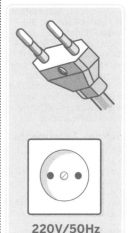

220V/50Hz

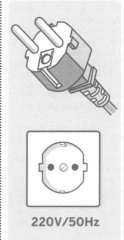

220V/50Hz

Embassies & Consulates

Foreign embassies and consulates are located in Ljubljana.

Australian Consulate (☎01-234 86 75; http://dfat.gov. au/about-us/our-locations/ missions/Pages/australian-consulate-in-ljubljana-slovenia. aspx; Železna cesta 14; ⊗by appointment)

Canadian Consulate (☑01-252 44 44; www.canadainternat ional.gc.ca/hungary-hongrie/ offices-bureaux/consulate_con sulat_.aspx?lang=eng; Linhartova cesta 49a; ⊗8am-noon Mon, Wed & Fri)

French Embassy (☑01-479 04 00; https://si.ambafrance.org; Barjanska cesta 1; ⊗8.30am-12.30pm Mon-Fri)

German Embassy (☑01-479 03 00; www.laibach.diplo.de; Prešernova cesta 27; ⊗9am-noon Mon-Thu, to 11am Fri)

Irish Embassy (☑01-300 89 70; www.dfa.ie/irish-embassy/slovenia; 1st fl, Palača Kapitelj, Poljanski nasip 6; ⊗9.30am-12.30pm & 2.30-4pm Mon-Fri)

Netherlands Embassy (☑01-420 14 60; www.netherlands andyou.nl/your-country-and-the-netherlands/slovenia/about-us/embassy-in-ljubljana; 1st fl, Palača Kapitelj, Poljanski nasip 6; ⊗9am-4.30pm Mon-Fri by appointment only)

New Zealand Consulate (☑01-200 93 37, Austria 43-1 505 3021; www.mfat.govt.nz; Dunajska cesta 199; ⊗8am-3pm Mon-Fri) Honorary consulate.

South African Consulate (☑01-241 77 00; www.dirco.gov.za; Nazorjeva ulica 6; ⊗by appointment) Honorary consulate.

UK Embassy (☑01-200 39 10; www.gov.uk/world/organisa tions/british-embassy-ljub ljana/office/british-embassy; 4th fl, Trg Republike 3; ⊗8am-4pm Mon-Fri, consular services by appointment)

US Embassy (☑01-200 55 00; https://si.usembassy.gov; Prešernova cesta 31; ⊗by appointment 9-11.30am Mon & Wed)

Emergencies

Slovenia's Country Code	☑386
Domestic Directory Assistance	☑1188
Ambulance & Fire	☑112
Police	☑113 (emergencies)
Road Emergency or towing	☑1987

Food

Slovenia has a highly developed and varied cuisine and a winemaking tradition that goes back to the time of the Romans. For more information, see Eat & Drink Like a Local, p33.

Health

There are no specific health concerns for travelling in Slovenia.

Availability & Cost of Health Care

Medical care in Slovenia corresponds to European standards and is generally good. Treatment at a public outpatient clinic is reasonable; doctors working privately will charge from €50 per consultation.

Medical Services

Every large town or city has a *zdravstveni dom* (health centre) or a *klinični center* (clinic) that operates from 7am to at least 7pm.

Pharmacies are usually open from 7.30am to 7.30pm or 8pm Monday to Friday, and at least one in each community is open round the clock. A sign on the door of any *lekarna* (pharmacy) will help you find the nearest 24-hour one.

Health Insurance

EU citizens are generally covered by reciprocal arrangements in Slovenia. They should carry their European Health Insurance Card. Other nationals are entitled to emergency medical treatment but must pay for it.

If you do need health insurance while travelling, we advise a policy that covers you for the worst possible scenario, such as an accident requiring an ambulance or an emergency flight home.

Health Insurance Institute of Slovenia (www.zzzs.si) Provides extensive information on healthcare providers and insurance options if you do happen to fall ill on your trip.

Environmental Hazards

Tick-borne encephalitis (TBE) Spread through tick bites, encephalitis has become a common problem. It is a serious infection of the brain, and vaccination is advised for campers and hikers who intend to stay in the woods for prolonged periods between May and September. For up-to-date information, visit www.masta-travel-health.com.

Lyme disease Another tick-transmitted infection not unknown in the region. The illness usually begins with a spreading rash at the site of the tick bite and is accompanied by fever, headaches, extreme fatigue, aching joints and muscles and mild neck stiffness. If untreated, these symptoms usually resolve over several weeks, but over subsequent weeks or months disorders of the nervous system, heart and joints might develop.

Mosquitoes These can be an annoyance, especially around lakes and ponds in the warmer months. Mosquitoes do not carry malaria, but can still cause irritation. Make sure you're armed with a good insect repellent and wear long-sleeved shirts and trousers around dusk in infested areas.

Water

Tap water is safe everywhere in Slovenia. If you are hiking or camping in the mountains and are unsure about the water, the simplest way to purify water is to boil it for 10 minutes.

EATING PRICE RANGES

The following price ranges refer to a two-course, sit-down meal, including a drink, for one person. Many restaurants also offer an excellent-value set menu of two or even three courses at lunch.

€ less than €15

€€ €15–30

€€€ more than €30

Insurance

➡ A travel insurance policy to cover theft, loss and medical treatment is a good idea. There is a wide variety of policies available, so check the small print. EU citizens on public health insurance schemes should note that they're usually covered by reciprocal arrangements in Slovenia.

➡ Some insurance policies specifically exclude 'dangerous activities', which can include motorcycling and even trekking, so check the small print.

➡ You may prefer a policy that pays doctors or hospitals directly rather than you having to pay on the spot

and claim later. If you have to claim later, make sure you keep all documentation. Some policies ask you to call back (reverse charges) to a centre in your home country, where an immediate assessment of your problem can be made. Check that the policy covers ambulances or an emergency flight home.

➡ Paying for your airline ticket with a credit card sometimes provides limited travel accident insurance, and you may be able to reclaim the payment if the operator doesn't deliver. Ask your credit-card company what it will cover.

➡ Worldwide travel insurance is available at www.lonelyplanet.com/travel-insurance. You can buy, extend and claim online anytime – even if you're already on the road.

Internet Access

Nearly every hotel and hostel will offer free wi-fi, and some still maintain a public computer on hand for guests' use. Most of the country's TICs offer free (or inexpensive) access; many libraries in Slovenia have free terminals; and many cities and towns have free wi-fi in the centre, including Ljubljana.

Language Courses

Centre for Slovene as a Second/Foreign Language (Center za Slovenščino kot Drugi/Tuji Jezik; Map p54;☑01-241 86 47; www.centerslo.net; Kongresni trg 12, Ljubljana; ◉9-11am & 2-3pm Mon-Fri) Full palette of Slovenian-language courses suited to short-term visitors or serious study. It holds a free 90-minute survival course in Slovenian every Wednesday from 5pm to 6.30pm at the Slovenian Tourist Information Centre.

Mint International House Ljubljana (☑01-300 43 00; www.mint.si; Vilharjeva cesta 21, Ljubljana) Reputable private school offering courses in Slovene.

Legal Matters

Persons violating the laws of Slovenia may be expelled, arrested or imprisoned. Penalties for possession, use or trafficking of illegal drugs in Slovenia are strict, and convicted offenders can expect heavy fines and even jail terms. The permitted blood-alcohol level for motorists is 0.05%, and it is strictly enforced, especially on motorways. Fines start at €300.

Alcohol may not be purchased from a shop, off-licence or bar for consumption off the premises between 9pm and 7am.

PRACTICALITIES

Weights & Measures The metric system is used.

Smoking Forbidden in all enclosed public spaces. Most pubs will have a smoking area outside. Vaping is legal, though banned in public indoor spaces.

Newspapers *Slovenia Times* (www.sloveniatimes.com) is a comprehensive English-language online newspaper.

Magazines *Sinfo* (www.ukom.gov.si) is a government-produced monthly e-mag about Slovenian politics, environment, culture, business and sport.

Radio Radio Slovenija broadcasts English news and weather updates throughout the day on various frequencies. Visit the RTV Slovenija (www.rtvslo.si) website.

TV The public broadcaster, RTV Slovenija, has three main channels; there are dozens of private broadcasters. English-language channels like CNN International and BBC are widely available.

CLAIMING TAX REFUNDS

Visitors who reside outside the EU can claim VAT refunds on total purchases of over €50 (not including tobacco products or spirits) as long as they take the goods out of the country (and the EU) within three months.

To smooth the process, inform the salesperson at the time of purchase that you intend to export the goods. To make the claim, the corresponding DDV-VP form must be correctly filled out. Retain the form and have it stamped by a Slovenian customs officer when you leave the country at the border (or airport).

You can collect your refund – minus a handling fee – from selected offices or have it deposited into your credit-card account. For more information see the Global Blue (www.globalblue.com) website.

LGBT+ Travellers

Slovenia has a national gay-rights law in place that bans discrimination on the basis of sexual preference in employment and other areas, including the military. In recent years, a highly visible campaign against homophobia has been put in place across the country, and same-sex marriage is allowed.

Ljubljana is the centre of gay life in Slovenia and is considered a reasonably tolerant city. Outside Ljubljana, there is little evidence of a gay presence, much less a lifestyle.

Several organisations are active in promoting gay rights and fostering cultural and social interaction. Foremost among these are ŠKUC (Študentski Kulturni Center, Student Cultural Centre; www.skuc.org) and **Legebitra** (☑01-430 51 44; https://legebitra.si; Trubarjeva cesta 76a, Ljubljana; ⏰noon-4pm Mon, to 6pm Tue & Fri, to 9pm Wed & Thu). Other sources of information:

➡ The Slovenian Queer Resources Directory (www.ljudmila.org/siqrd) contains a lot of info, both serious and recreational, but is in Slovene only.

➡ Out in Slovenia (www.outinslovenija.com), the first sports and recreational group for gays and lesbians in Slovenia, is where to go for the latest on outdoor activities and events.

Money

➡ One euro is divided into 100 cents. There are seven euro notes, in denominations of €5, €10, €20, €50, €100, €200 and €500.

➡ The eight euro coins in circulation are in denominations of €1 and €2, then one, two, five, 10, 20 and 50 cents.

➡ In practice, you may have trouble using large denominations over €50 for smaller purchases.

ATMs

ATMs – called *bančni avtomat* – are ubiquitous throughout Slovenia. If you have a card linked to either the Visa/Electron/Plus or the MasterCard/Maestro/Cirrus network and a pin code, you can withdraw euros anywhere.

Credit Cards

Credit cards, especially Visa, MasterCard and American Express, are widely accepted, and you'll be able to use them at restaurants, shops, hotels, car-rental firms, travel agencies and petrol stations.

Moneychangers

➡ Exchange your home currency for euros at banks, post offices, tourist offices, travel agencies and private exchange offices.

➡ Look for the words *menjalnica* or *devizna blagajna* to guide you to the correct place or window.

➡ Most banks take a *provizija* (commission) of 1%. Tourist offices, travel agencies and exchange bureaus usually charge around 3%.

Taxes & Refunds

Value-added tax (VAT) is a sales tax applied on the purchase of most goods and services. The standard rate is 22%, with a reduced rate of 9.5% on select items, such as accommodation, food, books and museum entrance fees. VAT will almost always be included in the price.

Tipping

Hotels Gratuity for cleaning staff completely at your discretion.

Pubs Not expected unless table service is provided.

Restaurants For decent service 10%.

Taxis Round up the fare to the nearest euro.

Opening Hours

Opening hours can vary throughout the year. We've provided high-season opening hours.

Banks 8.30am–12.30pm and 2pm–5pm Monday to Friday

Bars 11am–midnight Sunday to Thursday, to 1am or 2am Friday and Saturday

Restaurants 11am–10pm daily

Shops 8am–7pm Monday to Friday, to 1pm Saturday

Post

➡ The Slovenian postal system (Pošta Slovenije) offers a wide variety of services – from selling stamps and telephone cards to making photocopies and changing money.

➡ Newsstands also sell *znamke* (stamps).

➡ Many post offices have limited opening hours on Saturday.

➡ Find up-to-date postal rates on the postal service website: www.posta.si.

Public Holidays

Slovenia celebrates 14 *prazniki* (holidays) each year. If any of them fall on a Sunday, the Monday becomes the holiday.

New Year's holidays 1 and 2 January

Prešeren Day (Slovenian Culture Day) 8 February

Easter & Easter Monday March/April

Insurrection Day 27 April

Labour Day holidays 1 and 2 May

National Day 25 June

Assumption Day 15 August

Reformation Day 31 October

All Saints' Day 1 November

Christmas Day 25 December

Independence Day 26 December

Safe Travel

Slovenia is a safe country. The vast majority of crimes reported involve theft, so take the usual precautions.

➡ Be careful of your purse or wallet in busy areas like bus and train stations, and don't leave either unattended on the beach, or in a hut while hiking.

➡ Lock your car, park in well-lit areas and do not leave valuables visible.

➡ Bicycle theft is on the increase. Secure your bike at all times (or, even better, bring it indoors).

Telephone

Slovenia's country code is ☎386. Slovenia has six area codes (☎01 to ☎05 and ☎07). Ljubljana's area code is ☎01.

➡ To call a landline within Slovenia, dial the telephone number. Include the area code if the number you are calling is outside the area code.

➡ To call abroad from Slovenia, dial ☎00 followed by the country and area codes and then the number.

➡ To call Slovenia from abroad, dial the international access code, ☎386 (the country code for Slovenia), the area code (minus the initial zero) and the number.

Mobile Phones

Local SIM cards can be used in European, Australian and some American phones. Other phones must be set to roaming to work, but be wary of roaming charges.

Slovenia has several mobile carriers. All offer cheap, prepaid SIM cards. The three largest carriers are:

Simobil (☎040 929 301; www.simobil.si; Prešernov trg 2, Ljubljana; ◷8am-7pm Mon-Fri, 9am-1pm Sat)

Telekom Slovenija (☎01-472 24 60; www.telekom.si/en; Trg Ajdovščina 1, Ljubljana; ◷8am-7pm Mon-Fri, to 1pm Sat)

ADDRESSES & PLACE NAMES

Streets in Slovenian towns and cities are well signposted, although the numbering system can be confusing, with odd and even numbers sometimes running on the same sides of streets and squares.

In small towns and villages, streets are often unnamed, with houses simply numbered. Thus Ribčev Laz 13 is house No 13 in the village of Ribčev Laz on Lake Bohinj. As Slovenian villages are frequently made up of one road with houses clustered on or just off it, this is seldom confusing.

In Slovene, places with double-barrelled names such as Novo Mesto (New Town) and Črna Gora (Black Hill) start the second word in lower case (Novo mesto, Črna gora), almost as if the names were Newtown and Blackhill. This is the correct Slovene orthography, but we've opted to go with the English-language way of doing it to avoid confusion.

Slovene frequently uses the possessive (genitive) case in street names. Thus a road named after the poet Ivan Cankar is Cankarjeva ulica and a square honouring France Prešeren is Prešernov trg. Also, when nouns are turned into adjectives they often become unrecognisable. The town is 'Bled', for example, but 'Bled Lake' is Blejsko Jezero. A street leading to a castle (*grad*) is usually called Grajska ulica. A road going in the direction of Trieste (Trst) is Tržaška cesta, Klagenfurt (Celovec) is Celovška cesta and Vienna (Dunaj) is Dunajska cesta. The words *pri, pod* and *na* in place names mean 'at the', 'below the', and 'on the' respectively.

PRACTISING GOOD ETIQUETTE

Greetings On initial meeting, greet strangers with a firm handshake and maintain eye contact as you say hello. In a formal situation, don't address a person by his or her first name without asking permission.

Dinner parties If you're invited to someone's home for dinner, bring flowers or a good bottle of wine for the host.

Shoes Slovenes don't usually wear shoes inside the home; if you're visiting someone's home, offer to remove your shoes at the door.

Toasting The Slovene expression for 'Cheers!' is *Na zdravje!* (literally, 'To your health').

Telemach (☑080 22 88; https://telemach.si; Mestni trg 23, Ljubljana; ◷9am-7pm Mon-Fri, 8am-1pm Sat)

➔ Mobile numbers carry special three-digit prefixes, including 030, 031, 040, 041, 051, 070, 071 and 080. These numbers correspond, in some cases, to different mobile operators.

Time

Central European Time (GMT/UTC plus one hour)
Daylight saving time kicks in at 2am on the last Sunday in March and ends on the last Sunday in October.

City	Noon in Ljubljana
Auckland	11pm
Cape Town	1pm
London	11am
New York	6am
San Francisco	3am
Sydney	9pm
Tokyo	8pm

Toilets

➔ Finding a public lavatory is not always easy and when you do, you sometimes have to pay up to €1 to use it.

➔ All train stations have toilets, as do shopping centres and department stores. The standard of hygiene is good.

Tourist Information

Slovenian Tourist Board (www.slovenia.info)

Slovenian Tourist Information Centre (STIC; Map p54;☑01-306 45 76; www.slovenia.info; Krekov trg 10; ◷8am-9pm daily Jun-Sep, 8am-7pm Mon-Fri, 9am-5pm Sat & Sun Oct-May; ☏) Located in central Ljubljana.

Slovenian Tourist Information Centre (STIC; www.visitljubljana.si; Jože Pučnik Airport; ◷8am-7pm Mon-Fri, 9am-5pm Sat & Sun Oct-May, 8am-9pm Jun-Sep) Small kiosk at Ljubljana's Jože Pučnik Airport.

Ljubljana Tourist Information Centre (TIC; Map p54;☑01-306 12 15; www.visitljubljana.com; Adamič-Lundrovo nabrežje 2; ◷8am-9pm Jun-Sep, to 7pm Oct-May) In central Ljubljana.

Visas

➔ Citizens of several developed countries, including Australia, Canada, Japan, New Zealand and the US, only need a valid passport (no visa) if entering as tourists for up to three months within a six-month period.

➔ Nationals from other countries may need an entry visa. Visa applications must be filed with a Slovenian embassy or consulate, and visas are valid for stays of up to 90 days.

➔ For full details, see the website of the Slovenian

Ministry of Foreign Affairs (www.mzz.gov.si).

Volunteering

Several organisations can assist travellers seeking to volunteer in Slovenia.

GoOverseas (www.gooverseas.com) Lists several projects, mainly in environmental protection and community development.

Slovene Philanthropy (www.filantropija.org) Local group offering some volunteering opportunities in Slovenia and abroad in communal health and working with migrants.

Voluntariat (www.zavod-voluntariat.si) Student-oriented organisation offering both short- and long-term volunteering options.

Workaway (www.workaway.info) International organisation that matches in-country hosts with volunteers. Check the website for Slovenian listings.

Work

EU citizens do not require a work permit and are free to apply for jobs on the same basis as Slovenian nationals. Citizens of other countries can only work on the basis of a work permit and must normally be sponsored by a local company or institution.

For further details, see the website of the Slovenian Ministry of Labour, Family, Social Affairs and Equal Opportunities (www.mddsz.gov.si).

Transport

GETTING THERE & AWAY

Most travellers arrive in Slovenia by air, or by rail and road connections from neighbouring countries. Flights, cars and tours can be booked online at lonely planet.com/bookings.

Entering the Country

Entering Slovenia is usually a straightforward procedure. If you're arriving from an EU Schengen country, such as neighbouring Austria, Italy or Hungary, you will not have to show a passport or go through customs, no matter which nationality you are. If you're coming from any non-Schengen country, ie outside of the EU but also including Croatia, full border procedures apply.

Passports

EU citizens need only produce their national identity cards on arrival for stays of up to three months. Everyone else entering Slovenia must have a valid passport.

Air

Airports & Airlines

Ljubljana's **Jože Pučnik Airport** (Aerodrom Ljubljana; ☑04-206 19 81; www.lju-air port.si; Zgornji Brnik 130a, Brnik), 27km north of the capital, is the only air gateway for travelling to and from Slovenia. It's a small airport. The arrivals hall has a branch of the **Slovenia Tourist Information Centre** (STIC; www.visitljubljana.si; Jože Pučnik Airport; ☉8am-7pm Mon-Fri, 9am-5pm Sat & Sun Oct-May, 8am-9pm Jun-Sep), travel agencies and a bank of ATMs (located just outside the terminal). Several car-rental agencies, including international agencies like

Avis, Budget, Europcar, Hertz and Sixt, have outlets opposite the terminal.

Adria Airways (☑flight info 04-259 45 82, reservations 01-369 10 10; www.adria.si) From its base at Brnik, the Slovenian flag carrier serves more than 30 European destinations on regularly scheduled flights, including frequent connections to Munich, Frankfurt and Zürich; there are useful connections to other former Yugoslav capitals. Adria has an excellent safety record.

Air France (☑01-244 34 47; www.airfrance.com/si) Flights to Paris (CDG).

Air Serbia (☑in Serbia 386-1 777 43 90; www.airserbia.com) Flights to Belgrade.

EasyJet (www.easyjet.com) Low-cost flights to London (STN).

Finnair (☑in Finland 358-9 818 0888; www.finnair.com) Flights to Helsinki.

Lufthansa (☑04-074 77 37; www.lufthansa.com; ☉8.30am-

CLIMATE CHANGE & TRAVEL

Every form of transport that relies on carbon-based fuel generates CO_2, the main cause of human-induced climate change. Modern travel is dependent on aeroplanes, which might use less fuel per kilometre per person than most cars but travel much greater distances. The altitude at which aircraft emit gases (including CO_2) and particles also contributes to their climate change impact. Many websites offer 'carbon calculators' that allow people to estimate the carbon emissions generated by their journey and, for those who wish to do so, to offset the impact of the greenhouse gases emitted with contributions to portfolios of climate-friendly initiatives throughout the world. Lonely Planet offsets the carbon footprint of all staff and author travel.

5pm Mon-Fri) Flights to Frank-furt and Munich.

Montenegro Airlines (☑in Montenegro 382-20 405 545; www.montenegroairlines.com) Flights to Podgorica.

Turkish Airlines (☑04-206 16 80; www.turkishairlines.com) Flights to Istanbul.

Wizz Air (☑Slovenia call centre 090 100 206; www.wizzair.com) Flights to London (LTN) and Brussels.

Departure Tax

Departure tax is included in the price of the ticket.

Land

Slovenia is well connected by road and rail with its four neighbours – Italy, Austria, Hungary and Croatia. Bus and train timetables some-times use Slovenian names for foreign cities.

Border Crossings

➡ There are dozens of border crossings linking Slovenia with its four neighbours. The crossings to and from EU Schengen Zone members Italy, Austria and Hungary are open and passport checks are very rare.

➡ Travel in and out of Croatia is not part of the EU's Schengen Zone. Expect thorough passport checks and potentially long waits at the border from June to September.

➡ There are nearly 50 border crossings with Croatia, though some are only open during the day (8am to 8pm) or only accessible to EU citizens. The following crossings are open to both EU and non-EU travellers: Bregana, Macelj (Gruškovje), Rupa, Kaštel (Dragonja) and Pasjak (Starod).

Bus

Several long-haul coach companies operate in Slove-nia, connecting the country to destinations around Europe. This service is often cheaper and faster than trains, though can be less comfortable. Buses are also useful for reaching areas where train connections from Slovenia are deficient, in-cluding to points in Italy and Bosnia & Hercegovina.

Most international ser-vices arrive and depart from Ljubljana's **main bus sta-tion** (Avtobusna Postaja Lju-bljana; ☑01-234 46 00; www.ap-ljubljana.si; Trg Osvobodilne Fronte 4; ☉5am-10.30pm Mon-Fri, 5am-10pm Sat, 5.30am-10.30pm Sun). Maribor is an important departure point for trips north to Vienna and south to Zagreb and Belgrade. Slovenia's coastal cities, Piran, Koper and Izola, from June to September, have regular direct bus connections to points on the Croatian coast and to Trieste, Italy.

LONG-HAUL BUS COMPANIES

Following are some of the major coach companies that service points in Slovenia. Consult the websites for timetables, fares and buying tickets.

Flixbus (https://global.flixbus.com) Fast, clean and cheap, often with direct connections to major regional cities.

Arriva (www.arriva.si) Slovenian division of international bus line runs daily to cities in Italy, Austria, Croatia and Serbia.

Avtobusna Postaja Ljubljana (www.ap-ljubljana.si) From Ljubljana's main bus station, lists cheap and reliable services to a handful of popular cities, including Rome, Trieste, Zagreb, Vienna, Belgrade and Sarajevo.

Eurolines (www.eurolines.eu) Major European-wide operator.

POPULAR COACH DESTINATIONS

The most popular interna-tional destinations, along with reference fares and travel times. Departure and arrival points are at Ljublja-na's main bus station.

City	Cost (€)	Time (hr)	Km
Belgrade	40	8	532
Bratislava	40	6	450
Budapest	30	6	460
Frankfurt	80	11½	777
Munich	25	6	405
Rijeka	10	2½	136
Sarajevo	40	11	554
Split	40	8	528
Trieste	7	1½	105
Venice	30	3	250
Vienna	40	5	380
Zagreb	12	2½	150

Car & Motorcycle

Good roads and highways connect Slovenia with all four of its neighbours. Even though borders are open with Italy, Austria and Hunga-ry, motorists must still carry with them the vehicle's reg-istration papers and liability insurance and a valid driver's licence. Expect to show these documents at highway cross-ings with Croatia.

From the moment your ve-hicle enters Slovenia, you're obligated to display a road-toll sticker (p270). Try to buy a sticker at a petrol station near the border before you enter Slovenia or at the first big service plaza you see on the highway once you're in Slovenia.

Train

The **Slovenian Railways** (Slovenske Železnice, SŽ; ☑info 1999; www.slo-zeleznice.si) network links up with the European railway network via Austria (Villach, Salz-burg, Graz, Vienna), Italy (Trieste), Germany (Munich, Frankfurt), Czech Republic (Prague), Croatia (Zagreb, Rijeka), Hungary (Budapest), Switzerland (Zürich) and

BRINGING IN YOUR BIKE

There are no specific problems related to bringing in your own bicycle. Bikes can be transported on some international trains for a fee (€5 to €12 depending on the country). On online timetables, bike-friendly trains are normally designated by a bicycle symbol. Train carriages that can carry bikes are usually marked with a bicycle sign on the side of the car.

Serbia (Belgrade). The Slovenian Railways website has full information in English on current international connections.

DISCOUNTS & PASSES

International tickets on Slovenian Railways trains are valid for two months. Certain fares bought at special offer are valid for just a month, while others are valid only for the day and train indicated on the ticket. Half-price tickets are available to children between six and 12 years.

InterRail A 'Global Pass' from InterRail (www.interrail.eu) covers 30 European countries and can be purchased by nationals of European countries (or residents of at least six months). These passes only make sense for longer journeys, where rail will be the primary means of transport.

Sample prices for 2nd-class travel:

➡ Five days (within 15 days): €269

➡ Seven days (within a month): €320

➡ Ten days (within a month): €381

➡ Twenty-two continuous days: €493

➡ One month: €637
InterRail also offers a 'One Country Pass' valid for rail travel in Slovenia starting at €59 for three days of 2nd-class travel if taken within a month.

Passes are frequently discounted via the website. Discounts are available for passengers under 28 years.

Eurail It would be impossible for a standard Eurail pass (www.eurail.com) to pay for itself just in Slovenia. But non-European residents can consider a more

limited option that allows you to bundle rail travel within groups of neighbouring countries (eg Slovenia and Austria) over a fixed period of time. See the website for prices and options. Buy the pass before you leave home.

AUSTRIA, GERMANY & CZECH REPUBLIC

Both Ljubljana and Maribor are convenient departure and arrival points for connections to cities in Austria, Germany and the Czech Republic. Prices listed here are generally full fare, though many lines are discounted.

Austria To get to Vienna (€80, six hours, 441km) from Ljubljana there is the direct EC Emona (EC 150/151) train, or several other possibilities that require a change at Maribor or Villach, Austria. The EC Emona train also stops in Graz (€40, three hours, 221km); there are other connections to Graz that require a change at Maribor. Two direct trains daily travel from Ljubljana to Salzburg (€55, four hours, 280km); two additional trains require a change at Villach, Austria. Several trains daily link Ljubljana with Villach (€20, two hours, 102km).

Germany There are two direct trains daily, including an overnight sleeper, between Ljubljana and Munich (from €70, seven hours, 441km) via Villach and Salzburg; one carries on to Frankfurt (€180, 10 hours, 859km).

Czech Republic Rail travel is possible to Prague (€140, 11 hours, 700km), though connections normally require a change in either Villach or Maribor, and then again in Vienna.

CROATIA & SERBIA

Ljubljana is the main gateway for train travel south

to Croatia and Serbia. At the time of research, there were no direct rail connections to points in Bosnia & Hercegovina.

Croatia Several trains travel from Ljubljana to Zagreb (€20, two hours, 141km) via Zidani Most; two to Rijeka (€22, two hours, 135km) via Postojna, and three to Split (€63, eight to 12 hours, 456km), with a change at Zagreb.

Serbia Two trains daily travel to/from Belgrade (from €30, nine to 10 hours, 569km) via Zagreb.

HUNGARY

One train daily travels from Ljubljana to Budapest's Deli station (from €30, nine hours, 507km).

ITALY

Two trains daily link Ljubljana with Trieste (€8, 2¾ hours, 100km), via Postojna, Divača and Sežana.

SWITZERLAND

The overnight international train, MV414/415, links Ljubljana directly with Zürich (€89, 14½ hours, 730km) via Villach, Austria.

Sea

During summer it's possible to travel by sea between Piran and the Italian ports of Venice and Trieste. Purchase tickets and obtain information through the **Piran Tourist Information Centre** (TIC; Map p156; ☑05-673 44 40; www.portoroz.si; Tartinijev trg 2; ◷9am-10pm Jul & Aug, to 7pm May, to 5pm Sep-Apr & Jun).

Venezia Lines (Map p156; ☑05-242 28 96; www.venezialines.com) Runs a summer-only (usually mid-June to mid-September) catamaran service on Saturdays between Piran and Venice (adult/child €67/42, 3¾ hours).

Trieste Lines (Map p156;☎040 200 620; www.triestelines.it) Operates a daily (except Wednesday) catamaran from late June through August linking Piran's harbour to Trieste, Italy (€9.60, 30 minutes), and in the other direction to Rovinj, Croatia (€23, 70 minutes).

GETTING AROUND

Air

Slovenia has no scheduled domestic flights.

Bicycle

➡ Cycling is a popular way to get around.

➡ Bikes can be transported for €3.50 in the baggage compartments of IC and regional trains. Larger buses can also carry bikes as luggage.

➡ Cycling is permitted on all roads except motorways. Larger towns and cities have dedicated bicycle lanes and traffic lights.

➡ Bicycle-rental shops are generally concentrated in the more popular tourist areas, such as Ljubljana, Bled, Bovec and Piran, though a few cycle shops and repair places hire them out as well. Expect to pay from €3/17 per hour/day; you will usually be asked to pay a cash deposit or show some ID as security.

Boat

There are no internal boat connections within Slovenia.

Bus

➡ The Slovenian bus network is extensive and coaches are modern and comfortable. You can reach every major city and town, and many smaller places, by bus.

➡ A range of companies serve the country, but prices tend to be uniform: around €4/6/10/17 for 25/50/100/200km of travel.

➡ Buy your ticket from ticket windows at the bus station (*avtobusna postaja*) or pay the driver as you board. There are normally enough seats. The exception is for Friday and weekend travel, where it's best to book your seat (€1.50) a day in advance. Bus services are limited on Sundays and holidays.

➡ Timetables inside the bus station, or posted outside, list all destinations and departure times. If you can't find your bus or don't understand the schedule, get help from the information or ticket window (*blagajna vozovnice*).

➡ *Odhodi* means 'departures' while *prihodi* is 'arrivals'.

Car & Motorcycle
Automobile Association

Slovenia's national automobile club is the **AMZS** (Avto-Moto Zveza Slovenije; Slovenian Automobile Association; ☎roadside emergency 1987; www.amzs.si; Dunajska cesta 128, Ljubljana). For emergency roadside assistance, call ☎1987 anywhere in Slovenia. All accidents should be reported to the police immediately on ☎113.

Driving Licences

Foreign driving licences are valid for one year after entering Slovenia. If you don't hold a European driving licence, you might obtain an International Driving Permit (IDP) from your local automobile association before you leave.

Fuel

Petrol stations are usually open from 7am to 8pm Monday to Saturday, though larger towns have 24-hour services on the outskirts.

The price of *bencin* (petrol) is on par with the rest of continental Europe: standard unleaded 'EuroSuper 95' costs around €1.25 per litre.

BUS TIMETABLE ABBREVIATIONS

The following letters and abbreviations can help you sort out bus timetables. They are used to designate which days a bus line operates, and whether the route runs on weekends and holidays.

D Monday to Saturday

D+ Monday to Friday

N Sunday

NP Sunday and holidays

So Saturday

SoNe Saturday and Sunday

SoNP Saturday, Sunday and holidays

Š Monday to Friday when schools are in session

ŠP Monday to Friday during school holidays

V Daily

ROAD DISTANCES (KM)

	Bled	Bovec	Celje	Črnomelj	Koper	Kranj	Kranjska Gora	Ljubljana	Maribor	Murska Sobota	Nova Gorica	Novo Mesto	Postojna	Ptuj
Bovec	83													
Celje	131	207												
Črnomelj	147	223	130											
Koper	156	161	185	193										
Kranj	27	102	105	123	131									
Kranjska Gora	39	45	161	178	186	58								
Ljubljana	59	134	76	93	107	33	89							
Maribor	181	257	54	198	234	156	212	126						
Murska Sobota	245	320	118	266	298	219	275	189	64					
Nova Gorica	156	72	185	193	90	131	168	107	236	299				
Novo Mesto	127	202	95	32	171	101	157	69	151	246	173			
Postojna	102	131	131	139	59	77	133	53	182	245	60	118		
Ptuj	184	260	58	179	237	159	215	129	29	64	238	148	183	
Slovenj Gradec	164	188	50	191	217	138	185	108	71	135	218	146	163	75

Car Hire

➡ Hiring a car in Slovenia allows for greater flexibility than travelling by bus or train and makes it easier to access attractions outside of city and town centres.

➡ Rentals from international firms such as Avis, Budget, Europcar and Hertz are broadly similar; expect to pay from €40/200 per day/week, including unlimited mileage, collision damage waiver (CDW), theft protection (TP), Personal Accident Insurance (PAI) and taxes.

➡ Some smaller agencies have more competitive rates; booking via the internet is always cheaper.

➡ Rentals will normally also include the road-toll sticker, the *vinjeta*.

Insurance

Third-party liability insurance is compulsory in Slovenia. It will be included in the cost of your car rental. If you're travelling with your own car and the vehicle is registered in the EU, you're also normally covered. Other motorists must secure a 'Green Card' (www.cobx.org), indicating they have the minimum insurance coverage needed for legal travel around Slovenia.

Parking

➡ Parking is restricted in many city and town centres, meaning you'll usually have to pay to park your vehicle.

➡ The systems and rates can vary, but normally you pay at parking vending machines, which will spit out a ticket that you display on the car's dashboard.

➡ Ljubljana and other large cities also have underground car parks where fees are charged (€1.20 to €2.40 for the first hour and €0.60 to €1.80 per hour after that depending on the time of day). Parkopedia (www.parkopedia.com) is a handy website for finding available parking spots in Ljubljana.

ROAD TOLLS & THE VINJETA

➡ In place of highway tolls, all cars travelling on motorways must display a *vinjeta* (road-toll sticker) on the windscreen.

➡ Stickers cost €15/30/110 for a week/month/year for cars and €7.50/30/55 for motorbikes, and are available at petrol stations, post offices and TICs.

➡ A sticker should already be in place on rental cars.

➡ Failure to display a sticker risks a fine of up to €300.

Road Conditions & Hazards

➡ Roads are generally excellent. Big cities are usually linked by four-lane highways and motorways, which are well signposted. Petrol stations, parking areas and restaurants are spaced at convenient intervals for stops.

→ Some mountain roads, including the Vršič Pass in the Julian Alps, are closed in winter (November to April).

→ Always bring along a good road atlas or GPS navigation device (Slovenian roads are normally covered under 'Central European' maps). Bring your home GPS device or rent one with your car from car-rental agencies.

→ Expect heavy traffic on weekends and in July and August. This is especially true along the coast and at or near border stops with Croatia.

Road Rules

→ Drive on the right.

→ Speed limits for cars and motorcycles (less for buses) are 50km/h in towns and villages, 90km/h on secondary and tertiary roads, 100km/h on highways and 130km/h on motorways.

→ Seat belts are compulsory, and motorcyclists must wear helmets.

→ All motorists must illuminate their headlights throughout the day – not just at night.

→ The permitted blood-alcohol level for drivers is 0.05%.

Hitchhiking

Hitchhiking remains a popular way to get around for young Slovenes, and it's generally easy – except on Friday afternoon, before school holidays and on Sunday, when cars are often full of families. Hitching from bus stops is fairly common, otherwise use motorway access roads or other areas where the traffic will not be disturbed.

Hitching is never entirely safe, and we don't recommend it. Travellers who hitch should understand that they are taking a small but potentially serious risk.

Train

Domestic trains are operated by **Slovenian Railways** (www.slo-zeleznice.si). The network is extensive and connects many major cities and towns. Trains tend to offer more space and are more comfortable than buses, and can occasionally be cheaper. Trains are useful mainly for covering long distances. The railways website has a timetable and extensive information in English.

→ Purchase tickets at the train station (*železniška postaja*) or buy them from the conductor on the train (costs an extra €2.50).

→ An 'R' next to the train number on the timetable means seat reservations are available. If the 'R' is boxed, seat reservations are obligatory.

→ A return ticket (*povratna vozovnica*) costs double the price of a single ticket (*enosmerna vozovnica*). A 1st-class ticket costs 50% more than a 2nd-class one.

→ Large stations have luggage lockers (€2 to €3 per day according to locker size).

National Rail Network

Types of Trains

The following types of trains operate within Slovenia. Trains differ widely in terms of speed, comfort, amenities and ticket price. Ticket supplements for faster international trains, usually €1.80, are included in the fare. The abbreviations correspond to notations on timetables:

ICS – High-speed InterCity Slovenia trains travel between Ljubljana and Maribor throughout the year and to Koper from June to August. They have air-conditioning and buffet cars. Seat reservations required.

IC – High-speed InterCity trains are similar to ICS trains and cover long distances quickly. Normally offer food services and require an IC supplement, included in ticket price.

EC – High-speed EuroCity trains are similar to ICS and IC trains and connect important destinations, both in Slovenia and around Europe. Most have food services, and a supplement is included in the ticket price.

MV – Used to designate international trains. When travelling in Slovenia, an MV supplement is included in the fare.

EN – Designates EuroNight trains: long-distance international trains that run at night. Typically offer sleepers and couchettes; though can also be used for simpler travel within Slovenia. Seat reservations usually mandatory. Ticket prices include any supplements.

RG, LP – Used to designate slower and simpler regional and local passenger trains that connect cities and towns. Seat reservations and supplements not required.

Train Timetables

Most train stations will have a large central electronic timetable displaying upcoming arrivals and departures, which are also announced by loudspeaker and can be found on printed timetables within the station.

➡ Trains under the heading *Odhod* or *Odhodi Vlakov* are departures; *Prihod* or *Prihodi Vlakov* indicate arrivals.

➡ Other useful words are *čas* (time), *peron* (platform), *sedež* (seat), *smer* (direction) and *tir* (rail).

➡ Slovenian Railways (www. slo-zeleznice.si) has a handy online timetable, which includes fares.

Discounts & Passes

Slovenian Railways offers several discount schemes, including for weekend travel, and for students, families and travellers over the age of 60. See the website for details and restrictions. Some of the discounts:

➡ The 'IZLETka' flat-rate ticket (adult/child €15/7.50) allows for five days of unlimited travel on weekends and public holidays

➡ Travellers under 26 years can apply for a 30% discount on domestic travel within Slovenia.

➡ The Family RailCard reduces adult train fares by 40% and allows for children under 12 years to travel free.

➡ Travellers aged over 60 can qualify for 30% discount on train travel from Monday to Friday and 50% on weekends, though these benefits are restricted to Slovenes and permanent residents.

Slovenian Railways sells the InterRail Country Pass Slovenia from InterRail (www. interrail.eu), which is valid for rail travel in Slovenia only and available to residents of any European country (excluding Slovenia). The pass, which includes travel on ICS trains, is for three/four/six/eight days (€59/74/104/132) of 2nd-class travel within one month; those under 28 years pay €51/64/90/114.

Language

Slovene belongs to the South Slavic language family, along with Croatian and Serbian (although it is much closer to Croatia's northwestern and coastal dialects). It also shares some features with the more distant West Slavic languages through contact with a dialect of Slovak. Most adults speak at least one foreign language, often English, German or Italian.

If you read our coloured pronunciation guides as if they were English, you'll be understood. Note that oh is pronounced as the 'o' in 'note', ow as in 'how', uh as the 'a' in 'ago', zh as the 's' in 'pleasure', r is rolled, and the apostrophe (') indicates a slight y sound. The stressed syllables are indicated with italics.

The markers (m/f) and (pol/inf) indicate masculine and feminine forms, and polite and informal sentence options respectively.

BASICS

Hello.	Zdravo.	zdra·vo
Goodbye.	Na svidenje.	na svee·den·ye
Excuse me.	Dovolite.	do·vo·lee·te
Sorry.	Oprostite.	op·ros·tee·te
Please.	Prosim.	pro·seem
Thank you.	Hvala.	hva·la
You're welcome.	Ni za kaj.	nee za kai
Yes.	Da.	da
No.	Ne.	ne

WANT MORE?

For in-depth language information and handy phrases, check out Lonely Planet's *Central Europe Phrasebook*. You'll find it at **shop.lonelyplanet.com**, or you can buy Lonely Planet's iPhone phrasebooks at the Apple App Store.

What's your name?
Kako vam/ti je ime? (pol/inf) — ka·ko vam/tee ye ee·me

My name is ...
Ime mi je ... — ee·me mee ye ...

Do you speak English?
Ali govorite angleško? — a·lee go·vo·ree·te ang·lesh·ko

I don't understand.
Ne razumem. — ne ra·zoo·mem

ACCOMMODATION

campsite	kamp	kamp
guesthouse	gostišče	gos·teesh·che
hotel	hotel	ho·tel
youth hostel	mladinski hotel	mla·deen·skee ho·tel

Do you have a ... room?	Ali imate ... sobo?	a·lee ee·ma·te ... so·bo
cheap	poceni	po·tse·nee
double	dvoposteljno	dvo·pos·tel'·no
single	enoposteljno	e·no·pos·tel'·no

How much is it per ...?	Koliko stane na ...?	ko·lee·ko sta·ne na ...
night	noč	noch
person	osebo	o·se·bo

I'd like to share a dorm.
Rad/Rada bi delil/delila spalnico. (m/f) — rad/ra·da bee de·leew/de·lee·la spal·nee·tso

Is breakfast included?
Ali je zajtrk vključen? — a·lee ye zai·tuhrk vklyoo·chen

Can I see the room?
Lahko vidim sobo? — lah·ko vee·deem so·bo

DIRECTIONS

Where's the ...?
Kje je ...? — kye ye ...

What's the address?
Na katerem naslovu je? — na ka·te·rem nas·lo·voo ye

Can you show me (on the map)?
Mi lahko pokažete — mee lah·ko po·ka·zhe·te
(na zemljevidu)? — (na zem·lye·vee·doo)

How do I get to ...?
Kako pridem do ...? — ka·ko pree·dem do ...

Is it near/far?
Ali je blizu/daleč? — a·lee ye blee·zoo/da·lech

(Go) Straight ahead.
(Pojdite) Naravnost — (poy·dee·te) na·rav·nost
naprej. — na·prey

Turn	Obrnite	o·buhr·nee·te
left/right	levo/desno	le·vo/des·no
at the ...	pri ...	pree ...
corner	vogalu	vo·ga·loo
traffic lights	semaforju	se·ma·for·yoo

behind	za/zadaj	za/za·dai
far (from)	daleč (od)	da·lech (od)
here	tu	too
in front of	spredaj	spre·dai
near (to)	blizu (do)	blee·zoo (do)
opposite	nasproti	nas·pro·tee
there	tam	tam

EATING & DRINKING

What is the house speciality?
Kaj je domača — kai ye do·ma·cha
specialiteta? — spe·tsee·a·lee·te·ta

What would you recommend?
Kaj priporočate? — kai pree·po·ro·cha·te

Do you have vegetarian food?
Ali imate — a·lee ee·ma·te
vegetarijansko hrano? — ve·ge·ta·ree·yan·sko hra·no

I'll have ...	Jaz bom ...	yaz bom ...
Cheers!	Na zdravje!	na zdrav·ye

I'd like the ..., please.	Želim ..., prosim.	zhe·leem ... pro·seem
bill	račun	ra·choon
menu	jedilni list	ye·deel·nee leest
breakfast	zajtrk	zai·tuhrk

Question Words

How?	Kako?	ka·ko
How much/many?	Koliko?	ko·lee·ko
What?	Kaj?	kai
When?	Kdaj?	gdai
Where?	Kje?	kye
Which?	Kateri/Katera? (m/f)	ka·te·ree/ka·te·ra
Who?	Kdo?	gdo
Why?	Zakaj?	za·kai

lunch	kosilo	ko·see·lo
dinner	večerja	ve·cher·ya

Key Words

bottle	steklenica	stek·le·nee·tsa
breakfast	zajtrk	zai·tuhrk
cold	hladen	hla·den
delicatessen	delikatesa	de·lee·ka·te·sa
dinner	večerja	ve·cher·ya
food	hrana	hra·na
fork	vilica	vee·lee·tsa
glass	kozarec	ko·za·rets
hot	topel	to·pel
knife	nož	nozh
lunch	kosilo	ko·see·lo
market	tržnica	tuhrzh·nee·tsa
menu	jedilni list	ye·deel·nee list
plate	krožnik	krozh·neek
restaurant	restavracija	res·tav·ra·tsee·ya
spoon	žlica	zhlee·tsa
wine list	vinska karta	veen·ska kar·ta
with	z	zuh
without	brez	brez

Meat & Fish

beef	govedina	go·ve·dee·na
chicken	piščanec	peesh·cha·nets
clams	školjke	shkol'·ke
cod	oslič	os·leech
fish	riba	ree·ba
ham	šunka/pršut	shoon·ka/puhr·shoot
lamb	jagnjetina	yag·nye·tee·na
pork	svinjina	svee·nyee·na

poultry	perutnina	pe·root·nee·na
prawns	škampi	shkam·pee
squid	lignji	leeg·nyee
trout	postrv	pos·tuhrv
veal	teletina	te·le·tee·na

Fruit & Vegetables

apple	jabolko	ya·bol·ko
apricot	marelica	ma·re·lee·tsa
beans	fižol	fee·zhoh
carrots	korenje	ko·re·nye
cauliflower	cvetača/ karfijola	tsve·ta·cha/ kar·fee·yo·la
cherries	češnje/ višnje	chesh·nye/ veesh·nye
grapes	grozdje	groz·dye
hazelnuts	lešniki	lesh·nee·kee
orange	pomaranča	po·ma·ran·cha
peach	breskev	bres·kev
pear	hruška	hroosh·ka
peas	grah	grah
pineapple	ananas	a·na·nas
plum	češplja	chesh·plya
potatoes	krompir	krom·peer
pumpkin	bučke	booch·ke
raspberries	maline	ma·lee·ne
spinach	špinača	shpee·na·cha
strawberries	jagode	ya·go·de
walnuts	orehi	o·re·hee

Other

bread	kruh	krooh
butter	maslo	mas·lo
cheese	sir	seer
eggs	jajca	yai·tsa

pasta	testenine	tes·te·nee·ne
pepper	poper	po·per
rice	riž	reezh
salad	solata	so·la·ta
salt	sol	soh
soup	juha	yoo·ha
sugar	sladkor	slad·kor

Drinks

beer (lager)	svetlo pivo	svet·lo pee·vo
beer (stout)	temno pivo	tem·no pee·vo
coffee	kava	ka·va
juice	sok	sok
lemonade	limonada	lee·mo·na·da
milk	mleko	mle·ko
plum brandy	slivovka	slee·vov·ka
red wine	črno vino	chuhr·no vee·no
sparkling wine	peneče vino	pe·ne·che vee·no
tea	čaj	chai
water	voda	vo·da
white wine	belo vino	be·lo vee·no

EMERGENCIES

Help!	Na pomoč!	na po·moch
Go away!	Pojdite stran!	poy·dee·te stran
Call ...!	Pokličite ...!	pok·lee·chee·te ...
a doctor	zdravnika	zdrav·nee·ka
the police	policijo	po·lee·tsee·yo

I'm lost.
Izgubil/ Izgubila sem se. (m/f) — eez·goo·beew/ eez·goo·bee·la sem se

I'm ill.
Bolan/Bolna sem. (m/f) — bo·lan/boh·na sem

It hurts here.
Tukaj boli. — too·kai bo·lee

I'm allergic to ...
Alergičen/ Alergična sem na ... (m/f) — a·ler·gee·chen/ a·ler·geech·na sem na ...

Where are the toilets?
Kje je stranišče? — kye ye stra·neesh·che

SHOPPING & SERVICES

Where is a/the ...?	Kje je ...?	kye ye ...
bank	banka	ban·ka
market	tržnica	tuhrzh·nee·tsa

Numbers

1	en	en
2	dva	dva
3	trije	tree·ye
4	štirje	shtee·rye
5	pet	pet
6	šest	shest
7	sedem	se·dem
8	osem	o·sem
9	devet	de·vet
10	deset	de·set
20	dvajset	dvai·set
30	trideset	tree·de·set
40	štirideset	shtee·ree·de·set
50	petdeset	pet·de·set
60	šestdeset	shest·de·set
70	sedemdeset	se·dem·de·set
80	osemdeset	o·sem·de·set
90	devetdeset	de·vet·de·set
100	sto	sto

post office	pošta	posh·ta
tourist office	turistični urad	too·rees·teech·nee oo·rad

I want to make a telephone call.
Rad/Rada bi telefoniral/ telefonirala. (m/f) — rad/ra·da bee te·le·fon·nee·row/ te·le·fon·nee·ra·la

Where can I get internet access?
Kje lahko dobim internet povezavo? — kye lah·ko do·beem een·ter·net po·ve·za·vo

I'd like to buy ...
Rad/Rada bi kupil/ kupila ... (m/f) — rad/ra·da bee koo·peew/ koo·pee·la ...

I'm just looking.
Samo gledam. — sa·mo gle·dam

Can I look at it?
Ali lahko pogledam? — a·lee lah·ko po·gle·dam

How much is this?
Koliko stane? — ko·lee·ko sta·ne

It's too expensive.
Predrago je. — pre·dra·go ye

TIME & DATES

What time is it?
Koliko je ura? — ko·lee·ko ye oo·ra

It's (one) o'clock.
Ura je (ena). — oo·ra ye (e·na)

half past seven
pol osem — pol o·sem
(literally 'half eight')

in the morning	zjutraj	zyoot·rai
in the evening	zvečer	zve·cher
yesterday	včeraj	vche·rai
today	danes	da·nes
tomorrow	jutri	yoo·tree

Monday	ponedeljek	po·ne·de·lyek
Tuesday	torek	to·rek
Wednesday	sreda	sre·da
Thursday	četrtek	che·tuhrt·tek
Friday	petek	pe·tek
Saturday	sobota	so·bo·ta
Sunday	nedelja	ne·de·lya

January	januar	ya·noo·ar
February	februar	fe·broo·ar
March	marec	ma·rets
April	april	a·preel
May	maj	mai
June	junij	yoo·neey
July	julij	yoo·leey
August	avgust	av·goost
September	september	sep·tem·ber
October	oktober	ok·to·ber
November	november	no·vem·ber
December	december	de·tsem·ber

TRANSPORT

When does the ... leave?	Kdaj odpelje ...?	gdai od·pe·lye ...
boat	ladja	la·dya
bus	avtobus	av·to·boos
ferry	trajekt	tra·yekt
plane	avion	a·vee·on
train	vlak	vlak

One ... ticket to (Koper), please.	... vozovnico do (Kopra), prosim.	... vo·zov·nee·tso do (ko·pra) pro·seem
one-way	Enosmerno	e·no·smer·no
return	Povratno	pov·rat·no

1st/2nd class	prvi/drugi razred	puhr·vee/droo·gee raz·red
bus station	avtobusno postajališče	av·to·boos·no po·sta·ya·leesh·che

PLACE NAMES & THEIR ALTERNATIVES

(C) Croatian, (Cz) Czech, (E) English, (G) German, (H) Hungarian, (I) Italian, (P) Polish

Beljak – Villach (G)

Benetke – Venice (E), Venezia (I)

Bizeljsko – Wisell (G)

Bohinj – Wochain (G)

Brežice – Rhain (G)

Budimpešta – Budapest (H)

Čedad – Cividale (I)

Celovec – Klagenfurt (G)

Celje – Cilli (G)

Cerknica – Cirkniz (G)

Črnomelj – Tschernembl (G)

Dolenjska – Lower Carniola (E)

Dunaj – Vienna (E), Wien (G)

Gorenjska – Upper Carniola (E)

Gorica – Gorizia (I)

Gradec – Graz (G)

Gradež – Grado (I)

Idrija – Ydria (G)

Istra – Istria (E)

Izola – Isola (I)

Jadran, Jadransko Morje – Adriatic Sea (E)

Kamnik – Stein (G)

Kobarid – Caporetto (I)

Koper – Capodistria (I)

Koroška – Carinthia (E), Kärnten (G)

Kostanjevica – Landstrass (G)

Kranj – Krainburg (G)

Kranjska – Carniola (E), Krain (G)

Kras – Karst (E)

Krnski Grad – Karnburg (G)

Kropa – Cropp (G)

Lendava – Lendva (H)

Lipnica – Leibnitz (G)

Ljubljana – Laibach (G), Liubliana (I)

Metlika – Möttling (G)

Milje – Muggia (I)

Murska Sobota – Muraszombat (H)

Notranjska – Inner Carniola (E)

Nova Gorica – Gorizia (I), Görz (G)

Oglej – Aquileia (I)

Otočec – Wördl (G)

Piran – Pirano (I)

Pleterje – Pletariach (G)

Pliberk – Bleiburg (G)

Portorož – Portorose (I)

Postojna – Adelsberg (G)

Praga – Prague (E), Praha (Cz)

Ptuj – Pettau (G)

Radgona – Bad Radkersburg (G)

Radovljica – Ratmansdorf (G)

Reka – Rijeka (C), Fiume (I)

Ribnica – Reiffniz (G)

Rim – Rome (E), Roma (I)

Rogaška Slatina – Rohitsch-Sauerbrunn (G)

Rosalnice – Rosendorf (G)

Seča – Sezza (I) Peninsula

Sečovlje – Sicciole (I)

Škocjan – San Canziano (I)

Sredozemsko Morje – Mediterranean Sea (E)

Štajerska – Styria (E), Steiermark (G)

Soča – Isonzo (I)

Stična – Sittich (G)

Strunjan – Strugnano (I)

Trbiž – Tarvisio (I)

Trst – Trieste (I)

Tržaški Zaliv – Gulf of Trieste (E), Golfo di Trieste (I)

Tržič – Monfalcone (I)

Varšava – Warsaw (E), Warszawa (P)

Videm – Udine (I)

Vinica – Weinitz (G)

Železna Kapla – Eisenkappel (G)

first/last	prvi/zadnji	puhr·vee/zad·nyee
ticket office	prodaja	pro·da·ya
	vozovnic	vo·zov·neets
train station	železniška	zhe·lez·neesh·ka
	postaja	pos·ta·ya
I want to go to ...		
Želim iti ...	zhe·leem ee·tee ...	

How long does the trip take?
Koliko traja   ko·lee·ko tra·ya
potovanje?   po·to·va·nye

Do I need to change?
Ali moram presesti?   a·lee mo·ram pre·ses·tee

Can you tell me when we get to ...?
Mi lahko poveste   mee lah·ko po·ves·te
kdaj pridemo ...?   gdai pree·de·mo ...

Stop here, please.
Ustavite tukaj,
oos·*ta*·vee·te *too*·kai
prosim. pro·seem
I'd like to *Rad/Rada bi*
rad/*ra*·da bee
hire a ... *najel/*
na·*yel*/
najela ... (m/f)
na·ye·la ...

bicycle *kolo*
ko·*lo*
car *avto*
av·to
motorcyle *motorno kolo*
mo·*tor*·no ko·*lo*

Where's a service station?
Kje je bencinska
kye ye ben·*tseen*·ska

črpalka?
chuhr·pal·ka
I need a mechanic.
Potrebujem
po·tre·*boo*·yem
mehanika.
me·*ha*·nee·ka

GLOSSARY

(m) indicates masculine gender, (f) feminine gender and (n) neutral

AMZS – Avto-Moto Zveza Slovenije (Automobile Association of Slovenia)

bife – snack and/or drinks bar
breg – river bank
burja – bora (cold northeast wind from the Adriatic)

c – abbreviation for cesta
čaj – tea
cerkev – church
cesta – road

DDV – davek na dodano vrednost (value-added tax, or VAT)
delovni čas – opening/ business hours
dijaški dom – student dormitory, hostel
dolina – valley
dom – house; mountain lodge
Domobranci – anti-Partisan Home Guards during WWII
drevored – avenue
dvorana – hall

fijaker – horse-drawn carriage

gaj – grove, park
gledališče – theatre
gora – mountain
gostilna – innlike restaurant
gostišče – inn with restaurant
gozd – forest, grove
grad – castle

greben – ridge, crest
GZS – Geodetski Zavod Slovenije (Geodesic Institute of Slovenia)

Hallstatt – early Iron Age Celtic culture (800–500 BC)
hiša – house
hrib – hill

izvir – source (of a river, stream etc)

jama – cave
jezero – lake

Karst – limestone region of underground rivers and caves in Primorska
kavarna – coffee shop, cafe
klet – cellar
knjigarna – bookshop
knjižnica – library
koča – mountain cottage or hut
kosilo – lunch
kot – glacial valley, corner
kotlina – basin
kozolec – hayrack distinct to Slovenia
kras – karst
krčma – drinks bar (sometimes with food)

lekarna – pharmacy
LPP – Ljubljanski Potniški Promet (Ljubljana city bus network)

mali (m) **mala** (f) **malo** (n) – little
malica – midmorning snack
menjalnica – private currency exchange office
mesto – town

morje – sea
moški – men (toilet)
most – bridge
muzej – museum

na – on
nabrežje – embankment
narod – nation
naselje – colony, development, estate
nasip – dike, embankment
novi (m) **nova** (f) **novo** (n) – new

občina – administrative division; county or commune; city or town hall
odprto – open
okrepčevalnica – snack bar
Osvobodilne Fronte (OF) – Anti-Fascist Liberation Front during WWII
otok – island

pivnica – pub, beer hall
pivo – beer
planina – Alpine pasture
planota – plateau
pletna – gondola
pod – under, below
polje – collapsed limestone area under cultivation
pot – trail
potok – stream
potrditev – enter/confirm (on ATM)
prazniki – holidays
prehod – passage, crossing
prekop – canal
prenočišče – accommodation
pri – at, near, by
PZS – Planinska Zveza Slovenije (Alpine Association of Slovenia)

reka – river
restavracija – restaurant
rob – escarpment, edge

samopostrežna restavracija – self-service restaurant
samostan – monastery
Secessionism – art and architectural style similar to art nouveau
skanzen – open-air museum displaying village architecture
slaščičarna – shop selling ice cream, sweets
smučanje – skiing
sobe – rooms (available)
soteska – ravine, gorge
sprehajališče – walkway, promenade
stari (m) **stara** (f) **staro** (n) – old

stena – wall, cliff
steza – path
STO – Slovenska Turistična Organizacija (Slovenian Tourist Board)
stolp – tower
štruklji – dumplings
Sv – St (abbreviation for saint)
SŽ – Slovenske Železnice (Slovenian Railways)
terme – Italian word for 'spa' used frequently in Slovenia
TIC – Tourist Information Centre
TNP – Triglavski Narodni Park (Triglav National Park)
toplarji – double-linked hayracks, unique to Slovenia
toplice – spa
trg – square

ul – abbreviation for ulica
ulica – street

vas – village
večerja – dinner, supper
veliki (m) **velika** (f) **veliko** (n) – great, big
vila – villa
vinoteka – wine bar
vinska cesta – wine road
vinska klet – wine cellar
vrata – door, gate
vrh – summit, peak
vrt – garden, park
zaprto – closed
zdravilišče – health resort, spa
zdravstveni dom – medical centre, clinic
žegnanje – a patron's festival at a church or chapel
ženske – women (toilet)
žičnica – cable car
zidanica – a cottage in one of the wine-growing regions

Behind the Scenes

SEND US YOUR FEEDBACK

We love to hear from travellers – your comments keep us on our toes and help make our books better. Our well-travelled team reads every word on what you loved or loathed about this book. Although we cannot reply individually to your submissions, we always guarantee that your feedback goes straight to the appropriate authors, in time for the next edition. Each person who sends us information is thanked in the next edition – the most useful submissions are rewarded with a selection of digital PDF chapters.

Visit **lonelyplanet.com/contact** to submit your updates and suggestions or to ask for help. Our award-winning website also features inspirational travel stories, news and discussions.

Note: We may edit, reproduce and incorporate your comments in Lonely Planet products such as guidebooks, websites and digital products, so let us know if you don't want your comments reproduced or your name acknowledged. For a copy of our privacy policy visit lonelyplanet.com/privacy.

WRITER THANKS

Mark Baker

Thanks first to folks on the ground in Slovenia, including Najda Đorđević, Yuri Barron, John Bills, Jana Kuhar, Domen Kalajzic and family, Aleksandra Jezeršek Matjašič and Ana Vugrin. My Slovenian friends in Prague: Tjaša Čebulj, Zeljka Sok and Anjuša Belehar for their helpful suggestions. Finally, fellow writers Anthony Ham and Jess Lee, and my destination editor in London, Anna Tyler.

Anthony Ham

Many thanks to Romana Nared, Ana Petrič and Franc Mlakar in the Lož Valley, and to Saša and Jure in Idrija, as well as to all the staff at tourist offices across the country. At Lonely Planet, I am grateful to my editor Anna Tyler for sending me to such wonderful places, and to my fellow writers Mark and Jess for their wisdom. To my family – Marina, Jan, Carlota and Valentina: *con todo mi amor*.

Jessica Lee

Big thanks to staff at the tourist information centres across Slovenia for tips, advice and local knowledge. In particular the chirpy, friendly folk who staff the offices in Celje, Dolenjske Toplice, Murska Sobata and Ptuj went out of their way to help with answering my endless questions. Also a big thank you to Skanka and Igor, Petra, Daniel and Lea.

ACKNOWLEDGEMENTS

Cover photograph: Church of the Assumption, Bled Island (p91), Alan Copson/AWL ©.

THIS BOOK

This 9th edition of Lonely Planet's *Slovenia* guidebook was researched and written by Mark Baker, Anthony Ham and Jessica Lee. The previous edition was written by Carolyn Bain and Steve Fallon. This guidebook was produced by the following:

Destination Editor Anna Tyler
Senior Product Editors Grace Dobell, Elizabeth Jones
Product Editor Shona Gray
Senior Cartographer Anthony Phelan
Book Designer Virginia Moreno
Assisting Editors Sam Forge, Anne Mulvaney, Kristin Odijk, Tamara Sheward, Gabrielle Stefanos

Assisting Cartographer Katerina Pavkova
Cover Researcher Naomi Parker

Thanks to Bec Deacon, Carol Guy, Paul Harding, Benjamin Hoppe, Tuomo Huuskonen, Herb Leventer, Kate Mathews, Mazzy Prinsep, Kirsten Rawlings, Pam St Leger, Brana Vladisavljevic

Index

Map Legend

Sights

- Beach
- Bird Sanctuary
- Buddhist
- Castle/Palace
- Christian
- Confucian
- Hindu
- Islamic
- Jain
- Jewish
- Monument
- Museum/Gallery/Historic Building
- Ruin
- Shinto
- Sikh
- Taoist
- Winery/Vineyard
- Zoo/Wildlife Sanctuary
- Other Sight

Activities, Courses & Tours

- Bodysurfing
- Diving
- Canoeing/Kayaking
- Course/Tour
- Sento Hot Baths/Onsen
- Skiing
- Snorkelling
- Surfing
- Swimming/Pool
- Walking
- Windsurfing
- Other Activity

Sleeping

- Sleeping
- Camping
- Hut/Shelter

Eating

- Eating

Drinking & Nightlife

- Drinking & Nightlife
- Cafe

Entertainment

- Entertainment

Shopping

- Shopping

Information

- Bank
- Embassy/Consulate
- Hospital/Medical
- Internet
- Police
- Post Office
- Telephone
- Toilet
- Tourist Information
- Other Information

Geographic

- Beach
- Gate
- Hut/Shelter
- Lighthouse
- Lookout
- Mountain/Volcano
- Oasis
- Park
- Pass
- Picnic Area
- Waterfall

Population

- Capital (National)
- Capital (State/Province)
- City/Large Town
- Town/Village

Transport

- Airport
- Border crossing
- Bus
- Cable car/Funicular
- Cycling
- Ferry
- Metro station
- Monorail
- Parking
- Petrol station
- S-Bahn/Subway station
- Taxi
- T-bane/Tunnelbana station
- Train station/Railway
- Tram
- Tube station
- U-Bahn/Underground station
- Other Transport

Routes

- Tollway
- Freeway
- Primary
- Secondary
- Tertiary
- Lane
- Unsealed road
- Road under construction
- Plaza/Mall
- Steps
- Tunnel
- Pedestrian overpass
- Walking Tour
- Walking Tour detour
- Path/Walking Trail

Boundaries

- International
- State/Province
- Disputed
- Regional/Suburb
- Marine Park
- Cliff
- Wall

Hydrography

- River, Creek
- Intermittent River
- Canal
- Water
- Dry/Salt/Intermittent Lake
- Reef

Areas

- Airport/Runway
- Beach/Desert
- Cemetery (Christian)
- Cemetery (Other)
- Glacier
- Mudflat
- Park/Forest
- Sight (Building)
- Sportsground
- Swamp/Mangrove

Note: Not all symbols displayed above appear on the maps in this book

OUR STORY

A beat-up old car, a few dollars in the pocket and a sense of adventure. In 1972 that's all Tony and Maureen Wheeler needed for the trip of a lifetime – across Europe and Asia overland to Australia. It took several months, and at the end – broke but inspired – they sat at their kitchen table writing and stapling together their first travel guide, *Across Asia on the Cheap*. Within a week they'd sold 1500 copies. Lonely Planet was born.

Today, Lonely Planet has offices in Franklin, London, Melbourne, Oakland, Dublin, Beijing and Delhi, with more than 600 staff and writers. We share Tony's belief that 'a great guidebook should do three things: inform, educate and amuse'.

OUR WRITERS

Mark Baker

Mark Baker is a freelance travel writer with a penchant for offbeat stories and forgotten places. He's originally from the United States, but now makes his home in the Czech capital, Prague. He writes mainly on Eastern and Central Europe for Lonely Planet as well as other leading travel publishers, but finds real satisfaction in digging up stories in places that are too remote or quirky for the guides. Prior to becoming an author, he worked as a journalist for the *Economist*, Bloomberg News and Radio Free Europe, among other organisations. Find Mark on Instagram and Twitter @markbakerprague.

Anthony Ham

Anthony is a freelance writer and photographer specialising in Spain, East and Southern Africa, the Arctic and the Middle East. When he's not writing for Lonely Planet, Anthony writes about and photographs Spain, Africa and the Middle East for newspapers and magazines in Australia, the UK and US.

In 2001, after years of wandering the world, Anthony finally found his spiritual home when he fell irretrievably in love with Madrid on his first visit to the city. Less than a year later, he arrived there on a one-way ticket, with not a word of Spanish and not knowing a single person in the city. When he finally left Madrid 10 years later, Anthony spoke Spanish with a Madrid accent, was married to a local and Madrid had become his second home. Now back in Australia, Anthony continues to travel the world in search of stories.

Jessica Lee

In 2011 Jessica swapped a career as an adventure-tour leader for travel writing and since then her travels for Lonely Planet have taken her across Africa, the Middle East and Asia. She has lived in the Middle East since 2007 and tweets @jessofarabia. Jess has contributed to Lonely Planet's *Egypt*, *Turkey*, *Cyprus*, *Morocco*, *Marrakesh*, *Middle East*, *Europe*, *Africa*, *Cambodia*, and *Vietnam* guidebooks and her travel writing has appeared in *Wanderlust* magazine, *The Daily Telegraph*, *The Independent*, *BBC Travel* and Lonelyplanet.com.

Published by Lonely Planet Global Limited
CRN 554153
9th edition – May 2019
ISBN 978 1 78657 392 6
© Lonely Planet 2019   Photographs © as indicated 2019
10 9 8 7 6 5 4 3 2 1
Printed in Singapore